S0-AIO-491

EMORY UNIVERSITY STUDIES IN LAW AND RELIGION

John Witte Jr., General Editor

BOOKS IN THE SERIES

Faith and Order: The Reconciliation of Law and Religion
Harold J. Berman

Rediscovering the Natural Law in Reformed Theological Ethics
Stephen J. Grabill

*Lex Charitatis: A Juristic Disquisition on Law
in the Theology of Martin Luther*
Johannes Heckel

*The Best Love of the Child:
Being Loved and Being Taught to Love as the First Human Right*
Timothy P. Jackson, ed.

*The Ten Commandments in History:
Mosaic Paradigms for a Well-Ordered Society*
Paul Grimley Kuntz

Religious Liberty, Volume 1: Overviews and History
Douglas Laycock

Religious Liberty, Volume 2: The Free Exercise Clause
Douglas Laycock

Building Cultures of Trust
Martin E. Marty

*Suing for America's Soul: John Whitehead, The Rutherford Institute,
and Conservative Christians in the Courts*
R. Jonathan Moore

Theology of Law and Authority in the English Reformation
Joan Lockwood O'Donovan

Power over the Body, Equality in the Family:
Rights and Domestic Relations in Medieval Canon Law
Charles J. Reid Jr.

Religious Liberty in Western Thought
Noel B. Reynolds and W. Cole Durham Jr., eds.

Hopes for Better Spouses: Protestant Marriage and Church Renewal
in Early Modern Europe, India, and North America
A. G. Roeber

Political Order and the Plural Structure of Society
James W. Skillen and Rockne M. McCarthy, eds.

The Idea of Natural Rights:
Studies on Natural Rights, Natural Law, and Church Law, 1150-1625
Brian Tierney

The Fabric of Hope: An Essay
Glenn Tinder

Liberty: Rethinking an Imperiled Ideal
Glenn Tinder

Religious Human Rights in Global Perspective: Legal Perspectives
Johan D. van der Vyver and John Witte Jr., eds.

Natural Law and the Two Kingdoms:
A Study in the Development of Reformed Social Thought
David VanDrunen

Early New England: A Covenanted Society
David A. Weir

God's Joust, God's Justice: Law and Religion in the Western Tradition
John Witte Jr.

Religious Human Rights in Global Perspective: Religious Perspectives
John Witte Jr. and Johan D. van der Vyver, eds.

Justice in Love
Nicholas Wolterstorff

Hopes for Better Spouses

Protestant Marriage
and Church Renewal in
Early Modern Europe,
India, and North America

A. G. Roeber

WILLIAM B. EERDMANS PUBLISHING COMPANY
GRAND RAPIDS, MICHIGAN / CAMBRIDGE, U.K.

© 2013 A. G. Roeber
All rights reserved

Published 2013 by
Wm. B. Eerdmans Publishing Co.
2140 Oak Industrial Drive N.E., Grand Rapids, Michigan 49505 /
P.O. Box 163, Cambridge CB3 9PU U.K.

Printed in the United States of America

19 18 17 16 15 14 13   7 6 5 4 3 2 1

Library of Congress Cataloging-in-Publication Data

Roeber, A. G. (Anthony Gregg), 1949-
Hopes for better spouses: Protestant marriage and church renewal in
early modern Europe, India, and North America / A. G. Roeber.
pages   cm.   — (Emory University studies in law and religion)
Includes bibliographical references and index.
ISBN 978-0-8028-6861-9 (pbk.: alk. paper)
1. Marriage — History of doctrines.
2. Marriage — Religious aspects — Christianity.
3. Church renewal — Europe.   4. Church renewal — India.
5. Church renewal — North America.   I. Title.

BT706.R64   2013
261.8′358109 — dc23

2012045857

www.eerdmans.com

To Kumkum Chatterjee †2012

Esteemed Colleague and Friend

Memory Eternal

Contents

Acknowledgments

More than is always the case, I am especially indebted to a long list of colleagues and institutions for their help in bringing this project to publication. The generosity of the Fritz Thyssen Stiftung enabled me to return to Germany to make final, extended archival visits. Dr. Thomas Müller-Bahlke, Jürgen Gröschl, Brigitte Klosterberg, and the staff at the Francke Foundations in Halle have been especially gracious and helpful. To the archivists and staff at the University Archives of the University of Halle, the State Archive of Saxony-Anhalt in Wernigerode, the Archive and Library of the Saxon Church Province in Magdeburg, the Harzbücherei of Wernigerode, the staff of the Secret State Archives Prussian Cultural Heritage Foundation in Berlin-Dahlem, and the librarians and archivists of the State Library and Royal Archives of Copenhagen, especially Jen Nielsen and Eric Gobel, I extend my sincere gratitude. North American librarians and archivists at Northwestern University's Garrett Theological Seminary; the University of Chicago; the Lutheran Archives Center, Philadelphia; the Moravian Archives in Bethlehem, Pennsylvania; the Schwenkfelder Library in Pennsburg, Pennsylvania; and especially the Interlibrary Loan staff of the Pattee-Paterno Library at Penn State have been especially helpful in responding to requests for aid in securing rare documents and secondary literature. Susan Welch, Dean of the College of the Liberal Arts at Penn State, granted an extended leave of absence with generous research support from the Charles and Joyce Mathues Faculty Research Funds that enabled travel to Denmark and India.

Colleagues scattered across the globe have saved me from many a gaffe, and I am especially grateful to Will Sweetman, Robert Frykenberg, Kumkum

Chatterjee, Daniel Jeyaraj, Joseph Muthuraj, Heike Liebau, Father D. Amudhan, Maria Lazar, Peter Paul Thomas, the professors and students at the United Theological College, Bangalore, TBML College Poryar, and Gita Dharampal-Frick for advice and responses to my attempt to get the story of pietism and marriage in India right. Professor Dr. Wolfgang Breul provided the opportunity to present the argument to his colleagues and students in Mainz, and to him and Dr. Stefania Salvadori, and the participants in the discussions in Mainz and the 2011 American Society for Church History session where some of my argument was presented, I remain grateful for the many insightful exchanges on pietism and marriage in the territories of the Holy Roman Empire. Richard Helmholz commented on an early presentation at the Newberry Library's Early Modern Legal History meeting and continued to offer sage advice on the medieval backgrounds to the story, as did the participants in the Pietism and Community Conference at Emory University in 2006. My struggle with Danish law has been immensely helped by Per Andersen and Eric Gobel. Hermann Wellenreuther, Hartmut Lehmann, Peter Vogt in Germany, Paul Harvey, Mickey Mattox, Marianne Wokeck, Susan Klepp, Paul Peucker, Craig Atwood, Kate Carte-Engel, Jon Sensbach, Mark Noll, Jonathan Strom, Karen Kupperman, David Hall, and Kirsten Sword in the United States, have read chapters, made suggestions, or offered sage advice on how to navigate the shoals of a global approach to a difficult topic. My former doctoral student Axel Utz was especially generous in spotting sources and making suggestions for this project. My research assistants, Joel Waters, Ben Woodward, and Matthew Hill, have patiently combed through sources and references for me and responded with good grace and humor to all manner of requests for tracking down elusive data, and I thank them. John Witte took an early interest in the project, and I'm especially grateful for his support in placing the book in the Law and Religion series, as I am for the two detailed and valuable critiques offered by the anonymous readers. My special thanks to Linda Bieze and Tom Raabe at Eerdmans and to Kevin van der Leek and Professor Daniel Jeyaraj for the final version of the book's cover. The inadequacies of the book remain my own, but the long engagement with marriage debates would not have been sustainable without Pat's presence and the joys of our own marriage journey. May we still have many years!

A. G. ROEBER
University Park, Pennsylvania

Preface

Just as the series preface to the volume *Sex, Marriage, and Family in John Calvin's Geneva* explains, this book also seeks to "tell a story that is almost totally unknown."[1] Martin Luther's attempt to create a synthesis between the inherited canon law of marriage and his vision of the relationship between husband and wife that reflected the holiness conveyed by Christ to his church triggered, a century and a half after the Reformer's death, an enormous, global debate in early modern Protestantism that has been largely forgotten. Luther famously despised the canonical legal tradition and wanted to jettison it entirely. In actual practice, the marriage relationship he envisioned built upon, but quickly came to be frustrated by, the law of marriage.[2] I became curious a decade ago about marriage and the early modern Protestant renewal movement known as "pietism" when I learned that Philipp Jakob Spener (1635-1705) shared Luther's hopes and vision of the relationship between husband and wife as a partnership in which the couple pursued holiness together. Still, although Spener's famous "charter document," the *Pia Desideria*, proclaimed its "hope for better times for the church," marriage did not appear as part of that hope. Given the importance of the proper relationship between husband and wife in Spener's Lutheran tradition, this struck me as odd, and justification enough to appropriate Spener's

1. Don S. Browning and John Witte Jr., series preface to *Sex, Marriage, and Family in John Calvin's Geneva*, vol. 1, *Courtship, Engagement, and Marriage*, by John Witte Jr. and Robert M. Kingdon (Grand Rapids: Eerdmans, 2005), p. xviii.

2. John Witte Jr., *Law and Protestantism: The Legal Teachings of the Lutheran Reformation* (Cambridge and New York: Cambridge University Press, 2002), pp. 53-85.

title and to try to understand what happened to Luther's hopes and his own.[3] Whatever else one thinks of when remembering the Protestant Reformation, the marriage relationship, especially of the clergy, assumed transformative importance in the history of Western Christianity, and "the effect on this group is among the most significant social evidence cited to support notions of the Reformation as a rupture."[4]

Evangelical Lutherans did not claim to be interested in rupture. Still, in his trying to fashion a quasi-sacramental vision of marriage that emphasized the friendship and partnership of holy spouses, Luther broke new ground. The later dispute over how to understand the conjugal relationship of husband and wife left unresolved whether spouses encountered God there, and how that relationship was tied to the church. That ambiguity flowed from Luther's own theological struggle and his unfinished reading of Ephesians 5, which traditionally tied the marriage relationship to Christ's spousal connection to the church.

Anyone interested in the history of Christianity knows that an acrimonious and continuing debate over sexuality, gender, marriage, and the law threatens in the twenty-first century to split "global South" Christians from their Euro–North American counterparts.[5] Some scholars continue to hint that the Reformation is best understood as the first, if unintended, step toward "secularization." Because the debates on the marriage relationship and the church we reconstruct here have been forgotten, a recent analysis of Protestant morality has nothing to say about marriage, and pardonably (but erroneously) concludes that Protestants dismissed the possibility that any "positive remnant" of the image and likeness of God survived the Fall. Lutherans and Anglicans could not quite bring themselves to call marriage a "sacrament," but they tried hard to find a "quasi" standing for the godly estate, a quest some pietist renewers took up again a century and a half after

---

3. Phillipp Jakob Spener, *Pia Desideria, oder herzliches Verlangen nach Gottgefälliger Besserung der wahren Evangelischen Kirchen . . .* , ed. Kurt Aland (Berlin: Walter de Gruyter, 1964); the theme is more explicitly announced in Spener's *Behauptung der Hoffnung künfftiger besserer Zeiten in Rettung des insgemein gegen dieselbe unrecht aufgeführten Spruches Luk. 18.9* (Frankfurt: Johann David Zunner, 1693). For readers of English, a solid introduction to Spener is K. James Stein, *Philipp Jakob Spener: Pietist Patriarch* (Chicago: Covenant Press, 1986).

4. Susan R. Boettcher, "The Social Impact of the Lutheran Reformation in Germany," in *Lutheran Ecclesiastical Culture, 1550-1675,* ed. Robert Kolb (Leiden and Boston: Brill, 2008), pp. 305-59, at 346.

5. For an overview of the literature and issues, see Philip Jenkins, *The Next Christendom: The Coming of Global Christianity,* revised and expanded ed. (Oxford and New York: Oxford University Press, 2007), pp. 231-50.

Luther's death.[6] This book does not trace the history of pietist marriage. Rather, it reconstructs the battles between official theological belief and practice surrounding the marriage relationship that had been informed by the inherited canonical legal and secular traditions, and an unofficial theology of that relationship that Luther had articulated, Spener revived, and many ordinary believers found compelling — but one that eventually fell into obscurity. Luther had constructed that vision from his reflections upon medieval mystics and the iconic manner in which marriage reflected Christ's own relationship to his church. Unfortunately, the official theology's indebtedness to the law of marriage, secular and sacred, also quickly reasserted the authority of male heads of households, and linked the assertion of order to the need for social control and discipline exercised by princes over their subjects. Those perceived needs drove forward more contractual understandings of spousal relations and said little about how that relationship reflected Christ's own with his church — other than one of authority and submission. Unofficially, the more hopeful vision of spouses as friends manifested itself in sundry times and places, albeit without much support from the pastors and theologians one might have expected to entertain Luther's hopes.

The book concentrates on the version of "church" pietism identified with the town of Halle on the Saale River because the first explosive exchanges there touched off the broader, pan-Protestant debates. The hopes for a quasi-sacramental friendship marriage that Spener had advanced did not survive in the theology of his most famous student, August Hermann Francke, the justly famous founder of the Francke Foundations. Fifty-six miles west of Halle in the county of Wernigerode, the drive for social discipline over ungodly weddings and behaviors took its cues from Francke's center. That trend spread to the Danish colony in southeast India where Halle's missionaries (including relatives of Wernigerode's pastors) labored. In North America, Halle-trained pastors, many ordained in Wernigerode, fretted over the misbehavior of spouses while confronting a fellow alumnus Nikolaus von Zinzendorf and what turned into a scandalously hopeful understanding of the conjugal relationship and its holiness among his Moravian Brethren. The roots of modern Protestant disagreements about marriage lie in these bitter and inconclusive exchanges. Lutheran church

---

6. Brad S. Gregory, *The Unintended Reformation: How a Religious Revolution Secularized Society* (Cambridge, Mass., and London: Harvard University Press, Belknap Press, 2012), p. 207. Gregory somehow manages to overlook the centrality of marriage and the household as the most basic of Luther's "moral communities."

pietists refused to separate from the confessional, established institution linked to princes. More radical pietists did not hesitate to do so. Some adopted radical ascetic rejection of sexuality from start to finish; others appeared to condone a scandalously libertine view of sex unconstrained by the inherited laws of marriage. Both kinds of protagonists plausibly argued that Luther had been their mentor. Church pietists had to steer past these shoals in attempting to recover Luther's high view of Christian marriage and how it related to the church. The cessation of their efforts reflected unease about issues of human (especially female) sexuality, and the perceived need for a socially disciplined marriage and household. By neglecting Spener's pioneering insights, Protestant leaders left to future generations the unresolved task of reconciling the theology and law of the marriage relationship.

To understand what happened, we must do justice not just to the articulate theologians whose access to education and writing — and influence upon the laws of marriage — shaped the argument. We must also search for clues about the unofficial practices and perspectives of the less powerful and largely inarticulate believers. The result hopefully supports the late Jaroslav Pelikan's admonition: "Church history is always more than the history of doctrine, but it should not be less."[7] The key religious and legal propositions about the marriage relationship embedded in the official view most Protestants recognized might be summarized thus: marriage was divinely instituted and, as part of the pre-"Fall" of humans, spoke to God's concern for an ordered creation. Husbands and wives may have been partners once, but after Eden, authority and submission defined spousal roles. Sexual congress was licit in marriage; it contained lust and produced children, but even in marriage it could be the occasion for abuse by either husband or wife. The decision to enter marriage should proceed with parental consent and under the watchful eye of the secular authority; pastors of churches should bless such unions, but marriage belonged to that part of the two kingdoms identified with the prince, not with the preaching of the gospel. Adjudication of spousal disputes that might be the occasion for separation, or absolute divorce, fell under the jurisdiction initially of consistory or diocesan courts, but increasingly by the eighteenth century, especially in the English legal tradition, reformers pushed for common law, not ecclesiastical resolution to disputes. Although similar pressures and conflicts existed in the Continental legal families, Protestant church authorities

---

7. Jaroslav Pelikan, "An Essay on the Development of Christian Doctrine," *Church History* 35, no. 1 (March 1966): 3-12, at 11.

still exercised significant influence in regulating and adjudicating spousal relations and disputes.

Despite what both princes and pastors may have taught under these official norms, unofficial views differed considerably, over time, depending very much upon local and regional traditions and circumstances. Customary views of the spousal relationship among European Protestants remained deeply pragmatic, focused on the commonsense recognition that a stable household gave inhabitants a fighting chance to survive the constant dangers of illness, social and political instability, and sudden economic catastrophe. Since the option of entering a spousal relationship remained dictated by economic and social standing, not only in Europe but also in India and North America, unofficial views about spouses did not spurn official religious and legal norms, but those who held to unofficial values did not give their assent, whether open or grudging, to officials without calculating the possible long-term impact of what their social or political "betters" encouraged, or demanded. In the long run, the appeal to a more companionate spousal relationship that had always targeted the "middling sorts" of moderately well-off artisans, peasants, small merchants, and shopkeepers failed. It did so in part because official theology had never successfully confronted contrary behavior among the rich and the powerful, nor discovered how to extend such high hopes to the truly impoverished, marginalized, and powerless for whom marriage remained a vague hope, at best. Less articulate members of European, North American, or convert-Indian groups instinctively sought safety in tried-and-true wisdom inherited from the experience of their families' occupational and social identities. To transgress those boundaries, whether in Europe, India, or North America, was to risk social ostracism. A few small groups of Europeans by the late seventeenth century would do just that, opting for unsanctioned alliances that were completely ascetic, rejecting sexual activity altogether; others would flaunt the canonical and secular norms surrounding marriage that dared to suggest that sexual activity could be "sacramental" in itself, and not necessarily confined to a monogamous male-female relationship. Since the secular and the canonical law of marriage reflected the official, received tradition of preaching, the articulate carefully avoided acknowledging among social or economic inferiors any ambivalence or reservations they entertained about what the law of marriage might imply for hopes of better spousal relations. The appeal to order, in the long run, could preserve households and property, but an official endorsement of the spousal relationship's potential for helping ordinary husbands and wives find a path to holiness foundered in the face of the official tradition's own uncertainty about its own hopes for marriage.

By the late eighteenth century, some Protestant men and women managed to hope for deeper understandings of spousal relations, and some unofficially experienced it as a companionate friendship. But the official theology had not helped them to articulate those hopes.[8] That curious irony surrounding the debate about men, women, and marriage also unintentionally revealed a fragmented European Protestant understanding of the "church." Whatever else the Protestant Reformation had been about, it "protested" celibate clerical control and manipulation of access to God, including marriage. But the phrase "the priesthood of all believers" that appears to be the hallmark of Protestantism in the twenty-first century did not come into widespread use until the rise of the pietist movement. The increasing use of the phrase accompanied a renewed criticism of pastors, sacraments, and formal teachings after the Thirty Years' War. As one astute observer has written, "the Protestant Reformation left its heirs [with] no settled comprehensive system, only with many unresolved questions of principle and usage, not least in decisions relating to the body."[9]

Although scholars have traveled many avenues to explore what "the body" has meant in Christian experience, the sources that survive suggest that evoking associations with the human body in a physical sense, male and female, led believers to ponder the body of Christ, the church. But the emphasis upon an interior piety "of the heart" that had been so important in Luther's own conversion left some real ambivalence about whether the pursuit of holiness was an individual task or one best realized in the marriage bond. Perhaps one reason the pietist movement did not immediately tackle the issue is that by the 1670s Europeans who called themselves "evangelicals" were not as sure as Luther had been about the value of the body

8. The "continual dialectic" between official and unofficial forms of belief from late medieval and early modern European perspectives is insightfully probed by Robert W. Scribner, "Elements of Popular Belief," in *Handbook of European History, 1400-1600: Late Middle Ages, Renaissance, and Reformation,* ed. Thomas A. Brady Jr. et al., 2 vols. (Grand Rapids: Eerdmans, 1996), 1:231-62, at 239. On the importance of ritual practice as a measure of belief, see David D. Hall, "'Between the Times': Popular Religion in Eighteenth-Century British North America," in *The World Turned Upside Down: The State of Eighteenth-Century American Studies at the Beginning of the Twenty-First Century,* ed. Michael V. Kennedy and William G. Shade (Bethlehem, Pa.: Lehigh University Press, 2001).

9. David Tripp, "The Image of the Body in the Formative Phases of the Protestant Reformation," in *Religion and the Body,* ed. Sarah Coakley (Cambridge: Cambridge University Press, 1997), pp. 131-54, at 142.

and flesh. For Luther, "physicality accorded with the central emphases of his theology. One of the things that set Luther apart from many other Christian thinkers [was] his remarkably positive attitude toward the body, in all its aspects."[10] Many of his followers a century and a half later appear to have lost this vision.

This was no small matter, for Luther and his confessional tradition had not endorsed the notion that the individual believer enjoys immediate access to grace. At least formally, Lutherans (even when dismissing the Roman Catholic Church as a corrupt novelty) still needed recourse to a believing community and sacraments provided by a learned preaching ministry. Marriage sat awkwardly on the boundary between the worldly and the transcendent. Was marriage "graced," and if so, just how? What precisely was "grace," and what did it accomplish? Where was its visible sign that pointed to the gospel? Perhaps the sinner was merely declared "justified" by God. Perhaps the human condition was really "changed" only in the next life. But then what did Protestants mean when they called marriage a "holy estate," and what did they mean by the church?

The marital relationship thus became entangled in the larger questions of church renewal, but not by design. Today, hardly anyone would disagree that "at the same time that any marriage represents personal love and commitment, it participates in the public order."[11] In the seventeenth and eighteenth centuries, European public order centered on the claims of princely sovereignty and "the church" — and ambiguity about the meaning of the church guaranteed an explosion when pietist reformers pressed for a renewed, reinvigorated church made up of committed believers — most of them married — who practiced what they claimed to believe.

As the renewal movement of pietism spread beyond Europe, to India and North America, the public face of Christianity, and by extension, marriage, came to mean something quite different in those regions. What contemporary scholars refer to as "gender" "relies on and to a great extent derives from the structuring provided by marriage." But early moderns indebted to Luther's insights continued, at least at times, to think that it was "church" that could not be separated from the relationship of husbands and wives in marriage. We tend to think that what past generations took for

---

10. Lyndal Roper, "Martin Luther's Body: The 'Stout Doctor' and His Biographers," *American Historical Review* 115, no. 2 (April 2010): 351-84, at 384.

11. Nancy F. Cott, *Public Vows: A History of Marriage and the Nation* (Cambridge, Mass., and London: Harvard University Press, 2000), p. 1; and for the quotation below, p. 3.

granted about "male" and "female" illumines "relationships of power, say, between ruler and ruled or between empire and colony."[12] But evidence suggests that our understanding of marriage needs to expand beyond "relationships of power" to include the pursuit by pietists of a marriage relationship able to transcend social, political, and economic inequality between the partners and embrace companionate friendship and holiness. To the extent that the quest failed, this book locates the roots of the problem not merely or even primarily in social, demographic, political, or economic "forces." We do not need yet another book to remind us that such forces have always exerted pressure on marriage partners. Long after the debates on marriage had subsided in Europe, George Bernard Shaw offered his own biting observations on the pressures spouses could encounter in marriage, put into the mouth of Eliza Doolittle's father. When asked if he had no morals in selling his daughter for fifty pounds, Alfie could only reply: "Can't afford them, Governor. Neither could you if you was as poor as me." But the worldly-wise Doolittle, upon coming into an annual bequest and lamenting the triumph of "middle-class morality," nicely captured what Luther, Spener, and some pietists had hoped for about marriage: "I have to live for others and not for myself: that's middle class morality." How seventeenth- and eighteenth-century members of the "middling sorts" (and many of the lower orders) lived for others within their marriages must also inform our understanding of their hopes for better spouses.

Spener and those who followed in his train recognized how delicately they had to tread in raising the question of marriage in a "renewed" Protestantism. Shelves of books and essays interpret pietism on the European continent, and to a lesser extent in India and other lands where the movement took root. But pietists command little recognition in English-speaking libraries. Definitions usually emphasize "personal and practical 'heart religion' . . . prefigured in the works of Lutheran mystical writers," but given focus and energy by Spener at Frankfurt in the 1670s. They also include Bible study, emphasis on the priesthood of believers, the struggle for conversion of the heart, and concern for the poor and marginalized.[13] But by "pietists," we mean here first and foremost Protestants who "placed at the center of their

---

12. Joanne Meyerowitz, "A History of 'Gender,'" *American Historical Review* 113, no. 5 (December 2008): 1346-56, at 1347; and below, George Bernard Shaw, *Pygmalion*, act 1; act 5 (The Gutenberg Project: http://www.gutenberg.org/files/3825/3825-h/3825-h.htm [accessed 1 June 2011]).

13. Eamon Duffy, "Pietism," in *The Westminster Dictionary of Christian Theology,* ed. Alan Richardson and John S. Bowden (Philadelphia: Westminster, 1983), p. 447.

faith the genuine renewal of humanity, the recovery through holy living of the image and likeness of God lost through the Fall." But the burning question remained: Was this recovery an individual, purely internal renewal — or was marriage to a holy partner the actual occasion of the graced path to holiness?[14] Popular caricatures of pietists passed over marriage at first to focus on what critics saw as an obsession for law and order, for regulating lives, for denouncing card playing, dancing, and just about any other human enjoyment, and thus implicitly denying the holiness of life in this world — including marital holiness.

Asceticism and heart religion appeared to fit together nicely in the pietist movement because the Reformation had left unresolved the fundamental questions about who the Christian God is and what vestige of the image of God in human beings — male and female — connects them to God. Luther's attempt to synthesize his bold endorsement of the holiness of marriage with a revised canonical legal tradition proved to be an unstable compound, and its vulnerability the key weakness in his theological vision. Officially, Protestants could claim that they had liberated themselves from the shackles of canon law. Practically, they remained deeply indebted both to the canonical and the related secular laws that reaffirmed paternal authority and the subordination of wives.

Protestants affirmed that marriage continued to be the primary relationship God had intended for humans from the beginning. Roman Catholics, however, claimed that marriage remained bound to this world. Virginal celibacy pointed to the "higher" norm of a radically transformed human relationship to God. Some Orthodox Christian theologians whom pietist Lutherans encountered both in Europe and in India would probably have argued that such a question — did marriage or virginity occupy the "first place"? — was wrongheaded, and that both were equally acceptable paths on the journey toward holiness.[15]

The most sweeping attempt to summarize the meaning and purpose of "marriage" through the centuries concludes that it evolved from the negotiation stage among rival kinship groups as a means of controlling property and power. In the "early modern" era, according to some scholars, personal

---

14. Anne-Charlott Trepp, "Zur Differenzierung der Religiositätsformen im Luthertum des 17. Jahrhunderts und ihrer Bedeutung für die Deutungen von Natur," *Pietismus und Neuzeit: Ein Jahrbuch zur Geschichte des neueren Protestantismus* 32 (2006): 37-56, at 56.

15. For the opinion that the Catholic/Protestant debate is badly framed by a defective anthropology, see Vigen Guroian, "An Ethic of Marriage and Family," in Guroian, *Incarnate Love: Essays in Orthodox Ethics* (Notre Dame, Ind.: University of Notre Dame Press, 2002), pp. 79-114.

choice, attraction, and companionship superseded familial, church, and state "norms" that had linked marriage to communal order.[16] By the late seventeenth century, marital love probably claimed both aristocratic and plebeian loyalty as the fountain of happiness in this life; "it was in the domestic and personal sphere that people were most truly themselves."[17] But the story of the marriage relationship of husbands and wives and the early modern debates uncovered here call into question the notion that spousal relationships in marriage emerged through familiar "stages" and followed a fixed sequence of development.

Marriage has always remained a matter of the "public" realm and interest in any society. But the early modern pietists had to confront a troublesome dilemma: Was marriage, ordained by God before the Fall, therefore primarily a relationship in which the partners found not just one another but God himself in a godly household and, by implication, contributed to a renewed social order? Or, did the Fall so disrupt the marriage relationship that God turned it over to the prince as the agent responsible for maintaining worldly stability? Or, was there at least some validity in the medieval insistence that the church (and just what did this word mean?) — not just kinship groups or princes — blessed the union of man and woman?

This recovered story reveals that not much had changed since the sixteenth century at the level of "lived religion" or in the canonical law of marriage. True, a shift in legal norms technically relaxed the strictures on divorce and remarriage in Protestant lands. But the rejection of marriage as "sacrament" and (for some Lutherans and some Anglicans) its reemergence as a "lesser" sacrament actually intensified the regulation of marriage in Protestant Europe. That regulation — what historians have generally referred to as an attempt at social discipline — did not differ greatly from expectations in Roman Catholic lands.[18] All this changed with the advent of pietism. Hymns,

16. Stephanie Coontz, *Marriage, a History: From Obedience to Intimacy or How Love Conquered Marriage* (New York: Viking Penguin, 2005), pp. 145-60. Coontz (predictably) attributes the "change" solely to the "enlightenment" and market forces, not even mentioning the pietist movement.

17. Keith Thomas, *The Ends of Life: Roads to Fulfilment in Early Modern England* (Oxford: Oxford University Press, 2009), p. 188.

18. Witte, *Law and Protestantism,* pp. 203-55: "their new theology of marriage, though filled with bold revisions, preserved a good deal of the teaching of the Roman Catholic tradition. Their new civil law of marriage was heavily indebted to the canon law which it replaced" (p. 255). The literature on "social discipline" has produced its own reactions and critiques. I use the term here to refer primarily to church discipline even when noting disagreements between ecclesiastical and juridical leaders on the specifics and who should be in charge of such efforts. For an

broadsides, court cases, letters, and traces of iconography reveal how academic, judicial, and clerical concern connected with the lived experience of marriage and pushed the controversy about the relationship of husbands and wives to each other, and to the broader public realm, to crisis levels.

But if the crisis emerged in Europe, the disagreements intensified because of events far away. Protestant presence in southeast India and in the British North American colonies reshaped the initial exchanges in ways that the original protagonists could not have imagined. Particularly in non-Christian societies, "conversion [ranked] among the most destabilizing activities." Pietists advancing their views of marriage and renewal encountered stiff resistance in cultures with ancient beliefs — cultures that dismissed Protestants as latecomers peddling novelties.[19]

The quarrel about marriage thus quickly became a transoceanic dispute. The conflict came to be fought on European, South Indian, and North American ground. Pietist efforts at renewal forced to the foreground the question of whether marriage partially determined what it meant to be a Christian. Disputes about Christian marriage could not be easily confined to issues of "personal holiness" or even household order. Nor did any of the protagonists at first privilege individual choice, as if they intended to lay the groundwork for the companionate or romantic notions about marriage that triumphed by the nineteenth century.[20]

Ambivalence about the dignity of marriage in a Christian household and society served Europeans poorly when they carried their ideas to converted brothers and sisters elsewhere in the world. In India, they discovered that the definition of the marriage relationship of husband and wife paid strict attention to notions the Europeans would label "caste." Pious men and women in that vast country often pursued *bhakti* — personal spiritual devotion directed toward a spontaneous and loving relationship with God in

---

overview, see Ute Lotz-Heumann, "Imposing Church and Social Discipline," in *The Cambridge History of Christianity: Reform and Expansion, 1500-1660,* ed. Ronnie Po-Chia Hsia (Cambridge and New York, 2007), chapter 14, pp. 244-60. See also my assessment in A. G. Roeber, "The Law, Religion, and State Making in the Early Modern World: Protestant Revolutions in the Works of Berman, Gorski, and Witte," *Law & Social Inquiry: Journal of the American Bar Foundation* 31, no. 1 (Winter 2006): 199-227.

19. Gauri Viswanathan, *Outside the Fold: Conversion, Modernity, and Belief* (Princeton: Princeton University Press, 1998), p. xvi.

20. For example, T. H. Breen and Timothy Hall, "Structuring Provincial Imagination: The Rhetorical Experience of Social Change in Eighteenth-Century New England," *American Historical Review* 103, no. 5 (December 1998): 1411-39.

which neither the state nor the temple mattered much. Such persons seemed ideal candidates for conversion to pietism's religion of the heart. Converting Tamil views of marriage would prove to be more challenging.[21]

Pietist pastors trained at the Francke Foundations in Halle were ordained in the castle chapel above the small town of Wernigerode, and sent to India, or British North America. Those who had wanted to serve in India but ended up in the North Atlantic world encountered a disconcertingly tolerant, diverse, and Protestant public sphere. At first, they regarded marital relations among their transplanted flocks as a disordered situation in need of discipline. The Europeans who stayed on the Continent, the missionaries in India, and the pastors in North America persuaded themselves that the theological danger to "true Christianity" still lay in the Roman Catholic insistence on defining marriage as a sacrament in the control of a church whose leadership was unambiguously clerical, hierarchical, and celibate.

The propertied Protestant families in North America emphasized marriage's practical, useful character and also believed that it signaled cultural superiority to Africans and Native Americans, whom they increasingly excluded from their marriage rituals and from their churches.[22] By the late eighteenth century, demographic and social pressures also made marriage inaccessible to many of the marginal in pietism's European homeland. It functioned either as a private matter of companionate and affectionate choice for European elites, or it became an insignificant "estate" under the control of princes no longer interested in defending confessional markers. The sovereign's concern for maintaining an economic and social order that required undisrupted households — and the ordinary person's aversion to risking further economic marginalization — ended any hopes pietists had entertained for renewing Europe.

Concern for marital property and the law did not necessarily preclude

21. For an overview, see Robert Eric Frykenberg, "Christians and Religious Traditions in the Indian Empire," in *Cambridge History of Christianity VIII: World Christianities, c. 1815-1914*, ed. Sheridan Gilley and Brian Stanley (Cambridge: Cambridge University Press, 2006), pp. 29, 273-92, and more specifically, Richard Fox Young and Daniel Jeyaraj, "Singing the 'Sovereign Lord': Hindu Pietism and Christian Bhakti in the Conversions of Kanapati Vattiyar, a Tamil 'Poet,'" in *Halle and the Beginning of Protestant Christianity in India II: Christian Mission in the Indian Context*, ed. Andreas Gross, Y. Vincent Kumaradoss, Heike Liebau (Halle: Verlag der Franckeschen Stiftungen zu Halle, 2006), pp. 951-72.

22. For an insightful study of how non-European Catholics creatively used the different standing of marriage in Catholicism to their advantage, see Herman L. Bennett, *Africans in Colonial Mexico: Absolutism, Christianity, and Afro-Creole Consciousness, 1570-1640* (Bloomington and Indianapolis: Indiana University Press, 2003), pp. 79-191.

marriage companionate relationships, but the reform of marriage law in England among pietist allies also did little to advance a vision of the spousal relationship as a way of life leading to salvation.[23]

International Protestant debates over marriage collapsed as the pietist movement itself did. By shifting the definition of Protestant holiness toward the experiential and subjective, the renewal movement left unresolved the question of just why and how the marriage relationship itself was holy, a reflection of God's "ordered" estates in this world. As a result, marriage increasingly became a civil relationship that was not wholly secular, but one that left the relationship between husband and wife open to romantic, companionate, and, sometimes, adversarial interpretations, especially when touching property and inheritance, and thus also definitions of rights and privileges. Those interpretations said nothing at all about holiness.

The quarrel over marriage that continues today finds expression among European and non-European descendants of the pietists. Many details of this story remain to be worked out, and no attempt at a "master narrative" can possibly do justice to such an important and complex topic. Many readers will find plenty to quarrel about, especially my reading of Luther and Philipp Melanchthon. As someone who tried to read these theologians carefully from "within" their faith tradition but is now returning to them at a distance, I have become alert to aspects of Luther's struggle with marriage that I believe those in his tradition may not recognize. My reading of Luther, to put it in the simplest terms, forces me to conclude that he refused a nonspiritual reading of "nature." From first to last, I conclude he struggled to find the right language to allow his idea of the gospel to include marriage — because of its origins in the original creation plan — to be genuinely "divine by nature," if I can be so bold. This reading sets my conclusions firmly against a developed reading of Luther's anthropology (especially among German theologians), but I hope that the case I am arguing here, not merely about Luther, but about the consequences of his inability to resolve his di-

---

23. On the late-eighteenth-century patterns in Europe, see Raffaella Sarti, *Europe at Home: Family and Material Culture, 1500-1800,* trans. Allan Cameron (New Haven and London: Yale University Press, 2002), pp. 228-38; for the argument lamenting the lack of connection between property and expectations of marital companionship in much of the literature, see Rebekka Habermas, *Frauen und Männer des Bürgertums: Eine Familiengeschichte (1750-1850)* (Göttingen: Vandenhoeck & Ruprecht, 2000), pp. 259-65; for my own earlier attempts to trace the importance of familial inheritance practices and religious-political concepts, see A. G. Roeber, *Palatines, Liberty, and Property: German Lutherans in Colonial British America* (Baltimore and London: Johns Hopkins University Press, 1993; rev. ed. 1998).

lemma about marriage, will be clear and convincing. That reading, for reasons that will become obvious, also deeply affects my interpretation of the church pietists' struggle to articulate their hopes for the spousal relationship. At the least, I hope that the results of my curiosity will be sufficiently interesting to encourage others to improve upon my telling of the tale. This is, nonetheless, the story of where, how, and why the quarrel about the hopes for better spouses began.

Abbreviations

ADB	Allgemeine Deutsche Biographie (79 vols.; electronic to 2012)
AFSt [Bib]	Archiv der Franckeschen Stiftungen [Library] (Halle/Saale, Germany)
ALM/DHM	Archiv des Leipziger Missionswerks/Abteilung Dänisch-Hallesche Mission (Halle/Salle, Germany)
AuBKS	Archiv und Bibliothek der Kirchenprovinz Sachsen (Magdeburg, Germany)
BBK	*Biographisch-Bibliographisches Kirchen Lexikon* (33 vols.; 1975-present)
GStA	Geheime Staatsarchiv Preußischer Kulturbesitz (Berlin-Dahlem, Germany)
HSP	Historical Society of Pennsylvania (Philadelphia, PA)
LhaS-A (WH)	Landeshauptarchiv Sachsen-Anhalt Abteilung Magdeburg (Wernigerode Hauptarchiv)
LW	*Luther's Works* (55 vols.; 1958-65)
RGG	*Religion in Geschichte und Gegenwart* (4th ed., 8 vols)
Stab	Staatsbibliothek Berlin
UTC	United Theological College Archives, Bangalore, India
WA	*Dr. Martin Luthers Werke* (Weimar, 1883-1993)

Illustrations

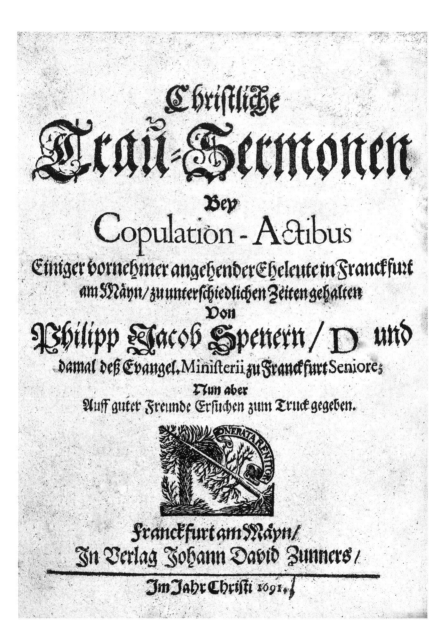

Figure 1: Frontispiece to Philipp Jakob Spener's *Marriage Sermons* (1691). Reproduced with the permission of the Francke Foundations, Halle, Germany (AFSt: 47E 11).

CHAPTER 1

Mystics, Marriage, and Early Lutheran Piety

In one of his many eloquent sermons, Martin Luther described the love of a man and woman in marriage as "the greatest and purest love of all loves." Unlike the "false love" that lusts after "money, property, honor" and mere sexual pleasure, and also unlike the mere "natural love" of paternal or filial relations, married love resembled the selfless love of God. Moreover, the mutual giving in marriage "is a union in faith. That is the basis and the entire existence of marriage that one gives oneself to the other and promises to be faithful." Fully aware of the less-than-ideal realities of marriage in his society, Luther still insisted that no one would ever know God truly or understand humanity correctly if he or she undervalued marital love. This primal "order," which God placed in his creation second only to the church formed by his relationship with Adam, undergirded Luther's anthropology, and profoundly influenced his understanding of an otherwise hidden and mysterious God.[1]

One hundred years after Luther's birth a Lutheran couple were married

---

1. Martin Luther, "A Sermon on the Estate of Marriage" (1519), WA 2:166-71; reprinted in *Luther on Women: A Sourcebook,* ed. and trans. Susan C. Karant-Nunn and Merry E. Wiesner-Hanks (Cambridge: Cambridge University Press, 2003), pp. 89-92, at 90, 91. As the editors point out, Luther here still preaches marriage as sacrament, then faithful companionship (fidelity), then progeny — classic Augustinian teaching, on which, see below.

Part of this chapter is taken from Roeber, "Marriage from 'Natural Sacrament' to Eucharistic Sign: A Canonical Recommendation for Pastoral Practice in North America in the Context of Orthodox–Roman Catholic–Protestant Mixed Marriages" (M.A. Theol. thesis, Balamand University, 2008). Cited with permission.

in Nuremberg. The letters exchanged by Balthasar Paumgartner and Magdalena Behaim reveal an intimate relationship of friendship, testified to by their routine use of the word "friendly" to describe their intimate marriage that "remained remarkably free and spontaneous."[2]

Luther would not have been surprised, however, by the grim alternative experience of marriage documented by the long-suffering pietist pastor's wife Beate Hahn Paulus. Her Württemberg diary recounts in harrowing detail the beatings she suffered at the hands of a drunken pastor-husband and how she survived by taking refuge in private devotions that had nothing to do with reflections on the joys of marriage.[3]

Theological Traditions

Where did Luther — who knew all about the brutalities of daily life — find his inspiration for such rhapsodic praises of the married estate? To reconstruct the anthropology of Luther and early Lutheranism, and to discern the Lutheran view of God's grace or life within the married estate, specialists direct us to late medieval European understandings of more ancient sources. But "how far back [should] one . . . go?"[4]

Luther scholars suggest that he faced a daunting challenge in rethinking the marital relationship. First, Luther inherited an anthropology deeply informed by the thought of Saint Augustine of Hippo and, more importantly, the misinterpretations of Augustine that were common among his successors in the Western Church. Contrary to later misreading of his reflections, the African bishop had been one of the more positive of the Latin Fathers in affirming the goodness of male-female relations. Even sexual activity, characterized by the irrational passions, was only "venially" sinful within the bonds of marriage. Nonetheless, on the singular point that Luther would advance and which Balthasar and Magdalena Paumgartner exemplified, Augustine was not helpful. Augustine deployed a classical Latin rhetorical device in his re-

2. Steven Ozment, *Magdalena and Balthasar: An Intimate Portrait of Life in Sixteenth-Century Europe Revealed in the Letters of a Nuremberg Husband and Wife* (New Haven and London: Yale University Press, 1989), p. 28.

3. Ulrike Gleixner, ed., *Beate Hahn Paulus. Die Talheimer Wochenbücher 1817-1829* (Göttingen: Vandenhoeck & Ruprecht, 2007). For details on this particularly unhappy marriage, see below, chapter 7.

4. Rebecca Probert, *Marriage Law and Practice in the Long Eighteenth Century: A Reassessment* (Cambridge: Cambridge University Press, 2009), p. 18.

flections on the "goods" of marriage that later vanished from memory. In that tradition, the last-named in a sequence occupied the place of greatest honor. Thus, in Augustine's ordering, the benefit or "good" of children occupied the first, and hence the lowest, purpose of the estate. In speaking of *fides* Augustine intended to elevate mutual trust in marriage as the second good, one that manifested the crucial virtue both partners needed to exercise before marriage could realize its potential as the third good — *sacramentum* — an iconic representation of Christ's relationship to his church. But Luther could not find in Augustine any notion of friendship between men and women. Whenever Augustine mentioned friendship, he appears to have had in mind Cicero's *Laelius de amicitia,* in which friendship was "nothing other than agreement on all matters divine and human, along with good will and affection." The phrase was typical of Ciceronian rhetoric, and its meaning cannot be divorced from its rhetorical form. But neither Augustine nor those who forgot his rhetorical sequence regarded marriage as a partnership of true friends. The most Augustine managed in his ruminations on the Genesis account of why Adam listened to his wife and not to God was the rather condescending observation that he did so out of a "certain amicable benevolence."[5]

Although God spoke to Adam, remarkably neither Augustine nor Luther, who followed the bishop's lead at so many critical interpretive junctures, noticed the lack of conversation between the spouses. In the mystical reading of Ephesians 5 that Augustine, Luther, and a host of other commentators shared, the husband in marriage stood in the place of Christ and the wife iconically represented the church. The absence of conversation between Adam and Eve should have elicited some commentary. If husbands and wives imitated Christ and his church, it was there, and not in the original spousal relationship, that the fullness of an iconic representation of friendship, partnership, and holiness finally emerged. But neither Augustine nor Luther ever provided such a

---

5. Cicero, *De amicitia* 20: "Est enim amicitia nihil aliud nisi omnium divinarum humanarumque cum benevolentia et caritate consensio." In *De bono conjugali* (written perhaps ca. A.D. 401) Augustine admits that mutual trust is a "good" but at the same time asserts that celibacy in marriage is preferable to sexual activity. For the comments on the Genesis passage, see Augustine, *De Genesi ad litteram libri duodecim* 11.42.59: "Non quidam carnis victus concupiscentia . . . sed amicali quidam benevolentia . . ." (www.augustinus.it/ricerca/index .htm; accessed 15 February 2012). I am grateful to Mickey Mattox for alerting me to the source; my interpretation, however, differs from his more generous description of this passage as denoting genuine "friendship." See Mattox, *"Defender of the Most Holy Matriarchs": Martin Luther's Interpretation of the Women in Genesis in the "Enarrationes in Genesis," 1535-45* (Leiden and Boston: Brill, 2003), p. 46.

commentary. Still, Luther would insist in his reading of Genesis that Adam's "righteousness was not a gift which came from without, separate from Adam's nature, but . . . it was truly part of his nature, so that it was Adam's nature to love God, to believe God, to know God."[6] And by extension, of course, it was in the nature of both Adam and Eve to love one another as well.

At the same time, not only the pagan world but also late Judaism eventually developed an eschatological vision that looked forward to "a messianic kingdom the citizens of which will have much offspring and attain old age," to be followed by a "second and final stage [that] will restore man's original immortality. Man's return to the angelic mode of being implies his loss of Sexuality. There will be no sex in heaven." By the thirteenth century, Thomas Aquinas could assert in his magisterial *Summa theologiae* (I; II:4:8) that neither sexual union nor friendship would be important in heaven, since "the blessed ones do not unite in order to promote communication among themselves." In affirming the "first order" of creation as a state of friendship between men and women, Luther had to look in more recent Christian sources. Despite an impressive contribution that finally surfaced in the *City of God,* Augustine's "vision of companionate marriage was not just balanced, but often overshadowed, by his emphasis upon the sexual and reproductive functions of marriage." It was this legacy Luther had to struggle to overcome, and he only partly succeeded in doing so. As a result, he never quite linked the marital relationship to a clear theology of the church, either. His successors would struggle with the same dilemma.[7]

6. Jaroslav Pelikan et al., eds., *Luther's Works,* 55 vols. (St. Louis: Concordia; Philadelphia: Muhlenberg, 1958-65), 1:165 (on Gen. 3:7) (hereafter *LW*).

7. On the long history of the problem of sex and holiness, and for the quotations, see B. Lang, "No Sex in Heaven: The Logic of Procreation, Death, and Eternal Life in the Judeo-Christian Tradition," in *Mélanges bibliques et orientaux en l'honneur de M. Mathias Delcor,* ed. Andre Caquot, Simon Legasse, and Michel Tardieu (Neukirchen: Neukirchener Verlag, 1985), pp. 237-53, at 241, 251. See also Dennis Trout, "Friendship, Friends," in *Augustine through the Ages,* ed. Allan D. Fitzgerald et al. (Grand Rapids: Eerdmans, 1999), pp. 372-73, on Augustine's late remarks on sexuality in *De civitate Dei* 22.15-19. See also Philip Lyndon Reynolds, *Marriage in the Western Church: The Christianization of Marriage during the Patristic and Early Medieval Periods* (Leiden, New York, and Cologne: Brill, 1994), pp. 241-58: "Because friendship is the end of marriage, the relationship that essentially constitutes marriage is itself a variety of friendship . . . but this fellowship is prior to sexual procreativity. . . . Augustine (rather like some modern feminists) believes that in our fallen condition, this relationship and sexual desire are mutually inimical" (p. 253). For the quotation on marital friendship, see Elisabeth Clark, "Adam's Only Companion: Augustine and the Early Christian Debate on Marriage," *Recherches Augustiniennes* 21 (1986): 139-62, at 139.

Because earlier reform movements and the canon law ignored the theme of friendship in marriage, Luther looked to the medieval mystics. Reformers of the eleventh century had divided human beings into groups of workers, warriors, and clergy. "Empathy for women in their writings about marriage and sexuality" was hard to find. Instead, "the only sexually active women to whom reformers really devote[d] much attention [were] prostitutes and the wives of priests . . . treated as symbols of sin . . . the latter increasingly . . . the targets of scorn and hatred."[8] The canon law Luther inherited did nothing to remedy this restricted depiction. But the theology and the canon law were not entirely congruent, and Luther's recourse to a mystical theological tradition enabled him to find a way toward his own conception of marriage without ignoring official teaching or at least parts of the canonical tradition.

When Luther thought about humans, male and female, he acknowledged a debt to Augustine, but he also had a secondhand knowledge of Thomas Aquinas and of the Latin Church's incorporation of Aristotle's philosophical methods into a "natural law" tradition.[9] Luther drew from this complex inheritance, but he also found help in mystical writings when he tried to explain the tension of "nature" and "grace" in marriage. To understand what he could and could not draw from medieval mysticism, however, it pays dividends to ask first what Luther meant when he wrote of "nature," and then to summarize the canonical tradition that failed (in Luther's view) to reflect the correct theology of marriage. Primarily, Luther, in speaking of nature, was concerned with its "relational" dimensions, and he returned repeatedly to the teaching that God had become human. In applying this insight to marriage, he was both conventional and innovative. No reformer in the sixteenth century wanted to concede that he was inventing anything new. The reformers insisted that they stood in continuity with the wisdom of the ancients. The Roman Church, not they, had indulged in innovation.[10]

The Lutherans, like their Roman opponents, were earnest in their claim to continuity with an ancient, apostolic church. But they had a problem — and Luther shared it. He believed, with perhaps the majority of sixteenth-

---

8. Megan McLaughlin, *Sex, Gender, and Episcopal Authority in an Age of Reform, 1000-1122* (Cambridge and New York: Cambridge University Press, 2010), p. 48.

9. See especially Denis R. Janz, *Luther and Late Medieval Thomism: A Study in Theological Anthropology* (Waterloo, Ontario: Wilfrid Laurier University Press, 1983), pp. 1-59.

10. On Luther's reliance on and disagreement with patristic sources, see Manfred Schulze, "Martin Luther and the Church Fathers," in *The Reception of the Church Fathers in the West*, ed. Irena Backus, 2 vols. (Leiden, New York, and Cologne: Brill, 1997), 1:573-626, and Eric Leland Saak, "The Reception of Augustine in the Later Middle Ages," in the same volume, 1:367-404.

century Christians, in the imminent second coming of Christ to a world in its "last days." Many of his contemporaries concluded that lasting marriages and families could not, in this mood of expectation, be all that important. But Luther's views on marriage and family had little to do with the "last things." He "horizontalized" Christian ethics and concluded that the sacraments of baptism, penance, and communion were crucial for living in the here and now. So also was marriage. He wanted to "show how to live a Christian life between-the-times."[11]

Eschatology was not the only problem. Luther and his beloved Katharina von Bora also scandalized many when they broke their monastic vows. "Luther's wedding marked a radical break . . . the Reformation had to take leave of the centuries-old ideal of the charismatic leader who, as an ascetic man of God, forsakes all things 'worldly.'"[12] Moreover, his pastoral advice to Landgrave Philip of Hesse shocked and horrified even his allies. The church would not condone Philip's divorcing his wife Christina, but to prevent the landgrave from continually bedding concubines, Luther agreed as a matter of emergency that Philip should quietly marry a second time. He refused, however, to allow Philip's case to create a new law of marriage. The issue would return to haunt the Protestant tradition by the end of the seventeenth century.[13]

Luther, in reflecting on what he found inadequate in the Latin tradition's understanding of "natural," found a solution both to the eschatological question and to the practical dilemmas of nature and grace partly through recourse to ancient and late medieval mystical sources. His quarrel with Augustinian and scholastic theology led him to a late medieval tradition of "German mysticism" that stimulated his thinking about the images of the bridegroom and the bride. Here he found a way to affirm the dignity of marriage — one of the two greatest orders of creation, as he preached — even though it was no sacrament. In his catechisms, his marriage ritual book, the official statement of the Augsburg Confession, and the hymnody of the sixteenth century, we catch glimpses of what he learned from the mystics and what pietist renewal leaders a century later were intent on recapturing.[14] Any

---

11. Heiko A. Oberman, *Luther: Man between God and the Devil,* trans. Eileen Walliser-Schwarzbart (New Haven and London: Yale University Press, 1989), pp. 80, 81.

12. Oberman, *Luther,* p. 282; on the scandal and the broader context of Luther's marriage, see pp. 272-89.

13. On the bigamy issue, see Oberman, *Luther,* pp. 283-89, and John Witte Jr., *Law and Protestantism: The Legal Teachings of the Lutheran Reformation* (Cambridge: Cambridge University Press, 2002), pp. 224-26.

14. Bernard McGinn, *The Foundations of Mysticism: Origins to the Fifth Century* (New

understanding of the importance of the mystical tradition, however, must presuppose a rudimentary knowledge of the development of marriage practices and the theological view of marriage in the earlier history of the church.

Liturgical Theology and Law

The Roman Church, as Luther knew it, had developed a long-standing tradition that preferred a eucharistic context for the marriage rite and a nuptial blessing. It also viewed the bishop or priest as the witness on behalf of the church. In this understanding, the marital partners "contracted" the marriage by mutual consent, giving it its "form," and the "substance" was held to be the union of the two who became "one flesh." This teaching kept alive the old pagan Roman legal maxim *consensus facit nuptias* (consent constitutes marriage), and the Latin theologians of the fourth and fifth centuries ratified such pre-Christian customs. But Augustine of Hippo also offered fresh contributions to the Christian view of marriage in his tract *On the Good of Marriage* (ca. 401). Even while reaffirming the Pauline teaching that celibacy was the higher calling for those who could undertake its rigor, Augustine identified "three goods" of marriage — *proles, fides, sacramentum* (progeny, mutual fidelity, sacrament). To determine a clear definition of just what "sacrament" meant for Augustine, we should follow the advice of those who have concluded that Augustine "posited a sacrament *in* marriage" but did not talk about a "sacrament *of* marriage." The absolute, permanent relationship of Christ to his church provided the bedrock for Augustine's musing on the mysterious aspects of marriage as he commented on Ephesians 5. While never explicitly pointing out how there might be a "visible word" in marriage as he did for baptism and the Eucharist, Augustine clearly regarded marriage as "more than a mere figure or symbol of Christ's union with the Church." Human marriage might be a pale reflection of the marriage between Christ and the church, but that did not make it any less sacred. What remained unclear, however, was the precise manner in which "nature" and "grace" worked together in the marital relationship [15]

York: Crossroad, 1991), pp. 243-62; Bernard McGinn, *The Flowering of Mysticism: Men and Women in the New Mysticism, 1200-1350* (New York: Crossroad, 1998), pp. 78-112; Bernard McGinn, *The Mystical Thought of Meister Eckhart: The Man from Whom God Hid Nothing* (New York: Crossroad, 2001), pp. 35-52, 114-61, 176-82.

15. Philip Lyndon Reynolds, *Marriage in the Western Church: The Christianization of Marriage during the Patristic and Early Medieval Periods* (Leiden, New York, and Cologne: Brill, 1994), pp. 241-311, quotations at 280, 288, 289.

But if Augustine contributed to the high hopes for marriage outlined in Ephesians 5, he also published darker reflections on marriage in book 2 of the 418 work *On Marriage and Concupiscence,* in which he associated marriage with desire tending to disorder. Augustine distanced himself from the even more negative views of marriage and sexuality of his mentor Ambrose and his contemporary Jerome, but his darker vision, inherited partly from Tertullian, overshadowed for his successors the positive assessments of marriage as an occasion for mutuality and transcendence that one finds in the writing of 401.[16]

In his essay *De anima (Concerning the Soul),* Tertullian had developed a doctrine of "original sin" *(vitium originis)* that included his "traducianist" view "that each soul is somehow generated from the parent's soul." Augustine dissented from a purely material interpretation of the soul's creation and "passing," but he accepted a "spiritual version of the same theory [that] fitted in best with his teaching about original sin."[17] He presented, therefore, an ambivalent view of marriage, emphasizing both its goods and its linkage to a fallen creation.

The later penitential tradition of the West that produced its own canonical history reflected the negative strain of thought represented by Jerome and Ambrose. Augustine's view of sexual congress in marriage as a positive good (albeit perhaps a "venial" sin when detached from any intention or possibility of procreation) suffered eclipse. The canonical tradition came to interpret Augustine as holding that "sexual intercourse was allowed but only between married couples when undertaken for the sake of procreation." An elaborate canonical body of regulation became so demanding that some have concluded that "a devout married couple could licitly have had sexual relations on fewer than forty-four days of the year, once the periods of abstinence required by both the woman's own physiological cycle, and those for major Church festivals, such as Lent and Advent, had been taken into account."[18]

---

16. David G. Hunter, "Marriage," in *Augustine through the Ages,* pp. 535-37.

17. On Tertullian's thought, see Eric Osborn, *Tertullian: First Theologian of the West* (Cambridge: Cambridge University Press, 1997), pp. 163-82; for Tertullian's theology and then Augustine's adaptation of the traducianist strain, see J. N. D. Kelly, *Early Christian Doctrines* (San Francisco: Harper San Francisco, 1978), pp. 174-78, 345. For the key text in Romans and "original sin," see Philip L. Quinn, "Disputing the Augustinian Legacy: John Locke and Jonathan Edwards on Romans 5:12-19," in *The Augustinian Tradition,* ed. Gareth B. Matthews (Berkeley and Los Angeles: University of California Press, 1999), pp. 233-350.

18. Sarah Hamilton, *The Practice of Penance, 900-1050* (Woodbridge, U.K.: Boydell Press, 2001), pp. 196-201, at 197.

This medieval Western tradition emanated not only from Latin patristic teaching but also, and more importantly, from tribal and kinship customs that defined marriage as an undertaking that was never "private" or "personal." Rather, spousal joining was always carried out within networks whose definition of "family" — the entire household including servants, apprentices, and in some cases more than one generation — endured in the West until the eighteenth century.[19]

Luther thus inherited not only a theology but also a canonical tradition that at times seemed at odds with unofficial, customary Christian behaviors. The two official expressions of belief, theological and canonical, coexisted uneasily — a circumstance that would make Luther's revisions difficult. The rite of marriage in the West, as in the East, developed regionally, and no one ceremony became universal in the first Christian millennium. The same proved true of the canonical legacies. Neither unambiguously stipulated that marital union was redemptive. The "darker" side of marriage did not dominate these rites, although some of the ceremonies still tended to point toward practices (such as veiling) that borrowed from the more "spiritual" qualities associated with consecrated virgins. Moreover, the rituals, even if asking spouses for mutual consent, underscored on balance the predominant right of the head of a kinship group (that later was transposed to the Christian bishop or priest) to permit and ratify the union of persons and properties. Thus, a bridal Mass for the region around the city of Rome seems to have existed early, and the surviving texts (from the last half of the seventh century) include a collect, a "secret" prayer, and a postcommunion prayer that emphasizes the good of children, Augustine's first, but least important, benefit. We have no corresponding documents either for the Gelasian or the Ambrosian rites, which refer only to a veiling, or *velati*. Similarly, the Mozarabic or Spanish tradition makes no mention of a Mass, although the presanctified Eucharist apparently was distributed to the bridal couple. By the eleventh century in some regions of the West, a marriage ceremony celebrated immediately before the Mass, *in facie ecclesiae* (in the face of the gathered church), kept alive the belief that marriage was a mystery cel-

---

19. On the difficulties in translating Mediterranean Christian teachings into the northern European cultural context because of these kinship networks and expectations, see James C. Russell, *The Germanization of Early Medieval Christianity: A Sociohistorical Approach to Religious Transformation* (New York: Oxford University Press, 1994); on "family" see David Gaunt, "Kinship: Thin Red Lines or Thick Blue Blood," in *Family Life in Early Modern Times, 1500-1789*, ed. David I. Kertzer and Marzio Barbagli (New Haven and London: Yale University Press, 2001), pp. 257-87, at 259.

ebrated within the believing community, but not as part of the Liturgy or Mass. The contractual basis for marriage in the West was clear from the comments of Saint Ambrose of Milan from the mid-300s onward; the practice of veiling came to be seen as an equivalent to the consecration of virgins, and a nuptial blessing (originally the only real rite of marriage in the city of Rome itself) was often sung. A wide variety of local customs nevertheless in all cases included the "giving of consent . . . part of the oldest Roman tradition on marriage (the *dextrarum iunctio*). . . . with hands joined, the couple express their own consent in a formula which is substantially that used in England since the Middle Ages and formerly used in many dioceses of France."[20]

These regionally varied rituals that surrounded spousal consent and the various edicts underlining the official, public character of marriage, which like baptism remained the concern of the Christian state and the church alike, illustrate why marriage remained dominated by the consent not just of spouses but also of the leaders of a kinship group, and hence, why marriage remained a matter of public concern. The early medieval customs that had once allowed couples to declare themselves married and to ask for the church's blessing afterward slowly gave way to a restoration of the more ancient custom evident in the insistence pioneered by the Corrector des Burchard von Worms around 1025 that defined marriage in "public" terms. By the thirteenth century, the German lands adopted the practice of having the priest meet the couple at the door of the church to ask if the marriage was uncoerced and if consanguinity rules stood in the way. By the sixteenth century, special "bridal doors" on the north side of the church in some cities of the empire depicted the wise and foolish virgins, and especially, the marriage of the first spouses, Adam and Eve. Between 1483 and the 1540s one booklet appeared that affirmed the more hopeful interpretation of nature pioneered by Augustine when he suggested that God had intended sexual intercourse and children to be a blessing even before the Fall. The innovations in marriage ritual that Luther would subsequently introduce (including the suppression of a nuptial Mass) did not change practice in Lutheran territories

20. Jean Evenou, "Marriage," in *The Church at Prayer: An Introduction to the Liturgy III; The Sacraments,* ed. Aime George Martimort et al. (Collegeville, Minn.: Order of St. Benedict, 1988), pp. 185-207, at 188, 190, 207, 204. On the variety of earlier practices, see Korbinian Ritzer, *Formen, Riten und Religiöses Brauchtum der Eheschliessung in den Christlichen Kirchen des ersten Jahrtausends* (Münster: Aschendorff, 1962), pp. 178-98, 231-32; Joseph A. Jungmann, *The Mass of the Roman Rite: Its Origins and Development,* trans. Francis A. Brunner, 2 vols. (New York: Benziger Press, 1951; reprint, Allen, Tex.: Christian Classics, 1986), 2:182, 185.

until pietists began to contest the opinion of "orthodox" Lutherans that a marriage was not to be thought correct unless the pastor had blessed the union.[21]

The role of priest or pastor in solemnizing the "joining together," popular in German-speaking Europe after the tenth century, may have had roots in an older Germanic legal custom of the advocate *(Fürsprecher)*, the neutral lay leader who had witnessed marriage agreements. The long process by which both Roman and ecclesiastical law gradually transformed German legal customs was incomplete in the sixteenth century. Village legal officers still "spoke" the law alongside the increasingly streamlined procedures that governed property issues and inheritance disputes, again keeping both the public aspect of marriage and its approbation by male authorities clearly in view.[22]

The Western medieval church attempted in this context to bring spousal relations more firmly under its own control. In the absence of a fully developed Trinitarian theology for marriage defined as sacrament, "canon law dominated the discussion," "even on the part of theologians."[23] Until the eleventh and twelfth centuries, the church was not clear about the sacramental status of the rite. The older canons did not require a priest, and canonists disagreed whether the exchange of formal promises or sexual intercourse "consummated" the union. By the time of the canonist Gratian's *Concordia discordantium canonum* (ca. 1140), the majority held that physical union was essential if done with mutual consent. Gratian insisted on both ritual consent and consummation. The unintended consequence removed marriage "from the control of the lay community" by defining consent. Contrary to the expectations of hierarchs and canon lawyers, "the lay community learned to exploit the exclusive role awarded consent to promote the interests of powerful families . . . ironically, then, growing attention to the role of

21. For background, see Bernward Deneke, *Hochzeit* (Munich: Prestal Verlag, 1971), pp. 17-22, 95-99, 101-2; on the remote origins of the medieval ceremonials, see Kenneth Stevenson, *Nuptial Blessing: A Study of Christian Marriage Rites* (New York: Oxford University Press, 1983), pp. 35-94, at 88-91. On the disputes over the necessity of pastoral blessing, see below, chapter 3.

22. On the priest's role and the older Germanic folk law customs, see Ritzer, *Formen, Riten*, pp. 316, 328-36; for a summary of the literature and the issues involved at the village level in the mix of various legal norms, see A. G. Roeber, "The Origin and Transfer of German-American Concepts of Property and Inheritance," *Perspectives in American History*, n.s., 3 (1987): 115-71, at 121-34.

23. Jaroslav Pelikan, *The Christian Tradition: A History of the Development of Doctrine*, vol. 3, *The Growth of Medieval Theology (600-1300)* (Chicago and London: University of Chicago Press, 1978), p. 211.

consent in marriage led churchmen right back to the importance of conjugal relations, ending where they had once begun."[24] The canonical tradition in the West, increasingly dominated by trained experts in the law, finally "distinguished among: (1) an exchange of promises to be married in the future, constituting a contract of bethrothal, which could be broken in certain cases . . . (2) an exchange of promises . . . constituting a contract of marriage; and (3) consent to intercourse following the marriage, constituting consummation of the marriage." The contract "remained vulnerable to dissolution" until after consummation. Thus, despite the church's efforts to place itself in the role of village elders, village and regional concerns for property and alliances worked to guarantee an increasing focus by canon law experts on "free will and related concepts of mistakes, duress, and fraud,"[25] the darker side of nature, human misbehavior, and marriage.

Gratian's chapters summarized the Augustinian tradition on the threefold "goods" of marriage, but by this time the canonist put "faithfulness" before "progeny" and the "sacramental" dimension. In so doing, he gave expression to the importance of contractual obligation and honesty, but contributed nothing to the notion of a "good" in which partners were achieving salvation together. Gratian brought together the "discordant" canons, but he did not number the sacraments. Peter Lombard's *Sentences* did, picking up on a numbering that had emerged by the time of his writings in the twelfth century.[26]

A century later, Pope Gregory IX set canonists to work to produce a compendium of papal decretals touching a wide variety of teachings. The 1234 work included chapters devoted to nuptial law, rights, and responsibilities.[27] These developments might have provided an opportunity to reexamine the "goods" of marriage, but instead they occurred at a time of tension

24. Irven M. Resnick, "Marriage in Medieval Culture: Consent Theory and the Case of Joseph and Mary," *Church History* 69, no. 2 (June 2000): 350-71, at 363-65; quotations at 370, 371.

25. Harold J. Berman, *Law and Revolution: The Formation of the Western Legal Tradition* (Cambridge, Mass., and London: Harvard University Press, 1983), quotations at pp. 227, 228. The canonical expressions did not completely overshadow the capacity to connect an anthropological approach to marriage and a more mystical understanding of sexual union and holiness in the church. See Bernard McGinn, *The Growth of Mysticism: Gregory the Great through the 12th Century* (New York: Crossroad, 1994), pp. 168-74, and Jean Leclercq, *Monks on Marriage: A Twelfth-Century View* (New York: Seabury Press, 1982).

26. Pelikan, *Growth of Medieval Theology,* pp. 209-12.

27. Emil Ludwig Richter and Emil Friedberg, comps., *Corpus juris Canonici, Pars Secunda: Decretalium Collectiones* (Leipzig: Bernhard Tauchnitz, 1881); *Liber Quartus Titulus I "De sponsalibus et matrimoniis."*

between the Latin West and Byzantine Christians. Among the eventual lists of "errors" the Byzantines attributed to Latins, two potentially touched on the holiness of spousal relations, and they prophetically targeted issues Luther would seize upon generations later. The Byzantines had condemned clerical celibacy for priests and deacons in the West, suspecting that its promulgation amounted to little more than an excuse for concubinage: even though priests "commit adultery and fornicate without hindrance, and although they have concubines, they still celebrate the Eucharist." The Byzantine popular prejudice in favor of the monk-bishop reflected a conviction that "an unmarried priest was better than a married one" but that, realistically, marriage contained lust among the lower clergy. That attitude among Western theologians extended to all clergy and contributed to their focus on the darker side of marriage's limited "good" and justification, and an attitude Luther himself struggled, not always successfully, to jettison.[28]

Later revisions of the canonical tradition in the West would outlaw "clandestine" marriages and sharpen the profile of marriage as sacramental to counter Protestant views, but the revisions did not substantively alter the canonical tradition that had emerged as a legal code by the 1200s. Most importantly, the Latin tradition did not revisit the question of marriage from the Council of Trent in the sixteenth century to the twentieth century. By around 1875, the church became worried about contraception but still taught that procreation defined the purpose of marriage, and held officially to the view that sexuality "was not integral to identity in any remotely positive way, but evidence of our nature's fallenness."[29]

Many scholars believe that "by the early fourteenth century the internal development of the *Corpus juris canonici* had reached its conclusion." Whether this is strictly true or not, from the twelfth century onward "canon law emerged as a discipline separate from theology." The complexities

---

28. Tia M. Kolbaba, *The Byzantine Lists: Errors of the Latins* (Urbana and Chicago: University of Illinois Press, 2000), pp. 40, 39. On the growing popularity of celibate bishops and the allure of monastic asceticism, see Claudia Rapp, *Holy Bishops in Late Antiquity: The Nature of Christian Leadership in an Age of Transition* (Berkeley, Los Angeles, and London: University of California Press, 2005), pp. 100-151; see also Andrea Sterk, *Renouncing the World Yet Leading the Church: The Monk-Bishop in Late Antiquity* (Cambridge: Harvard University Press, 2004).

29. Leslie Woodcock Tentler, "'The Abominable Crime of Onan': Catholic Pastoral Practice and Family Limitation in the United States, 1875-1919," *Church History* 71, no. 2 (June 2002): 307-40, at 314. For the literature on medieval canons touching on contraception, see P. P. A. Biller, "Birth Control in the West in the Thirteenth and Early Fourteenth Centuries," *Past & Present* 94 (1982): 3-26.

around "consent" produced litigation all over Europe, and that pattern helps to explain what would provoke the Protestant rejection of the late medieval syntheses. If the medieval debates failed to provide a unitary vision in theology or canonical tradition, much the same must finally be the judgment rendered upon Luther's rather heroic attempts to transcend the stalemate.[30]

Litigation surrounding marital disputes in the West showed pronounced regional variations by the late medieval period. Disputes from English church courts, for example, did not match Franco-Belgian examples, even though "the common academic training of the principal officers of the church courts in both countries and the availability of appeal, in some cases going all the way to the papacy," should have guaranteed "uniformity of application of the law." Variations came from different regions in Europe, but the difference in the "kinds of claims that were made before the courts, and the way in which the courts processed them," gradually emerged.[31] A north-south distinction appeared as Mediterranean Christians used the church courts to demonstrate that parents could control marriage choice, so there was less "litigation about marriage formation in southern Europe." By contrast, in the northern cities and regions that would come to accept the Reformation, restoration of parental authority and consent would come to play a significant role in Luther's high views of proper spousal relations. His preference for this aspect of the canonical tradition stemmed from his conclusion that the failure of the church to involve parents sufficiently in helping children seek out godly spouses had not served the Christian people of his region well.[32]

Evidence from our knowledge of surviving sermons, and on the basis of their own observation of popular understanding, the Reformers concluded that a more hopeful but pious view of spousal relations had not penetrated the hearts of believers. At least in part, the darker official theology and the impact of the emerging tradition of marriage law had contributed to that unfortunate state of affairs.[33] To "restore the ideal of the *ecclesia primitiva*

---

30. See Brian Tierney, "Canon Law and Church Institutes in the Late Middle Ages," in Brian Tierney, *Rights, Laws, and Infallibility in Medieval Thought* (Aldershot, U.K., and Burlington, Vt.: Ashgate, 1997), 6:49-69, quotations at 49, 51.

31. Charles Donahue Jr., *Law, Marriage, and Society in the Later Middle Ages: Arguments about Marriage in Five Courts* (New York: Cambridge University Press, 2007), p. 600.

32. Donahue, *Law*, pp. 598-632, at 632.

33. Pavel Blazek, *Die mittelalterliche Rezeption der aristotelischen Philosophie der Ehe: Von Robert Grosseteste bis Bartholomäus von Brügge (1246/1247-1309)* (Leiden and Boston: Brill, 2007), pp. 389-95.

was the goal of the Gregorian, Cistercian, and Franciscan reform movements of the later Middle Ages, as well as the Protestant Reformation," but the Reformers and later the pietists concluded that reform ideals had never been extended to include a more positive view of spousal relations. The evidence is mixed. Medieval historians seem to agree that the church never achieved a systematic teaching delivered at the local level that could have transformed the northern European understanding of Christianity. Accommodation to pre-Christian "world-accepting, folk-centered" religions guaranteed a kinship-oriented faith. Little evidence suggests that ordinary believers had abandoned this pragmatic view of faith by the sixteenth century. But the laity also did not merely tolerate the church's role in blessing marriage. They did look for support and affirmation of spousal relationships in the church's public, official ritual, even while defending their own customary views of the estate.[34]

Luther's Synthesis

To combat the disjunction between theology and the canonical sources, Luther drew on mystical writers who had fallen into disfavor with the rise of scholasticism in the thirteenth century. Luther scholars continue to disagree vigorously about the degree to which he remained in the debt of these authorities. But he never completely abandoned what he had learned from the neglected mystical sources in the West. Especially from the writings of the sixth-century Syrian known as "Pseudo-Dionysius," but also from Latin Catholic and German mystics, Luther learned to describe marriage as the "second estate" or created "order" in the world.[35] In the 1520s, to be sure, Luther fulminated against Dionysius. He dismissed his *Celestial*

34. See the argument and literature cited in Russell, *Germanization,* pp. 120-25, 138-40, 162-71; quotation at 189; 197-211, quotation at 211.

35. On "Pseudo-Dionysius" see McGinn, *Foundations,* pp. 157-85, and Alexander Golitzin, *Et Introibo ad altare dei: The Mystagogy of Dionysius Areopagita* (Thessalonica: George Dedousis's, 1994); on the possible political reasons for Pseudo-Dionysius's writings in his sixth-century context, see Rosemary A. Arthur, *Pseudo-Dionysius as Polemicist: The Development and Purpose of the Angelic Hierarchy in Sixth Century Syria* (Aldershot, U.K.: Ashgate, 2008); and more specifically on Luther's use and possible misunderstanding of these writings, Alexander Golitzin, "Dionysius Aeropagita: A Christian Mysticism?" *Pro Ecclesia* 12, no. 2 (Spring 2003): 161-212; and Bengt Hoffman, *Luther and the Mystics: A Re-examination of Luther's Spiritual Experience and His Relationship to the Mystics* (Minneapolis: Augsburg, 1976), pp. 56, 111, 120, 160, 193.

Hierarchy not only for its choirs of angels, but also because Dionysius "is more of a Platonist than a Christian. So if I had my way, no believing soul would give the least attention to these books. So far, indeed, from learning Christ in them, you will lose even what you already know of him. I speak from experience."[36]

But Luther depended on the mystical tradition Pseudo-Dionysius summarized.[37] Both writers agreed that God remained a mystery, wrapped in darkness and unapproachable light. For Luther, as for the ancient councils of Ephesus and Chalcedon, the mysterious God became comprehensible because the divine and human natures of Christ communicated perfectly with each other, without confusion, coercion, or contradiction.[38] Luther could not evade the image of the God-man doing chores for his human mother, the "God-bearer." And from there, it was but a short step to affirm marital love as the reflection of a salvation offered to both men and women by a God who had taken on flesh from a woman to restore the original purpose of the creation.

Pseudo-Dionysius appears, at first glance, an unlikely source for a hopeful theology of marriage. Scholars suspect that he probably defied Chalcedon and may have asserted that Christ had only one nature. Worse still, Dionysius, speaking to a monastic audience, ignored marriage. Still, from the Dionysian writings, subsequent Christians learned to think of the relatedness of created life and the divine. From his *Celestial Hierarchy* Luther learned that these sacred orders manifested God's beauty, in which human beings and angels would find their fulfillment. Though explicitly dismissing Dionysius, Luther drew on a neo-Dionysian revival in the Latin Church that began in the 1200s. For Luther, as for Bonaventure, the angelic and earthly hierarchies showed how "the inner powers of the soul" energized "loving union." And Luther, like his predecessor Thomas Gallus, took a dim view of

---

36. *On the Babylonian Captivity of the Church* (WA 6:497-573); here, *LW* 36:109.

37. Wilhelm Maurer, "Luthers Lehre von den drei Hierarchien und ihr mittelalterlicher Hintergrund," *Bayerische Akademie der Wissenschaften; Sitzbungsberichte* 4 (1970): 1-131, at 30-41. Maurer notes that Luther, despite describing marriage as the "fountain" of politics and society and the "seminary of the Church," in his commentary on Galatians discusses society and politics but not marriage and the church. Maurer concludes that contrary to Pseudo-Dionysius, the orders of creation exist for Luther in their function and activity, not as descriptions of social reality or states of "being."

38. See Schulze, "Luther and the Church Fathers," pp. 591-93; and in greater detail, Johann Anselm Steiger, *Fünf Zentralthemen der Theologie Luthers und Seiner Erben: Communicatio-Imago-Figura-Maria-Exempla* (Leiden, Boston, and Cologne: Brill, 2002), pp. 3-52.

human intellect as the proper site or focus for human attempts to develop the relationship to a "God [who] is unknowable but reveals himself as Love."[39]

How "unknowable" was God for Luther? God-as-Trinity was most obvious for Luther in God's "decision to create." But Luther argued that the created order could reveal God not as love but only as just and judge. The revelation of the Son in the incarnation made clear the revelation of the loving Trinity in creation. The continual creative activity of God, then, for Luther went beyond typical medieval boundaries. Luther saw "traces of the Trinity in all the created works, more than Augustine could ever have imagined," including marriage.[40]

No scholarly consensus has yet emerged on the definition of the "strain" of "mysticism" that Luther either admired or despised as he searched for support of his hopes for the created world. What no one disputes is that the late medieval German mystics like Meister Eckhart, but especially Johann Tauler and Henry Suso, brought the neo-Dionysian recovery of the 1200s into the sixteenth-century discussion. Their "mysticism of the ground" that emphasized simplicity, acknowledgment of spiritual poverty, and absolute obedience to God in suffering provided Luther with a powerful synthetic weapon.[41]

To see how this "mysticism of the ground" clarifies Luther's insights about marriage, we have to dispense with misleading juxtapositions of "nature" and "grace." A textbook summary would assert that after Augustine theologians saw God's grace behind any good human activity. The old Latin axiom "God crowns nothing in us other than his own gifts" had informed Augustine's theology that explained God confirming good carried out by humans according to their natural gifts. Luther accepted this ancient insight. Aristotelian methods of organizing Western theology, however, had encouraged some to conclude that this "gift" of grace was alien from mere creation, so that God had to "add" or "infuse" it into human nature. Luther rejected

---

39. McGinn, *Flowering of Mysticism*, pp. 78-85, at 79, 83, quotation at 81.

40. The above summarizes Christine Helmer, *The Trinity and Martin Luther: A Study on the Relationship between Genre, Language, and the Trinity in Luther's Works (1523-1546)* (Mainz: Verlag Philipp von Zabern, 1999), pp. 249-66, at 256, 262.

41. McGinn, *Mystical Thought of Meister Eckhart*, pp. 35-37; and see Anna Marie Wiberg-Pederson, "Justification and Grace: Did Luther Discover a New Theology or Did He Discover Anew the Theology of Justification and Grace?" *Studia Theologica* 57 (2003): 143-61; on the theology of the ground, see McGinn, *The Harvest of Mysticism in Medieval Germany (1300-1500)* (New York: Herder and Herder, 2005), pp. 390-404.

this notion in particular, because for him, "nature" is not a fixed, immobile "thing" "but rather . . . a relational concept. Thus human nature is corrupt only insofar as it refuses to ground its existence in God." Luther concluded that all men and women are trapped in a condition that obstructs the proper relation to God and the neighbor. He eventually concluded that the image of God partially survived in humans and made them "apt for the grace of God." Even apart from God's "crowning his own gifts" by reestablishing the right relationship through faith, "moral activity outside of grace is not totally without value . . . the pagan who does less evil than another will receive lesser punishment."[42]

Yet Luther could also be confusing when he wrote that nature was "relational" and therefore open to change. In his commentary on Galatians (1531), he emphasized an "imputed" righteousness and teetered on the edge of claiming total depravity, even to the extent of saying that the image of the devil had replaced God's image. Still, he could say that even without hope for perfection, the Christian was "holy." Believing that the Roman Church depicted God as an avenging judge, he insisted upon the free gift of Christ and the action of the Holy Spirit "by which the image of God has been renewed," making a genuinely "new creature" internally. Luther did not reconcile depravity and the possibility of renewal, and five years later in his *Disputation concerning Mankind* he wrote gloomily that the Fall destroyed any capacity for renewal. God had made a new relationship possible. Thus, human natural capacities and power had changed, but the change did not affect human actions. This distinction clarifies Luther's view of nature and grace, and hence of marriage. He rejected "total depravity" or the claim that "grace destroys nature" and therefore remained inclined toward a quasi-sacramental view of marriage. The distinctions were subtle, and contemporaries lost sight of them. Even today a scholarly neglect of Luther's insistence that humans are created for participation in the life of the Trinity helps explain why his teaching on the holiness of marriage as "not quite sacrament" also fell into obscurity. Within a few short years, Nicholas von Amsdorf, in criticizing Melanchthon's disagreement with Luther over the bondage of the will, forgot that Luther had restricted his focus on "bondage" to the theological

---

42. Janz, *Luther and Late Medieval Thomism*, pp. 6-33, at 9; my interpretation depends on Janz and Heiko Oberman, "Simul Gemitus et Raptus: Luther and Mysticism," in *The Reformation in Medieval Perspective*, ed. Steven Ozment (Chicago: Franklin Watts, 1971), pp. 219-51, rather than on Ozment, *Homo Spiritualis: A Comparative Study of the Anthropology of Johannes Tauler, Jean Gerson, and Martin Luther (1509-1516) in the Context of Their Theological Thought* (Leiden: Brill, 1969), pp. 87-216.

question of "who are we in the presence of God?" Von Amsdorf's attempt to rescue Luther from Melanchthon perpetuated a more pessimistic assessment of the marriage relationship as the meeting place between humans and God than Luther intended.[43]

Luther instead preached an elevated view of the created order. Perhaps because he was called to be a professor of Scripture, Luther ruminated on Paul's observation in First Thessalonians that human beings are body, soul, and spirit. For Luther, the human spirit comes from the Holy Spirit and biblical references to "flesh" meant "enmity to God." The flesh was not the body, since human beings remain this composite of body, soul, and spirit. Luther laid aside theological traditions that inherited from Greek speculation a distinction between the "higher" and the "lower" part of the soul. He especially disliked any tendency to locate the "higher" aspects of humanity in the intellect. Like the late medieval "nominalists," Luther insisted that the will was the problem, and if there was a "spark" from the original image that grounded the soul in God, it could be found in the heart and will. Unfortunately, the Fall meant that human hearts and wills always prompted a drive toward self-interest. Unaided by grace, reason could never discern the truly good and the conscience could not trust it. The will bent it always back toward the self. Because of this fallenness, Luther was not very interested in "nature" as such. He rather returned to the astonishing event in Bethlehem and concluded that the babe joined the divine and the human. There the eyes of faith could see that grace had radically entered "nature." Luther criticized theologians who (in his view) separated reason from will and analyzed conscience in isolation. He had no real interest in a Platonic, Renaissance humanism that pursued fine distinctions between reason and will. But while he fulminated against "scholastic" ideas of conscience, he admired Tauler and the anonymous author

43. Janz, *Luther and Late Medieval Thomism,* pp. 28-30. For the Galatians commentary quotations, see *LW* 26:229 and 431; 27:139-40, at 139, 136. On Luther's defense of the survival of the "image and likeness," see Simo Peura, "Die Teilhabe an Christus bei Luther," in Peura, *Luther und Theosis* (Helsinki and Erlangen: Luther-Agricola-Gesellschaft, 1990), pp. 121-61, who at 160 concludes that the actual "situation of humanity in this life does not basically change." For the von Amsdorf criticism of Melanchthon, see David C. Steinmetz, *Reformers in the Wings: From Geiler von Kaysersberg to Theodore Beza,* 2nd ed. (Oxford and New York: Oxford University Press, 2001), p. 55. For a more recent attempt to recover the importance of "image and likeness" and Luther's views on marriage that remain focused on Luther's debt to Augustine and the supposed primacy of procreation as marriage's purpose and holiness, see Paul R. Hinlicky, *Luther and the Beloved Community: A Path for Christian Theology after Christendom* (Grand Rapids and Cambridge, U.K.: Eerdmans, 2010), pp. 179-218, at 181-87.

of the *Theologia Germanica,* both of whom found in the soul some spark of the original image and likeness that God's grace could transform.[44]

Thomas Aquinas summarized for Luther (rightly or wrongly) the erroneous teaching on grace that Peter Lombard had pioneered in his *Sentences.* Thomas argued that created nature by itself could not merit eternal life, "unless there is added a supernatural gift, which we call grace." Whatever remains of the divine image in humans "subsists in humanity in our intellectual nature" for Thomas. But the gulf between God and the creation was so absolute in the metaphysics Thomas inherited from Aristotle that "Thomas [preferred] that his readers infer entities such as grace and happiness change their status, from uncreated to created, rather than claim that the creature becomes a composite of created and uncreated." In rejecting this notion of grace as "wholly alien" to humankind, Luther remained, despite later reservations, allied to medieval mystics, who taught him to find the "ground" for the relation between God and the creation. Moreover, late medieval German lay piety accentuated the humanity of Christ and his mother in ways that influenced Luther's ruminations on the incarnation and his convictions about marriage.[45]

Luther's fondness for the 1350 essay he attributed in his preface to the 1516 edition to "the illumined Doctor Tauler" is probably best explained by the central theme of the *Theologia Germanica* — "a dualism between selfwill and God's will, not between nature and spirit. God's living presence here on earth is more important . . . than the idea that God's spirit stands over against the material world."[46] Here Luther found the "ground" for his un-

44. John L. Farthing, *Thomas Aquinas and Gabriel Biel: Interpretations of St. Thomas Aquinas in German Nominalism on the Eve of the Reformation* (Durham, N.C., and London: University of North Carolina Press, 1988), p. 9; Herbert Olsson, *Schöpfung, Vernunft und Gesetz in Luthers Theologie* (Uppsala: Almqvist och Wiksell, 1971), pp. 270, 282-85, 454-56, 490-561; Brian Albert Gerrish, *Grace and Reason: A Study in the Theology of Luther* (Oxford: Oxford University Press, 1962), pp. 10-27, 153-67; Michael G. Baylor, *Action and Person: Conscience in Late Scholasticism and the Young Luther* (Leiden and New York: Brill, 1977).

45. Janz, *Luther and Late Medieval Thomism,* pp. 44-59; A. N. Williams, *The Ground of Union: Deification in Aquinas and Palamas* (New York: Oxford University Press, 1999), pp. 82-101, quotations at 86, 93, 95 citing the *Summa theologiae* I-II, q. 114, 2 resp. On the late medieval emphasis on the humanity of Christ and Mary, and the shift to a "spiritualized" Marian devotion to counteract Protestantism, see Donna Spivey Ellington, *From Sacred Body to Angelic Soul: Understanding Mary in Late Medieval and Early Modern Europe* (Washington, D.C.: Catholic University of America Press, 2001), pp. 54-56, 142-251.

46. I use here the most accessible English translation: *The Theologia Germanica of Martin Luther,* trans. Bengt Hoffman, introduction and commentary by Bengt Hoffman, preface by Bengt Hägglund (London: SPCK; New York; Paulist, 1980), pp. 42, 34-35.

derstanding of God's relationship with his created world, a relationship remarkably similar to the one Pseudo-Dionysius had pioneered. The Dominican Johannes Tauler was not the author of this work (as Luther supposed), but Tauler's eighty surviving sermons touched on similar themes. Tauler taught that humans can know only what God is not — and hence, the soul "knows" God by descending into the darkness of an unknowable God.[47]

Despite the reservations some scholars have expressed about the debt of Luther and the pietists to mystical thought, the "German Theology" served as the sourcebook for Lutheran reflections on grace and the creation for two centuries. It remained popular because it relied heavily on, and employed an engaging theology of, "the ground"; contrasted the old Adam and the risen Christ; asserted that God finds the divinization of his creation as the fulfillment of his own loving nature; praised the Eucharist; and insisted on radical obedience as the way to union with God — who is selfless love itself. Its popularity among Lutherans gave it a place on the Catholic Index of Forbidden Books on the eve of the Thirty Years' War. "Orthodox Lutherans . . . continued to read the book. The mystic John Arndt reedited an earlier printing based on Luther in 1597; his version had over sixty later printings. The German Pietists had a particular affection for the work."[48]

Tauler's mystical insights elevated a this-worldly and practical piety. Any attention given to the "innermost ground" of the soul can only come about in tireless love of neighbor and a willingness to imitate the suffering of Christ on behalf of others. Here, in the significance of Christ's passion and death — the profound mystery of the cross — Luther recognized a kindred spirit — and a model for the mysterious but holy relationship between husband and wife. Throughout his life, he admired Tauler because "the immediacy of God's presence was always part of his *Erfahrung* (experience)," and Luther's notion of grace as a relationship with the life of God, not an abstract quantity or quality "added" to nature, paralleled the teaching of the "German Theology." And nowhere was Christ's sacrificing love more exemplary, Luther concluded, than in the marriage relationship.

The "cure" for "nature," the treatise had concluded, was clear: "God assumed human nature or humanity. He became humanized and man became divinized. . . . God must become humanized in me. This means that God takes unto Himself everything that is in me, from within and from without, so that

---

47. For a representative sample, see Leopold Naumann, ed., *Ausgewählte Predigten Johann Taulers* (Berlin: W. de Gruyter, 1933).

48. McGinn, *Harvest of Mysticism,* pp. 392-404, quotation at 393.

there is nothing in me that resists God or obstructs His work." The peculiar dilemma of human beings "in nature" is that "the natural creature does not have in mind the Good as simply the Good, for the sake of the Good. It rather thinks of the Good as a particular Good that must be attained. . . . Man fancies himself to be what he is not. . . . He does not claim only what is God's insofar as God becomes man or dwells in a divinized person. No, he claims what is the innermost of God, God's prime mark, namely the uncreated, eternal Being."[49]

Luther's struggle with the terms "grace" and "nature" may seem remote from his teaching on the relationship between spouses. But his insights remained the standard to which Protestants repaired when they argued over their continuity or discontinuity with ancient and medieval Christians. Luther and his contemporaries were not radicals because they insisted on the primacy of marriage as the estate in which God called Adam and Eve to union with him. Nor were they radicals in refusing to tie ordained ministry to celibacy for the clergy — the Eastern Church had admonished the Latin Church about that in the seventh century. Their novelty lay elsewhere: in their claim that God's "grace and favor" acted immediately in the created elements of water, wine, bread, and the Word and therefore cut through any notions of "independent" or "natural" virtue. Luther rejected institutional "channels" controlled by clerical power that infused a "supernatural" quality into creation. His writings on marriage and its analogy with the relationship of Christ to the church reflected a mystical and graced view of the marital relationship. Pietists recovered such insights with excitement. Luther's debt to the "mystical tradition of the late medieval" formed his view of marriage, and "his theology is simply not understandable in its innermost content except against this background of its mystical roots."[50]

---

49. Hoffman, *Luther and the Mystics,* p. 119; Franz Posset, "Deification in the German Spirituality of the Late Middle Ages and in Luther: An Ecumenical and Historical Perspective," *Archiv für Reformationsgeschichte* 84 (1993): 103-26. Tauler sees the union of the human soul with the divine as a direct participation in the divine essence; for the quotations, *Theologia Germanica,* chapter 3, p. 63; chapter 38, pp. 115-16. For a more skeptical reading of the *Theologia Germanica*'s relationship to Luther, see Steven E. Ozment, *Mysticism and Dissent: Religious Ideology and Social Protest in the Sixteenth Century* (New Haven: Yale University Press, 1973), pp. 14-59.

50. Volker Leppin, "Transformationen spätmittelalterlicher Mystik bei Luther," in *Gottes Nähe unmittelbar erfahren: Mystik im Mittelalter und bei Martin Luther,* ed. Bernd Hamm and Volker Leppin (Tübingen: Mohr Siebeck, 2007), pp. 165-85, at 185, my translation. Lutherans were not happy with "sacramentals" and what they regarded as popular beliefs in theophanic conceptions of the world; they were less concerned about eradicating these notions than their Reformed counterparts. See Robert Scribner, "Ritual and Popular Religion in Catholic Germany at the Time of the Reformation," *Journal of Ecclesiastical History* 35 (1984): 47-77.

Luther had to confront the creation account in Genesis in any discussion of the spousal relationship and the "orders" of creation. The succession of teachings he wrote suggests that he may have initially jettisoned any notion of the "sacramental" from what he was tempted to see as a "worldly" relationship, only to retract that position and, in later writings of the 1530s, to recapture the quasi-sacramental, including both perspectives in his profoundly influential *Trau-Büchlein,* or *Marriage Booklet.* More than one scholar has suggested that as Luther had to confront the necessity of finding an evangelical substitute for Roman institutional forms of church life, he abandoned the more radical instincts of the early 1520s. Perhaps in the early church visitations of 1528, and beyond, he began to focus more on the continuities he saw between his own hopes for spouses and the best of what he could bring forward from the patristic and medieval theologians, shorn, as he hoped, from an oppressive canonical tradition.[51]

Philipp Melanchthon may have given the first set of lectures on Genesis at Wittenberg in November of 1523. Even if he did, "the shadow of Luther hung long over Lutheran interpretation of Genesis."[52] But Luther's contemporaries, especially Melanchthon, clung to the early dismissal of marriage's quasi-sacramental character, and thus changed Luther's more subtle views about marriage, possibly for political reasons. Seen as part of the long-established tension between the dual role of "church" and Christian princes, marriage could be interpreted, in a theology that spoke of "two kingdoms," as a secular compact undertaken by two people for "this-worldly" purposes. In Luther's sermons, his letters, his essay on the married estate, and his *Trau-Büchlein,* or *Marriage Booklet,* he took quite a different view.

In 1520, Luther in his treatise *On the Babylonian Captivity of the Church* had explicitly rejected the accepted interpretation of Ephesians 5:32 that had linked the "great mystery" of Christ to his church as the basis for teaching that marriage was a sacrament. What he missed, Luther wrote, was the "word of divine promise" *(verbum promissionis divinae)* that was necessary for any explicitly Christian rite to qualify as a true sacrament. After all, marriage had

---

51. On the shift in Luther's perspectives, and Melanchthon's role in preparing the "law and order" emphasis of the 1528 *Instructions for the Visitors of Parish Pastors,* see, for example, Martin Brecht, *Martin Luther: Shaping and Defining the Reformation, 1521-1532,* trans. James L. Schaaf (Minneapolis: Fortress, 1990), pp. 90-96, 266-72, 280-83. For further reflections on the fascination of Melanchthon with Roman law and "natural law" versus Luther's views, see Werner Elert, *Morphologie des Luthertums, Zweiter Band: Soziallehren und Sozialwirkungen des Luthertums,* 2nd ed. (Munich: C. H. Beck'sche Verlagbuchhandlung, 1953), pp. 334-38.

52. Mattox, *Defender,* pp. 273-75, quotation at 275.

been around since the beginning of the world, was known among all peoples, and could hardly be found only among those now under the "new law," that is, the members of the Christian church.[53] Two years later, in his treatise *The Estate of Marriage*, Luther again appeared determined to make a sharp break with the patristic and medieval consensus that had grown up around marriage. In this essay, he declared his distaste about saying anything regarding marriage, but it was the hopeless mix of worldly and spiritual matters and especially the "damned papal law" that persuaded him to write to quiet "confused consciences." Luther did not hesitate to speak both of the orders of creation and of an "implanted nature" that appeared to ground marriage firmly in God's plans for humanity from the beginning. Yet, in the second part of the presentation that dealt with divorce, Luther chose to overlook the fidelity of Christ to his church that had provided Augustine with the model for preaching the indissolubility of the bond between spouses. Luther's irritation with the canonical tradition led him through the argument to conclude that divorce on the grounds of adultery was after all approved by Christ himself. But in the third section of his treatise, in speaking of the holiness of marriage, Luther again avoided Ephesians, took his scriptural quotations overwhelmingly from the Old Testament, and concluded rather gloomily that sexual relations in marriage were always somehow sinful even if God protected them by his grace since the "order" of marriage was "his work."[54]

The publication of the New Testament that same year gave Luther the opportunity to comment again on the "sacramental" status of marriage in his gloss on Ephesians 5:32. Here, Luther repeated another's insight since his translation had depended upon Erasmus's second edition of the Greek New Testament published three years earlier. It had been Erasmus who observed that the Greek "mystery" pointed to something deeper and not as clearly explicit as the by-now accepted scholastic insistence upon an "outward sign" that "conveyed" grace. Luther's own use of the German word "secret" *(Geheimnis)* both distinguished marriage from baptism and the Lord's Supper, and also kept alive at least partially what earlier Christian writers had pondered, namely, the mysterious relationship between Christ and the church.[55] Although Luther scolded the Roman Church for not having paid sufficient attention to the Greek word "mystery," he offered no actual solu-

---

53. Luther, *De Captivitate Babylonica Ecclesiae*, WA 6:497-573, at 550.

54. Luther, "Vom ehelichen Leben," WA 10.2:275-304, pp. 275, 304.

55. On this issue, see Luther, *Die Deutsche Bibel* W.E, VII, p. 207; for the larger context, see Viggo Nörskov Olsen, *The New Testament Logia on Divorce: A Study of Their Interpretation from Erasmus to Milton* (Tübingen: Mohr Siebeck, 1971), pp. 7-8, 43-46.

tion to the Augustinian insight that marriage might "be" a sacrament that somehow "contained" the encounter between grace and nature.

What events or concerns may have caused Luther to have second thoughts about his initial willingness to break with the received standing of marriage as in some way sacramental, we cannot identify precisely. On the one hand, his *Marriage Booklet,* which appeared as a separate publication but at the same time as his 1529 *Small Catechism,* continued in its opening sentences to reflect what he had written at the beginning of the decade: marriage is a "worldly matter."[56] Nonetheless, as commentators have spotted, a central tension surfaces in this influential booklet since marriage is at one and the same time "worldly" and yet the "godly estate."[57] Luther's decision to decouple the ceremony from the reception of Eucharist undercut the tie to Ephesians 5 since common reception of the sacrament of the altar (undisputed in importance by Lutherans and Catholics) had long been accepted in both Latin and Byzantine Christianity as the normal conclusion to the marriage rite. Still, Ephesians 5 did find its way into the blessing Luther included in the booklet. But the "sacramental" in Luther's booklet is found in Christ's sacrifice of himself for the church. In more than one sermon, but especially one delivered at the marriage in 1536 of Caspar Cruciger, Luther could insist that Christ is not simply a kind of example that spouses are to emulate. Rather, as one summation of his sermons concludes, Luther would still see Christ as the one who "enters into the marriages of his believers above all as the mediator of grace and as sacrament."[58]

The "worldly" and the "quasi-sacramental," then, both appeared in this booklet that would inform almost all marriage legislation in Protestant Germany for two centuries. But the *Marriage Booklet*'s blessing and choice of words presupposed understanding of Luther's linkage of the creation and Fall in Genesis to Paul's letter to the Ephesians.[59]

---

56. Luther, *Trau-Büchlein,* WA 30.3:43-80, 74, "ein welltlich geschefft ist."

57. Albrecht Peters, *Kommentar zu Luthers Katechismen: Band 5: Die Beichte. Die Haustafel. Das Traubüchlein. Das Taufbüchlein,* with contributions by Rieder Schulz and Rudolf Keller, ed. Gottfried Seebaß (Göttingen: Vandenhoeck & Ruprecht, 1994), pp. 119-55, at 120.

58. Peters, *Kommentar,* pp. 143, 147, 152. Peters shares the opinion that Luther's "shift" back to a focus on Ephesians began with the 1528 instructions to those conducting parish visitations; see pp. 120, 150.

59. Mattox, *Defender,* pp. 70-71. On lay resistance and post-1525 acceptance of clerical marriage, see Marjorie Elizabeth Plummer, *From Priest's Whore to Pastor's Wife: Clerical Marriage and the Process of Reform in the Early German Reformation* (Burlington, Vt.: Ashgate, 2012), pp. 91-129.

The *Marriage Booklet* copied a prayer in the medieval Catholic nuptial Mass and elevated the "married estate" to the "signifier" of "the sacrament of your dear Son Jesus Christ and the church, his bride." This imagery, taken from Ephesians 5, prompted Luther's longest comment on the epistle, in which he stated that "the married estate is a sacrament and a spiritual sign of Christ and Christendom, that we all alike are one body with Christ as we believe, and his bride."[60] In the sermon preached at Cruciger's wedding, Luther repeated this sacramental assertion. These statements cohere with his statement in the *Marriage Booklet* that "weddings and the married estate are a worldly affair" because "nature" is relational. Moreover, despite a gradual evolution in Luther's opinions about the equality of women and men in the "original" married estate described in Genesis, he still recalled the Dionysian hierarchies. For Luther, God created human beings with the same capacity and destiny for union with God that Pseudo-Dionysius had affirmed. When speaking of "male" and "female" capacities, Luther again took aim at "reason" and the Neoplatonic preference for the "higher," that is, "rational," powers of the soul. He countered with the argument that reason was the inferior power. The real sign of the soul's higher destiny is the contemplative knowledge of God "where we effect nothing by our endeavor but merely learn and observe." These insights flowed from Luther's indebtedness to Augustine, Dionysius, and the medieval German mystical tradition. Despite his wrath at the damage he believed the canonical tradition had wrought on persons confused about marriage's holiness in the early 1520s, Luther's marriage rite still struggled to maintain the connection of ordinary, everyday spousal relations to the "mystery" Augustine and so many others had pointed to in their pondering of the Ephesians text.[61]

Human beings achieve the soul's higher destiny in ways that reflect the roles assigned by God. By linking Genesis and Ephesians 5, Luther tied the privileges and responsibilities of man and woman to the relationship of Christ to the church. The "original" relationship between God and human beings, and between men and women, rested, of necessity, not on coercion or domination but on "a spontaneous harmony of wills untainted by sin and self-centeredness." In his essay "On the Married Estate" Luther described this order of creation as unalterable. Its permanence reflects the created, relational desire of men and women for each other. In his lectures on Genesis, Luther condemned sodomy because it contradicted the attraction of the two sexes for each other, implanted by God himself. The normative quality of

---

60. WA 24:422; Mattox, *Defender*, pp. 71-72 n. 22; the English translation is my own.
61. WA 42:138; Mattox, *Defender*, pp. 79 and 102.

God's intent also rendered celibacy, for most males, highly unlikely. For, he argued in a letter to Wolfgang Reissenbusch, the "Word of God, through whose power procreative seed is planted in man's body and a natural, ardent desire for woman is kindled and kept alive . . . cannot be restrained either by vows or laws." Luther adopted the ancient Christian patristic view that God created men and women with an intrinsic yearning for union and companionship. Their yearning for God finds its reflection in the mutual yearning and the sacrifice of the self in marriage.[62]

Luther was not entirely comfortable with the consequence of such "yearning," namely, sexual intercourse, as his rather gloomy conclusion to the essay on the married estate suggested. He asserted that God overlooked the animal dimensions of a union that the Fall had corrupted, damaging the relationship between men and women. At his most daring, Luther insisted that Eve originally enjoyed equal dominion over the created world with Adam, and intercourse in the Garden was unsullied by lust. Only the Fall created a "subordinate" role for women, since a political order had to ward off warfare and social chaos. Later, confessional Protestants failed to use his insights to affirm the equality of the sexes, but to Lutheran dismay, radical reformers saw the connections. Between the 1670s and the 1740s, pietists drawn to friendship and companionate support in marriage also faced bitter polemics about the spousal relationship that would force them to make hard choices about the scope of such conclusions.[63]

The prophylactic against radical interpretation of the believer's access to the hidden and mysterious God took shape in the Lutheran "symbolic" books, primarily the Augsburg Confession (1530) and the *Small Catechism*

62. Mattox, *Defender*, pp. 74-92, quotation at 91. On Luther's observations on the reciprocal desire of men and women for union, see "The Estate of Marriage," *LW* 45:18; "Commentary on Genesis," Gen. 19:4 (*LW* 3:251-52); for the letter, see Theodore G. Tappert, ed., *Luther: Letters of Spiritual Counsel* (Philadelphia: Fortress, 1955), p. 273. On the patristic understanding of *epithymia*, see the sources and discussion in David C. Ford, *Women and Men in the Early Church: The Full Views of St. John Chrysostom* (South Canaan, Pa.: St. Tikhon's Seminary Press, 1996), pp. 12-73. For Augustine's views, see David Hunter, "Marriage," and Ann Maatter, "Women," both in *Augustine through the Ages*, pp. 533-37, 887-92; on Luther's differences with Augustine and his rejection of Augustine's view of Eve as created for the "servitude of love," see Mattox, pp. 94-95, 99. For the Jewish and Christian ruminations on the complexities of sexual love and celibacy, see Gary A. Anderson, *The Genesis of Perfection: Adam and Eve in Jewish and Christian Imagination* (Louisville, London, and Leiden: Brill, 2001), pp. 43-73.

63. For the limited impact of these dimensions of Luther's thinking on later commentators, see Philip C. Almond, *Adam and Eve in Seventeenth-Century Thought* (Cambridge: Cambridge University Press, 1999), pp. 149-70.

(1529) that located the graced estate within a visible, praying community. The hope entertained by the participants that the writing of the symbols would end strife over the meaning of the church, and by implication, marriage relations, turned out to be illusory. Pietists and their critics continued to cite these official theological statements, but questions persisted about the respective rights of princes and pastors to define marriage and resolve conflicts between spouses. The ambiguities enabled some to cast aside the theological emphasis upon the orders in creation, in which marriage enjoyed second status, and to deploy the canonical and secular legal tradition to turn the debate to the topic of the governing, preaching, and household "estates" in ways that largely ignored the perceptions of ordinary believers.

In the public symbolic statements of the evangelical Lutheran tradition, marriage appeared almost as an afterthought. Article XXIII of the Augsburg Confession rejected clerical celibacy but also implied that the purpose of marriage was to correct human frailty by preventing sexual wantonness. Only in response to Catholic criticism did Melanchthon's *Apology* (which became official teaching by 1537) improve its status when he allowed, in Article XIII on "the Sacraments," that marriage was an "Old Testament" sacrament but not on a level with baptism or the Lord's Supper. For later renewal movements, it was more important that Melanchthon insisted that identifying or numbering sacraments was not as crucial as using them correctly, in faith. Reaching back to Paul and Augustine, he noted that not the sacrament, but faith in the sacrament, made a man or a woman "just."

The Context of the Unofficial Synthesis

The late medieval German Catholics who heard Luther practiced a piety that concentrated on the humanity of Christ and his mother, the Virgin. Wedding customs and rituals that surrounded Luther in his youth and his early career as a priest and friar reveal his conservative views. They also showed the views of ordinary people about the validity of the Lutheran symbols. Despite claims of continuity with a medieval and ancient church, the Reformers said that real Christianization of the German-speaking peoples of Europe had awaited their program of revitalization.

Luther's positive views on marriage, and their adoption in the symbols, have suggested to some that his teaching convinced the laity because it assured them that they were more likely than celibate monks or clerics to find salvation. They seemed likely proponents of Luther's insistence that the married estate existed from the moment when God created man and woman. Such claims did challenge the medieval church's elevation of the celibate life, but anticlerical or antimonastic resentment does not fully account for the reception of Luther's teaching about marriage.

Moreover, it is far from clear that Lutheran preaching conveyed to its hearers a consistent message. The primacy of marriage in the "orders" of creation seemed less important when political order became the obsession. Unlike some others, Luther might not have turned his attention so decidedly away from the married order to the political order, but politics was only one dimension of the struggle. Ordinary people had inherited a panoply of folk customs and rituals, and these helped push Luther's claims about the quasi-sacramental dimensions of marriage into obscurity. The persistence of older customs and beliefs also accounts in part for pietists' later interest in Luther's insights, their exasperation about folk views of marriage, and their difficulty in sustaining "hopes" for better spouses and marriages.[64]

The daily experience of marriage and family reflected centuries of custom and strategies for survival. Most medieval and early modern German-speakers may have heard marriage described as an "estate" or "order," but the words probably directed their attention to the sometimes tense relationship between parents and children. Few of Luther's hearers would have thought about relationships between generations beyond the immediate one. Not until a full generation after Luther's death did the word for "grandparents" surface in the German language, and then only in northern and western areas of the empire. The practice was to describe biological ancestors solely in juridical and genealogical terms that conveyed nothing about parenthood. Nor did any special emotional attachment connect "grandparents" to "grandchildren" before the eighteenth century.[65] Nor was "nature" the glorious sphere of later romantics. Although other Europeans may have hoped for a return to the Garden, nothing in medieval or sixteenth-century sermons gave German-speakers any reason to believe they could either subdue the earth or recover a primal relationship with God, their spouses, or the natural world.[66] "Nature"

64. On the shift in emphasis to the political order, see Robert James Bast, *Honor Your Fathers: Catechisms and the Emergence of a Patriarchal Ideology in Germany, 1400-1600* (Leiden: Brill, 1997), pp. 122-31.

65. Erhard Chvojka, *Geschichte der Grosselternrollen vom 16. bis zum 20. Jahrhundert* (Vienna, Cologne, and Weimar: Böhlau, 2003), pp. 97-108.

66. See Jeremy Cohen, *"Be Fertile and Increase, Fill the Earth and Master It": The Ancient and Medieval Career of a Biblical Text* (Ithaca, N.Y., and London: Cornell University Press, 1989), p. 5: "rarely, if ever, did premodern Jews and Christians construe this verse as a license for

instead made their lives, as Thomas Hobbes later said, "solitary, poore, nasty, brutish, and short."[67] Only the knightly chivalric tale *Parzival* had identified love with marriage, and it fell out of favor during the Reformation.[68]

If sixteenth-century Protestants had second thoughts about the potentially sacral quality of marriage, the cause probably resided in demographic change. After recovering from the Black Death, Europeans expanded during a "long sixteenth century" "culminating in the crisis of the seventeenth." Demographers still disagree about details, but it seems that Europeans married earlier before 1600 than they did afterward, that central-to-northern European families were increasingly smaller, and that after 1620 the failure of agricultural technology triggered a stagnation or, in some regions, decline in population that ended only around 1720. During this demographic downturn (of which contemporaries were only vaguely aware) famine, disease, and warfare — all part of what some scholars now refer to as a "Little Ice Age" — limited the time of marriage, fertility, and illegitimacy. Early critics of Protestant family mores and morals reflected this population flux and instability. The downward spiral in population, greater in some regions than in others, hit the central-northern and southwestern territories of the Holy Roman Empire with particular force. In these regions, the renewal movement of pietism would find some of its most intense expressions.[69] As a result, the world in

---

the selfish exploitation of the environment," and: "exegetes of the Reformation period discerned little new in our verse . . . with a handful of rare and sometimes questionable exceptions, they never construed the divine call to master the earth and rule over its animal population as permission to interfere with the workings of nature" (p. 309). For a comparison of narratives about the Genesis story's impact on later human relations with "nature," see Carolyn Merchant, *Reinventing Eden: The Fate of Nature in Western Culture* (New York and London: Routledge, 2003), pp. 36-38, 66-69, 94-102.

67. Thomas Hobbes, *Leviathan; or, The Matter, Forme, & Power of a Common-wealth Ecclesiasticall and civill* (London: Andrew Crooke, 1651), p. 62; on Hobbes's eventual rejection of orthodox Christianity, see Richard Tuck, "The 'Christian Atheism' of Thomas Hobbes," in *Atheism from the Reformation to the Enlightenment,* ed. Michael Hunter and David Wootton (Oxford: Clarendon, 1992), pp. 129-30.

68. Wolfran von Eschenbach, *Parzival: A Romance of the Middle Ages,* trans. and ed. Helen M. Mustard and Charles E. Passage (New York: Vintage Books, 1971), pp. xiii-xiv.

69. Jan de Vries, "Population," in *Handbook of European History, 1400-1600: Late Middle Ages, Renaissance, and Reformation I; Structures and Assertions,* ed. Thomas A. Brady Jr. et al. (Grand Rapids: Eerdmans, 1994), pp. 1-50; Raymond Birn, *Crisis, Absolutism, Revolution: Europe and the World, 1648-1789* (Peterborough, Ontario: Broadview Press, 2005), pp. 3-9, 25-32; Thomas Robisheaux, "The Peasantries of Western Germany, 1300-1750," in *The Peasantries of Europe from the Fourteenth to the Eighteenth Centuries,* ed. Tom Scott (London and New York: Longman, 1998), pp. 111-42, at 116-19.

which laypeople heard Protestant teachings about marriage was one in which "not everybody could marry, a fact reflected in high rates of celibacy." Under such conditions a profoundly serious question emerged, namely, "who married, who remained single, who divorced, and who remarried?"[70]

Official theology and the canonical tradition never entirely tamed the excesses of popular rituals and views about the spousal relationship and could not control the demographic and economic fluxes that inevitably helped to intensify debates over spousal relations, obligations, and hopes. Emphasis on the "lawful" dimensions of marriage emerged in part because of the rowdy behavior of peasant and village marriage celebrations. In both the southern and the northern localities, optimistic Lutheran views collided with earthy practices. "Official" and "unofficial" religious practices and beliefs about marriage never fully diverged, but pastors lamented the distance between them. In both Catholic and Lutheran territories, the priest or pastor functioned as the accepted public figure to solemnize the ritual that bound individuals, families, and properties together. But the "luxury of cornucopian food, drink, and sensual license" did not cease, and many clergy began to stay away from revels they could not reform. The early Lutheran pastors' hope that they could reform popular practices probably ended by the late sixteenth century in stalemate. But pastoral hopes to renew religion by regenerating the spousal relationship did not die. Neither did local selectivity about the use of Luther's panegyrics on marriage. The Thirty Years' War reinforced late-sixteenth-century tensions and confronted pietists with a choice: either emphasize order and proper subordination in marriage as a mirror of a much-needed order in society and the state, or encourage the view of the spousal relationship as one of mutuality and spiritual help between the partners — as Luther had hoped when he ranked marriage in the created order second only to the church.[71]

Late-sixteenth-century manuals of piety and prayer suggest how little of Luther's hopes for marriage had outlived him to aid pietists in their hopes for renewal. The prayers, which date to the outbreak of the Thirty Years' War,

70. Antoinette Fauve-Chamoux, "Marriage, Widowhood, and Divorce," in *The History of the European Family,* vol. 1, *Family Life in Early Modern Times, 1500-1789,* ed. David I. Kertzer and Marzio Barbagli (New Haven and London: Yale University Press, 2001), pp. 221-56, at 221.

71. Susan C. Karant-Nunn, *The Reformation of Ritual: An Interpretation of Early Modern Germany* (London and New York: Routledge, 1997), pp. 6-42, quotation at 38; see also Günther Lottes, "Popular Culture and the Early Modern State in 16th Century Germany," in *Understanding Popular Culture: Europe from the Middle Ages to the 19th Century,* ed. Steven L. Kaplan (Berlin, Amsterdam, and Paris: Mouton De Gruyter, 1984), pp. 147-88, at 174-75.

omit reference to marriage, ignore "household" issues, and fail to mention the category of "family." They concentrate attention on individual piety. The disappearance of any focus upon spouses, however, occurs in these texts as part of a shift away from the piety of the Lord's Supper or sacraments and the presence of God in the created world. Manuals for pastors, as well, neglect sacraments or such "quasi"-sacramental rites as marriage. The trend instead focused upon individual meditative piety and subjective appropriation of the theology of the cross. It attenuated a large part of the influence of Tauler and the German mystics.[72]

Feminist scholars have long noted Luther's ambiguity about marriage, sexuality, and the roles of men and women. Most of them concluded that the princes and their allies in the chanceries neglected his intentions and imposed upon marriage an institutional identity useful for social discipline. Most feminist scholarship has also emphasized the negative consequences for women of contractual marriage. Whatever Luther may have intended, Protestant marriages ended up as less than liberating. Some scholars have accented the emergence of "companionate" marriage among Protestants, and others have emphasized that marriage was a sphere of shared labor. Still other scholars conclude, however, that a Protestant view of marriage as contract or "covenant" ended up crafting marriage and home as zones of exclusivity for women. Despite Luther's own somewhat more generous vision, his later disciples drew a "parallel between the microcosm of the family headed by the father, the territory presided over by the prince, and the universal macrocosm governed by God." Legally, culturally, and theologically, women remained subordinate, even if some of the propertied regarded marriage as a partnership. But local studies of marriage reveal that the Reformation probably did not dramatically change village customs, sometimes sardonic views of male-female relationships, or the relationship of men and women. Despite the efforts of princes, theologians, and pastors, many territories, Protestant and Catholic, remained hemmed in by local custom, with the clergy preaching "commonly high religious standards, with commonly inadequate means of implementation."[73]

---

72. For a summary of this shift and the scholarly literature, see Roeber, "Official and Non-official Piety and Ritual in Early Lutheranism," *Concordia Theological Quarterly* 63, no. 2 (April 1999): 119-43, and Amy Nelson Burnett, "The Evolution of the Lutheran Pastors' Manual in the Sixteenth Century," *Church History* 73, no. 3 (September 2004): 536-65.

73. Suzanne Zantop, "Trivial Pursuits? An Introduction to German Women's Writing from the Middle Ages to 1830," in *Bitter Healing: German Women Writers from 1700 to 1830; An Anthology,* ed. Jeannine Blackwell and Suzanne Zantop (Lincoln and London: University of Ne-

If Luther had taught that the spousal relationship reflected that of Christ to his church and yet had recognized the institution's practical, "this-worldly" dimensions, why did a dispute about marriage accelerate among the renewers of Protestantism by the late seventeenth century? Part of the answer lies with Philipp Melanchthon and his views about the "orders of creation." Despite their long friendship, Luther and Melanchthon diverged in their views of nature, grace, and marriage, and Melanchthon's thinking bequeathed a legacy that would dismay pietist reformers who wanted to nurture better spouses. The official theological and legal legacy on the spousal relationship provided a welcome support for both princes and pastors struggling to recover some sense of order in the aftermath of the Thirty Years' War. Ironically, however, the indifference or hostility among many ordinary believers to the demand for order manifested itself in the further cultivation of unofficial notions of the spousal relationship. Their speculations and experiments would further alienate them from renewers within the confessional churches and make the task of recovering and maintaining Luther's synthesis even more difficult.

---

braska Press, 1990), pp. 9-50, at 16; Susan C. Karant-Nunn and Merry E. Wiesner-Hanks, eds. and trans., *Luther on Women: A Sourcebook* (Cambridge: Cambridge University Press, 2003), pp. 12-14, 88-136, quotation at 89; Heide Wunder, *He Is the Son, She Is the Moon: Women in Early Modern Germany,* trans. Thomas Dunlap (Cambridge: Harvard University Press, 1998); Joel F. Harrington, *Reordering Marriage and Society in Reformation Germany* (Cambridge: Cambridge University Press, 1995), pp. 273-78, quotation at 277. For marriage and gender in early modern German scholarship, see Susanna Burghartz, "Umordnung statt Unordung? Ehe, Geschlecht und Reformationsgeschichte," in *Zwischen den Disziplinen? Perspektiven der Frühneuzeitforschung,* ed. Helmut Puff and Christopher Wild (Göttingen: Waldstein Verlag, 2003), pp. 165-85.

CHAPTER 2

Arguing with Aquinas?
Melanchthon, Mystics, and Marriage

Whatever Martin Luther may have thought about marriage, his brilliant coworker, Philipp Melanchthon, more decisively shaped Lutheran thinking about this "estate," thereby influencing pietists and other Protestants. Later pietist emphases on strict codes of behavior for spouses and rational reflection on the need for order and discipline in individual spiritual life, the home, society, and the state took their inspiration from Melanchthon.

Melanchthon's theological anthropology diverged markedly from Luther's. It is only a slight exaggeration to say that the official theology of marriage in Lutheranism that Melanchthon promulgated as the teacher of future pastors obscured key elements of Luther's insights and bequeathed much of the internal uncertainty within Protestant circles about the spousal relationship in the following century. But Melanchthon was not the sole culprit. By the time Melanchthon began his lectures to ministerial students, political and cultural events began to buttress Luther's willingness to jettison the claims of quasi sacramentality in spousal relations as his optimism about the freedom that should characterize ordinary Christian life collapsed in the uprisings of the mid-1520s among the unlearned peasantry. The older Luther did still speculate that before the Fall Eve had been the equal of her husband and that Christ's relation to the church modeled a proper marriage, but

Parts of this chapter were presented at the Sixteenth-Century Studies Conference in Denver, Colorado, in 2001; see also A. G. Roeber, "Pietists and the Orders of Creation," in *Interdisziplinäre Pietismusforschungen: Beiträge zum Ersten Internationalen Kongress für Pietismusforschung 2001*, ed. Udo Sträter et al., 2 vols. (Tübingen: Harrassowitz Verlag, 2005), 2:747-57.

"worries over establishing a secure ground for state authority seem to have far overshadowed interest in the sacramental signification of the married estate as an image of Christ."[1] The transition created tensions between "official" and "lived" Protestant views of marriage and between a view of it as friendship and mutual support and that of simply a relationship that needed to be regulated as part of a broader concern for social discipline and control. Both early reform-minded princes and pastors of the confessional church in the second half of the seventeenth century and especially the most eminent and influential of the "church pietist" writers, Philipp Jakob Spener, had to wrestle with these tensions.

The alienation of the peasants from Luther during the Peasants' War in the mid-1520s found expression within a decade in woodcuts that made both husbands and wives the objects of ridicule for the urban patrons who purchased depictions that cast doubt on the nobility of normal married life.[2] In the last decades of the sixteenth century, questions about the quality of peasant marriages surfaced in religious art that graced hymnals, as well. For example, the hymnal of Nicolaus Herman in the 1550s in Joachimstal reflected Luther's early esteem for the estate. Marriage of pious spouses would increase the number that would worship God. "God the Father sanctified it and Jesus the Son honored it." Praying that God would restrain Satan, "who attacks marriage," the hymn describes marriage as an estate enabling parents to enjoy "with their dear children the joys of heaven." Herman's devotions celebrated the reunion of families in heaven, as did the sermons of Johann Mathesius that emphasized "the unbreakable bond with which God has joined together parents and children." Only in seeing their children find eternal happiness did husband and wife "know the true and enduring joy of fatherhood and motherhood for the first time."[3]

Nonetheless, the woodcut illustrations on marriage that accompanied these hymnals and collections of sermons on the Sunday Gospels did not depict peasants as devoted couples. Even biblical figures like the married

---

1. Mickey L. Mattox, "Order in the House? The Reception of Luther's Orders Teaching in Early Lutheran Genesis Commentaries," *Reformation and Renaissance Review* (forthcoming); cited with permission of the author.

2. Keith Moxey, *Peasants, Warriors, and Wives: Popular Imagery in the Reformation* (Chicago: University of Chicago Press, 2004), especially chapter 3, "Festive Peasants and the Social Order."

3. Christopher Boyd Brown, *Singing the Gospel: Lutheran Hymns and the Success of the Reformation* (Cambridge: Harvard University Press, 2005), pp. 13-14; quotation of Herman's sequence at 63-64; of Mathesius's sermon at 113.

couple at Cana are "urban" or village residents more than representatives of the peasant estate. Luther and Melanchthon had doubted the capacity of peasants and villagers to become good married evangelicals. Such doubts surfaced again after 1648. The shift from a medieval, hierarchical model of family life to a model more attractive to the urban "middling sorts" meant that woodcut artists increasingly downplayed figures like Saint Anne, the grandmother of Jesus. She and other women were not equals, but still partners with their husbands in the shared burdens of begetting and bringing up pious children.[4] Allusions to the "cross" of marriage reflected anxieties about women who aspired to marital power and chided men who failed to be strong and responsible heads of households. Praise of paternal order permeated broadside literature throughout the sixteenth and seventeenth centuries.[5]

Never ordained, the son of an armorer, and a Swabian humanist, Philipp Melanchthon was neither a first-rate creative thinker nor an admirer of village and rural spouses. When it came time for him to marry, he chose the daughter of Wittenberg's mayor. His considerable linguistic and teaching abilities manifested themselves, however, in his capacity to organize systematically the thoughts of others. He presented his arguments on marriage within medieval categories associated especially with Peter Lombard, whose *Four Books of Sentences* had exemplified the ordering of theology into logical topics and categories for analysis.

In fairness to Melanchthon, he never forgot that "the clue to the Lutheran Reformation was the University of Wittenberg and Luther's activities as a university professor." The learned "adversary system in theology," practiced in the "disputation," nonetheless also deepened the gulf between "official" teaching on marriage and the hopes Protestant spouses could more easily draw from Luther's bold insights.[6]

4. On the transformation of the cult of Saint Anne, see Virginia Nixon, *Mary's Mother: Saint Anne in Late Medieval Europe* (University Park: Pennsylvania State University Press, 2004), p. 128. See the woodcut representations by Abraham Bach (among others) of marriage and society in the post-1648 era, in Dorothy Alexander and Walter L. Strauss, *The German Single-Leaf Woodcut, 1600-1700: A Pictorial Catalogue,* 2 vols. (New York: Abaris Books, 1977).

5. Kristina Bake, "Das Kreuz mit der Ehe: Häuslicher Gewalt in illustrierten Flugblättern der frühen Neuzeit," in *"Der Herr wird seine Herrlichkeit an uns offenbahren": Liebe, Ehe und Sexualität im Pietismus,* ed. Wolfgang Breul and Christian Soboth (Halle: Harrassowitz, 2012), pp. 78-96. I am grateful to the editors for allowing me to read the prepublication galleys of the essays.

6. George Wolfgang Forell, "The Formula of Concord and the Teaching Ministry," *Sixteenth Century Journal* 8, no. 4 (1977): 39-47, at 39.

By the time Luther and Melanchthon began their careers, medieval Catholic theology had developed a doctrine of creation that tied it to patristic sources and the Eastern Fathers. Both Hugh of St. Victor and Peter Lombard sought to understand "blessedness" or "well-being" as the destiny of humans created in God's image and likeness. It was, however, Thomas Aquinas whom Melanchthon and Luther accused of having misunderstood creation, humanity, and God's grace and favor. In the heat of battle, Protestants attributed to Aquinas a phrase that was not original to his work: "Grace does not destroy nature, but perfects it." (In all likelihood, Bonaventure was the first to use it, drawing on ancient writers like John Chrysostom.) More than Luther, Melanchthon moved away from any notion that humans participate in God's blessedness in this life and therefore enjoy transformation. Melanchthon said simply that by knowing God's benefits, one knows God. Luther remained, in the end, captivated by mystical Christian understandings of how humans "see" the natural world, a view that elevated men and women and their marriages. Melanchthon did not.[7]

The German scholar Wilhelm Dilthey may have been among the first to insist that the Reformation and the Renaissance contributed in equal measure to a new human-centered view of humanity. The German sociologist Ernst Troeltsch disagreed, arguing that the Reformation remained indebted to medieval mysticism and a conviction that everyday life had to be permeated by Christian principles and behavior. Melanchthon, both humanist and Lutheran theologian, has emerged repeatedly as the critical figure at the center of such competing understandings, and justifiably as the theologian who shaped Lutheran views of nature, humanity, and, by implication, spousal relations in marriage.[8]

Melanchthon believed that "Paul's letter to the Romans was the single most important book of the Bible." His commonplace method of explicating

7. See Fergus Kerr, *After Aquinas: Versions of Thomism* (Malden, Mass., Oxford, Victoria, and Berlin: Wiley-Blackwell, 2002), pp. 130-33, 138 on Bonaventure; 152-53 on divinization. On this sharp divergence between the two theologians, see variously Mickey L. Mattox, "Luther's Interpretation of Scripture: Biblical Understanding in Trinitarian Shape," in Dennis Bielfeldt, Mickey L. Mattox, and Paul R. Hinlicky, *The Substance of the Faith: Luther's Doctrinal Theology for Today,* edited and introduced by Paul R. Hinlicky (Minneapolis: Fortress, 2008), pp. 11-58, at 20-21; Wilhelm Pauck, "Luther and Melanchthon," in *Luther and Melanchthon in the History and Theology of the Reformation,* ed. Vilmos Vayta (Philadelphia: Muhlenberg, 1961), pp. 13-31.

8. Timothy Wengert, *Human Freedom, Christian Righteousness: Philip Melanchthon's Exegetical Dispute with Erasmus of Rotterdam* (New York and Oxford: Oxford University Press, 1998), pp. 5-20.

Paul taught generations of students about the graced, but not sacramental, standing of marriage.[9] His decision to move from his own early writing on Romans to a more systematic treatment of Lutheran thought stemmed in part from his students' enthusiasm. An unauthorized version in 1520 of his classroom musings on Romans upset him so much that he wrote not only "another introductory piece, *De studio doctrinae Paulinae*" *(O.1 the Study of Pauline Doctrine)*, but also a thematic treatment of Lutheran teaching.[10] Perhaps unduly influenced by the early Luther's disdain for notions of "sacrament" in marriage, Melanchthon in the treatise undercut the notion of marriage as the second of three orders of creation that Luther had built from mystical Christian teaching. Did his students, destined to be ministers, hear that marriage was the second of three orders — blessed before the Fall and reflecting the "image and likeness" of God — or did they follow Melanchthon's path and see it as part of the "worldly" kingdom regulated by the law, one dimension of the economic, political, and ecclesiastical ordering of "this world," separate from the gospel and its announcement of the heavenly kingdom?[11]

One clue as to what future pastors heard emerged in the way Melanchthon organized the *Loci communes theologici* ("Fundamental Theological Themes"). In his tangential remarks at the end of the lectures he touched briefly on the dimness of the original "image" of God after the Fall. Only here did he, in cursory fashion, discuss marriage. Questions about the remnants of "natural virtue" after the Fall remained problematic in Lutheran thought. On the one hand, by 1577 the *Epitome of the Formula of Concord* I:2 taught that "even after the fall our nature is and remains a creature of God." But Melanchthon in the 1521 "Themes" had preferred to emphasize the extent of the loss. Only Catholic criticism had prompted him to move marriage "up" in the numbering of the articles in the *Apology;* but all that re-

---

9. For the characterization of Melanchthon as an organizer of others' insights, see Heinrich Bornkamm, "Melanchthons Menschenbild," in *Philipp Melanchthon: Forschungsbeiträge zur vierhundertsten Wiederkehr sines Todestages dargeboten in Wittenberg 1960,* ed. Walter Elliger (Göttingen: Vandenhoeck & Ruprecht, 1961), pp. 76-90; for the citation on the importance of Romans, see Timothy J. Wengert, "The Biblical Commentaries of Philip Melanchthon," in *Philip Melanchthon (1497-1560) and the Commentary,* ed. Timothy J. Wengert and M. Patrick Graham (Sheffield: Sheffield Academic Press, 1997), pp. 106-48, citation at 133.

10. Wilhelm Pauck, ed., *Melanchthon and Bucer* (Philadelphia: Westminster, 1969), p. 7.

11. John Stevenson, "The Two Governments and the Two Kingdoms in Luther's Thought," *Scottish Journal of Theology* 34 (1981): 321-37; Stevenson argues that the three "hierarchies" (economic, political, ecclesiastical) are the actual basis for practical governance in the Lutheran territories of the empire and the basis for applying Luther's ethical teachings.

mained of the image for him was hope — a decisively truncated version of the medieval teaching, and one that never caught up with the more positive reinsertion of the Ephesians text Luther included in the blessing section of his marriage rite, thus conveying a much more nuanced view of spousal relations and how they were connected to the relationship of Christ and his church.[12]

Because he saw only a minimal survival of the image and likeness of God in humans after the Fall, Melanchthon sharply distinguished grace from nature, a decision that in its turn contributed to his omission of any separate category in his teaching schema for dealing with the sacraments. He was willing to reflect on the image and likeness of God among those who accepted the gift of grace. But he did not say exactly how such gifts could work on a nature that had been destroyed. He left no opening to say that one of the possible contexts could be the spousal relationship in marriage.

Melanchthon wanted to give students the tools to succeed in parish ministry. The aim of his pedagogy was to cultivate an educated pastorate, and he accented the persistence of natural law as a weapon against anyone who dared to disturb civil and political order. As a result, he turned only at the very end of his lectures to Luther's interest in the structure of family and marriage, giving it pride of place under "Of Worldly Authority" and belatedly referring to the spousal relationship as a "church of God," a godly condition in which the spouses labor to perform "a holy divine service."[13]

On the one hand, his students heard Melanchthon emphasize that "God . . . gave men light, namely, understanding of natural law through which we know that we should make and keep order in governments." On the other hand, he remained relatively silent about the graced quality of married life

---

12. Wengert, *Human Freedom,* pp. 88-89.

13. Robert Kolb, "Melanchthon's Influence on the Exegesis of His Students: The Case of Romans 9," in *Philip Melanchthon (1497-1560) and the Commentary,* pp. 194-215, at 209, 214-15; Wengert, "The Biblical Commentaries of Philip Melanchthon," pp. 106-48, at 133; Rolf Schaefer, "Melanchthon's Interpretation of Romans 5:15: His Departure from the Augustinian Concept of Grace Compared to Luther's," in *Philip Melanchthon (1497-1560) and the Commentary,* pp. 79-104; Markus Wriedt, "Pietas et Eruditio: Zur Begründung der Bildungsreformerischen Ansätze bei Philipp Melanchthon under besonderer Berücksichtigung seiner Ekklesiologie," in *Dona Melanchthoniana: Festgabe für Heinz Scheible zum 70. Geburtstag,* ed. Johanna Loehr (Stuttgart-Bad Canstatt: Frommann-Holzboog, 2001), pp. 501-20. For Melanchthon's comments see Clyde L. Manschreck, trans. and ed., *Melanchthon on Christian Doctrine: Loci Communes, 1555* (New York: Baker, 1965), pp. 71-75 on image and likeness; 112 on the purpose of marriage being reproduction and the control of lust; 311 for marriage as the locus for divine service.

except to scold the "idle monk" and praise men who bore the burden of "living as a father of a family, a burgomaster, or a soldier." In explaining natural virtue, Melanchthon wrote, under the heading of law, that the natural law guides civic order. But how much of natural virtue or the law written on the heart (Rom. 2:14) survived the Fall? Melanchthon gave no clear answer, leaving it to successors who would face it anew in strange lands. Reformed theologians, writing later on the topic, solved the problem by pointing to the complete "exteriority" of any "natural law."[14] Humans, no matter what their specific beliefs, could tell right from wrong on purely "worldly" matters — but not with regard to anything touching salvation. There was nothing wrong with affirming the limited "good" discernible in this life. Indeed, John Calvin and English Puritan commentators saw "the arts and sciences as evidences of traces of the image of God even in fallen humanity." Miracles in this understanding were possible only as "particular providences," for nature remained, in their view, a quasi-autonomous sphere separate from the functioning of the Spirit in the kingdom of grace.[15]

After many revisions of his book, Melanchthon finished the last version in 1555; he died five years later. Within a decade, his legacy fell under fire. By 1570, his son-in-law was arrested by the elector August because of suspicions that Melanchthon's views of nature and grace had undermined Lutheranism within and beyond his family circle. Lutheran battles over the person and work of Christ and the Lord's Supper seem distant from the question of spousal relations, but underlying all the battles stood the question: Can human beings grow toward union with God in this life? Melanchthon expounded his Christology and his view of the Lord's Supper in reaction against the Spanish theologian Michael Servetus, whose "disavowal of the eternal nature of the Son of God, the everlasting difference in nature of the Son of God from the Father and the doctrine of a God-become man" impelled one group of Lutherans to emphasize the mysterious "otherness" of God. But their insistence on the difference between a transcendent God and

14. Melanchthon, *Loci Communes*, pp. 325, 331, on natural law and secular occupations. On the Reformed resolution of this complex struggle to explain natural virtue, see David M. VanDrunen, *Natural Law and the Two Kingdoms: A Study in the Development of Reformed Social Thought* (Grand Rapids: Eerdmans, 2009).

15. Christopher B. Kaiser, *Creational Theology and the History of Physical Science: The Creationist Tradition from Basil to Bohr* (Leiden: Brill, 1997), pp. 164, 178-79. For where to place Melanchthon in the tradition of natural philosophy, see Sachiko Kusukawa, *The Transformation of Natural Philosophy: The Case of Philip Melanchthon* (Cambridge: Cambridge University Press, 1983), pp. 70-85.

creation excluded not only a physical presence in the Lord's Supper but also, perhaps unintentionally, any notion that marriage could be spiritually transforming. For Melanchthon's followers, John Calvin had been right, given the separation of grace and nature, to "locate" the body of Christ in heaven and not in material elements. By extension, whatever "sacramental" residues that Luther had attributed to marriage vanished.[16]

If Lutherans had not revised their views about natural and revealed theology after Melanchthon died, no pietist confrontations about what hopes could be placed in the spousal relationship would have been necessary. Some scholars have said as much, concluding that "there is nothing particularly original or new in the way . . . that the later Lutherans deal with the subject of natural and revealed theology." But such proved not to be the case. The theologian beloved by the pietists, Johann Arndt, recovered Luther's fascination with Tauler and the mystical strain. But Arndt was cautious about affirming the possibility of union with God because he knew that Tauler's mysticism was controversial and that the Wittenberg theologians had fallen into quarrels about the matter that lasted until the 1570s. Arndt downplayed contemplation and sacramental union. Instead, he urged individual believers to achieve "spiritual growth and moral improvement" through prayer and the exercise of moral virtues. He criticized the disconnection between doctrine and everyday life. But he did not restore a vision of the marital relationship as friendship or a shared journey in a context within which a quasi-sacramental encounter with grace actually occurred.[17]

Not only Arndt but also other late-sixteenth- and early-seventeenth-century commentators such as Johannes A. Quenstedt, David Chytraeus, Martin Chemnitz, Johann Gerhard, Abraham Calov, and Leonhard Hutter continued to feel the allure of the darker side of Augustine and Luther that found almost no remnant of grace in the natural state of human beings.

---

16. On this controversy, see Johannes Hund, *Das Wort ward Fleisch: Eine systematisch-theologische Untersuchung zur Debatte um die Wittenberger Christologie und Abendmahlslehre in den Jahren 1567 bis 1574* (Göttingen: Vandenhoeck & Ruprecht, 2006), p. 670, my translation, and see in general, 670-94.

17. For the opinion that changes in the teaching on the three estates were inconsequential, see Walter Behrendt, "Lutherisch-orthodoxe Ehelehre in der Haustafelliteratur des. 16. Jahrhunderts," in *Text und Geschlecht: Mann und Frau in Eheschriften der frühen Neuzeit,* ed. Rüdiger Schnell (Frankfurt am Main: Suhrkamp Verlag, 1997), pp. 214-29, at 222. Eric Lund, "Tauler the Mystic's Lutheran Admirers," in *Piety and Family in Early Modern Europe: Essays in Honour of Steven Ozment,* ed. Marc R. Forster and Benjamin J. Kaplan (Aldershot, U.K., and Burlington, Vt.: Ashgate, 2005), pp. 9-27, at 20.

Theologians who wanted to recover a more hopeful view of nature and of marriage's standing as the second of the prelapsarian orders needed to find a way to reject Reformed arguments that more logically and consistently defended the pessimistic view, and now attempted to find support in Luther's writings. By the seventeenth century, moreover, reports filtered into Europe about non-Christian peoples of conscience and natural virtue who honored marriage as more than a purely civic estate. Such reports required a theological response.

Melanchthon's own reaction to such reports in the late sixteenth century had reflected his continuing pessimism about the flickering remnants of the image of God left in humanity. Conceding that "the light of natural law was planted in man when he was created," he nonetheless concluded that "in the heathen it has been obscured, and they have allowed terrible sins which are contrary to the natural light in men, that is, contrary to the natural law. They have invented many gods and have imagined them to be eternal; they have even invoked dead men. They have allowed adultery and exchanges of wives."[18] The fusion of erroneous teachings about God with marital and sexual sin seemed clear enough to Melanchthon. But theologians in the following century would wrestle with the question of marriage among non-Europeans and wonder whether marriage practices indicated a glimmer of the original image and likeness of God in non-Christian cultures. Most assumed, as Melanchthon seemed to hint, that the "heathen" lay in a special kind of darkness. Like Nicolaus Hunnius (1585-1643) and Johannes Andreas Quenstedt (1617-88), most remained silent about the exact nature and standing of marriage among such people as indigenous Americans and Africans.[19]

Erasmus Sarcerius's massive treatise on marriage (1569), however, picked up Luther's insights that marriage existed before the Fall and is now universal, a common practice among Christians and non-Christians alike. Sarcerius could therefore describe marriage as a "high, great, and marvelous bond of the entire human society" because the bearing and rearing of children manifested God's presence in nature. God punishes those who marry close relatives as he had chastised ancient Troy, Thebes, Sparta, Athens, and the Greek and Asian lands because of the inhabitants' sexual immorality. Sarcerius did not, however, extend his understanding much beyond the early Luther insofar as he contented himself with writing that the purpose of mar-

18. Melanchthon, *Loci Communes,* p. 124.
19. For details, see Roeber, "Pietists and the Orders of Creation," pp. 747-57, at 748-50.

riage was to keep sexual impulses within honorable bounds. He explained that the word *Ehe* (marriage) was an old German word that also meant "laws" and "right" and should have been used as the word "old" and "new" "Testament" or "covenant" *(Eher)* was used. Such explications of marriage focused on its worldly and legal dimensions, and failed to recapture Luther's emphases on the internal dynamic of the spousal relationship. Instead, Sarcerius's treatise intensified the tendency to focus upon the structural and ordered social and political purposes of marriage.[20] Whether Sarcerius's writings that appear to be an extension of official Lutheran teaching on marriage found general acceptance, or whether in the face of the catastrophe of the Thirty Years' War they merely underscored the desperately felt need for seeking order in a crisis-ridden century, we cannot easily document.

The civil law of marriage in Europe certainly appeared to echo Sarcerius's perspective insofar as it likewise accentuated the public nature of the estate and elided betrothal and marriage into an indissoluble bond presupposing parental consent. But if civil authorities more often regulated marriage, the Protestant law of marriage had also opened the door to the intermarriage of "heathens" and Protestants since theologians did not identify baptism as a condition for marriage.[21] Official theological or canonical teaching, therefore, did not enjoy a complete monopoly in exercising influence on pastors and people. In territories within the Holy Roman Empire, seventeenth-century princes attended more and more to disciplining the behavior of households that seemed impervious to official demands and expectations for order and sobriety. The new emphasis appeared initially to be part of a program of renewal for Protestant communities. Rather quickly, however, the concern for order and discipline overshadowed any hope of recovering a teaching on the spousal relationship that reflected not just God's order, but also his love. The absence of emphasis upon the friendship of married partners who enjoyed a special blessing from God that deepened their ability to live in accord with the gift of justifying grace may have led some Protestants by the late seventeenth century to look for more radical insights into the nature of the marital bond. Both the official confessional theology and the secular legal impulse toward discipline would create a profound challenge for

20. Erasmus Sarcerius, *Corpus Juris matrimonialis Vom Ursprung anfang und herkhomen des heyligen Ehestandts was der seye wie er für zunemen anzusahen und Christlich zu volufüren* . . . (Frankfurt am Main: n.p., 1569), pp. 1, 2; see pp. 3-5 for his summary of Melanchthon, and for the definition, p. 9, "Was die Ehe sey."

21. John Witte, *Law and Protestantism: The Legal Teachings of the Reformation* (Cambridge: Cambridge University Press, 2002), pp. 232-55.

church pietists who soon discovered that their own hopes to restore Luther's synthesis appeared dangerous to many secular authorities. Princes alarmed by emerging groups of the pious had good reason to scrutinize views of marriage that threatened both official theological and legal norms, and transcended the bounds of unofficial village mores, to boot.

Several Protestant states tried to impose tighter controls over the behavior of their subjects in the last half of the seventeenth century. They had little confidence in self-regulation or a household order inspired by religion. It was clear by the early eighteenth century, however, that state disciplinary measures had achieved only modest success. Both Reformed and Lutheran states moved beyond the initial objectives of the theologians to the imposition of intrusive investigations of households. Into the first third of the eighteenth century, most states had to settle for whatever level of order they had managed to impose and to accept compromises with local customs and elites.[22]

Some have concluded that villagers and peasants paid scant attention to the "confessional" differences that preoccupied theologians in the late sixteenth and seventeenth centuries. Ordinary people naturally wanted to order and improve local conditions in the face of threats against communal stability. In some areas, like upper Hesse, the disruptions of the Thirty Years' War and confessional competition between Reformed and Lutheran pastors may account for growing attention paid to social order during a period when disputes about older, rural ways of dealing with property and marriage became more fractious.[23]

Family relationships in villages and the countryside also grew more complicated because families became larger, even exceeding the average size they had attained before 1618. They grew not because the number of children increased but because villagers saw "unrelated others" — servants, day laborers, and "indwellers" — as part of the family. As a result, discipline became stricter. Patterns differed from place to place, but several regions were like the lands of the Benedictine monastery of Ottobeuren in Upper Swabia where "an atmosphere of unprecedented strictness" surrounded marriage contracts and supervision of spouses. "Despite illegitimacy ratios even lower than the ones obtaining before the war, the punishment of extramarital pregnancy was much more ferocious during the later seventeenth century. Even when the couple

22. A. G. Roeber, "The Law, Religion, and State Making in the Early Modern World: Protestant Revolutions in the Works of Berman, Gorski, and Witte," *Law and Social Inquiry* 31 (Winter 2006): 199-227.

23. David Mayes, *Communal Christianity: The Life and Loss of a Peasant Vision in Early Modern Germany* (Boston and Leiden: Brill, 2004), pp. 360-74.

agreed to marry, they were often subjected to public humiliation."[24] At least initially, pastors and princes intent upon reform and discipline would become known for their legalistic condemnation of popular village behavior and high expectations for disciplined behavior within marriage.

This legalistic public face of what eventually came to be labeled pietism elicited satire, dismissal, and criticism from the outset. Preachers, sometimes allied with coalitions of married women, assailed male drunkenness, shift-lessness, sexual dalliances, frivolous amusements, excessive spending at baptisms, and the lack of youthful respect for parents, teachers, and clergy. Like their "Puritan" counterparts, some early pietists seemed to represent narrow, law-driven lives and joyless, oppressive marriages.

Christoph Matthäus Seidel (1668-1723), a student of Philipp Jakob Spener, seemed to exemplify this law-driven mentality when he wrote a programmatic approach for building congregational strength in the Mark Brandenburg. He placed his trust in law and order, certainly not in a loving marriage relationship, as the way to renewal. He spent twenty-six chapters teaching novice pastors strategies to awaken the piety of parishioners, and he consigned marriage to the "occasional" duties of the pastoral office, saying little about it except that the legal requirements should be observed.[25] Marriage should not occasion dancing, card playing, and excessive eating and drinking; it was to be celebrated in the church and not in homes (without a dispensation from the Brandenburg *Consistorium*). He wanted the ceremony to begin with a hymn and include a sermon and a prayer, but he addressed the content of the sermon only by saying that "the substance was about holy matrimony, since I regularly preached on the sayings and also after that the examples about marriage that are noted in Holy Scripture."[26] The announcement of banns was to follow the elector's laws, and the preacher was to pray that God would rule the couple with his Holy Spirit, lead them in the fear of God, and seal them in this "blessed estate."[27]

Seidel was not exceptional. His writings echoed attempts to discipline married life that had been undertaken for the previous thirty years several

24. Govind P. Sreenivasan, *The Peasants of Ottobeuren, 1487-1726: A Rural Society in Early Modern Europe* (Cambridge: Cambridge University Press, 2004), pp. 304-8, quotation at 307.

25. Christoph Mattäus Seidel, *Pietistischer Gemeindeaufbau in Schönberg-Altmark 1700-1708*, ed. Peter Schicketanz (Leipzig: Evangelische Verlagsanstalt, 2005), pp. 61-62, 65.

26. Seidel, *Pietistischer Gemeindeaufbau*, p. 61.

27. Seidel, *Pietistischer Gemeindeaufbau*, p. 62; he also notes that regulations of betrothals and weddings controlled the extravagance of clothing and that the wedding festivities were to last only one day — see p. 65, lines 15-20.

kilometers to the south in Saxe-Gotha. There the pastors were supposed to ask prospective marriage partners if they had studied the catechism, been drunk or quarrelsome before they entered the church, partied for more than two days, or engaged in "wild dancing and other frivolities." Only the emphasis placed upon proper pedagogy and methods of rearing children foreshadowed later pietist hopes for better spouses and households — an emphasis approved by the ruler "Ernest the Pious."[28]

Pastors in mid-to-late-seventeenth-century Rostock reflected the same preoccupations with regulation. The last-surviving member of this group, Heinrich Mueller, apparently (judging from the sermons that survive) preached on the "three estates" (pastors, rulers, citizens) in the Melanchthonian manner and ignored improved spousal relationships as a crucial instrument in the program for regenerating believers, the church, or the state. He issued a stern warning about a careless entrance into marriage that would lead to a lifetime of lamentation *(Wehe)*. His attack on thoughtless marriages paralleled his assault on the formalisms of the pulpit, baptismal font, altar, and confessional and must have struck a chord: the writing merited reissuing forty years after his death. His more lay-oriented colleagues Johannes Quistorp and Theophil Grossgebauer had remarkably little to say (judging from the sermons and treatises that survive) about the married estate as a source of the renewal for contemporary Christianity.[29]

Far to the south, the Württemberg community of Derendingen emerged as a pietist center of some 400 persons. In this territory, the Lutheran theologian of the duchy, Johannes Brenz, and his successors, Jakob Andreae and Lucas Osiander, had reaffirmed the "ubiquity" of Christ and hence his presence in the sacraments. By implication they lessened the gulf between "grace" and "nature." But they did not pursue the implications of such beliefs for recovering Luther's more expansive hopes for the marriage relationship. Local church court records, here and in other places marked by pietist sentiment

28. Veronika Albrecht-Birkner, *Reformation des Lebens: Die Reformen Herzog Ernsts des Frommen von Sachsen-Gotha und ihre Auswirkungen auf Frömmigkeit, Schule und Alltag im ländlichen Raum (1640-1675)* (Leipzig: Evangelische Verlagsanstalt, 2002), pp. 461-73, 483, 490-91, 533-34 on the interrogations and the emphasis on proper pedagogy for households.

29. Jonathan Strom, *Orthodoxy and Reform: The Clergy in Seventeenth Century Rostock* (Tübingen: Coronet Books, 1999), pp. 69-71, 230-39; for Mueller on the three estates, see his *Evangelisches Praeservativ wider den Schaden Josephes in allen drey Ständen* (Frankfurt and Rostock, 1681). For his warning, see *Ungerathene Ehe, oder Vornehmste Ursachen, so heutiges Tages Den Ehestand Zum rechten Wehestand machen* . . . (Hamburg: Johann Wolffgang Fickweiler, 1715); AFSt: S/A: 1344.

and activity, suggest a near fixation on order and control. A multitude of seventeenth-century regulations aimed at disciplining male and female behavior remain silent about the positive dimension of the spousal relationship. The condemnations of dancing, music, recreation, and strolling in the fields after Sunday services, however, do include an order that weddings were to be celebrated in silence.[30]

Admonitions about discipline in the marital relationship and the household at large were not peculiar to German-speaking Europe. The "precisionist" Puritans in the Church of England also produced "domestic conduct books" that surveyed duties in marriage and child-rearing principles while describing the home as a house of learning, correction, and prayer. Such treatises appeared also in the Netherlands where "numerous translations of English Puritan works for the advancement of a holy life style were published in the Dutch Republic." They may have echoed medieval Catholic themes.[31]

Still, such treatises and guidebooks left largely undeveloped the mystical roots that had nourished Luther, who affirmed the presence of God in the creation in ways foreign to both Melanchthon and the Reformed tradition. The departure from the fullness of what Luther had preached was not merely the result of oversight. On the contrary, these seventeenth-century writers feared for the social order if believers took friendship and partnership in marriage or "image and likeness" in theology too seriously. Mainstream Protestant theologians preferred to emphasize long-suffering, heroic, and obedient wives, and they indulged a barely concealed but "deep-seated fear of bodily passion as one of the enemies of conversion and spiritual rebirth." Radical separatists and "church" pietists would both attack precisely this demotion of marriage, but they would now seize upon wildly divergent aspects of what they imagined the Reformation teaching on spousal relations — and human sexuality — amounted to.[32]

---

30. Martin Brecht, *Kirchenordung und Kirchenzucht in Württemberg vom 16. bis zum 18. Jahrhundert* (Stuttgart: Calwer Verlag, 1967), pp. 86, 94-97; on the Württemberg theologians, see Hund, *Das Wort ward Fleisch*, pp. 694-98.

31. Leendert F. Groenendijk, "The Sanctification of the Household and the Reformation of Manners in England Puritanism and in Dutch Pietism during the Seventeenth Century," in *Confessional Sanctity (c. 1500–c. 1800)*, ed. Jürgen Beyer et al. (Mainz: Vandenhoeck & Ruprecht, 2003), pp. 197-218, at 200, 206.

32. On the move toward Lutheran-Reformed cooperation, see Bodo Nischan, *Lutherans and Calvinists in the Age of Confessionalism* (Aldershot, U.K., and Burlington, Vt.: Variorum, 1999); for Christian Thomasius's argument in favor of Lutheran-Reformed intermarriage, see

In the aftermath of the Thirty Years' War, those hoping to rejuvenate devastated communities also helped to define new notions of princely sovereignty, "humanity," the natural world, and ways of accounting for the varieties of human cultures.[33] Since the earliest renewers tended to be urban and literate, both men and women, they were familiar with commentary on men's and women's roles, their marriages, and their expectations that surfaced after the war. Johannes Praetorius, for example, criticized the excesses of the wealthy urban survivors, recounted the misery of everyday life, and conveyed the anxiety his male readers apparently felt about women managing the domestic sphere. Born in 1630 and writing for most of his life in Leipzig, Praetorius died in 1680 just as the early pietist movement was taking shape, but his satirical assessment of women conveyed both sympathy and condescension for women who lived on the other side of "a chasm created by gender," a chasm that excluded males, even the "Hausvater, the father and ruler of the domestic domain."[34]

The urbane world Praetorius described was one largely devoid of explicitly religious or doctrinal content. Praetorius scorned superstitions about the birth ritual and the care of the newborn; he described baptism as a largely social affair, and he revealed the lack of "gender solidarity in spite of the shared female experiences of marriage, birth, and managing the household. Not gender, but class divisions . . . shape the tone of the conversations."[35]

A far more radical attack on the sexual conventions of the urbane and the courtly, however, began to emerge only a few years after Praetorius's death. Between the 1680s and 1700, the term "marriage" became "a phenomenon with many and ambivalent meanings."[36] Both the unease that surrounded the "fleshly" aspects of marriage in Luther's own assessments and

Rechtmäßige Erörterung der Ehe-und Gewissens-Frage (Halle, 1689); for the quotation on fears of human sexuality, see Andreas Gestrich, "Ehe, Familie, Kinder im Pietismus. Der gezähmte Teufel," in *Geschichte des Pietismus IV: Glaubenswelt und Lebenswelten,* ed. Hartmut Lehmann (Göttingen: Vandenhoeck & Ruprecht, 2004), pp. 498-521, at 503.

33. Isabel V. Hull, *Sexuality, State, and Civil Society in Germany, 1700-1815* (Ithaca, N.Y., and London: Cornell University Press, 1996), expertly summarizes the literature on the *Hausvater* and the dependency of the rising states upon family fathers for "local sexual order" (p. 51) — but omits discussing the pietist renewal movement.

34. Gerhild Scholz Williams, *Ways of Knowing in Early Modern Germany: Johannes Praetorius as a Witness to His Time* (Aldershot, U.K., and Burlington, Vt.: Ashgate, 2006), pp. 3-4, 14-15, 169-217, at 169.

35. Williams, *Ways of Knowing,* pp. 188-192, 202, quotation at 191-92.

36. Willi Temme, *Krise der Leiblichkeit: Die Sozietät der Mutter Eva (Buttlarsche Rotte) und der Radikale Pietismus um 1700* (Göttingen: Vandenhoeck & Ruprecht, 1998), p. 394.

Melanchthon's tendency to emphasize the "worldly" functions of the estate under the categories of "law" and "gospel" now threatened to delegitimize hopes for incorporating the marriage relationship within a program of church renewal. In 1684 the fourteen-year-old Margaretha von Buttlar married Jean de Vesias and began what apparently was a nightmarish marital relationship that lasted ten years. Connected to the court life of Eisenach, the Vesias couple had ample opportunity to observe — and participate in — a life characterized by "confessional indifference, a spiritualized understanding of the church, [and] associated radical accusations of the established church." By 1695 she had fed her hunger for both sexual and religious fulfillment by taking a fourteen-year-old lover. She refused two years later to have sex with her husband any longer, and launched the beginning of a career that by 1700 exploded into scandal as she claimed that only by having sex with her could members of a growing radical society of followers be "purified" and encounter God.[37]

What became known as the "Mother Eva" scandal emanated from within the urbane and conventional Lutheran court life of post-1648 Thuringia. The radical views about sexuality and "marriage" revealed at least one dimension of what now appeared to be a growing crisis of indifference among persons whose receptivity to such startling notions showed that many remained unmoved by appeals to the "official" theology of Luther, Melanchthon, or their successors and the demands for ordered households generated by rulers as well. Antisacramentalism and a fascination for eschatology and prophecy now also emerged in these more radical groups. Not only the Mother Eva Society but also other less openly scandalous groups allowed a broader range of religious self-expression to educated women, such as Johanna Eleonora Merlau Petersen (1644-1724), and her husband Johann Wilhelm. In a few of these small groups, a Christology emerged that identified the human soul as feminine and described the Holy Spirit as "She."[38]

---

37. Temme, *Krise,* pp. 31-59, here 41, 59.

38. Hans Schneider, "Der radikale Pietismus im 17. Jahrhundert," in *Geschichte des Pietismus I: Der Pietismus vom sibzehnten bis zum frühen achtzehnten Jahrhundert,* ed. Brecht et al. (Göttingen: Vandenhoeck & Ruprecht, 1993), pp. 391-437, at 399-406. See also Lucinda Martin, "Women's Religious Speech and Activism in German Pietism" (Ph.D. diss., University of Texas at Austin, 2002); Martin notes the role of wealthy but gender-conventional female patrons in the church pietist movement in Halle (pp. 146-51). Pietist influence upon German Reformed views of marriage remains more difficult to establish. See J. Steven O'Malley, "Pietism at Herborn and Its Influence in the American Middle Colonies, with Reference to the Mediating Role of Philip William Otterbein," in *Interdisziplinäre Pietismusforschungen,* 2:781-90. I

49

The theological roots for such claims lay in ancient Christian writings as interpreted by sixteenth-century Protestant theologians, captivated by various strains of Western Christian mysticism. For late-seventeenth-century theologians and pastors struggling to remain within a confessional church, however, the willingness to tamper with accepted definitions of male and female identity, and even the image of the Trinity, intensified the need to say just what the right understanding of spousal relations and the iconic standing of marriage to the Ephesians 5 image consisted of.[39]

The most commonly read and favored texts church renewers found useful appeared at first to devote little attention to this critical question. Neither in its legal, "worldly" aspects nor in the reminder of how the spousal relationship was connected to the "great mystery" of Christ and his church did the estate hold pride of place. Inventories of estates reveal that literate persons attracted to various strains of pietism bought and read Johann Arndt's *True Christianity*, or the *Garden of Paradise*, Philipp Jakob Spener's *Pia Desideria*, and Thomas à Kempis's *Imitation of Christ*. Regional pietist writers produced updated prayer books and devotionals. Württemberg Lutheran pietists who read Johann Friedrich Starck's *Gebetbuch*, for example, found prayers of children for parents and parents for children, prayers for women in childbirth, and prayers at baptism or the Lord's Supper — but not a single prayer on behalf of spouses, words of gratitude or petition for the blessings of marriage, or even mention of the importance of the spousal relationship.[40] A cautious endorsement of the more mystical tradition would eventually resurface, but pietist authors had to be careful in writing or preaching about spousal relations in marriage since the Mother Eva scandal was not unique, nor even was it chronologically nor geographically the primary focus of potential trouble.

---

omit here the connections of radical German pietists to the Philadelphian movement in England. For the Sophia-logical influence from that tradition see Julie Hirst, *Jane Leade: Biography of a Seventeenth-Century Mystic* (Aldershot, U.K.: Ashgate, 2005), and Barbara Becker-Cantarino, trans. and ed., *Johanna Eleonora Petersen: The Life of Lady Johanna Eleonora Petersen; Written by Herself; Pietism and Women's Autobiography in Seventeenth-Century Germany* (Chicago and London: University of Chicago Press, 2005).

39. Johannes Wallmann, "Bernhard von Clairvaux und der Deutsche Pietismus," in *Zur Rezeption mystischer Traditionen im Protestantismus des 16. bis 19. Jahrhunderts: Beiträge eines Symposiums zum Tersteegen-Jubiläum 1997*, ed. Dietrich Meyer and Udo Sträter (Cologne: Rheinland-Verlag, 2002), pp. 1-23.

40. For an overview, see A. G. Roeber, *Palatines, Liberty, and Property: German Lutherans in Colonial British America* (Baltimore and London: Johns Hopkins University Press, 1993), pp. 88-94, 180-84, 385 nn. 15-18.

Some scholars interpret early "church" pietist silence on the relationship between spouses as an expression of unease among Lutherans with the mystical writers who had once attracted Luther. Church pietists could not easily reconcile Johannes Tauler, à Kempis, or the anonymous author of the *Theologia Deutsch* with Spener's insistence on direct, incontrovertible scriptural evidence for supporting mystical claims for union with God. Aware of hostile orthodox reaction to alleged perversion of Lutheran doctrine, Spener crafted the *Pia Desideria* in such a way that it did not include renewed marriage among the pathways to individual, church, and community reform. But pietists who looked to Luther nonetheless recognized the need for a more elaborate treatment of the estate. In Spener's careful maneuvering between the shoals of radical asceticism and rejection of the "fleshly" in marriage on the one hand, and the equally unacceptable sexual excess represented by Mother Eva on the other, the church pietists' attempt to recover Luther's hopes for spouses began to take shape.[41]

In Spener's catechetical sermons, published a decade after the *Pia Desideria,* he expanded on Luther's teaching on marriage in the *Small Catechism.* He wrote that marriage does not exist for procreation, but helps married couples toward salvation. God had called husband and wife to love each other and offer each other mutual help; their marriage should be permanent. Unlike the "orthodox Lutherans," Spener omitted the notion that marrying is primarily a social and political obligation — and he said nothing about procreation as the purpose of marriage. He did accept the canonical legal norms and a part of the official theology that placed men at the head of the household. And he called on women to catechize and educate children while supporting a "stronger emphasis on the spiritual-religious relationship in marriage." Nonetheless, church pietists, having inherited the medieval notions of "friendship" more than Luther's boldness, remained uncertain, as were their contemporaries among lyric poets, whether conjugal love could be reconciled to nobler "spiritual" friendship.[42]

---

41. Wallmann, "Philipp Jakob Spener und die Mystik," in *Zur Rezeption mystischer Traditionen,* pp. 129-47. My interpretations of Spener on marriage and the understanding of church pietists have been informed by, but do not agree in every respect with, Hans Schneider, "Understanding the Church: Issues of Pietist Ecclesiology" and "Marriage and Marriage-Criticism in Pietism: Philipp Jakob Spener, Gottfried Arnold, and Nikolaus Ludwig von Zinzendorf," both in *Pietism and Community in Europe and North America, 1650-1850,* ed. Jonathan Strom (Leiden and Boston: Brill, 2010), pp. 15-36 and 37-54, respectively.

42. This summarizes Ulrike Gleixner, "Zwischen göttlicher und weltlicher Ordnung. Die Ehe im lutherischen Pietismus," *Pietismus und Neuzeit* 28 (2002): 147-84, at 150-53, quotation at

Spener himself presents an almost classic case of caution mixed with a determination to recapture Luther's high view of marriage, a pattern reflected at times among authors happy with their own marriages. "One of the most important days in Spener's life was June 23, 1664. On the afternoon of that day he received his doctorate; in the morning, moreover, he took a wife." Spener never commented in public about his marriage. He may have originally intended not to marry; in any event, his wife, Suzanna Erhardt, remains an elusive figure about whom Spener said little. Perhaps she did not share his belief in the spiritual efficacy of marriage.[43]

In 1691, nevertheless, he published a collection of his sermons on marriage (see Figure 1). Spener dedicated the book to his wife in celebration of their years of partnership and their desire to enjoy the "marriage of the Lamb."[44] Like Sarcerius, Spener analyzed the etymology of the German word, noting that Hebrews, Syrians, Arabs, and Westerners all distinguished humans from other animals because of marriage. In primitive German the term *Ehe* meant a union, but in common understanding, he noted, it had acquired the meaning of "law" or "covenant," in part because of Luther's Bible translation. Plural marriage Spener denounced on the grounds of Jesus' admonition (Matt. 19:4) that "in the beginning it was not so" (p. 5). He defined the marriage bond as a covenant of unequal partners, one the head, one subordinate (p. 7), that did not require a priestly blessing (p. 10) because it was grounded in the order of creation and confirmed after the Fall by Christ (pp. 13-15). Against the profane who reduced marriage to a kind of whoredom, Spener invoked the image of marriage as a sign of Christ's headship of the church (Eph. 5:23). He added — and would emphasize — that headship required "reason" and never permitted tyranny; marriage was the work of the Trinity, the source of harmony (pp. 17-28).

Spener repeated the patristic view that Eve came from Adam's rib as a

152; on the later impact of the tension between conjugal love and friendship for the early Enlightenment, see Hans-Georg Kemper, *Deutsche Lyrik der frühen Neuzeit 5/II Frühaufklärung* (Tübingen: Niemeyer, 1991), pp. 160-61, 171-72.

43. K. James Stein, *Philipp Jakob Spener: Pietist Patriarch* (Chicago: Covenant Press, 1986), pp. 67-68, at 67; see also Johannes Wallmann, *Philipp Jakob Spener und die Anfänge des Pietismus* (Tübingen: J. C. B. Mohr [Paul Siebeck], 1970), pp. 176-77.

44. Philipp Jakob Spener, *Christliche Trau-Sermonen bey Copulation-Actibus. Einiger vornehmer angehender Eheleute in Franckfurt am Mayn zu underschiedlichen Zeiten gehalten* (Frankfurt am Main: Johann David Zunner, 1691). The publisher's cartouche showing the leaning tree boasts "though burdened, I resist." The following paragraphs are taken from the first edition, available online from the Bayerische Staatsbibliothek Digital project: www.bsb-münchen-digital.de (accessed 30 April 2011).

Figure 2. Halle's reprint of Philipp Jakob Spener's *Marriage Sermons* (1719). Reproduced with the permission of the Francke Foundations, Halle, Germany (AFSt: 46C 15 b).

sign that she was to be loved, her origin being near his heart. Christ had removed the curse from marriage, placed it within his scheme of salvation, bestowed the Holy Spirit on married couples, and — only at the end, Spener concluded — provided for the raising of children. Spener pioneered an approach that would find reflection in nearly all pietist-influenced hymnals of the next century: Christ as the spiritual Bridegroom provided a way of seeing the "bride as the human nature in Christ or the flesh" and marital union prefigured the union of the believing soul to Christ (pp. 32-62, quotation at 51). This *geistliche Vermählung* preoccupied Spener's successors, to the near exclusion of his own emphasis on friendship and partnership.

Marriage could be forbidden to no person, including the clergy. It was an "order of creation," but it also represented the social orders of those who ruled, who taught, and who oversaw households. This meant that its honorable standing required couples to love and help each other and to nurture children (pp. 120-22). It was no sacrament, since the Old Testament sacraments of circumcision and the slaughter of the paschal lamb found their Christian counterparts only in baptism and the Lord's Supper. Neither the Old nor the New Testament, moreover, attached a blessing to marriage (pp. 122, 162-63). But Spener deemed it nonetheless a holy estate, not a purely civic matter. He believed that Lutherans remained "in the middle way" between the excesses of both Rome and the ungodly (p. 161); marriage both extended grace and also pointed to the mysteries of the God who had instituted it (p. 164).

From time to time Spener returned in the sermons to the errors of the early church fathers (p. 294), singling out Jerome and Pope Siricius, who had tried to impose the rule of celibacy on the Western clergy. But he took aim also (p. 304) at anyone who would secularize the estate, even though he acknowledged that it contained "a political and worldly contract." But it was no mere contractual relation; it was a created order sanctified by Christ (p. 304).

The sermons aimed at comprehensiveness. Marriage entailed obligations, which God mandated for each partner (Eph. 5:33). Women were to be obedient, but obedience was to be Christian, so no woman was bound to suffer evil (pp. 171, 176-77). Spener said often that no woman was the servant of her husband and every husband had to be a "reasonable" head, called to lead by example, perhaps even to lay down his life for his wife (pp. 202-3, 217-20). Throughout, Spener admonished men more than women. Even when noting that a woman would be saved in childbearing (1 Tim. 2:15), he interpreted the passage to mean that even the "fleshly" side of marital life could be holy (p. 368).

Unlike some later pietists, Spener discerned holiness within the tangible and visible. Christ was the head of a universal church, some of which was visible in evangelical congregations of Europe, some of which included all who believed in an "unseen" manner (p. 217). His respect for the visible appeared in his continued approval of the bridal crown and floral circlets, which he described as ancient symbols both of honor and joy and of suffering, the crowns of martyrs (pp. 396-402).

Whether he preached on marriage or "awakening" or "regeneration," he accented permanence. This accent lay behind his insistence that the image and likeness lost in the Garden was being restored, in fact, that it "actually flowed into the soul and filled understanding, will, and affections," making believers "'divinized persons,' as the Greek church fathers had recognized. Spener spoke even of the 'inhabitation' *(Einwohnung)* of God's essence in the believer's soul."[45]

He adapted his ideas to his audiences. In a sermon preached at the remarriage of his pastoral colleague at the prestigious Saint Nicholas Church in Berlin, to which Spener had been called from Dresden, he said that women had the opportunity to show themselves as costly gifts who secured the conscience of men that God blessed the marriage. Both bride and groom were to remember that they were to bring into the world children who lived in obedience to their father. But Spener also added that marriage signified the soul's union with God, and mutual friendship and bodily health stood higher in God's plan for marriage than the mere begetting of children.[46]

Spener might have initially been silent about marriage as an instrument of renewal because he wanted to avoid bringing direct attention to conventicles. These small groups of intensely committed laity and clergy met for Scripture study, prayer, and mutual discipline. Princes and theologians reacted to them either with cautious endorsement or with outright hostility, including *Rescripts* intended to eliminate them. The Swedish Lutheran hierarchy, despite their early interest in Spener's work, became hostile by the early 1700s, and the *Riksdag,* convinced that even hostile bishops were too lenient, elbowed them aside and initiated an all-out campaign against conven-

---

45. Baird Tipson, "How Can the Religious Experience of the Past Be Recovered? The Examples of Puritanism and Pietism," *Journal of the American Academy of Religion* 43, no. 4 (December 1975): 695-707, at 703. The Eastern theologians would not have endorsed the idea that God's "essence" is joined with the creature, but rather that his uncreated "energies" are.

46. Spener, *Des Ehe-Standes Würde . . .* (Berlin, 1704), pp. 7-13; preached at the marriage of Peter Kalckberner and Barbara Cordula von Lauter (widow of Johann Paul Astman); AFSt 62F3.

ticles and suspect literature. That pattern repeated itself in varying degrees of severity in other principalities and urban centers of the Holy Roman Empire, even — to a degree — in deeply church pietist Württemberg (1733).[47]

Since the conventicles most often met in households, pietists regarded the attacks upon them as subversive of the household and its role as a "little church." That honor Luther had ascribed to the married estate, and Spener returned to it often to test whether a marriage was Christian or not.[48] When the Württemberg jurist Johann Jacob Moser published his 1734 essay on conventicles, he associated them with "God's children" and invoked the image of the household to describe them.

Early church pietist writings seldom transgressed the social and gender conventions of the seventeenth-century Reich. Spener's invocation of the "priesthood of all believers" in the *Pia Desideria* did not call for a radically altered role for women, married or unmarried. In his catechism lectures and in his counsels given to his own daughter, "Spener's own picture of the duties of the married woman was traditional and . . . in the Spener house religious duties or the insights of the woman played themselves out completely within the traditional structure." Neither did Spener's attitude change when he addressed the noblewomen whose patronage helped sustain the fledgling movement. He enjoined them also to fulfill obediently the duties of a wife.[49]

In his caution, Spener was by no means unique. Sermons that he and others preached before the Saxon elector in Dresden — thought by some the most important Protestant pulpit in the empire — rarely challenged social or political convention. Spener exercised theological and political influence more indirectly through his cultivation of eminent women such as Anna Sophia, the daughter of King Friedrich III of Denmark, and the elector's mother Sibylle Magdalene. In the sermons and exhortations, he remained silent about the duties of marriage, including the household table of duties in Ephesians 5 and 6. Instead, he merely admonished the courtiers to live up to their worldly authority and duties. Samuel Benedict Carpzov, his successor,

---

47. On the conventicles in southwest Germany, see Roeber, *Palatines,* pp. 75-88; on the Swedish campaign, see Ingun Montgomery, "Der Pietismus in Schweden im 18. Jahrhundert," in *Der Pietismus im achtzehnten Jahrhundert (Geschichte des Pietismus Vol. II),* ed. Martin Brecht and Klaus Deppermann (Göttingen: Vandenhoeck & Ruprecht, 1995), pp. 489-522, at 506-14.

48. Spener, *Trau-Sermonen,* pp. 129, 229, 245, 258-59, 353.

49. Cornelia Niekus Moore, "Obschon das schwächste Werkzeug: Die Darstellung der Frau im deutschen Pietismus," in *Interdisziplinäre Pietismusforschungen,* 1:37-53, quotation at 41.

accommodated himself to the elector August the Strong's weakness for mistresses, as did Carpzov's successors. By 1724, when Bernhard Walther Marperger began his duties, the pietists in this territory rarely criticized morals and did not endorse marriage as a pathway to renewal.[50]

The most plausible reason for Spener's hesitancy to define publicly marriage as a relationship, a quasi sacrament designed for mutual friendship, support, and holiness, however, can be found in the controversy surrounding the 1667 marriage of the Roman Catholic eunuch Bartolomeo Sorlisi to the Lutheran Dorothea Lichtwer. A full generation before the more famous Mother Eva scandal would challenge church pietists to distance themselves from such radical notions, this Saxon case showed the potentially explosive implications of examining the conjugal relationship and how it related to the "mystery" of Christ and his church. The ensuing uproar drew comment from the theological faculties of nearly every Lutheran university in the empire. The dispute prompted the Lutheran theologians of Königsberg in East Prussia and Greifswald in Pomerania to identify the primary purpose of marriage as mutual support and the containment of sexual desire, not the procreation of children. By the time Spener arrived in Dresden to take his post as *Oberhofprediger* in 1686, just after Mother Eva was embarking on her own miserable marriage, Sorlisi had died (1672), as had the elector Johann Georg II, who had bypassed his consistory to approve the petition to marry. The former court preacher Martin Geier, who supported Spener's appointment, had opposed the elector's decision and lobbied for annulment of a marriage he viewed as scandalous. Spener had to preach cautiously to Saxon auditors who vividly recalled the contention.[51]

Many of the Lutheran marriage canons maintained Catholic teaching regarding impediments. Sorlisi had been castrated as a postpubertal youth, so he argued (rather graphically) that he could consummate a marriage, thus trying to thwart canonists who saw the inability to consummate as a reason for annulment. Knowing that he would have to overcome canonical objections, Sorlisi adopted in his petition to the Leipzig Consistory the fictitious identity of a Swedish soldier as part of his strategy to prove his conjugal capacities.[52] But the heart of his argument lay in his declaration of "the

---

50. Wolfgang Sommer, *Die lutherischen Hofprediger in Dresden: Grundzüge ihrer Geschichte und Verkündigung im Kurfürstentum Sachsen* (Stuttgart: Franz Steiner, 2006), pp. 213-33 on Spener, and on Marperger, 263-79.

51. What follows summarizes Mary E. Frandsen, "*Eunuchi Conjugium:* The Marriage of a Castrato in Early Modern Germany," *Early Music History* 24 (2005): 53-124.

52. Frandsen, "*Eunuchi,*" p. 71. Here, I believe, Frandsen does not adequately understand

mutual love that he shares with Dorothea," and he denied that the primary purpose of marriage was procreation. Some Lutheran theologians accepted Augustine's trinity of marital characteristics — progeny, fidelity, and sacrament — but others did not. In any case, theological opinions from Strassburg, Giessen, Jena, Leipzig, and Wittenberg showed that "the views of Lutheran theologians on the ends (or goals) of marriage, and the number and order of these ends, were not absolutely consistent."[53]

The Jena theologians affirmed the procreative purpose, but mutual support occupied for them the traditional second good of marriage. The Prussian theologians reached far back into the patristic era to argue that the old covenant elevated procreation, the new covenant, spiritual children. After all, Matthew 19:12 had called some to celibacy. Without denying the three purposes or goods of marriage, the Königsberg writers employed a pre-Augustinian reordering: "If there is only one goal of marriage, it is mutual help; if there are two, the necessity of avoiding fleshly desire is added."[54]

Shrewdly aware of the potential for misspeaking, Spener avoided sermons on the topic of marriage in the early Dresden years. When he finally spoke out, he revealed a seventeenth-century Lutheran ambivalence about any move away from a biological and legal view of the estate. Such ambivalence pointed to the uncertainty about the identity of the Protestant church. Was it an institution or a community? The Sorlisi case drew heavily upon medieval canonical precedents, and the conservative Lutheran canonists seemed to agree with their Catholic opponents even about the order in which theologians should list the purposes of marriage. Luther, however, had defined Christians not so much in institutional terms but more as a community sharing an experience of God and communal life, including the married order

---

the canonical problem; for details on the impediments question, see Witte, *Law and Protestantism,* pp. 241-55; on the jurisdictions of the consistories in Saxony, see Tanya Kevorkian, *Baroque Piety: Religion, Society, and Music in Leipzig, 1650-1750* (Aldershot, U.K., and Burlington, Vt.: Ashgate, 2007), pp. 108-22. On the consistories and their background under Swedish influence as the courts with competence in cases of conscience, the clergy, and marriage cases, see Kjell Å. Modéer, *Gerichtsbarkeiten der schwedischen Krone im deutschen Reichsterritorium: I: Voraussetzungen und Aufbau 1630-1657* (Stockholm: A.-B. Nordiska Bokhandeln, 1975), pp. 140-46.

53. Frandsen, *"Eunuchi,"* pp. 78, 100.

54. Frandsen, *"Eunuchi,"* p. 108, quotation at 109. For a useful survey of Augustine's comments on marriage and its purposes that suggests the later loss of his own endorsement of mutual support and sexual activity even when procreation was not intended, see David G. Hunter, "Reclaiming Biblical Morality: Sex and Salvation History in Augustine's Treatment of the Hebrew Saints," in *In Dominico Eloquio: In Lordly Eloquence; Essays on Patristic Exegesis in Honor of Robert Louis Wilken,* ed. Paul M. Blowers et al. (Grand Rapids: Eerdmans, 2002), pp. 317-35.

and the household. Ambivalence about what terms like "marriage" and "family" might legitimately include, however, revealed, in its train, indecision about the nature of the church.

Spener during the 1680s also began to realize that theologians he initially thought of as potential allies appeared to harbor alarming interpretations of a "spiritualized" church that promised to stir up as much controversy as the Sorlisi case had. Spener's difficulties with Gottfried Arnold also complicated his endorsement of a more companionate vision of the spousal relationship in marriage. Arnold, a Lutheran pastor, was born in electoral Saxony in 1666, studied in Wittenberg, and then read Spener's *Nature and Grace,* which caused him to write the now-famous theologian in 1688 and to move a year later to Dresden, where he cultivated the aging Spener until taking a position in Quedlinburg in 1693. Arnold's emerging vision of an entirely "invisible" church seems to have developed during his association with more radical pietist cells during those years. Spener had left Dresden for Berlin in 1691 and helped to secure Arnold's position in Quedlinburg, but may well have been unprepared for the arguments that appeared in Arnold's massive *Unpartheiische Kirchen-und Ketzer-Historie* (1699).[55] The storm of acclaim and protest that greeted the book led Spener to write privately to Arnold expressing his disapproval.

Arnold sought to demonstrate that "confessional" approaches to Christianity betrayed the early vision of a "primitive" and apostolic church that knew no hierarchy, no sacraments, no set rites, in short, none of the "visible" marks that he traced to the disastrous era of Constantine the Great. "The identity of the Pietists up to this point received a new quality because of Arnold's historiography." Since Arnold insisted on citing original sources, he found little about marriage, for early sources describing marriage rituals or clarifying the standing of marriage as sacrament, or detailing spousal relations and the connection to Ephesians 5, were indeed scarce.[56] To identify the church as the Spirit-led *Stille im Lande* (the-quiet-in-the-land), however, as Arnold did, amounted to minimizing any reference to sacraments of any sort, including such visible external rites, orders, or estates as marriage.

Within a few years, Arnold's skepticism about such "externals" as clerics

---

55. *Unpartheiische Kirchen- und Ketzerhistorie,* 4 parts (Frankfurt am Main, 1699/1700). For further details, see Hans Schneider, "Der radikale Pietismus im 17. Jahrhundert," in *Geschichte des Pietismus I,* pp. 391-437, at 410-16.

56. Dirk Fleischer, *Zwischen Tradition und Fortschritt: Der Strukturwandel der protestantischen Kirchengeschichtsschreibung im deutschsprachigen Diskurs der Aufklärung,* 2 vols. (Waltrop: Hartmut Spenner, 2006), 1:23-69, quotation at 42, 54-61.

and sacraments encouraged a growing willingness among critics of the magisterial Protestant churches to question the role of pastors, even those as revered as Spener.[57] A younger generation of jurists even scrutinized Christian monogamy, and some pietist pastors began to doubt that proper marriages led to proper churches. The discussion drew the attention of one of Spener's successors among the "church" pietists: August Hermann Francke, who would also now have to confront the more radical attacks on marriage, mounted by both extreme ascetics and people church pietists could only understand as libertines.

Francke's early life in Lübeck and his subsequent education gave little indication of the celebrity that would emerge from his acceptance of the unpromising task of shepherding the small congregation in the village of Glaucha, outside the city walls of Halle. His founding of a refuge for orphans there nonetheless launched a new impulse for renewal not only in the Holy Roman Empire but also on the international stage. One interpretation of Francke's theology depicts him as a theologian of order, proclaiming a God of order and a creation that reflects that order.[58] In the massive number of "ordinances" for the Francke Foundations, one is tempted to see a law-driven mentality that manifested itself in "church orders, school orders, regulations for meals, and finally all the innumerable admonitions to the students for order."[59] But Francke saw God primarily as "teacher," not as "law-giver." He would initially think of such jurists as Samuel Pufendorf and Christian Thomasius as his allies, but he would discover that his agreements with them about the importance of education and the value of an ordered society led to no consensus about where marriage stood in God's order, or that of the "world."[60]

Francke may have at first shared Spener's admiration for Luther's complex view of marriage as a mixture of the worldly and the mystical. He initially seemed inclined toward the mystical tradition. His lectures on mystical theology in 1704 cited Tauler, Johann Arndt, and the medieval Dutch mystic

---

57. Euan Cameron, *Interpreting Christian History: The Challenge of the Churches' Past* (Malden, Mass., and Oxford: Blackwell, 2005), pp. 137-49.

58. Eduard Peschke, *Studien zur Theologie August Hermann Franckes* (Berlin: Evangelische Verlagsanstalt, 1964), p. 18; and see the extended discussion in Peter Menck, *Die Erziehung der Jugend zur Ehre Gottes und zum Nutzen des Nächsten: die Pädagogik August Hermann Franckes* (Tübingen: Niemeyer, 2001), pp. 95-102.

59. Peschke, *Studien,* pp. 95-97, quotation at 97.

60. On Pufendorf's role, see Pauline C. Westerman, *The Disintegration of Natural Law Theory: Aquinas to Finnis* (Leiden, New York, and Cologne: Brill, 1998), pp. 181-227.

Jan van Ruysbroek's treatise published in 1608 as *On the Ornament of Spiritual Marriages.*[61] But he grew wary after he discovered alarming tendencies toward radical mysticism in the thinking of his own spouse.

Letters between Anna Magdalena von Wurm and Francke suggest that the marriage was both happy and companionate.[62] But Anna Magdalena, instructed in part through correspondence with the radical pietist writer Johann Georg Gichtel, harbored more dangerous ideas than her spouse could express publicly. Von Wurm and Francke chose to be married in Quedlinburg, where Anna had lived since the death of her mother in 1693, the year Gottfried Arnold took up residence there. The town had a reputation for inspirationalist, prophetic, and even antinomian piety, and it may have influenced Frau Francke's view of marriage. She apparently subscribed to Gichtel's beliefs that the "reborn" woman enjoyed a particular relationship "to the heavenly Sophia — thought of as the male partner of the woman."[63] Gichtel himself achieved notoriety for his dissemination and interpretation of the sixteenth-century theologian Johann Jakob Böhme's teachings. But where Böhme had never insisted on fleeing a "fleshly" marriage in order to pursue union with the "heavenly Sophia," Gichtel did. Not surprisingly, this deeply ascetic interpretation fell back on one particular reading of the "bridegroom mysticism" of medieval Christian writers, and radicals read those sources with as much interest as they did (along with the "church" pietists) the new editions of the (supposedly) Tauler work, the *German Theology.* The emergence of a "marriage religion" in the writings of Arnold, the Petersens, the Mother Eva Society, and Gichtel had gradually crystallized by the 1690s, and Anna Magdalena apparently was drawn to these teachings. The profoundly different interpretations of what Ephesians 5 meant — fleeing all sexual activity in this life in favor of a union with the "spiritual body" of Christ, or realizing that "mystery" through sex with one (or more) partner — had now emerged as irreconcilable conclusions among renewal cells all identified by critics as "pietists." The crisis over the proper interpretation of what "union" with God meant and how it related to "marriage" now in-

61. Friedrich De Boor, "August Hermann Francke und die mystische Lehre von der geistlichen Trunkenheit," in *Interdisziplinäre Pietismusforschungen,* 1:155-70, at 160.

62. Unfortunately, Francke's letters to his future wife do not survive. For the details in this paragraph, see Erich Beyreuther, *August Hermann Francke 1663-1727: Zeuge des lebendigen Gottes* (Marburg: Verlag der Francke-Buchhandlung, 1956), pp. 137-46.

63. Martin Brecht, "August Hermann Francke und der Hallische Pietismus," in *Geschichte des Pietismus I,* pp. 439-539, quotation at 461. See also Aira Vosa, "Die Ehe bei Jakob Böhme und Johann Georg Gichtel," in *Liebe, Ehe und Sexualität im Pietismus,* pp. 81-88.

tensified, illustrating how difficult a task church pietist leaders faced in trying to distinguish their positions on spousal relations from these more radical views.[64]

Her surviving twenty-six letters suggest that both Anna Magdalena and Francke hoped that a notion of Christian friendship would undergird their marriage. But critics disapproved of their unequal social standing, a violation of the conventions surrounding friendship even between persons of the same sex. Living in this Quedlinburg pietist circle, she wrote no letters that openly reflected Spener's views, but Francke must have known from the outset that she had cultivated her own notions of marriage, and that they leaned in a potentially more radical direction.[65]

By 1715 Frau Francke made no secret that she disagreed with her husband's plan to marry their daughter Sophia to one of Francke's most promising disciples, Johann Anastasius Freylinghausen. Anna Magdalena boycotted the wedding. The picture of domestic harmony in Francke's marriage, in short, seems to be part of a later attempt at damage control — one that matches the suspicious indictment Francke had left of his congregation in Glaucha where he began his ministry in 1692. Among the 500 to 550 inhabitants of the village, very few Glaucha children found their way into his orphanage, despite his claims about its importance in the task of rescuing the children of the poor. Moreover, Francke became unpopular within three years because he excluded from communion members who drank alcohol. By 1704 that policy provoked outraged protest from the cantor Balthasar Bude and his wife, and produced an electoral order that forbade using access to the Lord's Supper as a disciplinary measure. That decision, at least, may have come as a relief to unhappy parishioners who had suffered, with Berlin's approval, Francke's imposition of Freylinghausen as adjunct pastor.[66]

Freylinghausen exerted an influence upon later pietists nearly as great as that of his father-in-law by compiling and publishing the massive hymnal, *Geist-reiches Gesangbuch*. From its publication in 1704, it reached the ordinary believer more profoundly than did his 1703 treatise *Grundlegung der*

---

64. The above summarizes the analysis of Temme in *Krise*, pp. 78-80, 362-417.

65. Katje Lißmann, "'. . . der Herr wird seine Herrlichkeit an uns offenbahren . . .'" — Die Eheschließung Anna Magdalena von Wurms und August Hermann Franckes (1694)," in *Liebe, Ehe und Sexualität im Pietismus,* pp. 152-70.

66. Veronika Albrecht-Birkner, *Francke in Glaucha Kehrseiten eines Klischees (1692-1704)* (Halle and Tübingen: Max Niemeyer Verlag, 2004), pp. 12, 34-35, 105-11; W. R. Ward, *Early Evangelicalism: A Global Intellectual History, 1670-1789* (Cambridge: Cambridge University Press, 2006), p. 46.

Theologie. Some may have noticed that he omitted hymns celebrating marriage except in the "spiritual" sense now favored by pietist writers who could attach varying meanings to the word.[67] Appearing just three years before the beginning of Danish-German mission efforts in Tranquebar on the southeast Indian coast, the hymnal Freylinghausen compiled aimed at revealing the foundations of the mystery of salvation. In classic Lutheran style, he wrote of the survival of the "image and likeness" of God and the "law written on the heart" that made it possible for fallen humanity to exercise "natural" virtue and to hear the "good news" of the Christian gospel. Unlike some pietist writers, however, he shied away from suggesting that the "natural" estate of marriage, as the image of the relationship between Christ and his church, could be transformative. Neither in the treatise nor in the hymns did he include marriage within the orbit of the "good news," confining it to the "worldly" realm of natural virtue. What survived for Freylinghausen was the bridegroom mysticism of the soul's union with God — an idea beloved by Johann Arndt. But Arndt's *Four Books on True Christianity* had treated marriage as a poor shadow of the marriage of Christ and the soul — not Christ and the church. In short, Arndt's position, while drawing like Luther on Tauler and other mystics, did not exalt marriage as one of the orders of creation, nor as the icon of Christ and the church. This lapse distinguished his approach from Luther's stronger view of marriage, and of the church, as well. In Freylinghausen's case, the decision to remain strictly within the bounds of discussing the individual soul's relationship to God may very well have stemmed from his awareness of the Mother Eva scandal. He would naturally have hesitated to link the version of church renewal now under way at Halle to the more volatile implications that notions of "union with God" and the ambivalent term "marriage" now held, given the notoriety of both ascetic and "libertine" radical pietist groups.[68]

67. Suvi-Päivi Koski, "Und singen das lied Mosis deß Knechts Gottes/und das lied deß Lamms — Apoc. XV:3. Zur Theologie des Geist-reichen Gesang-Buches (Halle 1704) von Johann Anastasius Freylinghausen," in *Geist-reicher Gesang. Halle und das pietistische Lied,* ed. Gudrun Busch and Wolfgang Miersemann (Tübingen: Niemeyer Verlag, 1997), pp. 184-203.

68. *Johann Anastasius Freylinghausens . . . Grundlegung der Theologie . . .* (Halle: in Verlegung des Waysenhauses, 1703), pp. 1-2; Arndt's classic text *Vier Bücher vom Wahren Christentum* (Frankfurt am Main, 1606; four volumes, Magdeburg, 1610) appeared in a final Latin edition in 1708 and received its first English translation by Anton Wilhelm Böhme in London in 1712. The references to marriage and Christ as the heavenly bridegroom occur in book V, part 2, chapters 1-7 in extended reflections that reflect Bernard of Clairvaux's bridegroom mysticism. On the complicated problem of Martin Moller's authorship of this chapter and its late addition to the *Four Books* (that nonetheless eighteenth-century readers would have

Freylinghausen dedicated the hymnal to the aristocratic women who occupied the imperial free secular *Stift* of Gandersheim and had proved to be allies of Halle's renewal efforts. The introduction described the church's fall to the papal Antichrist and the seeds of its recovery in the work of Amos Comenius and the Bohemian Brethren, whose wonderful hymns moved Luther. New collections in Erfurt, Darmstadt, Berlin, and Halle had inspired his collection. Freylinghausen retained the classic structure of the church year and then grouped the hymns according to the plan of salvation, adding songs appropriate to preaching, baptism, and the Lord's Supper. It included no "secondary sacramental" occasions and no wedding hymns, as such. Spiritual marriage identifying Jesus as the Bridegroom, however, occurred in thirteen hymns, and Freylinghausen also referred to chastity, "brotherly and general love," and "spiritual marriage." No heading touched on the wedding feast of Cana or other familiar scriptural texts about the spousal relationship in marriage per se. The pioneering association in hymnody of the "believing soul" to the bridegroom Christ had been laid down by Philipp Nicolai in 1599. His "Joyous Mirror of the Everlasting Life" bequeathed the text that Freylinghausen (and other pietist compilers after him) would include as the appropriate wedding hymn: "How Brightly Shines the Morning Star." Originally written as a meditation on Revelation 22:16 and Psalm 45, the piece, as Nicolai had made quite clear in the first published version, was a "wedding song" of the individual believing soul. No explicit, or implied, ecclesiology could easily be extracted from the hymn, and neither Freylinghausen nor any other commentator apparently ever attempted to relate it explicitly to the "mystery" of Ephesians 5. Moreover, the hymn appeared in the Halle hymnal as part of the "Morning Songs," further obscuring any public or official theological connection to marriage.[69]

---

accepted as coming from Arndt), see Wallmann, "Bernhard von Clairvaux und der deutsche Pietismus," in *Zur Rezeption mystischer Traditionen*, pp. 1-23, at 10-11.

69. Deanna Marie McMullen and Wolfgang Miersemann, eds., a reprint of the 1708 4th ed., 4 vols. (Tübingen: Max Niemeyer Verlag, 2004), Vorrede pp. 15-16; see headings 32, 36, 47, 54, and 56; for examples of the Bridegroom offerings, see vol. 2, pt. 2, nos. 594-96. "How Brightly Shines the Morning Star" is at vol. 1, pt. 2, no. 611, pp. 872-73. For commentary on Freylinghausen's understanding of humanity reflected in his works, see Suvi-Päivi Koski, "Zur theologischen Anthropologie der Freylinghausenschen Gesangbücher," in *Alter Adam und Neue Kreatur: Pietismus und Anthropologie. Beiträge zum II. Internationalen Kongress für Pietismusforschung 2005*, ed. Udo Sträter and Hartmut Lehmann et al., 2 vols. (Halle and Tübingen: Max Neimeyer Verlag, 2009), 2:597-610. Koski does not address the hymns on the marriage estate or for weddings. On Nicolai's work, see Temme, *Krise*, p. 396 n. 54; *RGG* 6, p. 292 with bibliography.

Local patriotism, at the least, might have inspired Freylinghausen to include the wedding hymn of Johann Olearius. Born in Halle, Olearius came from a long line of distinguished pastors and superintendents and had composed a hymn in thanksgiving for the end of an outbreak of plague. His son Johannes Andreas, although a theologian associated with the Leipzig "orthodox," sympathized with the Spenerian "church" variety of pietism, as did his brother Johann Gottfried. By the time of his own death in 1684, the older Olearius's text "Whosoever chooses marriage" ("Wer den Ehestand will erwählen") had earned its place among the favorites of at least some hymnal compilers. Unlike the more "soul-centered" hymn "How Brightly Shines the Morning Star," Olearius's text focused on the spousal relationship of the newly married couple. That they should begin their marriage with prayer, that God had blessed the "bond of love" and as a "mild father" would bring blessing, honor, joy, and prosperity — all were contained in his teaching and promises. After all, the hymn concluded, God himself had so ordained that "two hearts should find pleasure" in matrimony.

By 1725, the county of Oldenburg had published its new church order. Perhaps because it had been under Danish royal rule since 1676, and perhaps because of their distaste for the Halle variety of pietism that led to fractious relations within the Danish church into the 1720s, the Oldenburg clergy responsible for crafting the new church order explicitly forbade the use of "How Brightly Shines the Morning Star" and insisted that "Wer den Ehestand will erwählen" be used instead. Without detailing the precise nature of their prohibition, they contented themselves with the explanation "because of great misuse," and given the orthodox Lutheran tenor of the rest of their regulations of church services, including auricular confession, the anti-Halle implications were undoubtedly clear to the clergy expected to obey these mandates.[70]

---

70. On Olearius, see Hans Peter Hasse, *Olearius, Johannes, RGG,* 4th ed., VI (Tübingen: Mohr-Siebeck, 2003), p. 548; for the Danish context, including the protection given to mild pietism by King Christian IV and the resistance of more orthodox clergy, see Manfred Jakubowski-Tiessen, "Der Pietismus in Dänemark und Schleswig-Holstein," in *Der Pietismus im achtzehnten Jahrhundert,* ed. Brecht and Deppermann (Göttingen: Vandenhoeck & Ruprecht, 1995), pp. 446-71, at 449; for the Oldenburg issue, Gerhard Wintermann, *Die Zweite Oldenburgische Kirchenordnung von 1725 nebst Anhängen, im Auftrage des Ev.-luth. Oberkirchenrats in Oldenburg* (Göttingen: Vandenhoeck & Ruprecht, 1988), pp. 23-24, par. 7. On the regulation of confession and preparation for the Lord's Supper, see pp. 34-39. The text of Olearius's hymn continues to be in use in various hymnals today. For examples, see http://www .hymnary.org/hymnEGMG1894/page/194 (accessed 28 February 2012).

Freylinghausen missed or overlooked one hymn, however, that was to resonate in the subsequent debates over spousal relationships and the vexed question of Christ and the church. In 1698, three years before his death in Arnstadt, Thuringia, Adam Drese composed "Seelenbräutigam" ("Bride of the Soul"). Johann Sebastian Bach used Drese's work in 1736 in his cantata *Seelen-bräutigam, Jesu Gottes Lamm* (BWV 496). The melody for this reflection on the sacrifice of Christ as the Lamb of God and the bridegroom of each soul became so popular that one of Francke's students at Halle, Nikolaus Count von Zinzendorf, only a few years after he left the place, would use it for his own composition "Jesus, Still Lead On" ("Jesu, geh voran") (1721). As pietism evolved in the early eighteenth century, the absence in hymns of a clear teaching about Protestant spousal relations permitted even more speculative positions about the soul's relationship to Christ as the Bridegroom. That speculation had already worried princes and theologians and led to intensified scrutiny via princely regulations and pastoral control over the spousal relationship. Melanchthon's shadow would now fade in the heat of a blistering controversy between pastors and the legal advisers of princes. The terms of the ensuing debate extended far beyond the theological or canonical norms the sixteenth-century Reformers or their Catholic opponents had inherited. The unresolved tension between the "worldly" and the quasi-sacramental in the marital relationship had left the early church pietists ill-equipped to respond to the definitions of marriage promulgated by radical ascetics and "fleshly" celebrators of sexual congress. In attracting the attention of princes and jurists, the subject matter of spousal relations now threatened to enter dangerous territory none of the old combatants could have imagined.

CHAPTER 3

Pietism, Marriage, and Princely Sovereignty, 1670-1740

Casual students of Protestant Christianity remain unaware, for the most part, of Christian Thomasius. He was an ally and correspondent of Philipp Jakob Spener, an early admirer of the renewal movement, a critic of unenlightened witchcraft trials, and the stimulus for a ferocious eighteenth-century debate about marriage. He was known to early modern German scholars as a "moral philosopher, jurist, lay-theologian, social and educational reformer," but his writings on marriage, which kept his name before theologians and fellow jurists in the eighteenth century, are remembered by none of his professional heirs today. Even many historians have forgotten the debate on marriage that he helped to provoke.[1]

After the Thirty Years' War, the topic of marriage surfaced in an unexpected and unpleasant way, along with the question whether any spark of God's image and likeness survived the Fall. The debate at first looked like a rehearsal of old controversies about a "Christian law of nature." That question took on renewed urgency because a younger and brasher generation of

---

1. Ian Hunter, "Christian Thomasius and the Desacralization of Philosophy," *Journal of the History of Ideas* 61, no. 4 (October 2000): 595-616, at 595. See more fully, Hunter, *The Secularisation of the Confessional State: The Political Thought of Christian Thomasius* (Cambridge: Cambridge University Press, 2007). I have intentionally avoided using the problematic term "state" in favor of "sovereignty." For a summary of the continuing debates over the "composite state" or "baroque states" of Europe to 1750, see Nicholas Henshall, *The Zenith of European Monarchy and Its Elites: The Politics of Culture, 1650-1750* (Basingstoke, U.K., and New York: Palgrave Macmillan, 2010), pp. 7-27.

jurists and philosophers began to argue that monogamy was simply a cultural and historical accident, properly regulated by princes.

At the time these debates triggered an international response, Thomasius had come to be associated with the pietist leaders at the new university at Halle and with August Hermann Francke, who enjoyed the patronage of the elector of Brandenburg/king in Prussia. Unexpectedly, the nearby county of Wernigerode, annexed by Prussia in 1714, had allied itself to the Halle renewal movement. The small territory's ruling family enjoyed close ties to the Danish court, and quickly became involved with a grand experiment beyond the bounds of Europe. The Danish monarch had already asked Halle's leaders to procure missionaries to the Danish East India colony in Tranquebar in 1705, and Wernigerode's pietist pastors had relatives who would join that renewal and missionary effort by the 1730s. The pastors in Wernigerode and the missionaries to India would turn their attention to marriage reform in part because of Thomasius. As a result of his work, a concern to bring spousal relations under a form of social discipline threatened to eclipse any emphasis on marital friendship. The vision of Luther and the hopes Spener had for marriage now fell into deeper peril.

Thomasius counted among the most promising of a younger seventeenth-century generation of university scholars, so his writing on marriage carried weight. Pietist theologians would have preferred to ignore it. The question of the marriage relationship and public authority threatened to aid opponents who accused them of teaching Catholic notions of grace and sacraments. The question also threatened to unglue compromises between princes and theologians that placed marriage in the "worldly" realm but still celebrated it in the church as a godly estate. Thomasius had a reputation, especially after his exile from Saxony in 1690, as a defender of pietism, but it did not last long. He rejected the teachings of his father Jacob and Jacob's most illustrious student, Samuel von Pufendorf, and defended views about marriage that took him far outside pietist circles.

The elder Thomasius and Pufendorf had posited a guardedly optimistic view of humanity because of an "underlying multidimensional image of man." In contrast to classic Lutheran theology, Pufendorf affirmed a human characteristic of "sociability." The notion that humans "naturally" sought out a life together, regardless of any dependence on the companionate relationship of Adam and Eve before the Fall, struck some as a dismissal of the original goodness of creation. Pufendorf's argument, they retorted, could lead to the view that human companionate instincts resulted solely from the need for survival in a hostile world. Perhaps stung by the controversy, the younger Thomasius by 1700 "had given up the principle of 'reasonable love' in favor of a more pessimistic anthropology."[2] He also caused his former pietist allies difficulty when he attacked the teaching that marriage as one of the three estates might be the prince's primary responsibility to protect, but pastors and theologians should also have a hand in guiding and judging it. Church pietists had agreed, with some reservations, with the inherited two kingdoms teaching, the view Thomasius now seemed to disdain. In truth, they would have preferred not to antagonize the princes by raising the issue. They were not to be granted that luxury.

In 1695, while Francke quarreled with his congregation in Glaucha, Thomasius's student Enno Rudolph Brenneisen defended a dissertation that portended trouble. Thomasius served as his supervisor for "The Right of Protestant Princes regarding Indifferent Matters or *Adiaphora*." But it was not really just "external" liturgical ceremonies Brenneisen defended as the province of princes. Orthodox Lutheran jurists, led by Benedict Carpzov (1595-1666), whose monumental *Jurisprudentia Ecclesiastica seu Consistorialis (Ecclesiastical or Consistory Law)* was to go through seven editions by 1721, set the terms of the debate. Brenneisen admitted that by reputation alone, Carpzov and his students were "authors fit to terrify their opponents, and all of them deny that the prince by virtue of his supreme authority can change or abrogate church ceremonies and indifferent matters."

He also noted that the imposing Martin Havemann had defended episcopal oversight of marriage law and declared it "impious to leave cases concerning matrimony to the judgment of jurists, or to have them sent to faculties of law." It did not help Brenneisen that both theologians and princes — on both sides of the battle — now defined the three estates as "the clerical, the political, and the economic." These categories actually referred to functions and qualities within society. Luther, in contrast, had begun with the created orders of the church, marriage, and the state, defining the third as a consequence of the Fall. Brenneisen also complicated matters by arguing that within the society of the family "the conjugal, the paternal, and the domestic" could be identified as "three estates."[3]

---

2. Michael Kempe, "The Anthropology of Natural Law: Debates about Pufendorf in the Age of Enlightenment," in *The Anthropology of the Enlightenment*, ed. Larry Wolff and Marco Cipolloni (Stanford: Stanford University Press, 2007), pp. 252-61, at 254-55, quotation at 255.

3. Brenneisen's dissertation is available in English in Christian Thomasius, *Essays on Church, State, and Politics*, ed. Ian Hunter, Thomas Ahnert, and Frank Grunert (Indianapolis: Liberty Fund, 2007), pp. 49-127, quotations at 79, 81, 83-84; on Carpzov's work and its impact in Saxony and Thomasius's controversial role there and his correspondence with Spener begin-

The definition of marriage and the God-willed nature of spousal relations eventually brought Thomasius and Francke into conflict. In 1707, Thomasius wrote an introduction to Hugo Grotius's *Right of War and Peace*. The piece revealed Thomasius's disdain for mystical tradition in Lutheranism. Identifying Pseudo-Dionysius as the mischief-making source for Clement of Alexandria and other unproductive "enthusiasts," Thomasius also criticized *German Theology*. Arguing that "Luther's entire doctrine and his life show that he was not a mystical theologian," Thomasius charged that the Württemberger Johann Valentin Andreae, an otherwise "clever and thoughtful theologian," had also fallen "into the hands of the mystical theology of those ignorant times."[4] Thomasius's and Francke's readings of Luther were bound to clash, but the conflict began in the context of marriage.

Francke's relationship with Thomasius soured for many reasons, but pride of place goes to Francke's influence on Thomasius's wife. Upon hearing Francke preach on the necessity of a personal experience of conversion, Auguste Christine Thomasius began to fear so much Francke's insistence on private confession that she left his church and put herself under the care of the more mainline orthodox Lutheran pastor David Olearius. Thomasius, incensed about her crisis of conscience, informed Francke that he would not approach the Lord's Supper again unless he was excused from private confession. Shortly thereafter he began attending the services of the Reformed congregation in Halle.[5] Thomasius also now became aware of just how explosive the spousal relationship and sexuality could be for the public realm as Johann Friedrich Mayer unleashed his attack on all forms of pietism in 1705, using the Buttlar scandal as his platform. A full account of the judicial proceedings against the Buttlar group found its way to the Halle law faculty in 1706. Although Thomasius was not immediately involved in formulating a judgment on the Buttlar case, he published in 1725 an edited version of the proceedings along with his own commentary. By that time, his confrontation with the Halle theologians had already become the stuff of legend.[6]

Thomasius's alienation from Francke made it easier for him to move

---

ning in 1685, see Tanya Kevorkian, *Baroque Piety: Religion, Society, and Music in Leipzig, 1650-1750* (Aldershot, U.K., and Burlington, Vt.: Ashgate, 2007), pp. 115-22.

4. Thomasius, "On the History of Natural Law until Grotius," in *Essays on Church, State, and Politics*, pp. 1-48, 36-41, citation at 40, 41.

5. Werner Schmidt, *Ein vergessener Rebell: Leben und Wirken des Christian Thomasius* (Munich: Eugen Diederichs Verlag, 1995), pp. 178-80.

6. Willi Temme, *Krise der Leiblichket: Die Sozietät der Mutter Eva (Buttlarsche Rotte) und der Radikale Pietismus um 1700* (Göttingen: Vandenhoeck & Ruprecht, 1998), pp. 15, 26-27.

forward with plans to unseat the theologians from the councils of state power. Part of that plan included the publication of a dissertation in defense of concubinage in 1713. He had already published an essay on the crime of bigamy in 1685, but the controversy over that treatise paled by comparison with the firestorm his new essay set off. Members of the faculty of law and theology competed to see who would rebut Thomasius's speculation.[7] The controversy brought public attention also to a discussion about polygamy associated with the Danzig jurist Samuel Friedrich Willenberg between 1713 and 1717. Monogamy seemed suddenly to be under attack.

Thomasius especially offended the pietists because he refused to concede any difference between polygamy and polyandry. That refusal appeared as ominous to those who argued for a "Christian" natural law as it did to those who believed that a law of reason testified against polyandry since men seemed willing to provide only for their own children, not for those of other males.[8] Thomasius intended to dislodge the influence of theologians in political and social policy, and the question of polygamy was a mere pretext. But since many saw him as sympathetic to pietism, the pietists feared that his views would undercut their attempts to defend the sanctity of the marital relationship as a means of renewing churches.

Luther had emphasized a pre-Fall existence of the church (God talking with Adam) and marriage as an unsullied order of creation. Thomasius read the evidence differently. For him, "the first form of social life was the *coaeva societas* that existed between God and Adam. . . . if Adam had recognized an obligation to obey certain commands of God, then a social relationship between God and man was implicit in the moment of Creation."[9]

Thomasius nevertheless lost interest in debating about the influence of pre-Fall conditions on social institutions like marriage. For him, marriage was interesting only as an expression of natural law understood as "the com-

7. For a summary of the controversy surrounding his treatise and his relationship to Pufendorf and the pietists, see Martin Gierl, *Pietismus und Aufklärung: Theologische Polemik und die Kommunikationsreform der Wissenschaft am Ende des 17. Jahrhunderts* (Göttingen: Vandenhoeck & Ruprecht, 1997), pp. 425, 429, 461, 484-85. For the broader context surrounding the tensions between jurists and theologians, see Kevorkian, *Baroque Piety*, pp. 99-122.

8. See Stephan Buchholz, "*Erunt Tres aut Quattuor in Carne Una:* Aspekte der neuzeitlichen Polygamiediskussion," in *Zur Geschichte des Familien-und Erbrechts: Politische Implikationen und Perspektiven,* ed. Heinz Mohnhapt (Frankfurt am Main: Vittorio Klostermann, 1987), pp. 71-91, at 80-81, 87-88.

9. T. J. Hochstrasser, *Natural Law Theories in the Early Enlightenment* (Cambridge: Cambridge University Press, 2000), p. 114.

mand to do all those actions that promote sociability."[10] But his increasing skepticism about the "natural" human capacity for sociability made him a liability for church pietists. One of the sharpest orthodox Lutheran critics of Halle's theology, Valentine Loescher, denounced any notion that marriage partners still reflected "image and likeness," for, as he saw it, the evangelical church "knows of no image of God after the fall. . . . the principle of renewal to God's image is . . . not the image itself, or the spark, or the so-called true humanity, but the grace of our Lord Jesus Christ."[11]

Assaulted by the likes of Loescher, still smarting from the aftershocks of the Mother Eva scandal, and worried by the controversy over Thomasius's treatise, Francke hesitated. Johann Gustav Reinbeck alerted Francke in September 1713 that he would reply to Thomasius. Francke read the manuscript, but his hesitations prompted Reinbeck to request its return. Reinbeck published it in Berlin the following year. The same hesitation marked Francke's response to the attack on Thomasius by Justus Henning Böhmer (1674-1749), an eminent Protestant jurist, who happened to agree with Thomasius's judgment that canon law was older both in conception and reception in the Holy Roman Empire than Justinian's Roman law. Thomasius had used this point to fashion a weapon from canon law with which to undermine the approach of Carpzov. Francke's close colleague and ally Joachim Lange read Böhmer's manuscript and concluded that it did not distinguish sufficiently among concubinage, polygamy, and prostitution. Böhmer proceeded anyway, publishing his views in a larger work on Protestant church law.

Böhmer and Reinbeck attacked Thomasius's defense of concubinage and also argued that the purpose of marriage had to be discerned by assessment of its condition before the Fall. Johann Michael Lang took up Böhmer's argument, writing that the unsullied original state of nature was "the only ground of a true law of nature" and that true Christians should "seek the renewal of the Godly Image in the teaching and strength of Jesus Christ." He concluded that the present state of nature was like that of a sick person; that God only tolerated such external or civil contracts as divorce and remarriage; and that it was almost as bad to entrust matters of marriage to secular jurists as to the Roman pope.[12]

---

10. Hochstrasser, *Natural Law Theories*, p. 119.

11. Valentine Loescher, *The Complete Timotheus Verinus*, trans. James L. Langebartels and Robert J. Koester (Milwaukee: Northwestern, 1998), p. 164. The original volumes appeared in 1718 and 1721.

12. The above summarizes the following: AFSt H:C 320, Böhmer to Francke, February

Church pietists continued to worry that Thomasius's dismissal of the pre-Fall state of nature's significance undermined the sanctity of the marital relationship as blessed by God in Genesis and reaffirmed by Christ. By the 1730s Böhmer wrote a preface to an old 1704 treatise, *Concerning the Remnants of the Sacrament in Matrimony,* by his former colleague Johann Samuel Stryk (d. 1715). Stryk had criticized the orthodox Lutheran vision of marriage as neither fully sacred nor secular. His title revealed as much. Stryk devoted some 320 pages to examining marriage after the Fall, insisting that it was not called *der heilige Ehestand* (the holy marital estate) for nothing. As Melanchthon had conceded, marriage had something of the sacramental about it. Marriage contracted against divine and human law could not be blessed or favored. But Stryk denied that any institutional, "sacramental" standing could be bestowed on marriage by clerical authority, rejecting Carpzov's argument that a pastoral blessing *(priesterliche Copulation)* contributed to "the perfection and substance of marriage." The Leipzig Consistory had demanded the use of the phrase as early as 1616 in its public regulation of marriage in electoral Saxony. Stryk refused to endorse this quasi-sacramental position that seemed to rely upon the role of the pastoral office because it implied that a ritual form, and not God's original actions in the orders of creation, grounded the sanctity of marriage. Too much attention to external ceremony could lead to a distraction from the right understanding, that marriage constituted one of the primary orders. The true holiness of marriage could be found in that external example of the married man and wife, the one that pointed to the interior mystery of Christ's relationship to his church.

The official Lutheran canon law tradition did indeed rely upon Ephesians 5, as Stryk insisted in his treatise; those familiar with Luther's marriage prayer would have found the argument familiar. However, the official tradition had left the details of the "substance" of the matrimonial bond in the

---

1716; Böhmer's treatise is *Jus Ecclesiasticum protestantum, usum Modernum juris canonici . . .* (Halle, 1717); it includes the treatise on matrimony: part I: cap 1:11; Joachim Lange to Paul Anton, Francke Nachlaß, Stab/F 13, 2/9: 76; letters of Reinbeck to Francke, Stab/F 17,2/13:10 and 11 (August to December 1713) and Stab/F 17:2/13:13 and 14; Reinbeck, *Die Natur des Ehestandes und verwerfflichkeit des dawieder straitenden Concubinats . . .* (Berlin: Johan Andreas Rüdiger, 1714), pp. 7, 10-12, for his "image and likeness" arguments; AFSt 47:C: 19:15; and his *Theologische Gedancken von der Heiligkeit des Ehestandes wider den unheiligen Concubinatum* (Berlin, 1714) [AFSt 64 B 3 (#22)]; I. M. Lang, *Daß die Divortia, oder Ehescheidungen jure naturae verbothen sey . . .* (Berlin, 1716) (AFSt 46 E 12), p. 9, quotation at 12, and against both jurists and Catholics, 21-23.

hands of consistories and pastors, and the details of the contract and care for "worldly goods" in the jurisdiction of secular judges. Stryk argued, however, that marriage could either be "a civil negotiation" or a sacrament, but no half-spiritual "condition or estate." In fact, Stryk had laid out the argument that "pietist private holiness and a creative lay faith make marriage the 'little church within the church.'" To avoid mere "ceremonialism," he suggested that private reception of the Lord's Supper in houses was preferable to pompous services in large churches that could not adequately reproduce the love feasts of early Christians. Their heirs in the pietist movement now needed to make their own homes and marriages the settings for the sanctification of the awakened.[13]

These debates and the cautious endorsement of companionate marriage by pietist pastors trained in Halle found a hearing among ordinary villagers and households by the 1720s. In the duchy of Holstein, the consistorial court responsible for hearing petitions for separation and divorce now included members who had been trained at Halle under Stryk and Böhmer. In the 420 cases that came before the court between 1650 and 1770, the pastors, not city or village officials, dealt with the quarrels. Böhmer's treatise on church law stood on the shelves of at least two of the judges. Their intention to uphold the sanctity of the marital relationship made them sympathetic toward women, whose complaints about the unchristian behavior of their husbands undergirded demands for divorce on the grounds that a loveless and brutal marriage violated its very nature.

Complaints of violence in the household (mixed with those of abuse of alcohol) characterized marriage problems at the lower level of the social order. The more affluent and educated women complained of long absences or desertion, but only rarely of adultery or infidelity. They also brought complaints of the absence of compassionate cooperation and financial support before the pietist pastors. In their defense, they pointed to Luther's views of a woman's right to be treated with respect, and suggested that the failure of the

---

13. Johann Samuel Strykius, *De Reliquiis Sacramenti in Matrimonialibus . . .* (Halle, 1733), quotations at pp. 325, 336, and preface, 13; 329, 346-52; and chapter II:IV on the iconic "external" image of marriage. I have used this later edition in the Francke Foundations libraries to include the posthumous use to which the original 1704 essay was still being put a generation later. The above paragraph also summarizes Buchholz, *Recht, Religion und Ehe: Orientierungswandel und gelehrte Kontroversen im Übergang vom 17. Zum 18. Jahrhundert* (Frankfurt am Main: Vittorio Klostermann, 1988), pp. 246-81, at 246-47, 265-67; 269 on the probable authorship of the first, 1704 essay; see 280-81 on the shared jurisdiction of Protestant canonical law against which Stryk was fulminating.

male heads of household to live up to Lutheran standards justified their petitions for release from a relationship that had ceased to be true marriage. Private confession was still a norm in this territory, and the women used auricular confession to air marital disputes. Among the poor, husbands behaved badly; bigamy occurred when husbands left home to work and remained so long that they were presumed dead; adultery occurred in only sixty-seven cases brought equally by men and women but mostly from people at the upper end of the social scale.[14]

The recourse by aggrieved spouses to courts had long preceded the rise of pietism. In the towns of Sweden and Denmark before the Reformation, "the marriage ceremony performed by a priest *in facie ecclesiae* had gained importance in . . . marriage customs." Most of the commoners who petitioned for dispensations of marriage before the Reformation came "from the Duchy of Schleswig, where the peasants were relatively wealthy, self-aware and independent landowners" who consumed "status products, including papal dispensations," and who "found it necessary to confirm the ownership of their land by complying with ecclesiastical norms."[15] "Desertion or malicious abandonment of one party had been a valid reason for breaking an engagement already in canon law. That the Reformation introduced desertion also as grounds of divorce probably facilitated the dissolution of the betrothal."[16]

Still, in these regions, nobody before Thomasius had questioned the assumption that marriage meant the union of one man and one woman. Despite the bitterness of the exchanges over polygamy — which produced at least nine published attacks on Thomasius's *De concubinatu* — Thomasius visited Francke in July of 1714, aware that his position as professor of canon law and his appointment as *Director perpetuus* of the university in 1710 enhanced his power and influence. He could afford to be generous. Francke, Lange, and the pietist faculty had urged the *Reichshofrat* in Vienna to intervene through its fiscal agent on the grounds that Thomasius's essay had insulted the Catholic clergy of the Reich. Thomasius knew that the new

---

14. Alexandra Lutz, *Ehepaare vor Gericht: Konflikte und Lebenswelten in der frühen Neuzeit* (Frankfurt am Main: Campus Verlag, 2006), pp. 8-15; on the various courts and marriage law, 59-83; on the use of confession and communion, 93-94; on the types of complaints, 111-26; on the influence of the Halle jurists, 133-38; on the arguments of women based on religious identity, 183-88, 284-86.

15. Mia Korpiola, *Between Betrothal and Bedding: Marriage Formation in Sweden, 1299-1600* (Leiden and Boston: Brill, 2009), pp. 223-61, at 224, 226-27.

16. Korpiola, *Between Betrothal,* p. 320.

Brandenburg elector, Friedrich Wilhelm I, would tolerate no challenge to his role as the ultimate interpreter of the law in his territories. In the previous summer the elector had already confirmed Thomasius's argument that the *Reichshofrat* could not function as the court of first instance for any charge against the estates or persons of the Reich.[17] Moreover, both the theology and law faculties of the university finally agreed that for the sake of public order the disputes had to end. Two commissioners who had been ordered to investigate the controversy had complained to Berlin that the theologians had attempted to bypass them and to approach the king directly.[18]

The initial dispute over polygamy in Halle, however, only rehearsed what now became clear — the growing power of the Prussian monarchy over all aspects of religious life, including disputes that emanated from spousal relations and attempts to reform them. In the year the Hannoverian dynasty began in Britain, Prussia "mediatized" its medieval vassal territory, the county of Wernigerode. This annexation (with retention of limited privileges and title by the former ruler) meant that the Hohenzollerns now imposed their will in matters relating to marriage and the church in this county with more success than they enjoyed among "ordinary Prussians" in Brandenburg itself. Subjects there managed to resist both electoral and aristocratic incursions on village customs and social order.[19] The obscure mountainous county in the Harz profoundly influenced the international debates over spouses, though not by design.[20]

The town itself, numbering between three thousand and four thousand souls in the eighteenth century, boasted a city charter dating from 1229. Perched on the northeastern edge of the Harz Mountains, it had grown up at the foot of the Agnesberg, which overlooked two valleys, accounting for the fortified settlement at its summit since the ninth century. Two major trade

17. For details, see Schmidt, *Ein vergessener Rebell*, pp. 187-94.

18. Martin-Luther-Universität Halle-Wittenberg Archiv Rep. 3: III: 1/3 306, Untersuchung über die Disputation des Prof. Christian Thomasius über das Konkubinat 1701-1716, 20 July 1713, 26 and 27 recto and verso.

19. William W. Hagen, *Ordinary Prussians: Brandenburg Junkers and Villages, 1500-1840* (Cambridge: Cambridge University Press, 2003), especially chapter 8, "Policing Civic and Social Order, 1700-1760."

20. The summary that follows depends upon sources in the GStA; the LhaS-A (Magdeburg and Wernigerode); Stadtarchiv Wernigerode and the AFSt. A popular but accurate overview of the ruling family's relationship to Prussia is Konrad Breitenborn, *Im Dienste Bismarcks: Die politische Karriere des Grafen Otto zu Stolberg-Wernigerode* (Berlin: Verlag de Nation, 1986); this relies on Heinrich Drees, *Geschichte der Grafschaft Wernigerode* (Wernigerode Kommissionsverlag von Paul Jüttners Buchhandlung, 1916).

routes intersected in this region, and the emperor by the fourteenth century charged the count of Wernigerode with keeping open the road that linked Quedlinburg, Blankenburg, and Ilsenburg to Harzburg and the imperial city of Goslar. The trade routes gave rise to the town. The territory was compact; the count was lord of 58 percent of the land, and peasants had evolved into nearly free agents by the late seventeenth century. The peasants guarded "ancient" privileges jealously and regarded any change with deep suspicion — an attitude that extended to customs surrounding marriage.

By midcentury Wernigerode, like its wealthier and larger neighbor Hildesheim to the northwest, faced a burgeoning population and increased demand for food just as demand for traditional handwork products began to diminish. Like its neighbors, Wernigerode's small producers and poorer residents would suffer from the spike in food prices due to Prussia's involvement in the Seven Years' War. The resulting inflation intensified debates over the care of the resident poor, wandering ex-soldiers, and widows and orphans. These sufferings, however, came at the end of a much longer debate over the behavior of spouses and how weddings should be conducted.

The concern for families, sexual morality, and the care of orphans had emerged even before Brandenburg asserted its power and consolidated its economic and political grip on the county. Strictly speaking, as a medieval vassal territory, the county fell under the legal oversight of the *Altmark*. The *Kammergericht* in Halberstadt had overseen administrative matters. Even after the 1714 mediatization the count retained the right to constitute lower courts with the right of appeal to the *Kammergericht*.

Representatives of the guilds had initiated a complaint in 1656 against Count Heinrich Ernst (1638-72), and a commission from Brandenburg in 1657 attempted to sort out the demands, which had to do with the naming of the city and the appointment of pastors, teachers, and anyone serving the church. Count Ernst of Wernigerode (1672-1710) successfully defended his rights, but the dispute brought his difficulties to the attention of the elector's advisers in the chancellery. In exchange for increased vigilance in pursuing anyone who dodged collection of an excise tax, Berlin reiterated the count's privileges over the partially deserted cloisters of Ilsenburg and Drübeck. But the appearance that the count actually retained local control over church matters would prove to be wholly illusory.[21]

21. See Otto Hintze, "Einleitende Darstellung der Behördenorganisation und allgemeinen Verwaltung in Preußen beim Regierungsantrit Friedrich II" (Berlin, 1901), pp. 425-26, vol. 6:2 of *Acta Borussica: Behördenorganisation und die allgemeine Staatsverwaltung Preußens im 18. Jahr-*

Upon the death of Count Ernst in 1710, the succession fell to his nephew Christian Ernst (1710-71), son of Ludwig Christian and Christine, duchess of Mecklenburg-Güstrow. It was the redoubtable pietist Christine who shaped the future of a church pietist attempt to reform marriage ritual and encourage more sober, godly spouses. Her son Christian Ernst would succeed her under a Prussian annexation she fought bitterly to prevent. In the person of Prussia's brilliant legal counselor, Samuel Freiherr von Coccejus (1679-1755), she met her match. Justly known for his key role in drafting the early version of a revised law code between 1749 and 1751, Coccejus oversaw the "project" Frederick II would impose upon Silesia, although the rehearsal in Wernigerode proved that official legal and ecclesiastical sanctions from above did not produce uniform compliance, among clergy or people.

The 1714 document of "mediatization" bore all the hallmarks of a cleverly designed legal instrument that preserved the illusion that the counts of Wernigerode still maintained their traditional privileges. In actual fact, the text referred to those rights as *"privitive"* or "private rights" to distinguish them from public law. The count and his consistory could publish edicts that touched on religious matters, but Prussia tolerated no ambiguity about its authority over church-related matters. In his notes making the case for "improvement of the administration of justice," Coccejus had referred already to a 15 December 1694 edict on betrothals and marriage matters that he regarded as far too open to confusing interpretations. He noted that the king had, since the beginning of his reign, desired a general law reform, but much local variation in the widely dispersed provinces had frustrated a design Coccejus was now about to impose.[22]

---

hundert, pt. 1, ed. Ernst Posner et al. (Marburg and Berlin, 1970), pt. 2, ed. Peter Baumgart and Gerd Heinrich (1982). See also Drees, *Geschichte,* pp. 45-50; GStA: HA I: Rep. 8 188v.; "Streitigkeiten zwischen Rat und Burgerschaft zu Wernigerode," 1647-1657; on the rights to the cloisters, Rep. 8. 188t; and the review of these agreements on 19 May 1714 Receß. Idem VII HA Allg. Urkundens. Belehnungen d. Landsh. Wernigerode Nr. 189. See also Gerd Heinrich, "Staatsaufsicht und Stadtfreiheit in Brandenburg-Preußen unter dem Absolutismus (1660-1806)," in *Die Städte Mitteleuropas im 17. und 18. Jahrhundert,* ed. Wilhelm Rausch (Linz: Donau, 1981), pp. 155-72.

22. On Coccejus, see Hans Hattenbauer and Günther Bernert, eds., *Allgemeines Landrecht für die Preußischen Staaten von 1794 O. Textausgabe* (Berlin: Luchterhand, 1970), pp. 11-13; GStA: HA I: Rep. 92 Nachläße (Cocceji) Nr. 2; 12 r.-21 v. LhaS-A (WH) Rep. H: Stolberg-Wernigerode HAB: 43 Fach 4, Nr. 13; for the Countess and allies see Allgemeine Deutsche Biographie (Onlinefassung) Historische Kommission bei der Bayerischen Akademie der Wissenschaften: http://www.biographie.de/artikelADB_pnd115373128.html; http://de.wikisource.org/wiki/ADB: Neuss, Heinrich Georg. On the relationships between Prussia, Wernigerode, and Denmark, see

The widowed countess Christine von Mecklenburg-Güstrow pleaded with the emperor to preserve the rights of her son Christian Ernst: the elector of Brandenburg, she said, had no right to transgress the privileges of a knight of the empire. Her erstwhile ally had been the superintendent Heinrich Georg Neuß, who had died two years before the mediatization. A native of Elbingerode, he had spent his childhood in Wernigerode but was educated in Blankenburg, Osterwieck, Quedlinburg, and Halberstadt before returning to the scene of his childhood in 1675 as a private teacher having taken his theological training in Erfurt. Befriended by Philipp Jakob Spener, Neuß was recommended to Count Ernst of Stolberg-Wernigerode for the post of superintendent, membership on the county's consistory, and the senior pastorate at Saint Sylvester. An impatient pietist reformer, the superintendent had quickly alienated the townspeople and the members of the town council and only survived because of Christine's protection. Her own sister, married to King Fredrik IV of Denmark, saw to it that recruits for the pastoral office in Wernigerode were supplied to Dargun, the territory in Mecklenburg. Intent on making certain that young Wernigerodans were sufficiently catechized before being admitted to the Lord's Supper, Christine had already ordered rigorous examinations before, most likely at Neuß's urging. Wernigerode historically had aligned itself with the conservative Lutheran faculty at Wittenberg and had exhibited no prior tendencies to alter Reformation theology or piety. But Neuß commenced work in 1712 on a revision of the hymnal that revealed a pietist agenda. The new collection retained the old feasts and hymns for Epiphany, Purification, Annunciation, the death of Mary, and the feasts of Saint Michael and Saint John. The collection did not overly emphasize themes of "rebirth." But in the second half of the 1,512-page work, the pietist intent began to emerge. Influenced by Freylinghausen's Halle hymnal, Neuß omitted any hymns that addressed the spousal relationship other than the favored "How Brightly Shines the Morning Star." Neither in this edition nor in the important 1735 revision did wedding hymns that actually spoke to the spousal relationship, as Olearius's had, merit inclusion. Prayers for various occasions (first communion, confirmation, before a journey, and thanksgiving upon being bled by a physician) were deemed more important.[23]

Stefan Harmann, *Die Beziehungen Preußens zu Dänemark von 1688 bis 1789* (Cologne and Vienna: Böhlau, 1983), pp. 109-44, for the early eighteenth century.

23. The original title is *Wernigeroedisches Geang Buch Begrieffend 800. Geistreiche so wol Alte als Neue Auserlesene Lieder/in IV. Theile ordentlich abgetheilet; Wie auch jedes Lied mit dem*

By 1723 the deceased superintendent's shade hovered over the church services and, now, a new rite for the celebration of marriage. Some of the regulations once again appeared to preserve traditional practices: pastors were to be available on the confessional stools on Fridays, and the faithful were to pay the absolution penny willingly out of love for their spiritual fathers. Baptisms were to be done in the church only and punctually at 11:00 A.M. But in regulating the celebration of marriage, the new ritual reaffirmed the canonical laws that widows and widowers had to settle the property claims of first-marriage heirs before being married in the parsonage. Young people had to have the consent of their parents. And to the indignation of both prospective marriage couples and some pastors, the regulation stipulated that the "so-called *Polter abend* is to be completely abolished . . . marriage is to be performed at 11:00 A.M. and if the married partners are late by 12:00 Noon they are to pay a two Thaler fine." Moreover, the rules abolished the old custom of giving *Morgenbrot,* since it led to "much strife and disorder," as did dancing before the wedding meal. By 10:00 P.M. everyone was to retreat to their houses and the old custom of "night music" was now banned.

The ritual for marriage directed that if the prospective couple were of high social standing, music could be played at the very start of the service, which was to be followed by a sermon and a prayer. Music could be played before the pronouncement of marriage, and again, at the end. But if the couple came from the ranks of the ordinary subjects, one organ piece only was to be played and the schoolboys were to sing "How Brightly Shines the Morning Star," the hymn that carried the sense of the individual soul's relationship to Christ. Since the new pietist-inspired orphanage was to be the beneficiary of fines imposed on those who violated these norms, no one could miss the pietist intent — and pietist beneficiaries — behind these innovations.[24]

Besondern Innhalt und Clave Cantus, nebst noethigen Registern und gewoehnlichen Collecten, auf Gnaedigst Anordnung/Samt einer Vorrede Und kleinem Gebet-Buch Versehen/Und zu Ermunterung Gottgefaelliger Andacht also aussgefertiget (Wernigerode: Verlegt und zu finden bey Johann Christoph Willebald, 1712); Harzbücherei Wernigerode, UG 1 1712; UG 11; Walter Beyse, "Das Wernigeroeder Gesangbuch von 1712" (theol. diss., Halle, 1926), pp. 22-27, 39-40. Beyse's work is invaluable since in the 1920s he had access to the (as yet) undisturbed Archiv des Wernigerodischen Konsistoriums and the Stolberg-Wernigerode family archive, both of which have since been scattered.

24. Landeshauptarchiv Stolberg-Wernigerode Hauptarchiv B, MD 9-2 H 92 43 Fach 2 #10, Eine neu abzusagende Kirchen-Agende betreffend de 1723; "Ordnung, wie es in allen Kirchen Unserer Grafschaft Wernigerode gehalten werden solle," pp. 13-18; 15, 16, 17; #21, Die Copulation geschiehet folgender Weise. . . . The custom of breaking up crockery to ward off evil spirits and the obligation of the bridegroom to pick up the accumulated mess are similar to the French

Over the course of the next decade, attempts to keep the affairs of the church and the laws and rituals regarding marriage, bequests, poor relief, and pious foundations in local hands failed.[25] By March of 1726 the elector Friedrich Wilhelm lost patience when an *Advocat* in open court admitted that he did not respect the mediatization; a warning was issued promising punishment if the elector were not explicitly named as the head of the church and overall *Landesherr* in Wernigerode. Three years earlier Friedrich Wilhelm had warned the count that he would enforce his role as the ultimate authority in the county by any means he deemed appropriate, a not-so-veiled threat to deploy a military force to make his point.[26]

By 1730 the limited authority of the Wernigerode consistory over marriage became even more obvious. As the year came to an end, Berlin issued an edict aimed at curbing excessive celebrations at weddings. Friedrich Wilhelm wanted to eliminate all vestiges of Catholic ritual, and his scrutiny created dissension even within Wernigerode's consistory. Into these increasing tensions, a native-born son, Liborius Zimmermann, an alumnus of the local Latin school, now entered. Zimmermann had studied at Halberstadt and Jena, where he fell under the influence of the former Halle theologian and professor Johann Franz Buddeus and experienced "conversion." His awakening had been spurred in part also by his friend Augustus Spangenberg, Buddeus's secretary. Spangenberg joined the Moravian movement and in 1731 helped secure for Nikolaus Count von Zinzendorf an initial warm welcome in Wernigerode. By 1727 Zimmermann obtained the post of court chaplain in his hometown and then accepted a call to Halle, although he continued to serve as a member of the consistory. The pietism of the court

---

charivari. The presentation of baked bread in honor of the newly married fell under attack because of pietist aversion to cost and luxury. See Oswald A. Erich and Richard Beitl et al., eds., *Wörterbuch der deutschen Volkskunde,* 3rd ed. (Stuttgart: Alfred Kröner Verlag, 1974), pp. 649-50.

25. For the original act of "mediatization" and the protests, see GStA: HA: VII Allg. Urkundens #189; Rep. 8 Nr. 188aa 1689-1736, pp. 46-160. For more details on the gradual encroachment into Wernigerode's attempts to continue regulating poor relief under its presumed authority in church matters, see A. G. Roeber, "Constitutions, Charity, and Liberalism by Default: Germany and the Anglo-American Tradition," in *Republicanism and Liberalism in America and the German States, 1750-1850,* ed. Jürgen Heideking and James A. Henretta (New York and Washington, D.C.: Cambridge University Press and the German Historical institute, 2002), pp. 73-89, and more generally, Silvia Maier, "Studien zur Geschichte des Waisenhauses in Wernigerode im 18. Jahrhundert" (M.A. thesis, University of Leipzig, 1993), pp. 16-25.

26. GStA: HA: Rep. 8 Nr. 188aa (von Stolberg), 1730-1748, 123 recto 22, April 1723; pp. 135-48 (13 March 1726).

intensified; the townspeople and rural residents stiffened their resistance. By 1734 the count ordered that some matters of a party nature were "not to be sent to all members of the Consistory."[27] Zimmermann, who died in 1734, had produced a number of essays and reflections that found avid readers in pietist circles, including admirers in Great Britain. But the piece most often reprinted, though filled with images of "mother love," the faith of children, and the importance of "fidelity" (Treue), concentrated exclusively on individual struggle. Zimmermann remained silent about marriage as an estate in which the awakened soul might also find Christ.[28]

Strife over religious ritual and the law of marriage in Wernigerode reflected broader tensions within Brandenburg-Prussia. Halle's theologians did not approve of "the Elector's high-handed tampering with the Lutheran liturgy. . . . But others within the pietist establishment supported the king in his policy and contributed enthusiastically to its framing and implementation."[29] Despite the appearance of cautious personal reconciliation between Thomasius and Francke, Friedrich Wilhelm appeared determined to assert authority over marriage, regardless of local customs, privileges of the clergy, or reform objectives of pietists. The debate over marriage now widened not only to local jurisdictions such as Schleswig or Holstein or Wernigerode, but also beyond the control of either Thomasius or Francke, or the elector, and beyond the bounds of the empire.

As late as 1733, the Halle faculty appears to have missed the signals coming from Berlin. They continued to endorse the claims of the count

27. GStA: HA: Rep. 8 Nr. 188aa, von Stolberg 1689-1736, 29 December 1730, *Edict wegen Hochzeiten und Kindauffen . . .* (100, verso); Landeshauptarchiv Sachsen-Anhalt (Wernigerode), Rep. H: Stolb-Wern. HA B 43 Fach 2 Nr. 17 2, 6 (23 December 1730; 25 December 1730); Nr. 12, "Verordnung an das Consistorium . . ." (24 March 1734). On Friedrich Wilhelm's campaign and some Lutheran pietist lobbyists' attempts to resist the imposition of Reformed ceremonies, see Benjamin Marschke, *Absolutely Pietist: Patronage, Factionalism, and State-building in the Early Eighteenth-Century Prussian Army Chaplaincy* (Tübingen: Max Niemeyer Verlag, 2005). For details on Zimmermann, see the ADB sketch (online) at: http://de.wikisource.org/wiki/Zimmermann,_Liborius.

28. Brecht, "Der Hallische Pietismus," in *Der Pietismus im achtzehnten Jahrhundert (Geschichte des Pietismus Vol. II)*, ed. Martin Brecht and Klaus Deppermann (Göttingen: Vandenhoeck & Ruprecht, 1995), p. 329; Zimmermann, *Die Überschwängliche Erkentniß Jesu Christi als der richtige, leichte, und selige Weg zu einer Warhen Kraft im Christenthum* (Halle, 1731); the English edition appeared in London in 1772 as *The Excellency of the Knowledge of Jesus Christ. . . .*

29. Christopher Clark, "Piety, Politics and Society: Pietism in Eighteenth-Century Prussia," in *The Rise of Prussia, 1700-1830*, ed. Philip G. Dwyer (Harlow, U.K.: Pearson Education, 2000), pp. 68-88, at 83.

that the 1714 mediatization gave him some say over church matters without his consistory's need to obtain prior consent from Berlin. A case brought by a son of a second marriage and his mother to see if a third marriage had been legally correct, however, forced the issue. The regulations of marriage in Wernigerode by 1719 had no provision for Prussia's prior or *ex post facto* approval.[30]

In Wernigerode, as was true in most other territories, marital disputes, questions of consanguinity, and sexual scandals consumed most of a church consistory's time. Occasionally, members dealt with accusations of spousal abuse or adultery. Catherina Walls had brought her husband Malthasar Mitteldorff before the court in 1717 for calling her an old whore and a thief, and wishing to bring her to the devil — as her neighbors could attest since they knew she had to flee. Demanding separation and annual support, she pressed her case over the next five years until he was ordered to produce fifty thaler, since she was in danger of starvation. Two years earlier, the wife of a young pastor was prosecuted for an affair with a young officer stationed in the town. In another instance, Henriette Sophia Friderique von Caprivi successfully brought Bodo Georg Henrich von Gadenstaedt to heel for having promised matrimony and reneging. He coupled his threat to take his case on appeal to Berlin by invocation of a seventeenth-century order of the late count that two single persons intending to marry were to do so publicly and that private promises were invalid. The law faculty at Helmstedt found in favor of von Caprivi, but she insisted that she be declared not guilty of having engaged in clandestine marriage promises. Asked by the Wernigerode consistory if the court in Berlin wished to become involved, Berlin in this instance allowed its mediatized authorities to resolve the case.[31]

But the threat of intervention in marriage affairs by Berlin exploded in the late 1720s in a case that dragged on for more than a decade. It illustrated how the attempt to impose an official theology of pietist sobriety on village weddings and spousal relationships could create political shock waves. It also sent a warning to the Halle theologians that they needed to revise their support for the authority of their ally the count over marriage matters and to signal clearly that they recognized Berlin's authority over

---

30. LhaS-A (WH) B 43 Fach 4 Nr. 16 p. 4.

31. LhaS-A (WH) H 9-2 B 50 Fach 6-7 Nr. 3, Acta Consistorialia in Sachen Cathrinen Walls . . . ; Fach 6/7 Nr. 13, Ad Acta Inquisitionis Catharinen Elisabets Fridericin; H 9-2 50 Fach 6/7 Nr. 20, Henriette Sophia Friderique von Caprivi contra Bodo Georg Henrich von Gadenstaedt 1715·in puncto promissu matrimonii.

the control of marriage, a control that had nothing to do with objectives of pietist renewal.[32]

The new marriage ordinances imposed by the count and his pietist allies did not enjoy the support of all the pastors in the territory. Among the opponents, none was more vocal than Johann Mauritius Müller, who occupied the comfortable and prestigious pulpit in Drübeck. Located on the trade route that linked Wernigerode to Goslar, and nestled in the shadow of an imposing former Benedictine cloister in Ilsenburg in which the counts sometimes lived, Drübeck proved to be a dangerous place from which to resist the count and his pietist reforms. Any criticism of pietist innovations could not be hidden for long, given the village's proximity to the count's residence and his circle of pietist allies. The case that dwarfed all the other causes that came before the consistory began when the pastor was accused of performing the marriage of a soldier who had not secured the consent of his superior officer. Müller disingenuously pled ignorance of the law, noting that Prussian rescripts on the matter had not been publicly printed and distributed.

Unimpressed, the consistory ordered him to appear, but the question that seemed to preoccupy the count (and behind him, by implication, Berlin) was whether the pastor owed the *Fiscus* a fine for his carelessness. Only in the course of many postponements and appeals to the law faculties in Frankfurt and Aldorf, theologians in Helmstedt, and the *Oberconsistorium* in Berlin did it become clear that more was at stake here. The pastor (among other lapses) had allowed his wife and daughter to dance in honor of the newly married couple at a village wedding. By 1735 Count Christian Ernst, tired of appeals and delays, ordered his *Forst-Secretarius* to pursue the pastor vigorously, an order blocked by more maneuvering on the pastor's part.

A year later it was the *Fiscus*'s Johann Martin Runde who had to appear before the consistory. Müller's *Advocat* had two years earlier demanded the restitution of his client's good name, seeking court costs at the expense of the *Fiscus*. Since the case had already dragged on so long, it might be better,

---

32. The following paragraphs summarize the holdings in LhaS-A H 9-2 Fach 6/7 Nr. 17, *Acta in causa Fisci Denuncierter Johan Maritium Mueller Past. Druebeck Denuncienten de 1728*, a huge file running to more than 300 pages, and Nr. 15, *Acta in causa Fisci refe. Pst. Druebeck Johann Maurit. Mueller 1724*, the latter containing the initial accusation and the pastor's claim that he was ignorant of needing the consent of a soldier's superior officer to marry and his 31 March petition noting that Prussian law on the issue of superior officers' consent had not been legally published; also the 11 May 1726 notification for the pastor and accusers to appear before the consistory over the question of money owed the *Fiscus*.

some advised, to impose a decree of nullity on the whole affair. Berlin had signaled in 1730 that it expected the consistory in Wernigerode to sort out the case and not to allow further appeals. As of January 1739, however, no clear resolution appeared to be possible.[33]

Such hostility to pietist attempts to root out village marriage customs to create more sober spouses could not hope to succeed. Müller had appealed directly to Chancellor Caprivi, hoping to use his authority against Superintendent Johann Heinrich Gutjahr, who had in 1724 imposed a sentence to bear all costs of the accusations, "against my knowledge and will," which he considered *summa injuria.* No less an authority than Spener himself, the aggrieved pastor claimed, would have denounced this sentence as "unchristian." He could not acquiesce in conscience to obey authorities who engaged in such behavior. Despite the years of strife, however, Müller discovered that the pietist network of informers was more powerful than he. A young theological student from Halle, E. L. Schultze, ostensibly being prepared for service in the pietist mission in Tranquebar, informed on him in the course of raising contributions for the Danish-German workers in India. Müller lost his pastorate.[34]

Uncertainty about who exercised final authority over marriage continued to produce strife that enmeshed local pastors throughout the next decade. The pastor of Apperode, Theophilus Wilhelm Stieren, fell afoul of the law when the count's pietist ally Jacob Hildebrand, pastor of Saint Sylvester's in Wernigerode, attempted to explain what went wrong when Heinrich Christian Bartels, a sawmill worker temporarily in town, wanted to get mar-

---

33. LhaS-A H 9-2 Fach 6/7 Nr. 17 pp. 154-55 recto and verso on the appeal to the *Oberconsistorium;* p. 301 for Christian Ernst's order from Hannover; p. 236, 15 July 1733, for the demand from the *Advocat* for restoration of the pastor's good name; p. 138 for the decree from Berlin demanding resolution in Wernigerode of the case; p. 1, dated 23 January 1739, to 6 verso rehearsing the case and noting the appeals to Frankfurt, Helmstedt, and Aldorf.

34. LhaS-A H 9-2 Fach 6/7 Nr. 17, p. 304, for the letter to Caprivi dated 8 January 1724; for the evidence that it was Schultze who had informed the superintendent of Müller's continued refusal to publish marriage banns according to law, p. 5 recto; for Schultze himself, who by 1739 appears to have been working with C. M. Mölling, who had replaced Müller as pastor in Drübeck, see AFSt/M 3 H 12: 48, 1739 letter of Mölling to Gotthilf August Francke, and AFSt/HC 802:5, 4 July 1739, Francke to Schultze. Despite the evidence that he was being so trained, no evidence survives to indicate that Schultze served in Tranquebar. Andreas Cyriacus Breithaupt in Wernigerode provided another direct link to India in the person of his cousin, Johann Christian, in Tranquebar; the marriage issues in both locales, however, do not appear to have been broached in any correspondence. See, for example, AFSt/M 3 H 65: 84, Breithaupt to Gotthilf August Francke, 18 December 1764.

ried. Bartels announced his intention to take the Lord's Supper and notified Hildebrand that he had a fiancée in Apperode, a village under the legal authority of Halberstadt that lay within Brandenburg-Prussia, just outside Wernigerode's territory. He wanted banns to be proclaimed for the third time and asked if it were true that he had to have banns announced in Wernigerode. Hildebrand warned him that the pastor in Apperode could not marry him until he showed evidence of the proclamations to both pastors. Bartels retorted that he had lived a number of years in Harzburg, had approached the authorities in Hasserode, and had given the pastor in Apperode the proper notifications — why did he need to do more? Hildebrand had to write the consistory to determine what the law said.

Count Christian Ernst turned to his chancellor Caprivi for legal advice to determine the balance between Prussian and Wernigerode law and privileges. In his report to the consistory, Caprivi summarized the opinion of the Prussian authorities in Halberstadt, and the resulting concession that Hildebrand should proclaim the banns three times in Saint Sylvester's to speed a resolution to the case, even though Bartels and the pastor should have known about this beforehand. Pastor Stieren, stung by the implication that he had done anything wrong, protested that he knew nothing of a Prussian royal edict that demanded reciprocal evidence of the banns. Was Bartels under Wernigerode's authority simply because he happened to be working there? Hildebrand noted, however, that the Halle jurist Justus Henning Böhmer had taught that reciprocal proclamation was necessary. Hildebrand pleaded his actions as justified under his immediate authorities, namely, the consistory in Wernigerode. But since Hasserode was *unmittelbar,* that is, directly, Brandenburg-Prussian, the Brandenburg edicts on banns were in full force there. But were they in Wernigerode? Did Hildebrand and the consistory have the authority to demand a prior reciprocal announcement of banns in the face of a concession by the Halberstadt authorities who believed this could be dispensed with?[35]

35. AuBKS: II G 6 805 1748, *Acta die von dem pastore zu Appenrode Theophilo Wilhelm Stieren wiedrrechl. Unternomenen Proclamation . . . ,* pp. 1-17; 8-11 recto and verso contain Hildebrand's summary of the case to the consistory; cf. 9-10 recto and verso for the citation of the Brandenburg edicts; 10 verso and 11 recto for the citations to Böhmer's *Jus Parochialis;* 11 recto for the appeal of Hildebrand to the authority of the consistory in defense of his actions; 17 for Christian Ernst's observations on Caprivi's handling of the contacts with Halberstadt. By July of 1748, issues pertaining to marriage and pastors in Brandenburg-Prussia were removed from the *Oberconsistorium* and placed under the jurisdiction of the *Kammergericht.* For a copy of the edict see AFSt: 144:B 3 (1).

These jurisdictional disputes that began with the mediatization coincided with Francke's greeting his missionary Bartholomaeus Ziegenbalg, who returned from the Indian subcontinent to give his report on progress among the Tamil-speakers of the region. Francke had long been impressed by Ziegenbalg's profound knowledge of the welter of religious beliefs and practices among South Indians. But he was not prepared to hear about the worship of many gods, notions of sexual union within a pagan godhead, or the practice of plural marriage. These matters remained especially sensitive in the wake of the Thomasius affair and in the context of the widening disputes in nearby Wernigerode and Berlin. As early as 1709, Ziegenbalg's response to a question put to him about polygamy had alerted Francke to the potential for mischief if the reports paid too much attention to sexual sins and scandalous marriages among both Europeans and Tamils in the Danish mission area.

Ziegenbalg had reported that "because all of their Gods have many wives," the Indians did not regard polygamy as immoral. Still, to avoid impurity that came from sexual contact with others outside the appropriate social group, and because Indians had to wait sometimes years before being allowed to marry, it was not uncommon that a man might take "one or two wives from an inferior order." It was sufficient that the man's parents and a few close friends considered the marriage "valid." Ziegenbalg had to admit that in his opinion, these pagans were so inclined to sin against the sixth commandment and were so attached both to whoring and to polygamy that "they do not gladly convert to our religion." Nor did the Danish trading company officials object. Worse still, they turned a blind eye to sexual immorality among their own coreligionists. Francke could only hope that disputes over sexual sins and marriage and the role of princes, Christian or pagan, in determining religious belief would not engulf the fragile mission. He did not need questions about marital relations and illicit sex emanating from Halle's favored mission outpost to put the entire complex of his Foundations at risk just as the pietist reform movement in Wernigerode was gathering steam.[36]

Francke's anxiety grew more acute because he feared that bad publicity about sex and marriage would also alarm Halle's British allies who had become supporters of the India mission. A financial and political realist, Francke needed his English admirers to continue investing both funds and

---

36. For the details of Ziegenbalg's works and the complicated question of its censorship, see below, chapter 4. For the letter here, see Arno Lehmann, ed., *Alte Briefe aus Indien: Unveröffentlichte Briefe von Bartholomäus Ziegenbalg 1706-1719* (Berlin: Evangelische Verlagsanstalt, 1957), p. 121.

personnel in the Danish colony's pietist experiment. If they had grounds to suspect internal disagreements among the clergy about a matter as critical as instruction in Christian marriage, the backers might curtail support. Anglican funds by 1714 supplemented the aid from Denmark and patrons such as the count of Wernigerode, whom Francke encouraged to cultivate his connections to the Danish court.

Both Danish and British Protestants took a special interest in this, the most important Protestant challenge to Catholic missionary dominance in India, a mission that enjoyed the full support of the Danish Lutheran monarch Christian IV. The pro-Whig faction in English politics had also watched Halle's social experiments, and by 1701 Francke became a corresponding member of the Society for the Propagation of Christian Knowledge (SPCK). Predominantly a lay-led organization, the brainchild of Thomas Bray, the SPCK also attracted Anglican clerics and bishops, including the propagandist for the Glorious Revolution, Bishop Gilbert Burnet.

These lay-led movements gathered together clusters of the devout intent upon moral and social reform. But events now showed that the inherited canonical law of England and its official theology of marriage were proving to be just as problematic as the Lutheran version on the Continent. Unfortunately, an embarrassing revelation now surfaced about one of the more eminent SPCK clerics who turned out to have been on the wrong side of controversial questions — such as marriage. Gilbert Burnet died in 1715 hard on the heels of the intense exchanges on marriage between pietists and Thomasius. But his ghost now arose to haunt his admirers and supporters not only in Britain but also in German-reading circles on the Continent, and the topic was marriage, its definition and regulation. Had English concerns over marriage not intersected with the debates on the Continent, the issue probably would not have caught the attention of an international Protestant readership. Protestants were worried about the dangers of Catholicism, and they yearned for reports of successful Protestant missionary efforts abroad. Nonetheless, by 1738 a translation of an essay by Burnet reached German readers. Its title was sufficiently threatening: "Is a Plurality of Wives in Any Case Lawful under the Gospel?" Burnet had managed to suppress it during his lifetime. But the piece surfaced by the 1720s in the midst of controversy in Britain over marriage reform. It was clear that something more than the ominous possibility of a Catholic succession to the English throne or the state's control of marriage in the interest of a Protestant monarchical succession had spurred Burnet's ruminations.

Burnet seems to have recognized the difficulty the Church of England had faced in defining marriage. On the one hand, some Anglicans, influenced by the Augsburg Confession and the Lutheran reduction of the sacraments to two (or three, in some versions, which included auricular confession), had remained as unhappy as Lutherans in seeing marriage demoted to the status of an ambiguous, godly estate. These more conservative Anglican theologians at first took comfort because the Crown endorsed their views. Thomas Cranmer tried, without any success, to woo King Henry VIII away "from his steadfastly traditional view of human life as a progress towards God through the steady performance of God's commands." When the "Bishops' Book" *(The Institution of a Christian Man)* was finally ready for promulgation, the king demanded that it note the status of marriage in the Garden of Eden. On the basis of its prelapsarian status alone, "it outranked the sacraments instituted in the New Testament." Cranmer fought this position as steadily as he could, and won, at least to the degree that marriage remained among the "lesser" sacraments. From 1537, as Cranmer moved out of his "Lutheran phase" toward the Reformed understanding of nature and grace, "that was the last to be heard of matrimony's chances of promotion."[37]

Burnet had, for his part, speculated in his youthful opinion about the status of matrimony and asked whether New Testament teachings indeed canceled Old Testament norms. His audacity in suggesting that the lack of an explicit scriptural prohibition of polygamy left the question open to royal discretion led him into deeper waters than he could have imagined. Unfortunately for him, his youthful opinion would now end up being wrenched from its original context and inserted into the widening eighteenth-century circle of Protestant debate over marriage. Probably formulated in 1671 when the eager young Scots scholar was flattered to be asked to provide a legal brief to John Maitland, earl of Lauderdale (perhaps on behalf of King Charles II), the piece had later embarrassed its author. At least according to one account, Burnet by 1696 abashedly disowned his earlier argument. When he finally wrote his monumental *History of My Own Time,* he stoutly defended the official Anglican theology of the "sacramental" side of matrimony. His version of the English law of marriage also noted that "in the latter ages of popery, when marriage was reckoned among the sacraments, an opinion grew to be received, that adultery did not break the bond, and that it would only entitle to a separation, but not the dissolution of marriage." Under Thomas Cranmer's influence, the statute of Edward VI finally allowed a second marriage "upon a

---

37. On the 1530s developments, see Diarmaid MacCulloch, *Thomas Cranmer: A Life* (New Haven and London: Yale University Press, 1996), pp. 181-236, quotation at 212.

divorce for adultery." But a century later, Burnet concluded, "a skeptical and libertine spirit prevailed, so that some began to treat marriage only as a civil contract, in which the parliament was at full liberty to make what laws they pleased; and most of King Charles's courtiers applauded this, hoping by this doctrine that the king might be divorced from the queen."[38]

Unfortunately for Burnet's posthumous reputation, his original brief appeared in English publication in 1731. Thomas Salmon, an amateur geographer and historian, pounced on the piece. He had already written a blistering review of Burnet's *History* when the volume on pre-Revolution England appeared in 1724. That same year, Salmon had published his own interpretation of Protestant marital history entitled *An Essay concerning Marriage.* Committed to proving that friendship among husband and wife lay at the heart of marriage, Salmon nonetheless regarded marriage as primarily contractual. Borrowing heavily both from Grotius and Pufendorf, Salmon surveyed the authority of husbands, noting that "man does not seem at the Creation to have had any Dominion over the Woman." Dismissing defenses of polygamy and concubinage of the sort being promulgated by jurists like Thomasius, Salmon still argued for a more liberal teaching on divorce, but on grounds of a betrayal of friendship. He insisted that marriage constituted a meeting of minds, not bodies; it required more than ritual and mere consent. Rejecting Catholic teaching, Salmon noted that "the Protestant Divines say it is no Sacrament, but an Ordinance of God instituted in Paradise, and signifies the mystical Union between Christ and his Church." But Salmon backed away from pushing this teaching any farther. He fell back at the end on the safer official canonical legal argument that the "essence" of marriage can be found in "the free mutual Consent of both Parties, being of Age and Ability to contract." The Reformed influence on the Anglican liturgy clinched his arguments: the purposes of marriage were, in order, procreation, a remedy against lust, and (only finally) mutual support.[39]

---

38. Gilbert Burnet, *A History of His Own Time* (London: William S. Orr, 1850), pp. 600-601; this edition includes both volumes of the *History;* the first volume originally appeared posthumously in 1724. On the original context of Burnet's legal opinion, see T. E. S. Clarke, *A Life of Gilbert Burnet Bishop of Salisbury* (Cambridge: Cambridge University Press, 1907), pp. 103-4.

39. Thomas Salmon, *An Essay concerning Marriage* (London: C. Rivington, 1724), pp. 38-39, 53-54, citations at 72, 153, 155; on Anglican Liturgy, 159. I cannot conclusively prove that Salmon is identical with the later rector of Tavistock and author of essays on marriage reform. For that possibility, see Hermann Wellenreuther, *Repräsentation und Großgrundbesitz in England 1730-1770* (Stuttgart: Klett-Cotta, 1979), pp. 193-94, 204, 250.

The norm of mutual support in English marriages, however, remained muddled not only in Salmon's thinking, but also in the official theology and the canonical and secular law of Britain. A Protestant monarchy and ecclesiastical establishment had learned from the late medieval tradition to interpret "marital discord in terms of female resistance to male authority." A culture of local shaming had monitored households, holding men responsible for moderate correction of wives, and scorning them if they resorted to violence that failed to attain its aim. Ecclesiastical demands for documented abuse to justify separation from table and bed *(a mensa et thoro)* remained so strict that before strife reached the courts "English villages had an effective system of dealing with marital strife . . . punish(ing) domestic violence through public humiliation."[40] Moreover, no matter what official theology and law might say, by the eighteenth century the gentry and aristocracy, at least unofficially, judging from their letters and essays, appeared to accept married love "as a principal source of human fulfillment."[41]

The willingness of church courts to tackle marital disputes and accusations of sexual infidelity declined after the Restoration of the monarchy when "the focus of prosecutions shifted strongly to breaches of the religious code." The standard explanation is that as the church courts shied away from the "correction of sexual behavior, and of defamation cases," the various Societies for the Reformation of Manners briefly filled the breach. By the mid-1720s they also had failed. Now, the secular, local courts were expected to handle such issues almost exclusively.[42]

It is in this context that the strife over the spousal relationship among pietists on the Continent and in the Danish mission intersected with British controversies over the law of marriage. Although marriages had some standing before the law even if they were mere contracts *per verba de praesenti* (from the words of those present), along with "non-Anglican marriages and clandestine marriages," in practice, "clandestine marriage might carry all of the same legal rights as a regular marriage, but it exposed the parties to cer-

---

40. Sara M. Butler, *The Language of Abuse: Marital Violence in Later Medieval England* (Leiden and Boston: Brill, 2007), pp. 259-65, at 265, and citing at 262, Joy Wiltenburg, *Disorderly Women and Female Power in the Street Literature of Early Modern England and Germany* (Charlottesville: University Press of Virginia, 1992), p. 97.

41. Keith Thomas, *Ends of Life: Roads to Fulfillment in Early Modern England* (Oxford and New York: Oxford University Press), p. 217, and on marriage and male-female friendship, 198-220.

42. R. B. Outhwaite, *The Rise and Fall of the English Ecclesiastical Courts, 1500-1860* (Cambridge: Cambridge University Press, 2006), pp. 81, 100-101.

tain penalties, and those that took place outside a church might well be difficult to prove." The reform of the canons governing marriage in 1604 had made it possible to enforce a contract provided "both parties to the contract agreed that they had entered into a contract in words of the present tense, and no third parties were involved." By 1696 two Marriage Duty acts imposed serious financial penalties (£100 per offense) on Anglican clerics who performed or allowed another cleric to perform the marriage ceremony without the canonically correct proclamation of banns and proper license. By the time the Halle pietists began to converse with British reformers, then, "there was certainly no tradition of marrying outside a recognized place of worship . . . [and] it is clear that the story of clandestine marriage in the seventeenth century is one of commitment to marrying in church, if not necessarily the church that the canons would have prescribed." Nonetheless, the accelerating demand in the early eighteenth century for more marriage reform would increasingly reflect the interests of "the propertied men who made up Parliament" and worried about "their minor children marrying without their consent or knowledge."[43]

Did such British concern for marriage reform reflect a concern for defending its theological standing, and a recognition of real friendship and partnership between husband and wife? Pietist observers may well have had reason to doubt that this was the case, as do we. The determination of British reformers to impose order on an institution that seemed susceptible to the pressures of unscrupulous males intensified in 1724, when the first volume of Burnet's *History* appeared and an irregular marriage brought the matter to public attention. Despite the efforts of both Crown and the church, English and Scottish marriage laws had remained unsettled; marital disputes ended up less and less in ecclesiastical courts and more in the hands of local justices of the peace or commissioners of courts of conscience. English law dictated that the parties had to freely consent, be of age, and not violate the rules of consanguinity before contracting a legal first marriage.[44] Regular marriages included the publication of banns and a ceremony before the parish priest. But reformers were alarmed at the multiplication of irregular marriages and the conflicts they caused. Many of these unions depended solely upon vague oral statements and implied promises of a future union.

43. Rebecca Probert, *Marriage Law and Practice in the Long Eighteenth Century* (Cambridge: Cambridge University Press), pp. 19, 205, 28, 175-76, 206.

44. Leah Leneman, "The Scottish Case That Led to Hardwicke's Marriage Act," *Law and History Review* 17, no. 1 (Spring 1999): 161-69, at 162.

Such was the case when Magdalen Cochran secretly married John Campbell at Paisley Abbey. She may have understood why he asked her to keep the marriage from the knowledge of his patron the duke of Argyll. She did not expect that eighteen months later he would irregularly marry Jean, the woman he had been living with for twenty years, even though he had admitted his marriage to Jean, raised three children with her, and convinced everyone that they were lawfully husband and wife.

The case of Campbell against Cochran did not enter the courts until 1746, but the details already known in the 1720s had troubled reformers, who deplored this kind of clandestine marriage and deeply regretted the unsavory reputation of clergy willing to perform marriages for a fee despite the threat of fines. If the clergy would not exercise proper oversight of marriage, then perhaps it was high time that the laity in Parliament did. Reformers observed that Scottish law had continued to recognize clandestine marriages as legal if both parties consented, while English law after 1695-96 fined the participants in such marriages, including the clergy caught performing them. "Fleet" marriages (performed in the area surrounding the Fleet prison by debtor clergy) were notorious, as were the marriages at the Gretna Green blacksmith's shop just over the border in Scotland — a favorite recourse of English elopers. Both moved reformers to seek clearer definitions of marriage and a firmer consensus about its regulation. By the early 1730s, the older traditions of English law on the rights of women in marriage slowly shifted as the result of arguments carefully construed to make novel notions appear as if they were ancient. The older treatise *Baron and Feme: A Treatise of the Common Law concerning Husbands and Wives,* issued in 1700 and again in 1719, now gave way in popularity to *A Treatise of Feme Coverts; or, The Lady's Law,* which first appeared in 1732.[45]

The gist of the new definitions of married women boiled down to an attempt to assure wives that they had some control over their real and personal property despite the legal disabilities that came with marriage. In truth, both the impact of these reforms and the audience at whom the new treatise was aimed do not suggest that friendship and partnership in a quasi-sacramental relationship lay at the heart of the reformers' concerns. The treatise enjoyed

---

45. Leneman, "The Scottish Case," pp. 163-64; Rebecca Probert, "The Impact of the Marriage Act of 1753: Was It Really 'A Most Cruel Law for the Fair Sex'?" *Eighteenth-Century Studies* 38, no. 2 (2005): 247-62; Kirsten Sword, *Wives, Not Slaves: Marriage, Authority, and the Invention of the Modern Order* (Chicago: University of Chicago Press, forthcoming), chapter 3 on the possessory rights of husbands in marriage and the changing status of the *feme covert*. (I am grateful to Professor Sword for allowing me to read and cite her work prior to publication.)

a readership almost exclusively male, and the information, which was directed to "all practitioners of the Law, and other curious Persons," dwelt in prurient detail on "Rapes, Polygamy, and stealing of Women." *The Lady's Law* revealed growing interest in revising the law of marriage, but it remains far from clear whether married women were now, as a result, thought of as partners and friends or still as subjects of their husbands, especially in cases of marital discord and dispute over married property.[46]

One year after the appearance of *A Treatise of Feme Coverts,* Sir Nathaniel Curzon headed the parliamentary committee that used a 1730 clandestine marriage as a justification for investigating the defects of ecclesiastical courts.[47] The committee could look back on the previous decade for plenty of evidence that a reform of marriage law had been postponed too often. The serial bigamist Constantia Phillips, who began her career by entering "into a marriage of convenience in 1722 at the age of fifteen with a soldier called Francis Delafield," gradually became notorious, upon the publication of her autobiography in 1748/49 and in a tract written by the Reverend Henry Gally. Whether a concern for morals, or property, prompted the parliamentary investigators to rethink the issue of debt, the need for aggrieved husbands to maintain control of marital property remained a question of some debate. The combined impact of events since the 1720s, however, led Lord Hardwicke to push forward the bill that became the Hardwicke Act in 1753 (26 George II cap. 32). The collective impact of these judicial cases raised doubts about the possibility of genuine friendship and partnership in marriages at an "official" level even as literary tastes increasingly demonstrated sympathy for affectionate and companionate images of married life. Could married women be sued for contracts made as *feme sole* traders or equitable separate traders, even if their husbands had the power to grant such status? The courts reached no consensus. Whatever their disagreements, however, they tended to uphold the integrity of debtor-creditor agreements.[48] The issues were commercial and legal, not theological. Nevertheless, eighteenth-

46. Sword, *Wives, Not Slaves;* for the original citation, see *A Treatise of Feme Coverts; or, The Lady's Law. Containing all the laws and statutes relating to women* . . . (London: In the Savoy: printed by E. and R. Nutt, and R. Gosling, [assigns of E. Sayer, Esq]; for B. Lintot, and sold by H. Lintot, 1732), pp. vi-vii.

47. Outhwaite, *Rise and Fall,* pp. 107-13, at 113.

48. Karen Pearlston, "Married Women Bankrupts in the Age of Coverture," *Law & Social Inquiry* 34, no. 2 (2009): 265-99; the older standard work on the Hardwicke Act is R. B. Outhwaite, *Clandestine Marriage in England, 1500-1850* (London and Rio Grande, Ohio: Hambledon Press, 1995).

century Protestants, English and German, would have agreed that "the concept of a secular marriage in the common law was still a long way off."[49]

German pietists could not have been wholly unaware of these developments. Halle's London representative Friedrich Michael Ziegenhagen did not initially take notice of Salmon's annoyance with Burnet, or, more accurately, his few surviving papers do not reveal that he did. The British disputes did not find their way into Ziegenhagen's correspondence with Halle. Ziegenhagen worried about English Deism, Catholicism, and Reformed notions of predestination. His surviving sermon texts ignored the wedding feast at Cana, Ephesians 5, Matthew 19, and any other text about marriage or divorce. His estate left no treatises on marriage or sexual ethics, save, perhaps, Buddeus's 1715 *Institutes of Moral Theology*.[50]

But in 1738, when the Burnet legal opinion appeared in German translation as *A Defense of Polygamy,* the Weidemann booksellers, eager for customers, printed Burnet and followed it with Salmon's essay, "because of its exhaustive treatment, translated into German." German readers may have been pleased to see Pufendorf cited so liberally; they may not have been so happy with Salmon's observations on marriage in Germany: German women "are very obsequious to their Husbands, have less Command in their Houses than *English* and *French* Women, and are not allow'd the upper End of the Table." Besides, he sniffed, the costs of a wedding in Germany are ruinous.[51]

The ambivalent standing of marriage — with regard to the authority of princes and its location on the border between "two kingdoms" of theology, the standing of European Protestant women within matrimony, and the apparent preference of some pietists for lifelong celibacy — had now spread like a cancer well beyond the confines of the original dispute between Tho-

---

49. Maebh Harding, "The Consequences of Lord Hardwicke's Act in Ireland: An Unholy Confusion of Church and State," in *Crossing Legal Cultures,* ed. Laura Beck Varela, Pablo Gutierrez Vega, and Alberto Spinosa (Munich: Martin Meidenbauer, 2009), pp. 217-26, at 226.

50. This paragraph summarizes my reading of the uncatalogued AFSt "Teilnachlaß Ziegenhagen und Pasche Laufzeit 1700, 1720-1792," Karton 5 Verschiedne Briefe, Karton 2 (that includes a catalogue of books, though undated and hence, perhaps, not simply Ziegenhagen but belonging also to his coworkers Pasche or Albinus). I am greatly indebted to Jürgen Gröschl for making these newly discovered sources available with a superb index of contents.

51. On Salmon (1699-1767) see H. C. G. Matthew and Brian Harrison, eds., *Dictionary of National Biography* (Oxford: Oxford University Press, 2004), 48:734-35. The German version of Burnet's piece is entitled *Eine Vertheidigung der Polygamie . . .* (Leipzig: Weidemann, 1738); it appeared in English in 1731. Salmon's essay is *Die Wichtigkeit des Ehestandes* (Leipzig, 1738). For Salmon's description of German marriages, see *An Essay,* p. 263. I have used the Newberry Library's Frankfurt 1740 edition (K 74.776).

masius and Francke. Wernigerode's count would manage to attract Danish financial support for his own goal of copying Halle's orphanage, opening his own version in 1737. He, too, was by that time allied to Britain and supported the SPCK-Augsburg experiment in resettling Protestants in the experimental colony of Georgia in North America. The Danish mission in Greenland also attracted Wernigerode's attention. But unhappily for Halle, Wernigerode, the Danish Crown, and British Protestant reformers, unforeseen contributions to the debate over marriage now intruded from the very place upon which all had set their hopes for the spreading of the true gospel. In the confrontation with numerically superior Catholics in the non-Christian environment of southeastern India, a brief attempt to transcend the official pietist theology of marriage ran headlong into a transplanted jurisdictional dispute between church and state over who regulated marriage. Pietist hopes for better spouses faltered in the face of European doubts that converted Tamil women qualified as wives for Europeans, and the doubts of converted Tamils themselves about the wisdom of contracting marriage with European Protestants. All these uncertainties would undercut the restoration of Luther's synthesis and propel the understanding of spousal relationship further along the path toward its standing as a civil matter.

CHAPTER 4

Polygamy and Pietism:
The India Mission Shapes the Debate

In 1762, an account by the missionaries Johann Philipp Fabricius and Johann Christian Breithaupt appeared in Europe, updating Danish-German efforts to convert the Tamil-speaking population of southeastern India. They detailed how the late Johann Lucas Niekamp (d. 1740) had registered his delight at the arrival of two unexpected visitors to the pietist mission community in Tranquebar. An unnamed Syrian Orthodox priest and an Armenian companion arrived and asked permission to enter the library. Most likely, they journeyed from the modern state of Kerala that had served as the point of contact between Syrian Orthodox Christians and their Indian congregations since the sixth century (at either Kodungallur [Cranganore] or Kollam). The rediscovery of the tomb of Saint Thomas at Mylapore in the early 1500s had given rise to a Jesuit presence by the 1540s, and at least in their suspicions about the Portuguese Jesuits, the pietists, their British allies at Madras, and their Oriental Orthodox counterparts shared something in common.[1]

---

1. Johann Lucas Niekamp, *Kurzgefaßte Missions Geschichte oder historischer Auszug der Evangelischen Missions-Berichte aus Ostindien, von dem Jahr 1737 bis zu ende des Jahrs 1767 fortgesetzt von Michael Meier, Prediger zu Garz bei Ruppin* (Halle, 1772), p. 498. The original source is "Bericht über das Jahr 1762 von Johann Philipp Fabricius und Johann Christian Breithaupt," AFSt/M 2H 14: 1. On the Syrian-Indian connection and the tomb of Saint Thomas, see Ines G. Zupanov, *Missionary Tropics: The Catholic Frontier in India (16th-17th Centuries)* (Ann Arbor: University of Michigan Press, 2005), pp. 87-107. For a history of marriage rites and customs among the Syro-Malabar Catholic communities, see Mariamma Joseph, *Marriage among Indian Christians* (Jaipur and New Delhi: Rawat Publications, 1994). The Kerala traditions, however, shed little light even comparatively upon marriage customs in Tamil Nadu, on which, see

97

The Syrian priest presided over a Liturgy in Syrian and pronounced himself especially pleased when given a copy of the Gospel accounts of the passion of Christ in his own language. The incident reflects, in miniature, a sustained but deeply ambivalent interest among the pietists about Eastern Christians. On the one hand, the Armenian merchant community and the Syrian Orthodox Christians seemed like natural allies for Protestant missionaries harboring an animus against the Portuguese Roman Catholics. But pietist Lutherans serving in the Danish enclave regarded with distaste the Orthodox ceremonies, their sacramental worship, and their willingness to incorporate indigenous rituals or practices into Christian marriage. Catholics were worse, observed Niekamp. They performed ceremonies without catechizing their converts or explicating God's word. They seemed to imitate the pagans in encouraging pilgrimages that featured a picture of Saint Francis Xavier carried about on a wagon surrounded by 100 persons who entertained gawking onlookers with wild gesticulations and dancing.[2] Not without reason, therefore, did the pietist Lutherans in India rejoice when a number of their most promising converts came not from the non-Christian but from the already-converted, mostly unmarried Catholic population.

The battle among European Protestants about what their official theology and received canonical tradition said about the marital relationship arrived as an unwanted import on the southeast coast of the Indian subcontinent. Both preexisting Indian Christianity and the overwhelmingly complex familial, social, and political realities of the Tamil-speaking territory in which they labored would also now push the official view about spousal relations more rapidly in a "civil" direction. Protestant perceptions of pre-Reformation Christianity had helped to fashion in the course of the eighteenth century a new convention of imagining "Eastern" Europe and "Eastern" lack of "civilization."[3] Those convictions did not aid Protestants interested in church renewal to integrate easily the prior experience of Eastern or Roman Catholic Christians, or to accept the Tamil people's culture as one that could express pietist hopes for better spouses. Only a few years before the mission within the Danish trading outpost in Tranquebar began, pietist pamphleteers de-

---

below. For a survey of the issues surrounding the apostle Thomas and India, see George Nedungatt, S.J., *Quest for the Historical Thomas Apostle of India: A Re-reading of the Evidence* (Bangalore: Theological Publications in India, 2008).

2. Niekamp, *Missions Geschichte*, p. 461.

3. Larry Wolff, *Inventing Eastern Europe: The Map of Civilization in the Mind of the Enlightenment* (Stanford: Stanford University Press, 1994), pp. 4, 89-143.

scribed with enthusiasm the journeys of Czar Peter the Great through Europe. They rejoiced that the Roman Church, after failing to trick the Greek Christians into submission through flattery and bribery, had now turned toward Russia. To the pietists' delight, Rome had more than met its match in Peter. The former Halle professor Johann Franz Buddeus wrote from Jena that Czar Peter was determined to root out superstition in Russia, and he cheered Peter's attack on the cult of the icons (as much a plague, Buddeus wrote, among the Orthodox as among the papists). He had decided to abolish the Russian Patriarchate because he understood that the bishops were capable "of robbing the crown, the scepter, yes life itself" if they could but work their will. Union with Rome would be unthinkable for a czar committed to reason, one who understood that Rome's superstitious ways were hardly to be distinguished from "pagan blindness."[4]

"Pagan blindness" was what the pietist missionaries expected to find in India. Their perceptions and expectations loom especially dark and heavy over the task of understanding what the Tamil people themselves believed about their society, about their divinities, and especially about sexuality and marriage in the early eighteenth century. Not a single surviving document gives a firsthand account by convert Tamil men or women. Yet profound changes were occurring in Tamil society even before the arrival of Halle-trained Protestant missionaries in 1706, and they intensified afterward. The Tamil-speaking people had long before developed their own modulation of the so-called *varna* system of Brahmanical social and religious beliefs. The missionaries, for their part, carried convictions about the spousal relationship shaped by a bruising confrontation with Danish legal institutions and the ambiguous relation in which marriage stood to church authority.

The descriptions of both Tamil beliefs and missionary perceptions come mainly from Bartholomaeus Ziegenbalg. He provided an extraordinary output of written documentation for Europeans. He also contributed to the flourishing of Tamil as a printed, literary language in southeast India. But his notions about the society of the Indian subcontinent, and then about marriage, cannot be divorced from the European debates. Because of events in both Europe and Tranquebar, spousal relations and sexuality emerged as controverted topics with international consequences. By midcentury, among European missionaries, an unofficial theology of marriage seemed to find

---

4. Johann Franz Buddeus, *Erörterung der Frage ob eine Vereinigung der Römisch-Catholischen und Russischen Kirchen zu hoffen sey? . . .* (Jena, 1719), pp. 3, 8, 13 (AFSt [Bib]: 145 H 11).

room for the notion of the spouse as genuine friend — a glowing if dying ember of Luther's or Spener's vision of the estate. Officially, however, events within Tamil society and conflicts within the Danish-German missionary cadre paved the way for a darker, pessimistic assessment of spouses that tied marriage to legal institutions erected to ensure discipline and moved understanding of the estate to a final definition as a "civil matter."

I

As Christianity had spread eastward from Roman-occupied Palestine, three Tamil kingdoms (Chera, Chola, Pandya) enjoyed maritime exchanges with the Roman Empire and southeast Asia. Those trading networks intersected with the herding and agricultural economies that dominated the region. Most people in the area (Tamil Nadu today) around the Pandyan capital depended upon the waterways and wells of the region. The ecology of these kingdoms dictated the social order that secured the chieftains' properties through matrilineal succession by marriage of cousins in the first or second degree of kinship. Cementing the power of familial groups, these local networks had deep roots that resisted novel Christian teachings on monogamous marriage.

Long before the arrival of Christians, the Dravidian culture of this part of the subcontinent had selectively absorbed various northern influences including Brahmanical, Buddhist, and Jain teachings. Arriving Europeans found particularly baffling and frustrating the absence of a central political or religious authority. In some of the five rural districts that surrounded Tranquebar (Tarangambadi) or were nestled in the Kaveri delta near Cuddalore or Madras (Chennai), Europeans could find Brahmin practices flourishing next to *bhakti* devotional rituals that believers performed in private areas to prevent the pollution of their god. That tradition included women as well as men and flourished alongside local temple cults associated with deities like Ayanar or Amman — entities invoked to ward off disaster. Although a temple cult did exist alongside the political bureaucracy at Thanjavur (the state that encompassed most of the pietist area around the Kaveri River delta), Europeans miscalculated if they thought that the conversion of such worthies in these centers would necessarily influence the widely dispersed rural and fishing village inhabitants of the Coromandel coastal areas or the villages farther inland. Far from being the rigidly structured and "unchanging" society later Europeans would imagine "India" to

100

be, the society of the southeastern parts of the subcontinent had taken on its structure from practical necessity, a pattern Ziegenbalg recognized because of his own village and rural background in the rolling countryside of the Lausitz in southeast Germany.[5]

Nonetheless, the missionaries aspired to replace the religious beliefs and practices of this society with their own. By 1809, however, only a paltry 40,000 Indian Christians of all confessions occupied the region, despite a century of labor by Danish, German, and English missionaries and their Indian counterparts. The triumph of British forces over the French by 1763 and the absorption by 1845 of the Danish enclave where the pietists had labored hardened the later misapprehensions of "Hinduism" and the invented word "caste" that tell us almost nothing about the world earlier European observers had encountered. When late-eighteenth-century British observers began questioning indigenous people about the history of southern "India," Lionel Place and Francis Whyte Ellis discovered that "contrary to what both the British and local individuals claimed in their normative, utopian descriptions," the area had enjoyed a thriving economic and trading history among independent states.[6]

Portuguese Catholics — and most especially Jesuits — had enjoyed a big head start among Europeans in the attempt to understand the diverse peoples and social relationships of this vast subcontinent. Their presence at Cochin (Kozhikode, in Kerala) and Goa gave them more than a century's advantage over Protestants in having developed both trading networks and indigenous convert groups. But both Catholics and, belatedly, Protestants discovered that Brahman scholars regarded Christianity with barely disguised contempt because of its novelty and lack of deep historical roots. "Hindu," originally a term that in today's parlance we would understand as "secular," may have originated from the corrupted Persian "Sindhu" to designate the peoples beyond the Hindus River. The Sanskrit-influenced cultures in the north of the subcontinent had gradually adopted the *varnasrama* that ancient Greek observers had struggled to comprehend, suggesting a sevenfold stratification of society as the best way of understanding what by the eighteenth century may have constituted "3,000 different groupings within the

---

5. The following paragraphs summarize the arguments found in Gita Dharampal-Frick, *Indien im Speigel deutscher Quellen der Frühen Neuzeit (1500-1750): Studien zu einer interkulturellen Konstellation* (Tübingen: Max Niemeyer Verlag, 1994), pp. 228-42, and at 232-34 on Ziegenbalg's background in the Lausitz.

6. Eugene F. Irschick, *Dialogue and History: Constructing South India, 1795-1895* (Berkeley, Los Angeles, and London: University of California Press, 1994), p. 77.

Hindu society." In any event, the leaders of the various geographic regions probably "believed that simply reckoning things by Christian ideas was shallow by comparison with Hindu notions, whose era stretched back much farther into antiquity."[7]

The admiration for antiquity had also informed sixteenth-century Protestant humanists like the cosmographer Sebastian Franck, who would make much of the hierarchical and stable qualities of "India." But such idealizations missed the functionality of the various priestly, peasant, herding, handworking, or warrior elements in society that made much more sense to the peoples living in that part of the world. By the time seventeenth-century German descriptions of the subcontinent began to circulate, the importance of religious teachers (the role attributed to Brahmins) reflected the values of the Protestant German authors as much as these figures did the functioning of society. The pragmatic functional nature of the four *varnas* that Ziegenbalg would transcribe into German *(Brahmaner, Tschaddirer, Waschier, Tschuddirer)* shed little light on the various occupational groups within these *varna* terms.

Ziegenbalg skipped over occupational details of the *varna* categories and the *jāti (Geschlechter)* (families) in order to make sense of differences in status among the social groups. This decision put distance between his own pietist-influenced preference for productive, hardworking *shudras* as opposed to Brahminical "priestly" types he knew had been cultivated by the nearby French Jesuits at their outpost in Pondicherry. Arriving Catholic and Protestant Europeans sometimes did manage to get straight the ninety-eight subcategories of the "right" *(valangai)* and left *(idangai) Geschlechter (jāti,* or families), that is, the agricultural and skilled craftsmen groups. Ziegenbalg appears to have understood aright the seventy-one "families" that composed the majority of the categories the Tamil themselves understood as *shudra*. In the Tamil region even categories that in the north were of "lower status" were still *shudra (kurawer, paraiyar,* and *karaiyar)*. Brahmins in the north disdained these groups who ate dogs, cats, mice, and other "revolting" animals.[8]

Assuming with Ziegenbalg the functionality of the social categories in the Tamil society he now entered, we may also (just barely) be able to recon-

---

7. Dharampal-Frick, *Indien,* p. 183; Irschick, *Dialogue and History,* p. 107.

8. Dharampal-Frick, *Indien,* pp. 229, 231, 234; Gita Dharampal-Frick, "Zur Frage des 'Kastensystems': Die Proto-Ethnografie Bartholomäus Ziegenbalgs und der vorkoloniale Diskurs über Indien," in *Mission und Forschung: Translokale Wissensproduktion zwischen Indien und Europa im 18. Und 19. Jahrhundert,* ed. Heike Liebau, Andreas Nehring, and Brigitte Kolsterberg (Halle: Verlag der Franckeschen Stiftungen, 2010), pp. 207-25, at 211-12, 215.

struct the bare outlines of Tamil expectations about spouses. Not surprisingly, the Tamil thought of family and community primarily in relation to social, economic, and political cohesion and survival.[9] Ziegenbalg concluded realistically that the notion of *jāti* (i.e., family group), though not "essential" to the religious beliefs summed up by the term "Hinduism," nonetheless connoted a "belongingness" so compelling that "escape from . . . a family was unthinkable. From one's birth onward, the individual learned that, unless bonds were violated in one terrible way or another, such bonds were not just for life, but for eternity." Marriage outside the family and community could destroy the lives of those who embarked on it.[10]

South Indian marriage did not depend on the dominance of the groom's patrilineal family as was true in the north, but rather "upon the lineage of the groom's mother. This matrilineal system seems to have been much older than that which had evolved from Sanskritic traditions. . . . The southern system, sometimes called 'cross-cousin' marriage — also rested upon a regular formula for preferable and proper marriage . . . [where] a girl could not be married to her mother's younger brother, nor to a son of her brother, nor again, finally, to a son of her father's sister." In such a social system, the extraordinary influence of a mother-in-law over both husband and son had to be carefully negotiated even though the death of her husband rendered such a "true wife" *(satī)* devoid of status in favor of her daughter-in-law. She became a "walking corpse" without voice or physical profile.[11]

Tamil custom dictated the fixing of bride-price, the erection of the *pandal* or bamboo wedding pavilion, the use of the *tali* (the string with amulet tied around the neck of the bride by the groom), and the practice of the bridegroom's mother bestowing upon the new couple the *arati* or blessing.

9. The following paragraphs depend upon the observations contained in Paul Roche, "The Marriage Ceremonies of the Christian Paraiyans of the Kumbakonam Area, India," *Asian Folklore Studies* 36, no. 1 (January 1977): 83-95; V. James, "Marriage Customs of Christian Son Kolis," *Asian Folklore Studies* 36, no. 1 (January 1977): 131-48; Lionel Caplan, "Bridegroom Price in Urban India: Class, Caste and 'Dowry Evil' among Christians in Madras," *Man*, n.s., 19, no. 2 (June 1984): 216-33; Karin Kapadia, "Marrying Money: Changing Preference and Practice in Tamil Marriage," *Contributions to Indian Sociology* 27 (1993): 25-51; Isabelle Nabokov, "When the Dead Become Brides, Gods, and Gold: Marriage Symbolism in a Tamil Household Ritual," *Journal of Ritual Studies* 10, no. 1 (1996): 113-33; Ines G. Zupanov, "Lust, Marriage and Free Will: Jesuit Critique of Paganism in South India (Seventeenth Century)," *Studies in History* 16 (2000): 199-220.

10. Robert Eric Frykenberg, *Christianity in India: From Beginnings to the Present* (Oxford: Oxford University Press, 2008), pp. 35-43, at 36, 37, 43.

11. Frykenberg, *Christianity*, pp. 40, 43.

The ceremonial cooking of rice in more affluent families and the serving of separate dinners or *pandhi* for children, men, and finally women marked the occasions. These latter customs, "remnants of their Hindu past," would be scrutinized for reconciliation with the missionaries' demand for sobriety and dignity in the marriage ceremony.[12]

Tamil beliefs about the status of women included "associations between a woman's demonic possession and her desire for forbidden sexuality [that] seem to run very deep." Most ominously, "it is not women as a whole but predominantly new brides who are most at risk . . . the spirits known as *pēys* [demons] indisputably cause the gravest psychic disorders, inducing their married victims to reject their spouses."[13] Elaborate ceremonies and rituals were intended to "make fit" a person, but especially women since "the natal relatives of an unmarried female need to protect themselves from the consequences of any sexual activity in which she may engage, particularly with partners of unsuitable status . . . [and] bridegrooms and their families need to be sure of the status and personal purity of their brides," since only when sure of these conditions can the entire family be reassured about "the status of a woman's offspring."[14]

The ceremonies that accompanied *kaliyanam* — a word that can mean, besides "wedding" or "marriage," "virtue" or "good character" — were far more elaborate for the Brahmin *varna* "twice-born" than for the *shudras,* the fourth of the *varna* schema that constituted the majority population of the Tamil region. The perceived danger of female sexual power and the attendant rituals pointed to the "importance of divine marriage," which included "the nightly cohabitation of god and goddess, [that] allow[ed] creation to be portrayed more acceptably, as divine sexual intercourse within wedlock." The Tamil ideal of chastity *(karpu)* in marriage existed right alongside the many stories of sexually aggressive goddesses to present a world in which "purity brings power, but exercise of that power diminishes purity: conversely, power is potentially impure and violent, and must be restrained."

12. Roche, "The Marriage Ceremonies," pp. 85, 86, 89, 91-92, quotation at 95.

13. Isabelle Clark-Decès, "From Wasteland to Bus Stand: The Relocation of Demons in Tamilnadu," in *Tamil Geographies: Cultural Constructions of Space and Place in South India,* ed. Martha Ann Selby and Indira Viswanathan Peterson (Albany: State University of New York Press, 2008), pp. 173-97, at 175. The "demon" is usually understood as a female failed lover and perhaps a suicide; see 176-77; Isabelle Nabokov, "Expel the Lover, Recover the Wife: Symbolic Analysis of a South India Exorcism," *Journal of the Royal Anthropological Institute,* n.s., 3 (1997): 297-316.

14. Anthony Good, *The Female Bridegroom: A Comparative Study of Life-Crisis Rituals in South India and Sri Lanka* (Oxford: Clarendon, 1991), pp. 1, 5.

Just so, in the world of humans, the changing status of women through four stages (virgin, married, barren, widow) testified to the profound power women held over life itself, their "fertility . . . dangerous unless it is properly controlled and regulated by men. The four roles are not alternatives, but stages in the lives of all women. All begin adulthood as virgins; all should marry; in every marriage barrenness is an initial cause for anxiety; and every woman should outlive her husband . . . the rituals . . . serve, precisely, to make and effect transitions from one such stage to the next."[15]

Despite concern over female sexual purity in marriage, Tamil expectations about the exact status of women remain opaque. Even in the Mughal Empire, the role of powerful women — in sharp contrast to their counterparts, for example, in the Ottoman Empire — remained largely hidden. Despite the later appearance of women whose domestic and marital standing gave them and their children considerable power, "one's overwhelming sense remains that of the women's profound invisibility."[16] Until the early eighteenth century, married women had exercised influence over male sexual behavior in Tamil society in ways not all that different from their village counterparts in the German southwest territories. This influence apparently diminished in some degree by the time the pietists arrived among the Tamil. Whether the arrival of more European traders contributed to the destabilizing of traditional women's roles, or whether, as some have argued, a cyclic rise and fall in the power and social role of women happened to coincide with the European penetrations of the subcontinent, remains an unresolved question.[17]

The "sacred geography" of the Tamil, whose devotions and beliefs depended upon "orientation to place . . . [was] fundamental to Tamil religion

---

15. Good, *Female Bridegroom,* pp. 244-56, at 250, 251, 254, and 255.

16. Ruby Lal, *Domesticity and Power in the Early Mughal World* (Cambridge and New York: Cambridge University Press, 2005), pp. 222-26, at 225.

17. For a survey of the literature on the contested question of women in Indian society and the reasons for changing status, see Gita Dharampal-Frick, "'Audiatur et altera pars' — Aspekte der indischen Frauengeschichte," in *Südasien in der "Neuzeit": Geschichte und Gesellschaft, 1500-2000,* ed. Karin Preisendanz and Dietmar Rothermund (Vienna: Verein für Geschichte und Sozialkunde & Promedia Verlag, 2003), pp. 129-52; the influence of women at the court in Thanjavur suggests that the border between the "private" and the "public" sphere was particularly fluid in the Tamil regions, a pattern that would have challenged Europeans whose village cultures increasingly restricted even married women's control over male sexual misbehavior and subjected women increasingly to male-dominated instruments of "law" (pp. 138-39, 142). On the changing legal patterns in the German-speaking villages of Europe, see Roeber, "The Origins and Transfer of German-American Concepts of Property and Inheritance," *Perspectives in American History,* n.s., 3 (1987): 115-71.

in ways that are not shared by Hindu and other religious traditions in other regions of India."[18] What persisted in the marriage ritual and what converted Tamils would have constructed as a mixture of inherited and adopted customs elude us. The Tamil practice of inviting deceased parents to the first marriage of a child, for example, reflected the conviction that ancestors should be present at any important ritual. This custom remained widespread outside of Brahmin circles, complete with the offering of *pongal* (a delicacy made of sweetened rice and milk) and the use of "bridal symbolism" for the dead who are asked to protect and "perpetuate the family."[19]

The strong preference for "bilateral marriage" (also termed "sister-exchange") among non-Brahmin Tamils also reflected moral ideals that would have suggested to Europeans that they could reconcile their Christian ideals with "the values of equality and reciprocity of the non-Brahmin Tamils" in which "the subordination of women is relatively mild." The absence of dowry among non-Brahmin women, the preference for "bridegroom wealth" exchanges among the nonpropertied, and the identification of Tamil women with their mother's household (not their father's), combined with the agricultural work women did alongside husbands, encouraged a somewhat more egalitarian sense of household that the European pietists recognized as vaguely similar to peasant relationships in Europe. They believed, however, that even this sense of the household could be improved through the education of women.[20] (See Figure 3.)

The complexity of the kinship systems and the subtle distinctions within "cross-cousin marriage" had put considerable obstacles in the path of Portuguese Catholic missionaries. The Catholics, too, had been forced to address the issue of spousal relationships squarely. Even today, observers have noted that "not all cross-cousins are marriageable: a woman must marry her terminological senior and a man his junior." Eventually, Catholics allowed converts "by special dispensation" to marry first cousins with "each family paying a small fine to the church."[21] Observations upon marriage as the linchpin that anchored men and women within a social-familial network lay

18. Selby and Peterson, introduction to *Tamil Geographies,* pp. 1-16, at 8.

19. Nabokov, "When the Dead Become Brides," pp. 113, 115, 116, quotation at 126.

20. Kapadia, "Marrying Money," p. 29, quotations at 34, 36, 37; Caplan, "Bridegroom Price," pp. 216, 220, 223, 224-25.

21. Good, *Female Bridegroom,* p. 75. For a summary of Catholic canon law on consanguinity and the conditions for dispensation from impediments, see William E. Pinto, *Law of Marriage and Matrimonial Reliefs for Christians in India: A Juridical Evaluation of Canon Law and Civil Law* (Bangalore: Theological Publications in India, 2000), pp. 78-80.

Figure 3. "Portuguese" and Tamil school boys and girls (from Nicolaus Dal's 1729 sketches, colored by an unknown hand). Reproduced with permission of the Francke Foundations, Halle, Germany (AFSt/M B 5:4).

at the heart of the debates over syncretism, and they also determined how much Europeans could accept what they would eventually call "caste" without undermining the Christian teaching that God is no respecter of persons. Catholics endured this unresolved controversy over "Malabar Rites" that continued even after the 1744 decision to send special missionaries among the *paraiyar*. But the Catholics persisted in denouncing "caste" as a concept and practice grounded in religious belief, even while making concessions to the customs that defined social communities in India.[22]

How much did Tamil marriage and family practices produce syncretism

22. Will Sweetman, "Colonialism All the Way Down? Religion and the Secular in Early Modern Writing on South India," in *Religion and the Secular: Historical and Colonial Formations,* ed. Timothy Fitzgerald (London, U.K., and Oakville, Canada: Equinox, 2007), pp. 117-34, at 120-27. Jesuit missionaries argued for a reversal of the 1744 bull until the suppression of the Society in 1773. For further details, see Jean Lafrenez, *History of Pondicherry Mission: An Outline,* ed. and trans. P. A. Sampathkumar and Andre Carof (Chennai: University of Madras Department of Christian Studies, 2000), pp. 19-33.

among converts? One clue survives in the curious question of the culture of memory. The absence of gravesites of eighteenth-century Protestant converts poses a serious interpretive issue. Both precise astrological and genealogical charts might have guided at least the more socially prominent Tamils in making marital alliances. The capacity to memorize hymns and poems had long played the same important role among the "Thomas Christians" of India as it had among their "Hindu" neighbors. But at the lower end of Tamil society, few persons may have been able to tell the missionaries details about grandparents or the dates of their deaths. The absence of Tamil Christian gravesites for the eighteenth century testifies to the lack of resources for maintaining them. Moreover, unless early converts specified their wishes, their "Hindu" relatives would have cremated the bodies; even if burial took place, this occurred outside the village resident areas, and the unmarked graves could be forgotten. If missionaries worried about the degrees of consanguinity that were enforced in Europe, they had to question Tamil converts among many of the fishermen and workers who may not have been able to respond. Given the absence of interest in family burial sites, Tamils were even less likely to be concerned about the location of a spousal burial site, even if a Christian marriage had been performed.[23]

23. The existence and knowledge of the astrological and genealogical charts have been suggested by Gita Dharampal-Frick (correspondence to author, 29 October 2011); Good, *Female Bridegroom*, pp. 76-77, found that local Tamils might know the immediate descent "branch" but not wider "clusters" of relationships; my conclusion here that those of the non*varna* orders in society even today do not value such information reflects my survey of all surviving Christian gravesites during February-March 2011 in Chennai, Cuddelore, Tharagambadi, Tanjour, Poryar, Mel Pattambakkam, the French Catholic village of Karaikall, Nagapattinam, and the Catholic pilgrimage center at Vailankanni, and interviews with Professor Maria Lazar and Father D. Amudhan, who asserted the absence of Tamil interest in familial memory, as did pastors S. Navaraj Abraham, S. Reid, S. Sudharsan, and Mr. George Manuel of Tranquebar. The oldest Tamil pastors' graves are commemorated in the Old Cemetery in Poryar where a tablet notes "Ambrose" (1777), Ryappan (1797), and Xavier (1817). The gravesites of the Tamil pastors Aaron and Diogo in the original Jerusalem Church have since been lost to the sea. On the gravesites of European Christians, see J. J. Cotton, *List of Inscriptions on the Tombs or Monuments in Madras Possessing Historical or Archaeological Interest* (Madras: Government Press, 1905), who noted on p. iii that this comprised only a "select list of monumental inscriptions relating to Europeans buried in the Madras presidency . . . all epitaphs of adults earlier than 1800." See also Karin Kryger and Lisbeth Gasparski, *Tranquebar Cemeteries and Grave-Monuments* (Copenhagen: Royal Danish Academy of Fine Arts, School of Architecture Publishers, 2003). On the patterns of spousal memorials among Europeans, see below, chapter 7. On the importance of memorization of hymnody and poetry, see Nedungatt, *Quest for the Historical Thomas Apostle of India*, pp. 355-67, at 358-59.

A second example of possible syncretism suggests that the missionaries sometimes succeeded in keeping marriage a simple, and hence, visible but still mixed marker of boundaries that helped to create a fragile sense of Christian community. In the areas away from the coast, "rural Christians often conducted very simple ceremonies in their home that consisted only in reciting the Lord's prayer and a relative's tying the south Indian symbol of marriage, the *tali*, around the neck of the bride." But such a ceremony might easily become consonant with Hindu customs, as was the case when husbands approached the village *panchayat* to allow parties to dissolve their marriage and seek another partner.[24]

The use of the *tali* — at first condemned by Zieganbalg but tolerated by his successors — had an importance beyond its immediate indication that a woman was married. A temple official in Tiruvallur explained that social and political standing could be signaled by saying that "his taudoo [Telugu 'tadu'] will be entirely cut off." The removal of the *tali* when a woman lost her husband signaled she had lost the status her husband enjoyed because of his occupation and standing in the community. There existed, then, a symbolic, one might even venture sacramental, dimension of "exterior" signs that pointed to both an "interior" reality of relationship within the family and communal groups, and the larger, public dimension of order and property. So important is the symbol of the *tali* even today that a woman who abandons her marriage is immediately ostracized and labeled by a Tamil term that means "she who does not know how to live a life." Some women would still display a saffron string to indicate that they once enjoyed the marital standing in the community.[25]

Since so many of the early converts to European Protestantism came from only the moderately well-off or the impoverished groups of Tamil society, the absence of elaborate ritual or the consumption of food at a convert Tamil Christian wedding might have been familiar to those who knew they would never enjoy the sumptuous wedding ceremonies of the wealthy. More importantly, the simplicity of the Protestant marriage rite stood in sharp contrast to the elaborate temple ceremonies open to the social elites at Madurai, for example, where the fish-eyed goddess Meenakshi was believed (at least by Europeans) to copulate with Sundareshwarar, her spouse, a flesh-

---

24. Eliza F. Kent, *Converting Women: Gender and Protestant Christianity in Colonial South India* (New York: Oxford University Press, 2004), pp. 164-97, at 169.

25. On the use of the term and its broader meaning, see Irschick, *Dialogue and History*, p. 57.

and-blood priapic version of the god Shiva. It was imperative for Protestants to isolate their converts from these marital ceremonies and from the syncretistic errors of the Catholics.

The first reports from the Indian mission that circulated in German, Latin, and French throughout Europe only a few years after the mission's planting in 1706 revealed both the formidable levels of "pagan blindness" about marriage and the disturbing head start enjoyed by Catholic missionaries. The reactions by German pietists against Thomasius's defense of concubinage reflected long-rehearsed polemics against Roman Catholic teachings. Catholic defenses of celibacy and the sacramental character of marriage both signaled to Protestants Rome's interest in monetary gain. Protestant hostility surfaced now in the Indian context with denunciations of "heathen" marriage rites and practices.

Most Europeans, whether Catholic or Protestant, elided concubinage with polygamy in their censures of "Indian marriage." They did so because notions of sexuality and family that differentiated Christian beliefs from non-European cultures had been the topic of European reflection since the sixteenth century. Eighteenth-century Franciscans in California, for example, demanded compliance "in matters of marriage and sexuality," establishing the conditions for "a terrific and tragic conflict" because "the Children of Coyote" occasionally "practiced polygyny, now and then engaged in extramarital sexual relations, and from time to time dissolved their marriages." Only a few years later, Russian Orthodox contacts with the First Peoples in Alaska revealed how slowly "the practice of polygamy, especially common among the wealthy aristocracy, would change."[26]

II

The Halle-trained pietists who arrived in 1706, however, discovered in their fellow Europeans the Danes no interest in Protestant evangelizing, and just as little in maintaining Christian sexual morality or marital fidelity. Protestant teaching on marriage provoked harsh reactions initially, not from Tamil-speakers, but from the Danish East India Company authorities. Partly

---

26. Steven W. Hackel, *Children of Coyote, Missionaries of Saint Francis: Indian-Spanish Relations in Colonial California, 1769-1850* (Chapel Hill: University of North Carolina Press, 2005), see especially chapter 5, pp. 182-227, quotation at 182; Sergei Kan, *Memory Eternal: Tlingit Culture and Russian Orthodox Christianity through Two Centuries* (Seattle and London: University of Washington Press, 1999), p. 88.

to counterbalance Portuguese influence, the Mughal rulers had offered trade concessions to other European nations. But England's East India Company (1600) and the Dutch *Verenigde Oost-Indische Compagnie* (1598) remained weak and fragile. The Danish East India Company (1620) maintained only a precarious foothold within a forty-square-kilometer area with one walled city and fifteen villages perhaps numbering 30,000 persons by 1706.

In return for an annual tribute, Danes gained their trading center, Tranquebar. Despite the presence of a Danish Lutheran pastor, company officials expressed hostility to the Halle missionaries. The Danish monarch Frederik IV had secured the services of the Halle-trained students Heinrich Plütschau and Bartholomaeus Ziegenbalg, but he had not seen fit to inform the company's board of directors of his religious zeal. The board therefore tried to undermine the Halle-staffed mission. Within a few years, marriage — and the question of who was responsible for its proper order, and marital relations, among Tamils, and between Europeans and Tamils — exploded into a public controversy.

Within six years Ziegenbalg had mastered enough of the Tamil language to investigate with some real insight the religious beliefs and practices of the Indian subcontinent. Some 200 indigenous people had become converts by 1712, an impressive increase from the baptism in 1707 of five Tamils held as slaves by the Danes. From this initial vantage point in 1706, the pietist efforts extended to Tanjavur by the 1730s and to Tirunelveli by the 1770s; by the end of the century they had penetrated to Travancore and Serampore.[27]

The relationship of the Danish Company to the monarchy — and hence to the question of who spoke with authority on the law of marriage within

---

27. On the background to the Halle-trained mission's beginnings, see Martin Brecht, "August Hermann Francke und der Hallische Pietismus," in *Geschichte des Pietismus: Der Pietismus vom siebzehnten bis zum frühen achtzehnten Jahrhundert*, ed. Brecht et al. (Göttingen: Vandenhoeck & Ruprecht, 1993), pp. 440-540, at 527-29; Daniel Jeyaraj, *Inkulturation in Tranquebar: Der Beitrag der frühen dänischhalleschen Mission zum Werden einer indisch-einheimischen Kirche, 1706-1730* (Erlangen: Verlag der Ev.-Luth. Mission, 1996); D. Dennis Hudson, *Protestant Origins in India: Tamil Evangelical Christians, 1706-1835* (Richmond, U.K.: Eerdmans, 2000); on the pre- and post-1700 political struggles for control of the area, see Robert Eric Frykenberg, "Raja-Guru and Sishiya-Shastriar: Christian Friederich Schwartz and His Legacy in Tanjavur," in *Halle and the Beginning of Protestant Christianity in India I: The Danish-Halle and the English-Halle Mission,* ed. Andreas Gross, Y. Vincent Kumaradoss, Heike Liebau (Halle: Verlag der Franckeschen Stiftungen, 2006), pp. 471-96, at 471-72 and 474-78. On the Dutch Phillipus Baldaeus's problematic 1671 history of the Tamil region, see Jarl Charpentier, "The Brit. Mus. Ms. Sloane 3290, the Common Source of Baldaeus and Dapper," *Bulletin of the School of Oriental Studies, University of London* 3, no. 3 (1924): 413-20.

the narrow confines of their trade concession territory — remained a matter of dispute because Danish law itself was evolving. In theory, the first Danish law code should have clarified the relationship,[28] but both monarchical authority and the oversight of marriage remained complicated in Denmark and in Tranquebar. Illiterate bailiffs and an absence of qualified recorders frustrated the drive toward creating courts of record in Denmark itself, and not until 1736 did a royal decree make a degree in law from the university in Copenhagen the indispensable qualification for jurists who increasingly controlled both local and higher courts in the realm. Despite the creation of a new Supreme Court *(Højesteret)* by 1660, legal privileges that had been written into the original charter still protected entities such as the Danish East India Company from royal legal authority.[29] Jurisdiction in any cause having to do with the internal matters of the Company remained protected under paragraph twelve of the Company regulations, a proviso continued after the reorganization of the Company in 1698. Appeals to the Danish high court were restricted to cases involving those convicted of a capital offense and facing the death penalty. In its reconstituted form, the Company boasted six governors, a number that dropped again by one in the next incarnation of the organization in 1732. The governors could be prosecuted in the courts for mismanagement, a penalty threatened at least twice in the early seventeenth century. As the monarchy tightened its grip on the legal system, more elaborate oaths of obedience to the Crown were stipulated. At the same time, throughout the Company's various lives, the Crown apparently respected the principle of limited liability, and during the seventeenth and eighteenth centuries the company "assumed that limited liability required royal approval in the form of an Oktroj (royal charter) or some similar concession." In the attempt to lure investors, Danish law placed the power of management in the hands of the shareholders and their general meeting. Management on the site — that is, in Tranquebar, and at other outposts — had to balance the wishes of investors at home with royal orders. The mon-

---

28. Per Andersen, "'Os iletrados': Juízes da Dinamarca na primeira modernidade" ["'The unlettered': Judges in early modern Denmark"], in *História Social dos Juristas na Primeira Modernidade: Europa e América, 1500-1800* [The social history of early modern lawyers], ed. Hermann Nébias Barreto (Belo Horizonte, Brazil: Editora Tempus, 2013), pp. 1-26, at 1. I thank Professor Andersen for allowing me to read and cite the prepublication English translation of the essay.

29. Andersen, "Os iletrados," pp. 2-5; Svend Ellehoj, "Rettens geografiske virkefelt," in *Højesteret 1661-1961,* ed. Povl Bagge, Jep Lauesen Frost, and Bernt Hjele (Copenhagen: G.E.C. Gad, 1961), pp. 100-102.

arch exercised strong influence, but commandants sometimes resisted. In the opinion of some scholars, "the king's influence was very strong . . . so that the company had more of the nature of a royal project than a private initiative which gathered capital from many investors." That reality, however, did not prevent commandants from frustrating royal wishes — especially after the arrival of the missionaries.[30]

The arriving Halle pietists, scornful of Catholic syncretism and toleration of pagan practices, had their hands full both with the Company and with Tamils who had inherited their own culture's beliefs about spousal relations. Within four years of their arrival, the missionaries counted 2,000 Muslims who worshiped in two mosques in the villages and town, dwarfing the 500 Roman Catholic converts. The vast majority of inhabitants frequented five temples, the majority dedicated to Shiva, a minority to Vishnu. Ziegenbalg recognized that marriage between the two groups was rare and that any Christian challenge to notions of who constituted a proper spouse could result in complete isolation for a convert. Among the radical practices promoted by the missionaries, perhaps none had more far-reaching implications than their determination to teach young women in pietist schools in their own language both Lutheran Christian doctrine and practical subjects. At the end of such training, however, women were supposed to marry fellow Christians — a daunting challenge for the future of the missionary experiment.[31]

Ziegenbalg's attempt to teach Tamils why their beliefs about spouses had to be reformed now surfaced in an important early catechetical approach he summarized for his European mentors. He wrote, in the Tamil language, a succinct history of salvation that showed "Scriptural evidence

30. Karsten Engsig Sørensen, "The Danish East India Company," in *VOC 1602-2002: 400 Years of Company Law,* ed. Ella Gepken-Jager, Gerard van Solinge, and Levinus Timmerman (Deventer, Netherlands: Kluwer Legal Publishers, 2005), pp. 107-30, at 127-28, 130.

31. See Daniel Jeyaraj, "The History of the Lutheran Churches in India during the Eighteenth Century: An Overview," *Lutheran Quarterly* 17 (Spring 2003): 77-97; on the 121 students in schools and the 354 members and catechumens, see Bartholemew Ziegenbalg and Johann Ernst Gründler, *Brevis Delineatio Missionis Operis, quod ad propagandam vivam Christi cognitionem et promovendam verae Pietatis Praxin inter Paganos Orientales et praecipue inter Damulos virtute divina Tranquebariae geritur* (Tranquebar, 1717), pp. 3-4, 8-9, AFSt: H:146; for the details on the early settlement and population of the area and Ziegenbalg's treatment of the religions of South India, see Daniel Jeyaraj, trans. and ed., *A German Exploration of Indian Society: Ziegenbalg's "Malabarian Heathenism"; An Annotated English Translation with an Introduction and a Glossary* (Chennai and New Delhi: Mylapore Institute for Indigenous Studies and the Indian Society for Promoting Christian Knowledge, 2006), pp. 2, 23-24.

revealing how loathsome heathenism is and how those rooted in it may be saved." In his sweep through history, Ziegenbalg explained how Christianity would rescue the Tamils from "spiritual ignorance" *(akkiyanam)* by contrasting their polytheism and rituals with the story of the one God revealed in Genesis. But while using Paul's letter to the Romans to condemn sexual immorality (Rom. 1:21-32), Ziegenbalg summarized the story of Genesis with breathtaking speed. God did create humans in his image, he instructed the Tamils. In explaining the loss of the "divine image and splendour," he omitted any clarification of marriage as the first of the "orders" God had intended for the world. Indeed, his summary omitted speaking of "male and female" altogether.[32]

Ziegenbalg's major purpose — to spotlight the error of polytheism and idolatry — caused him to postpone explaining Luther's understanding of marriage as the second of the prelapsarian orders. Ziegenbalg instinctively understood that tackling male-female relationships and marriage too early could constitute a fatal misstep. His indictment of spiritual blindness under present Indian false religion moved next to idolatry and then to "witchcraft, legerdemain, the art of hoodwinking by magic," and only at the end to the evils of pagan marriage. "When they marry," he observed, the misguided of India "marry not only among blood relations but also marry two or three women. All kinds of sins such as debauchery, adultery, carnal desires, quarrels and litigations are very widely prevalent in this country. There are no priests who could advise and counsel these people who commit such sins. There are no arbiters who can give punishments suitable to such sins. There are examples to show that everyone lives according to their whims and fancies and lustful desires." He concluded with a classic pietist morphology: hear the Word of God; examine your conscience; repent of sins against God and neighbors; take refuge in Christ as the only true God and the salvation from sin and death; be baptized, renounce sin and spiritual blindness; attend services and receive "with proper preparation" the Lord's Supper; be vigilant against backsliding — and, finally, "reverently do the things pertaining to the body, the deeds of

---

32. For the text, written and then printed at Tranquebar in 1713 in English translation as "The Abomination of Paganism, and the Way for the Pagans to Be Saved," see Andreas Gross, Y. Vincent Kumaradoss, and Heike Liebau, eds., *Halle and the Beginning of Protestant Christianity in India III: Communication between India and Europe* (Halle: Verlag Der Franckeschen Stiftungen zu Halle, 2006), pp. 1453-65, at 1453. Ziegenbalg intentionally omitted the creation of male and female since this would have compelled him to discuss divine coupling in Śaiva cosmogony, which he denounced elsewhere as indecent.

the five senses, the affairs of the family and those matters connected with society according to the decrees of true Scripture."[33]

These writings, among the first from the Danish-German mission in India, reveal more by what they omit than by their exhortation. In an early report to British supporters, Ziegenbalg and fellow missionary Johann Ernst Gründler had confidently expected that the distribution of proper religious books "accompanied with the Operation of the holy Spirit" would turn Indians "away from their abominable Idolatry unto the Living God." But their hopes that by so doing they could produce "wise Governors in the state, faithful Ministers of the Gospel in the Church, and good members of the Common-wealth in Families" reflected the classic Melanchthonian "distant third" position marriage held among the three estates. Ziegenbalg, indebted to Freylinghausen's collection of hymnody, was also a close reader of Johann Arndt. He may also have hesitated to break any new ground for which he could not see support in those who had influenced him.[34]

Since so many of the early converts to Halle's version of Lutheran Christianity had already been baptized as Roman Catholics, the challenge of explaining marriage's standing among God's orders did not immediately demand attention. But if a marriage ceremony did occur within the Danish settlement, the Danish Lutheran ritual of 1685 remained mandatory, and its language remained unambiguous in conveying just that teaching, despite the stark simplicity of the new Jerusalem Church's interior that lacked images or a crucifix, perhaps intentionally to put distance between the pietists and their Roman Catholic and "Hindu" competitors.[35] The Danish-Norwegian ritual for marriage prescribed a ceremony that still ended with a prayer remembering that God the "heavenly Father" made man and woman and instituted marriage. It kept Luther's wording from his wedding booklet, reminding all present of the sacrament of Christ's relationship to the church his bride, of which marriage was the symbol or icon ("og den hellige kirkes, hans bruds, sakramente"), and asking God's blessing on the newly married couple.[36]

---

33. Ziegenbalg, "Abomination," pp. 1459, 1460, and 1462-64, at 1463.

34. *A Letter to the Reverend Mr. Geo. Lewis* (London, 1715), AFSt: H: 146; pp. 25, 2, 1. On Ziegenbalg's indebtedness to Freylinghausen and Arndt, see Daniel Jeyaraj, trans. and ed., *Genealogy of the South Indian Deities: An English Translation of Bartholomäus Ziegenbalg's Original German Manuscript with a Textual Analysis and Glossary* (London and New York: RoutledgeCurzon, 2005), pp. 11-16.

35. Hudson, *Protestant Origins in India*, pp. 50-51.

36. See Anders Nørgaard, "The Mission's Relationship to the Danes," in *Halle and the Beginning of Protestant Christianity I*, pp. 161-207. For the text of the 1685 service, I am grate-

Marriage, both in its celebration and its maintenance as an estate of a godly society, had already by 1706 produced a long history in Danish-Norwegian laws that had taken shape since the Reformation. Marriage decrees in 1582 in Denmark and in 1589 in Norway brought local variations under a degree of control. Although adultery had been the sole basis for dissolution before 1589, desertion "became the most common reason for divorce in the seventeenth and eighteenth century, and the majority of these cases were initiated by women, who often had been left in poverty when their husbands left." The cases resembled those of the Holstein consistory court. Ziegenbalg and his associates could not have been ignorant of these trends. Yet, these European Protestants now had to face a group of indigenous, powerful states with marriage customs that profoundly challenged whatever hopes for spouses the pietists brought to the Indian subcontinent.[37]

According to much later reports, converted Tamils were expected to celebrate marriage in the most unobtrusive way possible. Missionaries retained seating arrangements in worship that respected the segregation of the sexes and the "castes." Their communities were satisfied to take a bridal couple into the modest church buildings unaccompanied by ceremonies or fanfare.[38] Ziegenbalg wrote that a simple procession to the church by the bridal pair (but not including parents) included a sprinkling with rose water, followed by a hymn, a sermon, the exchange of a promise, and the invocation of the Trinity. A closing hymn and a return home to a meal accompanied by the consumption of betel arak (a green leaf and relative of the Muscat nut)

---

ful to the theological librarian in Copenhagen, Minna Giesel, for securing a copy of *Danmarks og Norges Kirke-Ritual . . .* (Copenhagen, 1685); chapter 8, "Om forlovelse og aegteskab," and to my colleague Richard Page for advice on comparing the Danish to the German original. The English rendition would be that God is asked to "bless them with the fruit of life . . . [for] therein is symbolized the sacrament of your dear Son Jesus Christ with the Holy Church, his bride." For the German and a discussion of Luther's reliance upon the Latin, Gregorian sacramentaries, see Albrecht Peters, *Kommentar zu Luthers Katechismen Band 5: Beichte, Haustafel, Traubüchlein* (Göttigen: Vandenhoeck & Ruprecht, 1994), pp. 148-55. So far, Ziegenbalg's Tamil translation of this marriage service has eluded identification in any archive.

37. See Anne Irene Riisoy, *Sexuality, Law, and Legal Practice and the Reformation in Norway* (Leiden and Boston: Brill, 2009), pp. 13-21, 173-79, quotation at 174, for a discussion of Danish law; Holger Fr. Rordam, ed., *Danske Kirkelove: Samt Udvalg af andre Bestemmelser vedørende Kirken, Skolen og de Fattiges Forsørgelse fra Reformationen indtil Christian V Danske Lov, 1536-1683*, 3 vols. (Copenhagen: Selskabet for Danmarks Kirkehistorie, 1883-89).

38. For a summary of the correspondence and description, see Jeyaraj, *Inkulturation in Tranquebar*, pp. 245-50.

116

incorporated local custom. A mild narcotic, the plant perhaps conveyed the "peaceful" disposition of the newly married couple.[39]

The significance converted Tamil Lutherans placed upon observing proper ritual in religious rites besides marriage suggests that the pietist demand for simplicity in the marriage rite may not have been accepted without resistance. Two brothers asked the missionaries to be allowed to hire drummers to accompany a deceased Tamil Christian to the burial site, to give alms to the poor, and to light lamps as was customary among both Catholics and non-Christians. Otherwise, they observed, the pietist Christians would be scorned for behaving as if they "were burying a cat." The hiring of male drummers to make the actual procession to the graveyard (as opposed to the women who engaged in elaborate wailing and performance of "crying songs") forced the missionaries to acknowledge that a stringent abolition of indigenous ritual might endanger the credibility of their version of Christianity among potential converts.[40]

As early as 1712, Ziegenbalg had already expressed concerns about how to handle difficult questions surrounding marriage and wrote to Johann Joachim Lange asking for advice. The Halle theologian replied that he and Francke had pondered the questions and were glad that some of their observations could be of use to the missionaries. But it was not indigenous Tamil marriage customs, but European misbehavior, that preoccupied the missionaries.[41] Danish criticism of the mission had prompted Ziegenbalg to turn to British supporters, resulting by 1710 in what became the Halle-English mission effort. But the involvement of the Church of England, complete with what was still, in theory at least, a quasi-sacramental theology of

39. Jeyaraj, *Inkulturation in Tranquebar,* pp. 245-47. Most of the description relies on the *Hallesche Berichte* I 7: Cont. 368, HB I 4, Cont. 161, conveyed to Europeans in 1709.

40. Jeyaraj, *Inkulturation in Tranquebar,* pp. 245-47. This summarizes the *Hallesche Berichte* I 7: Cont. 368, HB I 4, Cont. 161. For the funeral incident, see *Hallesche Berichte* III 26: Cont. 40; and Jeyaraj, p. 252. On the male drummers and crying songs see Isabelle Clark-Decès, *No One Cries for the Dead: Tamil Dirges, Rowdy Songs, and Graveyard Petitions* (Berkeley, Los Angeles, and London: University of California Press, 2005).

41. ALM/DHM3/5a:15 (Halle, 3 December 1712), Lange to Ziegenbalg and Plütschau. Unfortunately, the letter, like many of the materials in the Leipzig archival collections now at Halle, is nearly illegible. The same applies, as Jeyaraj pointed out, to the critical instructions regarding marriage questions from Christian Wendt, the secretary of the *Missionskolleg* in Copenhagen, in 1724. See Jeyaraj, *Inkulturation in Tranquebar,* pp. 249, 423. The response noted here appears to address questions surrounding the controversy that erupted when Ziegenbalg and Plütschau had intervened in 1708-9 on behalf of an illegitimate child of a Danish soldier and a Tamil woman and a Tamil widow indebted to a Catholic employee of the Danish company.

marriage, did not reflect a commitment to better spouses among European traders in India.

The marriage registers that survive from 1713 to 1729 for the East India Company indicate that no more than 6 marriages per year, and more to the point, in the second half of the eighteenth century a paltry 1,581 marriages, were solemnized in Bengal among the Europeans. By contrast, baptismal records of illegitimate children reveal a substantial practice of cohabitation with indigenous women. Although "less than 7 percent of all European men were known to be married while serving in India, substantially more, anywhere from 20 to 50 percent, were known to be involved in some sort of sexual liaison with a local woman."[42] Brahmin scorn for this European behavior, coupled with tensions over social/caste agreements and customs, forced the issue of spousal relations and sexual sin increasingly to the fore among Ziegenbalg's problems.

Two years before the emergence of the United English East India Company in 1709 in Madras, a wedding transgressed the boundary between the right-hand and left-hand "castes" in the so-called black town that revealed how explosive the question of proper spouses could be. The procession had led to a riot among the Tamils and resulted in the intervention of the Company's Madras council. Despite a new constitutional basis for the Company that implied a heightened degree of royal and parliamentary oversight, in either old or new form the Company claimed to exercise sovereignty, not the Crown. So confident of its own prerogatives over all matters — including the adjudication of marital disputes and behavior — were the English company's representatives that "Upon arriving at Masulipatnam, John Pitt . . . refused to salute or acknowledge as legitimate the royal standard flying on Fort St. George." Ziegenbalg would now discover in similar fashion that even royal Danish support for his attempt to put teeth into the law of marriage and to demand sexual discipline among Europeans in order that they exemplify Christian piety and marital fidelity did not translate into compliance by the Danish East India Company commandants.[43]

Brahmin scorn for European sexual license in their midst made it almost impossible for the pietist missionaries to hold up the estate of marriage as Luther had portrayed it (more richly blessed than any other). Ziegenbalg for his

42. Durba Ghosh, *Sex and the Family in Colonial India: The Making of Empire* (Cambridge: Cambridge University Press, 2006), pp. 39, 40.

43. Philip J. Stern, *The Company-State: Corporate Sovereignty and the Early Modern Foundations of the British Empire in India* (Oxford and New York: Oxford University Press, 2011), pp. 174, 173, 165.

part blamed the Brahmins for most of what he found wrong on the Indian subcontinent. But Ziegenbalg's struggle to understand the local culture and rituals of the *paraiyar* (agricultural) and *cuttirar* (artisans, merchants) Tamils also drew a cautious response from Francke himself. Most of Ziegenbalg's readers in Europe only dimly understood the peculiarity of the Tamil region's religious and social categories. In contrast to northern India where both Brahman and Sanskritic culture had deep roots, in South India "not only was the Brahmin population fairly small but there had been a substantial resistance to Brahminism and Sanskritic culture in earlier times." Ziegenbalg grasped this faster than most other Europeans. The fact that the property-owning "castes" were summarily reduced to the designation *shudra* meant that the *vellalar* were (in classical Brahmin terms) nothing better than menial servants. In the Tamil region, they were property owners and self-consciously far superior to the *paraiyar.* These two ranks of society remained Ziegenbalg's major targets for conversion.[44]

Ziegenbalg sent his magnum opus, an exhaustive examination of "Malabar heathenism," to Europe in 1711. His analysis of South Indian society and his 1713 work on the panoply of South Indian gods attracted Francke's attention just as the uproar over marriage in which Halle was embroiled intensified and as Wernigerode's new superintendent began his campaign of encouraging pietist sentiments among the county's faithful. Francke decided to allow only a select few of his most trusted allies full access to Ziegenbalg's works. Pressed by the success of his Foundations, Francke turned oversight of the Tranquebar mission to Christian Benedikt Michaelis, an accomplished member of the Oriental College since 1702, an adept in both biblical languages and the Amharic/Ge'ez of Ethiopia — but not conversant with the Tamil culture of the Indian subcontinent.[45] Michaelis reacted nervously to Ziegenbalg's work. He noted especially the sexual immorality of the people and their trust in "good works," and argued against the broad dissemination of the two books.[46]

---

44. Ravindiran Vaitheespara, "Christianity, Missionary Orientalism and the Origins of Tamil Modernity," in *Halle and the Beginning of Protestant Christianity in India II: Christian Mission in the Indian Context,* ed. Andreas Gross, Y. Vincent Kumaradoss, Heike Liebau (Halle: Verlag Der Franckeschen Stiftungen zu Halle, 2006), pp. 973-1017, at 976.

45. On Christian Benedikt Michaelis, see the entry by R. Kittel in Johann Herzog and Albert Hauck, eds., *Realencyklopädie für protestantische Theologie und Kirche,* 3rd ed. (Leipzig: Hinrichs, 1903), pp. 53-54; for Michaelis's reaction, see Jeyaraj, *A German Exploration of Indian Society,* pp. 53, 35.

46. Dharampal-Frick, *Indien,* pp. 100-105, 353. On the circumstances surrounding the

The censorship of Ziegenbalg's efforts was complicated. Francke allowed his views of Hinduism to have rather wide dissemination.[47] Ziegenbalg's conviction that Hinduism was monotheistic — based on the Tamil source *Tirkāla cakkaram*[48] — appealed to Francke, and parts of the introduction to Ziegenbalg's first works did appear in the *Hallesche Berichte* of 1710. Ziegenbalg also laid special "stress on the high moral standards of the Hindus," but he had to mention[49] "the depiction of the undifferentiated unity of the divine in the sexual union of a divine couple."[50] The overtly sexual nature of the divine — even if one supreme being predominated — undercut the Christian doctrine of monogamy. Although a spiritual "elite" in India might eschew polygamy and the sexual antics of "gods," the prevalence of such beliefs among the South Indian peoples accounts for the hesitancy with which Francke and his contemporaries viewed the writings of their colleague on the southeast coast of India.

To complicate matters further, Ziegenbalg may not have understood the long debates among Brahmins over the relative values of polygamy and monogamy. By the seventeenth century, a Tamil version of the story of Amator, who had been baptized in 1608, related how powerful family pressures could be deployed to persuade converts from Christianity to renounce their faith. Efforts by the converted Jesupattan to abolish polygamy in his caste had produced mixed results. The decision of tribal headmen to adopt monogamy may have been "an example of the process of Sanskritization." Monogamy and polygamy had served as indigenous status markers in Indian society long before the European Protestants arrived. Some could have interpreted the Protestant demand for monogamous marriage as an opportunity for achieving better social rank in Tamil society; others could have seen it as an

---

writing and selective publication of Ziegenbalg's two massive works, see Jeyaraj, *Genealogy of the South Indian Deities,* pp. 1-34, and Jeyaraj, *A German Exploration of Indian Society,* pp. 1-58, especially at 44.

47. Will Sweetman, "The Prehistory of Orientalism: Colonialism and the Textual Basis for Bartholomäus Ziegenbalg's Account of Hinduism," in *Halle and the Beginning of Protestant Christianity in India II,* pp. 923-49.

48. *Bibliotheca Malabarica: Bartholomäus Zigenbalg's Tamil Library,* ed. and trans. Will Sweetman, with R. Ilakkuvan (Pondicherry: French Institute of Pondicherry, 2012).

49. Sweetman, "Prehistory," pp. 931-32, at 932, 934. For the complex history of the authorship and importance of the moral teachings in the *Tirukkuṟaḷ* for Tamil literary history and European assessments of Tamil culture, see Stuart Blackburn, "Corruption and Redemption: The Legend of Valluvar and Tamil Literary History," *Modern Asian Studies* 34, no. 2 (2000): 449-82, especially for Ziegenbalg's and the Jesuit Constantin Beschi's assessments at 455, 458, and 468.

50. Sweetman, "Prehistory," p. 943.

inconvenient and irrational choice that threatened social and economic well-being.[51]

In attempting to detail the major festivals of the South Indians to Europeans, Ziegenbalg carefully described the feast of Tirukaliyāṇam. Depicting the events of each succeeding day, however, Ziegenbalg explained the purpose of the feast only at the end of the description: in honor of Īśvara, or Shiva, but as he uncomfortably noted, in honor of an occasion when "Īśvara caused his consort Pārvatī to be born as a daughter to Teṭcakaṉ or Dakṣa. Afterwards, when she was twelve years old, he married her again and took her to his [abode] Kailāsa."[52]

Ziegenbalg also noted the mid-January festival of Pongal, celebrated on the first day of the month of *Tai,* a rice harvest festival honoring the cattle that did the hard work in the fields, observed by every religious group among the Tamils. The newly harvested rice was boiled with milk and offered to the sun before being consumed in large quantities by celebrating devotees.[53] If one reads Ziegenbalg's two books in tandem as he intended, one cannot escape the conclusion that despite his observations on many aspects of Tamil life and society, spousal relations remained a profoundly difficult topic. As a result, Johann Lucas Niekamp's review of what the missionary efforts had accomplished thirty-four years into the story focused primarily on the problem of idolatry and the challenges of sexual morality and of *jāti,* the familial community strictures and customs of "caste."[54]

In his two great works, Ziegenbalg could not forbear to return — repeatedly — to his sense of embarrassment and barely concealed outrage at the sexual antics of the South Indian gods and their worshipers. In the 1711 work on Malabar heathenism, Ziegenbalg expressed admiration for the *ñanikal (Gnanigol,* i.e., "wise") because they among all the South Indians understood the importance of "interiority" and "reject[ed] all divine beings

51. Ines G. Zupanov, *Disputed Mission: Jesuit Experiments and Brahmanical Knowledge in Seventeenth-Century India* (Oxford and New Delhi: Oxford University Press India, 1999), pp. 218-24, 325-26, quotation at 223.

52. Jeyaraj, *Genealogy of the South Indian Deities,* p. 173.

53. Jeyaraj, *Genealogy of the South Indian Deities,* p. 221; for the description of Pongal, see Wilhelm Caland's German edition of the *Malabarisches Heidenthum* (Amsterdam: Koninklijke Akademie van Wetenschappen, 1926), p. 140.

54. See Daniel Jeyaraj, "Mission Reports from South India and Their Impact on the Western Mind: The Tranquebar Mission of the Eighteenth Century," in *Converting Colonialism: Visions and Realities in Mission History, 1706-1914,* ed. Dana L. Robert (Grand Rapids and Cambridge: Eerdmans, 2008), pp. 21-42, at 26-27.

and the [external] ways of [religious] life." In introducing Europeans to Brahma, Ziegenbalg recounted the story of the sage Vasistha, "born by a whore whom Brahma had slept with," a tale so outrageous that even the South Indians themselves "confess that their religious scripture has an impure origin." The gods' misbehavior proved them to be "partly adulterers, partly lewd beings, partly thieves, partly arrogant spirits and partly miserable beings . . . this is because one reads in their stories that the deities have indulged in adultery and caused children to be born out of wedlock."

Their followers sinned accordingly since, "among the South Indians, the sin of adultery is very common indeed." The wealthy attempted to escape the cycle of their sins "by giving their own daughters in marriage to poor men and entrust them with enough wealth to begin their [decent] life." Marriage could thus be a release from reincarnation if one married in the right "caste," but Ziegenbalg constrasted the scandal of Brahma's two concubines and the curse of his wife with the superiority of the Śaiva Hindus like Civavakkiyar, who disdained image worship and who alone possessed "a reasonably correct perception of the nature of bliss."[55]

Two years later, in the *Genealogy of the South Indian Deities,* Ziegenbalg expanded upon his original guarded comments by admitting that "we reluctantly spend our time examining the heathen foolishness because it contains many immodest and offensive histories." Just how offensive those stories were was not left to the imagination of European readers. Samtānalakshmī, the goddess of marriage, appeared in his explanations alongside Bhūmidevī, the goddess of the earth, whose son Manmatha Ziegenbalg identified as the "god of carnal love or Cupid." Lust stirred up in women by Manmatha was matched by the mischief of his consort Rati, "Venus," and "just as her husband inspires unchastity in women, she is unchaste with men."

Ziegenbalg did attempt to explain that the "supreme being" or Parāparavastu contained both male and female energy but signaled his admiration for the Jain and his distaste for South Indian devotion by explaining that the central image of the supreme being "everywhere in the temples is the Linga. It represents both kinds of sex organs which nature wishes to keep hidden. It is worshipped in all the temples of the Śivabhaktikāras three times daily with drink, food and burnt offerings made by the Brahmins."

55. Jeyaraj, *A German Exploration of Indian Society,* pp. 77, 84, 100, 118, 123, 221, 222-23, 225-26. Jeyaraj's translation seems to imply that Ziegenbalg meant the "Jains" in describing those who rejected the use of images. Ziegenbalg, when he does mean "Jains," uses the Tamil *camanar.* See the review of Jeyaraj's edition of the *Genealogy* by Will Sweetman in *Contemporary South Asia* 16, no. 1 (March 2008): 122-23, at 112.

Ordinary men and women, Ziegenbalg concluded, were easily taken in by a notion that what happened in the realm of the gods and that of men was identical even though no one could understand why the gods should be interested in sexual activity and the propagation of children. Only the elite among the South Indians correctly concluded that this was a kind of image or ideal type; "though the common people accept the stories written about the gods as true the educated people protest against them and state that all these things are narrated of the gods symbolically."

Ziegenbalg's observation of South Indian sexual behavior, however, led him to conclude that most of his potential converts understood their gods' activities as anything but symbolic. The prevalence of dancing temple girls devoted to Subramanya persuaded him of this. So, for that matter, did the devotion to Lakshmi and Bhūmidevī, the consorts of Vishnu. Even though Lakshmi was the goddess of marriage and wealth, she was named "Mahalaksmi," and the "Śivabhaktikāras place her image in the temple of Īśvara and worship her everywhere." For him, she was hard to distinguish from Manmatha, the kindler of lust among women, and Rati, who exercised malign influence on the lusts of males.[56]

The local village gods, Ziegenbalg knew, were far more important to ordinary believers than the denizens of the larger temples. But here too, Ziegenbalg began his explications by noting that Māriyamman, the great local guardian and protectress against measles and smallpox (who could nonetheless visit these afflictions upon those who did not sufficiently venerate her), was feared along with the demon Kāttaruṇaṇ, a Brahman bastard raised by a pariah and "given to adultery" who "disgraced all the Pariah-women of the same place . . . [so that] people [were] afraid of Kāttaruṇaṇ more than of Māriyamman." The over 330 million minor gods were as bad, their behavior testifying that they were "unholy, sinful, unsound and filthy and [were] against all wisdom, holiness, righteousness and truth. . . . one might wonder how, having such a [high degree of] natural understanding, the South Indians could believe in such foolish fables."

Among these, the father of Devendra copulated with a female giant, bringing forth the giants known as the Acuras. Devendra himself ravished the wife of a sage and was cursed by having his body sprout 1,000 vaginas, but to spare him excess humiliation, these appear to humans as eyes. Ziegenbalg contrasted such outrages with Jains and their understanding of marital virtue and insight. He rhapsodized in his writings about Jain belief in a wisdom that

---

56. Jeyaraj, *Genealogy of the South Indian Deities,* pp. 40, 44, 81, 85, 99, 103.

can be obtained by men who still live a chaste married life, have some profession, and make the offerings. This *Jnana* (wisdom) manifests itself in a person of true virtue. Those who are married and live in the world but follow the principles of virtue can be considered wise people. "In general, he is a wise man who knows what god has commanded and does accordingly."[57]

The European pietists' information on the status of marriage, women, and human sexuality appears to have come exclusively from male interlocutors. What these men chose to convey, and what they hoped the Europeans would understand or do in return, remains unclear.[58] The challenge of understanding marriage among the Tamils was also complicated because many of the early converts were servants or slaves who could not marry. The problem, from the perspective of Ziegenbalg and Gründler, was that these people could not marry legally but they could and did engage in sexual activity without incurring the disapproval of their masters, since through such "unclean sleeping together" the number of the slaves increased.[59]

Ziegenbalg continued to focus his studies on the educated, but still lower, orders of Indian society, and 147 *shudras* (*chattier* caste) constituted over half of the convert population of 250 Christians, who were divided on language lines between "Portuguese" and "Malabar" groups by 1720.[60] As he reminded European critics shortly before his death, pretending to attend to purely "spiritual" needs of the Indians would not do. Ziegenbalg concluded that missionaries "also have to see to it that the bodily needs of most of them are redressed."[61]

Ziegenbalg's empathy for the bodily necessities and realities of everyday life among his potential converts may have stemmed in part from his own decision to marry. In so deciding he violated the wishes of Francke, who opposed marriage for missionaries. Francke's problems with his own marriage may have influenced his negative reaction to the wives of other pastors. He seems to have preferred the apostolic witness of Paul for his missionaries, despite his own choice.

57. Jeyaraj, *Genealogy of the South Indian Deities*, pp. 122, 146, 148, 153-58, 161.

58. James Lockhart, *Of Things of the Indies: Essays Old and New in Early Latin American History* (Stanford: Stanford University Press, 1999), p. 99 on the concept of "double mistaken identity."

59. AFSt/M II C 5: 21; cited also in Jeyaraj, *Inkulturation in Tranquebar*, pp. 209-11 n. 220.

60. Hugald Grafe, "The First Lutheran Indian Christians in Tranquebar," in *Halle and the Beginning of Protestant Christianity in India I*, pp. 209-28, at 213.

61. AFSt/M I C 11:15; see for a discussion of the sharp exchanges produced in 1719 by such criticism, Nørgaard, "Mission's Relationship to the Danes," pp. 189-91.

From the perspective of the women who first served as missionary wives in India, Maria Dorothea Ziegenbalg and Utilia Elisabeth Gründler enjoyed mutual support but had no public duties in the ministry of their husbands. Indeed, Francke forbade them to have any. The strict separation of the "private" from the public sphere in the missionaries' own households suggests why European writing on Tamil spousal relations showed such little understanding of or sympathy for the role of Tamil women. Nor did the pastors' wives serve as models or teachers of Indian convert women. That oddity did not reflect doubts about the European women's social or educational backgrounds. Among the missionary women who married the Halle pastors, most were "daughters of pastors or civil servants in the Empire or Denmark, the very young daughters of Halle missionaries in India, daughters of merchants and of employees of the Danish, English and Asiatic East India Companies in India, as well as daughters of officers in the armies of these trading companies, besides widows and widowed missionary wives living in India."[62] Most would have expected to have conventional marriages, but perhaps more of an active role as a pastor's wife as they had observed in Europe than what Francke appeared to be willing to concede to them in Tranquebar.

The same ambivalence regarding the role of wives extended to Halle's British supporters. By the time the Society for Promoting Christian Knowledge told the English mission at Madras how the missionaries Benjamin Schultze, Johann Ernst Geister, and Johann Anton Sartorius were to comport themselves, the Society found it unnecessary to mention marriage and the support of spouses. In the 1735 description of "the good Disposition and Behaviour necessary in a Protestant Missionary," sound learning and piety took pride of place. They were to consult with each other, baptize, catechize, preach, avoid ambition for worldly profit, and honor "those that are the Seniors." Not a single counsel, not even a mention, of Christian marriage accompanied the Society's admonitions other than a final warning that the men were to flee "all lusts and Pollutions of the world." The apostolic model

---

62. Erika Pabst, "The Wives of Missionaries: Their Experiences in India," in *Halle and the Beginning of Protestant Christianity in India II,* pp. 685-704, at 686. Ziegenbalg was delighted with his marriage and made a point of including greetings not only from his own but also from Gründler's spouse in a Latin letter to the SPCK sent shortly before his death. See UTC-Bangalore Library Archives, SPCK Film Vol 2, 15 January 1719, p. 176, "Bina nostra dilectissima bene valent, Tibi, Tuaquae Dilectissimae ac filiolo cum nobis a DEO O.M. omnem anima et corporis praeponita cum precibus." Dorothea Ziegenbalg was just as positive about her marriage "with my dearest husband and he with me." See her 10 October 1716 letter in *Halle and the Beginning of Protestant Christianity in India III,* pp. 1363-65, at 1364.

of mission — the long-standing Protestant fascination with Paul in particular — continued to shape missionary efforts in Europe despite the hesitation to endorse Catholic praise for celibacy.[63]

In truth, however, a barely concealed tension over spouses in Christian life that had simmered quietly for some years exploded by 1713. The episode revealed that the mission would not tolerate intermarriage of European pietists with converted Tamil women. The immediate case in its turn triggered a series of moves toward the "Europeanization" of the mission effort and toward the official legal and theological teaching that marriage was solely a civil matter, quite contrary to Ziegenbalg's initial hopes and convictions.[64]

In October of 1708 Ziegenbalg had rejoiced at the arrival of a new missionary, Johann Ernst Gründler, accompanied by a thirty-one-year-old theology student who had paid his own way to India. Throwing himself into the work of the mission, Polycarp Jordan took on the task of handling the money and property affairs of the experiment but struggled with the Tamil language, a task for which he showed little aptitude. He enjoyed more robust health than the other Europeans, and in Ziegenbalg's opinion could have worked in India forever. But without prior warning Halle learned on 6 October 1713 that Jordan intended to take the first Danish ship available and return to Europe. His decision was all the more unsettling since Plütschau also returned, leaving Ziegenbalg and Gründler shorthanded. The real reason for Jordan's return, however, was kept a secret in both Halle and Copenhagen: he intended to marry a converted Tamil girl. Upon the refusal of his European coreligionists to approve of his intent, he decided to leave India for good.[65]

Dismayed at Jordan's decision, Francke sent New Year's greetings with the announcement that Jordan was to be ordained in Tranquebar. He

63. "Instructions for the English Missionaries," original AFSt 2: C: 2 9, London, December 1735, reprinted in translation in *Halle and the Beginning of Protestant Christianity in India III*, pp. 1391-1400, at 1392, 1394, 1399. See on the apostolic model, Hanco Jürgens, "German Indology *Avant La Lettre*: The Experiences of the Halle Missionaries in Southern India, 1750-1810," in *Sanskrit and Orientalism: Indology and Comparative Linguistics in Germany, 1750-1958*, ed. Doug McGetchin, Peter Park, and Damodar SarDesai (New Delhi: Manohar, 2004), pp. 43-84. I am grateful to Will Sweetman for alerting me to this source.

64. Anders Nørgaard, *Mission und Obrigkeit: Die Dänisch-hallische Mission in Tranquebar 1706-1845*, trans. Eberhard Harbsmeier (Gütersloh: Gütersloher Verlagshaus-Gerd Mohn, 1988), pp. 109-40.

65. Jordan's career can be followed in Arno Lehmann, ed., *Alte Briefe aus Indien: Unveröffentlichte Briefe von Bartholomäus Ziegenbalg 1706-1719* (Berlin: Evangelische Verlagsanstalt, 1957), pp. 108, 136, 154, 220, 257, 332, 381, 401.

should, Francke urged, "in the name of the Lord stay where he is and not weaken." Unimpressed, Jordan returned to Europe, where he became the object of a whispering campaign in which he was rumored to entertain a special aversion to marriage. Writing from Merbitz in July of 1716 to Francke, the outraged Jordan made it plain that even with the blessing of his superiors, "I am not willing to marry," but this had nothing to do with an aversion to the estate, nor because of rumors being bruited about that since all the missionaries now wanted to marry he would shortly take a wife.

More to the point, he was dismayed to learn that in Halle and Berlin word spread that he had slandered the work of the mission, doubting that a single soul among the heathen had been successfully converted. Suspecting Ziegenbalg of trying to embarrass him, Jordan informed Francke that the disparagement of the mission's success could be gleaned far more easily from the massive correspondence from Tranquebar than it could from any words he had spoken. In any event, he was determined never again to say anything about India. And about his intent to marry a Tamil woman in India, Jordan was as good as his word; he never mentioned the subject again — nor did his patrons.[66]

Within a year of Jordan's departure, Ziegenbalg approached the *Missionskolleg* in Copenhagen for permission to erect a consistory court that would handle marriage matters, a request they approved. The court incarnated the dilemma over who should investigate spousal misbehavior and whether the estate lies primarily within the civil or the religious domain. The Danish law revision of 1683 had solidified the absolutist claims of the monarchy advanced in 1660, and Christian V's code outlined the bounds of ecclesiastical law. The capacity of the Danish East India Company to resist the claims of this royally grounded code by appealing to the privileges of their own charter mirrored in many respects the behavior of the English East India Company.[67]

---

66. The above paragraph citations are from AFSt/M 1C8: 3, from August Hermann Francke, 1 January 1715; Jordan to Francke, AFSt/M 1 C 9: 35, quotation at 1 recto; Rigsarkivet Kopenhagen 600 Trankebar-missionen 1712-1740 Efterretninger om missionen Nr. 2 (6 October 1714 and 18 December 1714) (pp. 46, 47). They contain the terse notification by Ziegenbalg and Gründler that Jordan had decided to return and that he would have to settle accounts with Francke since he had received an additional thirty-six Reichstaler as a salary supplement. I can find no surviving evidence of the name of the intended bride; she probably came from the "Portuguese" Jordan was instructing, the Tamils who spoke a Portuguese creole. Subject to Danish law, this group lay outside Tamil social, family, and political structures.

67. I thank Professor Per Andersen of the University of Aarhus for guidance on the stand-

The court for Tranquebar matched almost exactly the Danish *Tamperret* or court for matrimonial causes that emerged after the Reformation. Each diocesan court included both clergy and a lay judge, the latter the royal administrative officer for the area. Meeting four times a year *(quatuor tempora)*, the *"tamper"* courts (in the vernacular) dealt with marriage cases until, in the second half of the eighteenth century, they were abolished and their jurisdiction given over to the secular, royal courts. The conventional view that this newly established court in Tranquebar balanced the "two kingdoms" doctrine of Luther is belied by the fragmentary evidence from adjudicated cases and by the evidence that it was anxiety over the sexual immorality of Tamil women that emerged as the primary focus of the court's activities.

At the level of official law, the sitting court included the missionaries, but the king's order stipulated that the commandant of the Company preside at any session, following the model of a Danish diocesan court. Ziegenbalg brought back the royal order establishing this *Kapitelgericht* along with his own new wife — whom he had married even though Francke refused to officiate at the wedding. Ziegenbalg's apparent triumph, however, immediately ran into the refusal of the Company's commander Christen Brun Lundegaard to preside over the court. He argued that he had received no orders to do so from the Company's own directors *(Vorstand)*.

His refusal revealed a deep lack of deference to the civil as well as the religious authority of an absolute Lutheran monarch who, like all other such princes, at least officially exercised the role of *summus episcopus*. Official theology and royal authority apparently did not impress Lundegaard. Nor did the Crown choose to contest the Company's tenacious obstruction of an ecclesiastical court introduced into its territory. As in Denmark, this quasi-*Tamperret* court's leading officer was bound to follow Danish law as laid out in the code of 1683, but the law allowed some individual judicial discretion. On this basis, the court in Tranquebar exceeded the strict limits of its founding as a marriage tribunal. Tensions about jurisdictional ques-

---

ing of the court; see Andersen's essay "Elegant Jurisprudence in Seventeenth Century Denmark: Cross-Border Influences on the Authorship of Scavenius, Resen and Bornemann," in *Clio Themis: Revue électronique d' histoire du droit* (accessed 15 June 2011: http://www .cliothemis.com/Elegant-Jurisprudence-in). The legal records holdings of the Ostindisk Compagni, 1618-1730 in the Rigsarkivet do not include the records of the *Kapitelgericht* that so far have eluded identification. I am grateful to archivist Eric Gobel for also checking the Danish Chancellery *(Danske Kancelli)* and the *Missionskollegiet*. Specific cases or decisions from the surviving legal papers of the Company are noted below.

tions, however, faded in significance compared to disputes about the "Europeanization" of the mission. The marriage tribunal provided the forum for these disagreements.[68]

Ziegenbalg did not — mercifully — live to see the near collapse during the 1720s of his efforts to convert the Tamils, nor the use of the consistory court in ways he could never have approved. Yet, what really was his theology of marriage? His pragmatic assessment of Tamil society and his equally practical arguments for needing a wife suggest that he regarded a spouse as a helper, of course, but perhaps also as a true friend. Since his married life was so short — a mere five years — his views remain nearly as difficult to recover as those of his Tamil congregants. Gradually, Ziegenbalg came to recognize the importance of the peasant landowners and warrior contingent of Tamil society (the *vellalar*), but his initial refusal to segregate these persons of higher standing from the *paraiyar* and his disdain for the use of the *tali* as a symbol of marital standing gradually gave way to a more depressed if realistic assessment of how familial and social alliances worked in the Tamil world. At one level, one might understand the pietist fondness for "interiority" as a confirmation that Ziegenbalg, like Francke and the other Halle authors who had responded to Thomasius, preferred to think of marriage in such a "spiritual" manner that he never quite succeeded in reconciling that ideal with the "earthly" dimensions of sex and friendship.[69]

The struggle to integrate interiorized spirituality with bodily existence remained an unresolved dilemma, not only for Ziegenbalg but also for his

68. This summarizes Nørgaard, *Mission und Obrigkeit,* pp. 101-40; his reliance upon the "two kingdoms" solution is on pp. 113-15. The history of the church courts for Denmark to 1683 can be followed in Rordam, *Dankse Kirkelove;* for more detail on the actual functioning of these courts, see Anne Riising, "Tamperrettens function og dompraksis," in *Festskrift til Johan Hvidtfeldt, Arkivvaesenet,* ed. Peter Kr. Iversen, Knud Prange, and Sigurd Rambusch (Copenhagen: Arkivvæsenet, 1978), pp. 393-412. I am grateful to Per Andersen for this reference. The extant legal records of the company are located in the Rigsarkivet, Ostindisk Compagni, 1618-1730: Tranquebarske Justisprotokoller 1690-1732: VA XIV 5 fasciles (in very poor condition; several documents are missing).

69. I wonder, therefore, about Dharampal-Frick's conclusion when she suggests that his description of the "families" within Tamil society and the observation that no one could marry outside of them did not imply a positive or a negative judgment. See *Indien,* p. 239, citing Ziegenbalg; Wilhelm Caland, ed., *Ausführliche Beschreibung des Malabarisches Heidenthums darinnen aus dieser heiden eigenen Schriften ihre Principia und Lehr-satze sowohl in Theologicis als Philosophicis umständlich entdecket und zur dienlichen Unterricht dem geliebten Europa communicirt warden . . .* (Amsterdam: Akademie van het Wetenschappen, Verhandelingen Afd. Letterkund, N.R. 25-3, 1926; orig. Tranquebar, 1711, handwritten), p. 198.

successors. In part, Johann Arndt's classic *True Christianity,* which Ziegenbalg read for his nightly devotions, may have contributed to the tension. At least some commentators have concluded that Arndt's concern for "hidden wisdom" led him so far into the speculative that many of his contemporary Lutheran critics suspected that he held to a notion of a "heavenly body of Christ" that was radically separate from the mere "flesh of Adam." Such ancient Christian heresies had been condemned, for they separated the human and divine natures of Christ. Ziegenbalg avoided stumbling by maintaining his commitment to Lutheran dogmatics. But the tension in his generation's struggle with the earthly surroundings of South Indian life and his prospective converts' obvious dedication to the pursuit of spiritual truth remained unresolved, especially in the area of marital relations.[70]

III

These unresolved tensions grew into outright divisions that began to trouble the SPCK patrons, an ominous portent of events that between 1720 and 1750 moved the hopes for better spouses into the arena of civil and legal control. Joseph Collett, governor of Fort St. George, had communicated to the Society his conviction that the missionaries enjoyed all the protection and help "that is in our Power to give them," but "the Prejudice & Interests among the Malabar" appeared to be "so strong that it seems impossible to Surmount them by the bare force of reason . . . being expelled [from] their respective castes is to them what Exomunicon [*sic*] is to us." Rather than concentrating on the practical question of how to preach the gospel in the face of "caste" prejudices, however, Collett criticized what he saw as increasingly divisive theological disputes among the missionaries — divisions that expressed themselves in disagreements about how to encourage Christian behavior among the converted.

Rehearsing his unhappiness in a letter written ten years after his initial 1716 experience, he admitted that his criticism of the missionary journal reports might offend some, but he remained adamant. To William Stevenson, the Anglican chaplain in Madras, he quoted extensively from his original let-

70. See Hermann Geyer, "'Die pur lautere Essenz und helles Licht': Verschmelzung von Alchemie und Theologie in Johann Arndt's 'Vier Büchern vom wahren Christentum'" (1605-10), in *Antike Weisheit und kulturelle Praxis: Heremetismus in der Frühen Neuzeit,* ed. Anne-Charlott Trepp and Hartmut Lehmann (Göttingen: Vandenhoeck & Ruprecht, 2001), pp. 81-101, at 97.

ter sent to Ziegenbalg and Gründler in which he had asked: "Why are useless Controversies and Scholastick Notions brought into the remote parts of the world? . . . Here we ought to preach neither the Doctrine of Luther, nor Calvin, nor of any Church, but only the Doctrine of Jesus Christ." Divisive theological disputes ought to be banned from the mission field, since they are "a Reproach to Christians, a stumbling Block to Unbelievers and do the greatest Disservice to Religion."[71]

The English insistence upon a pragmatic and simple approach to spreading Christianity provides a context for understanding why the debates about the exercise of authority over Christian marriage turned into more than a theoretical exchange. Surviving letters from men and women destined for the rigors of foreign missions included conventional expressions of thanks addressed to August Hermann or Gotthilf August Francke (for arranging their meetings and subsequent marriages), but they universally avoided speaking of marriage's theological or legal standing. They concentrated instead on the estate's pragmatic value for pastoral labor, emphasizing often the need for mutual support and understanding in conditions of severe physical and psychological stress. They confirmed the growing emphasis upon the "this-worldly" and purely legal-contractual view of spousal relations.[72]

The reason for this pragmatic shift lay in the arrival in 1719 of the Danish pastoral candidate Nikolaus Dal, the German-speaking pastor Benjamin Schultze, and the unordained student Johann Heinrich Kistemacher. Within a year, Kistemacher found himself hauled before the *Kapitelgericht,* presided over by the colony's commandant. Since the court was authorized only to allow missionaries to oversee the discipline of marriage issues among converts, the trial was patently irregular. Even the most liberal reading of the Company's prerogatives under Danish law would not justify what amounted to using a diocesan court as a general court of inquiry for the Company's purposes, even if invited to do so by Schultze. Strictly speaking, the Company should have called its own court into session; the willingness of Schultze — and the commandant — to use the *Kapitelgericht,* however, stood as a signal for Schultze's conviction that European institutions and authorities had to advance more aggressively the objectives of missionary activity.

---

71. UTC-Bangalore Library Archives, SPCK Correspondence, Vol. 2: #5624, 19 September 1717; Nr. 9156, 21 February 1726/27. On Collett's dismissive view of religious controversies (Christian or non-Christian), see Stern, *The Company-State,* pp. 175-76.

72. For examples, see the letters of Maria Catharina Koeppen and her husband Johann Ulrich Koeppen to Francke, Francke Nachlaß, Stab/F 13,1/3, 21, 24, 25 (1723); see also Pabst, "Wives of Missionaries," pp. 690-95.

Forced to apologize to the "Europeanizing" and tyrannical Schultze, who had taken an intense dislike to him, Kistemacher saw his career in Tranquebar effectively ended before it began; he died unordained two years later. More ominously, Schultze, who was to be twice spurned when he offered marriage to the widow of the recently deceased Gründler, turned increasingly against Dal. Nikolaus Dal, for his part, became so embittered over the trial that he denounced Schultze in the most derogatory terms as a murderer of the "unhappy student" *(unseelige Student)*. Incensed at Schultze's attempt to impose a European-style consistory that targeted Tamil women, he began to consider marrying one of these converted fellow Christians.[73]

Dal's decision to marry an indigenous woman sprang, as he explained in a later letter, from several conclusions he had reached about the dangers of marrying European women. The salary of a missionary was insufficient to support a European wife. But far more serious was the fate of European children who would have to be sent back to Europe since otherwise they "can only be raised to become soldiers and sailors." Intending to avoid these perils, Dal announced his intentions in 1723.[74] Unfortunately for Dal, the invited interference of the Company in the legal affairs of the mission produced a sharp rebuttal from the *Missionskolleg,* authored by the jurist and *Kanzleirat* Seyr Mahling. The mission, he reminded everyone, was legally accountable to the king solely through the college.

August Hermann Francke contributed his strong endorsement of Mahling's point of view, and the *Missionskolleg* reinforced their argument a few months later in a letter sent to the Company commander in Tranquebar. Despite the attempt to sort out the boundary between the legal privileges of the missionaries and the Company, however, no one clarified the precise standing of marriage in this dispute and just who exercised jurisdiction over marital relations, separations, and divorce.[75] But Dal's loathing for Schultze un-

73. Nørgaard, *Mission und Obrigkeit,* pp. 134-35; Dal to Christian Benedict Michaelis, 1 September 1725: AFSt 1B 1 p. 2; see also AFSt I H 3:9 1722/14/3 to Francke.

74. AFSt/M 1 H 3: 24, 13 September 1723, and B 2:43 Dal to Francke, 20 September 1725, 1 verso.

75. Nørgaard, *Mission und Obrigkeit,* pp. 130-32. Wilhelm Germann, *Ziegenbalg und Plütschau: Die Gründungsjahre der Trankebarischen Mission: Ein Beitrag zur Geschichte des Pietismus nach handschriftlichen Quellen und ältesten Drücken,* 2 vols. (Erlangen: Verlag Andreas Deichert, 1868), 1:245-46, omits entirely the furor around Polycarp Jordan's marriage plans. Germann agrees that Gründler and Ziegenbalg opposed intermarriage (1:292 n. 1) and recounts Dal's letter to Lange but dismisses Dal as far too critical. Germann's laudatory comments about the "restoration period" of the mission are confined to Pressier and Walther; they do not include Dal; see pp. 340 n. 1, 374.

doubtedly contributed to the dashing of his hopes for a Tamil spouse. Schultze's account of his colleague's plans hinted darkly at sexual misbehavior. In October of 1725 in a letter to the Danish mission authorities, Schultze explained that Dal was furious at the inspector of the schoolchildren, Otto Friedrich Radewitz, because Radewitz had — at the request of Dal's prospective in-laws — requested that he act as their young daughter's protector. Although, Schultze wrote, Radewitz could not discover what Dal "in his closed room had arranged with the little black girl," rumors had spread among the entire student body, and Dal blamed Radewitz for foiling his plans.[76]

Stung by the opposition — if not outright plotting — of his coworkers and European authorities, Dal penned a sardonic inquiry to Lange in Halle, asking the pietist leader why he had stipulated in a 1708 letter to Tranquebar that only Germans and Danes could provide wives for missionaries, but at the same time called the Tamil "dear brothers and sisters." For Dal, this appeared far too much like the foundation stone for Schultze's despising the Tamil as "black beasts." Despite his undoubted record of successful labor in the Portuguese congregation, Dal had to wait until 1730 for ordination.

Three new missionaries, Maxim Bosse, Christian Friederich Pressier, and Christoph Theodosius Walther, suspected (correctly) that Schultze's version of events misinformed authorities in Europe. Reporting to the privy councillor and president of the *Missionskolleg*, Johann Georg von Holstein, in 1726, they rehearsed the entire affair, urging Dal's ordination and declaring that "he is completely free of the Indian maiden. She has now married a soldier from our Portuguese congregation." An earlier report the previous October had already confirmed that Dal was prepared to help the mother of the young girl find a suitable spouse. The young girl's name (Francesca), her eventual marriage, and the allusion to her family's Nagapattinam residence all suggested that she had come from one of the formerly Catholic groups evangelized by the Danish-German Lutherans. But Schultze's letter had caused sufficient pause in Europe that Dal never did receive a reply to his query even though the three newly arrived missionaries pleaded with Halle and Copenhagen to answer him for his own peace of mind. Dal eventually secured ordination; his marriage plans were permanently foiled. In later years, he continued to enter withering remarks in his diary about Schultze's inappropriateness for mission work, his disdain for the dark-skinned Tamils,

76. AFSt/M1 B2: 18 Schultze to the *Missionskolleg*, Copenhagen, Tranquebar, 11 October 1725, p. 3.

and his "steel-hearted nature" and carelessness about burying people without following the Danish ritual customs — but Dal never again broached the spousal issue.[77]

The Tranquebar court, when it did act, however, targeted Tamil women. It opened its sitting with punishment of a woman for whoring, and two years later a slave woman who had borne a fourth illegitimate child was put into the stocks and doused with water. Despite the early denunciation of "caste" by Ziegenbalg, the social stigma of public humiliation (applied almost solely to Tamil women exclusively from the lower orders who constituted the converted) reflected a long pattern of European legal sanctions against marginal and shameful persons and professions.

As problematic cases of marital and sexual behavior preoccupied the court, the *Missionskolleg* in Copenhagen mandated in 1724 that only a mixed bench composed of the missionaries could make decisions on marriage issues. The order repeated the need for the presence of the commandant of the fort or, in his absence, the consensus of his privy council.[78] In applying to Denmark for the erection of this version of the *Temperret* court, the missionaries had extended to the Tamils under their control within the Danish territory the European pattern of dealing with social outcasts, which included community sanctions, denunciations, and hearsay. Even though Danish law had never received Roman law to the extent that this had become the case in the German territories of the empire, in matters of punishment the Tranquebar court reflected a pattern that in Europe had for some time mixed ecclesiastical law with revisions of Roman law.[79]

---

77. AFSt/M 1 B 2:49, 27 October 1725, to Consistory, p. 17 recto; Copenhagen, Royal Library Folio 389 Missionsvaesenet 1702-1746 Ledreborgske Haandskriftsamling, 20 October 1726, from the three missionaries to von Holstein p. 3 recto; and p. 5 for the 20 October 1725 letter; on Schultze's disdain for correct burial customs, Dal to Lange, 19 June 1725, AFSt/M 1 H 3:3; for Dal's later continued negative assessments of Schultze, Dal's Diary for 1740 including a letter to Johann Michael Ziegenhagen, 10 January 1740: AFSt 1 B 1 to B 2: 2 E 45 (Film 595), pp. 0066-0069. The young woman's husband was one of the soldiers in service to the Danish East India Company; most of the women in this group were servants or slaves in the Danish households. For a laudatory reading of Schultze, see Peter Vethanayagamony, "'I Appeal to the Whole of Christendom': The Place of Benjamin Schultze in the History of [the Lutheran-Anglican] Cooperation during the Second Quarter of the Eighteenth Century (1719-1743)" (Ph.D. diss., Lutheran School of Theology Chicago, 2006), pp. 140-83.

78. Jeyaraj, *Inkulturation in Tranquebar*, pp. 248, 418, 419-23.

79. On these patterns, see Maria R. Boes, "Public Appearance and Criminal Judicial Practices in Early Modern Germany," *Social Science History* 20, no. 2 (1996): 259-79, and Kathy Stuart, *Defiled Trades and Social Outcasts: Honor and Ritual Pollution in Early Modern Germany*

The overreliance upon the court may have reflected what Dal denounced to the *Missionskolleg* already in September of 1723. He complained that the missionaries had to rely upon supposedly converted Tamils as catechists even when their behavior in no way reflected Christian beliefs. Explaining that they could not get along without one such man, Dal nonetheless reported the scandal that surrounded the catechist's decision to take an infant, "the fruit from the body of one of his other wives," and to "transfer it to the body of his wife." Dal wanted the missionaries to be able to use the penitential church canons rather than civil legal measures to punish such behavior, but, as he bitterly observed in 1725, Schultze had not called a conference for four years, and had allowed the custom of the communal prayer meeting, or *Bettstunde,* to lapse as well.[80]

The highly sanitized observations of activities in Tranquebar that made their way into the published *Halle Reports* avoided sexual and spousal topics among the newly converted. The missionaries referred to the subject only in carefully veiled terms. The 1728 report noted that while twenty-six people died during the year, eleven were married, of whom at least two couples were either bondsmen *(Leibeigene)* or slaves. The missionaries were uneasy with such marriages: "since through such slave marriages considerable evil can be prevented, one may convey to the Christian authorities the assurance that with time, more such examples will follow."[81] Both the need to reassure European civil authorities in the Danish colony and concerns about patrons in Europe stand behind such curt summaries.

Since not all such marriages lasted, it was not immediately clear whether the women partners thought of them as Tamil second marriages or whether they more closely resembled the widespread practice of concubinage that the pietists especially deplored among the Europeans. They felt that the bad example set by the Europeans materially undermined their own efforts to

---

(Cambridge: Cambridge University Press, 1999), p. 64: "infamy was seen as a material quality that permeated the physical being on a person — much like nobility ran in the blood — and determined a person's condition in this world." On the distinctions and similarities of Danish to Roman and German law, see Ditlev Tamm, *The History of Danish Law: Selected Articles and Bibliography* (Copenhagen: Djoef Publishing, 2011), pp. 80-83.

80. AFSt 1B1 Dal to Christian Benedikt Michaelis, 1 September 1725, p. 2; Dal's Diary II E 46 for 1732-34 referring to the 15 September 1723 report to the *Missionskolleg* on the catechist incident, p. 3; on the preference of Dal and the newly arrived missionaries for church discipline and not the court, Copenhagen, Royal Library Folio 389, *On Missionsvaesenet (Ledreborgske Haandskriftsamling),* 20 October 1725, pp. 19-20.

81. *Hallesche Berichte* III, no. 26, introduction, 5-6 (1728).

support an ordered marriage life among the newly converted. Especially after they abandoned Ziegenbalg's initial hope to transcend issues of caste, the Danish-German missionaries increasingly accepted the existence of *jāti*, regarded it as purely social or conventional, and as their pragmatic and Europeanized agenda developed, accepted that marriage across caste lines was wholly impractical. The Danish jurist and, after 1721, secretary of the *Missionskolleg* in Copenhagen, Seyr Mahling, had answered the series of queries about marriage law sent from India by Schultze and Dal, questions that reflected the tensions among the missionaries themselves over how stringently to attempt control over marriage inside their limited jurisdiction.[82] Polygamy and the potentially fatal consequences of mixed marriages between Christians and pagans, and between Catholics and Lutheran pietists, figured among the major concerns of pietist missionaries as they adjudicated cases among the converted.[83]

By 1729 the commander of the colony agreed to create a quasi-policing force that would attempt to report incidences of whoring, gaming, and missing services in which the missionaries themselves were not involved. This "special court" remained under the control of the consistory/*Tamperret*; the missionaries restricted themselves to marriage cases. The commander was to preside at such sessions, determining all punishments. But nonmarital questions now demanded urgent attention. Serious famine broke out in the region in 1728-29. As conditions deteriorated, the Danish East India Company was dissolved. The missionaries, upon learning of the reconstitution of the company, petitioned in 1732 that the court be reaffirmed but allowed to extend its jurisdiction beyond marital disputes and irregularities.

The peculiar history of this court reflects the general pattern that "the personal law principle was widely accepted . . . in Asia. Thus foreign merchants were granted the privilege of living under and of settling their disputes according to their own laws. This was not seen as an infringement of the sovereignty of the local ruler, but rather as a means of attracting commerce without losing control over it." Nevertheless, the Danish experiment casts some doubt over the broad generalization that "to the late eighteenth century there was no serious European endeavor to develop jurisdiction over an indigenous population according to their own law. Nor were there attempts on a large scale to extend European law to the subject popula-

---

82. AFSt: ALM/DHM 8/16:35, 18 November 1724.

83. See, for example, Benjamin Schultze, *Drey und zwanzigste Continuation des Berichts der königlichen Dänischen Missionarien in Ost-Indien* (Halle, 1728), pp. 941-46.

tion."[84] The missionaries seem in fact to have wanted — especially in the area of spousal sexuality — to do precisely that.

They were frustrated in this because the Danish company, while not seeking to impose European law extensively, nonetheless recognized, as did their English rivals and later successors, that corporate bodies with their rights and immunities exercised at least some control and legal authority over behavior, both their own and that of their trading partners, specifically in criminal matters. They did not intend to see this privilege put at risk by ceding significant control over the law of marriage to ecclesiastical courts and theologians in Tranquebar, any more than Thomasius was willing to tolerate interference from theologians in the law of marriage within Europe.[85]

The pressures that now confronted the missionaries brought delicate questions before the consistory that, while related to marriage, also illustrated that the competence of a European-style court could never be extended into the neighboring towns of Tanjavur or Madurai, where local village assemblies and headmen dealt with marital matters. Although the rice-producing area of the Kivari delta had been subject to cycles of bounty and drought-driven famine before, the increasing presence of European traders and rivalries probably conspired in the 1730s to drive up the price for rice even as another of the downturns in the agricultural cycle hit the area.

The Roman Catholic Jesuit Constantin Beschi, increasingly irritated by the loss of some of his people to the "plague" of Danish pietists, composed an essay explaining the Catholic faith during the famine years of 1728-29. Beschi predictably defended the veneration of the saints and the Virgin and the use of images. Appealing to the argument from antiquity, he dismissed Protestants as latter-day innovators before turning to the sacraments. The seven sacraments of the Catholic Church, he noted, included matrimony, and it was emphatically not polygamous but between one man and one woman and indissoluble. In standard post-Tridentine fashion, Beschi compared the marriage of man and woman to Christ's marriage to his church

84. Jörg Fisch, "Law as a Means and as an End: Some Remarks on the Function of European and Non-European Law in the Process of European Expansion," in *European Expansion and Law: The Encounter of European and Indigenous Law in 19th- and 20th-Century Africa and Asia,* ed. W. J. Mommsen and J. A. De Moor (Oxford and New York: Berg, 1992), pp. 15-38, at 23.

85. Philip J. Stern, "Bundles of Hyphens: Corporations as Legal Communities in the Early Modern British Empire" (paper read at the Symposium on Comparative Early Modern Legal History "New Perspectives on Legal Pluralism," Newberry Library, Chicago, 23 April 2010); and more extensively, Stern, *The Company-State,* pp. 142-206.

(Eph. 5). Adopting the polemics that had long characterized Catholic-Lutheran sparring in Europe, Beschi denounced Luther's willingness to allow a husband to divorce his wife for refusing sexual congress and his infamous endorsement of Philip of Hesse's bigamy that revealed the fruit of Protestant error.

The agricultural crisis now revealed new and alarming sexual and marital behavior among the Tamil converts. By 1733-34 Halle's theologians turned for advice to the Orphan House physician Johann Juncker in response to a dilemma outlined in letters from Benjamin Schultze, Christian Friedrich Pressier, and their colaborers. Because of the agricultural and economic crisis, the established custom of Tamil women renting themselves out as wet nurses to supplement meager incomes had taken an ominous turn. Even with the consent of a husband, the missionaries reported, the poor convert women now found that when they were taken in as wet nurses among the wealthier Hindus, they were expected to abort their own legitimate infants "through a mixture of chalk and spider web." In another case, a bound servant and maid had been allowed to live together as man and wife, but the servant was then accused of adultery. His defense was that he both was and was not married because his "wife" had to give her milk to satisfy the child of her owner and refused sexual intercourse with him. Was it permissible for a Christian woman who was nursing to sleep with her husband without damaging her own fetus's chances of survival? Some ethical and medical authorities said yes, others vigorously denied this.

Such questions were so potentially fraught with both moral and political implications that Pressier pleaded that a decision should be addressed *"to me alone"* (his emphasis). Juncker's four-page response rehearsed the theological and medical opinions and concluded that continued cohabitation during a time of lactation and new conception posed no danger. Christians ought to be able to contain their fleshly lusts, of course, but more damage to the marriage bond might well result if total abstinence were demanded of men. Gotthilf August Francke added his comments to Juncker's professional opinion. Christian mothers were bound to see to the nourishment of their own children first. But Francke admitted that he suspected that the situation in Tranquebar might well be different since mothers there were accustomed to suckle their children longer than was customary in Europe. He shrewdly guessed as well that poverty was the underlying issue. In the end, he could only refer to Juncker's medical opinion and avoided any theological conclusions about the morality of impoverished Christian women who were now forced to choose between maintaining sexual relations in their marriage and giving up their positions as wet nurses among the wealthier Hindus.[86]

The new European-trained physician in the Tranquebar settlement, Samuel Benjamin Cnoll, avoided this dispute and apparently confined himself to demonstrating the superiority of European over Tamil medical knowledge. In medicine as well as theology, the earlier openness to learning from Tamil practices and wisdom regarding social and marital customs increasingly gave way by the 1730s to "the movement towards suppression which the invading European culture carries out against traditional societies and their cultural forms in the overseas colonies."[87]

Gottfried Wilhelm Obuch's report to his superiors, written a generation after Ziegenbalg's passing but only a few years after Obuch's arrival in 1737, reflected the increasing emphasis on the practical utility of marrying, whether among transplanted Europeans or newly converted Tamils. Despite his recent marriage, Obuch had remarkably little to say about the event. Composing a report in English that was also copied in German, Obuch detailed his labors among recent converts, "preparing 50 for communion at Christmas." The growing awareness of the British North American colonies among Halle pietists revealed itself in Obuch's curiosity about an (unnamed) countryman who was supposed to go to Pennsylvania "and in what condition he lives in."

---

86. The above paragraphs summarize AFSt/M 1318; Pressier's letter, 15 December 1733; Juncker's four-page (unpaginated) *Gutachten;* Gotthilf August Francke's remarks dated 11 October 1734. The fair copy of these notes is in ALM/DHM 2/4:56, but the rough notes are more legible given the poor condition of the Leipzig Mission documents. On the rice production prices and surrounding political-economic patterns for the 1730s, see Axel Utz, "Cultural Exchange, Imperialist Violence, and Protestant Renewal Efforts: Local Perspectives from Tanjavur and Lenape Country, 1720-1760" (Ph.D. diss., Penn State University, 2011), chapter 4, pp. 88-92. On Beschi, see Leon Besse, *Father Beschi of the Society of Jesus, His Times & His Writings* (Trichinopoly: St. Joseph's Industrial School Press, 1918), pp. 84, 88-97, 193-95; Beschi's *Veda-Vilakkam* appeared in 1728; running to some 250 pages and reprinted many times since, it appears to have been the only place where he attacked the Lutherans specifically on the topic of matrimony. I am especially indebted to Father Dr. D. Amudham of the Shrine Retreat House at Vailankanni for conversation on Beschi's work and for checking the original edition for confirmation of Beschi's attack on Lutheran theology of marriage. For Beschi's importance for Tamil language studies, see Albertine Gaur, "Father Beschi and His Grammar of High-Tamil," *British Museum Quarterly* 32, no. 3/4 (Spring 1968): 103-8.

87. I base my conclusions here upon unsuccessful attempts to locate in the Halle archives Cnoll's responses to the Pressier plea for advice or his comments to Juncker. On the overall pattern described here, see Josef N. Neumann, "Tamil Medical Science as Perceived by the Missionaries of the Danish-Halle Mission at Tranquebar," in *Halle and the Beginning of Protestant Christianity in India III,* pp. 1135-54, at 1153.

But as for himself, Obuch couched his identity in classic pietist humility: "I live till this Date in that place and condition the marvelous Providence has appointed me for, and God be thancked [*sic*], well enough." One would scarcely think that a fairly momentous day in his life had just occurred given his next remarks. "In Things belonging to this Life has happened nothing with me but what I mentioned in my last, viz. the marriage which was finish'd the 15th of march 1740 and I am in the unalter'd mind, I wrote to you by it."[88]

In addition to revealing that he had, in Melanchthonian Lutheran fashion, been catechized to think that marriage pertained exclusively to the "things belonging to this Life," Obuch's silence about marriage extended to his report to unconverted relatives as he explained his own new religious convictions and urged them to consider a truly awakened Christianity. Barely six months into his new life, neither his marriage, nor his wife, nor her place in his religious convictions deserved notice in his exhortation. Given the lack of attention he gave to his own marriage in his correspondence, it is hardly surprising that no surviving sermons or reports from the first half of the eighteenth century focus on the importance of this "estate" among the newly converted Christians of India. The absence of parental consent, the lack of financial support, and the danger of converting to a religion that could potentially cut spouses' ties with the broader familial, financial, and social networks remained the bundle of serious problems the missionaries recognized as major impediments to their hopes for the pietist experiment.[89]

The lack of focus on any transformative or holy dimension of spousal relations survived even Obuch's own accounts. At his death in 1745, eulogizers neither praised his marriages nor held them up as models for emulation to European or Indian believers. That same silence characterized the whole series of reports on the progress of the missions that appeared throughout the eighteenth century.[90] The omission is all the more arresting when compared

88. AFSt: M/1B 28 #78 1 verso and 3 verso, Obuch to Johann Heinrich Michaelis; German translation included with the original English copy, 30 December 1740. Obuch had not received word that his correspondent, a major figure in the Halle *Collegium Orientale,* had died at Halle on 3 October 1738. The unnamed Pennsylvania pietist was not Heinrich Melchior Mühlenberg, who only learned in September of 1741 that Francke and Ziegenhagen wished him to accept the call to the three Lutheran congregations in the proprietary North American colony, and would not be sending him to India.

89. AFSt: M/1B 28, Letter 69, Obuch to his relatives (torn edges and partially illegible), 29 September 1740.

90. For Obuch's death, see Johann Lucas Niekamp, *Kurzgefaßte Missions Geschichte oder historischer Auszug der Evangelischen Missions-Berichte aus Ostindien, von dem Jahr 1737 bis zu*

to the concerns of the missionaries themselves, who went to great pains to seek the intervention of the Halle fathers in procuring a proper spouse for their labors among non-Christians.

Pietist attempts in the first decades of the century to broaden the understanding of the spousal relationship beyond the legal-contractual and the this-worldly pragmatic virtually ceased in southeastern India by midcentury. The scarcity of Christian parents compromised one of the major advances Lutherans cherished in their marriage tradition — the involvement of parents. The European legacy of public betrothal and marriage — a custom shared with Tamil tradition — gave, at least partially, "the community as a whole — civil authorities via the pastor, extended family via the parents — warning of an alliance about to be concluded." Especially for pietists intent on linking "awakened" families to one another by marriage, the paucity of converted extended families in India presented a daunting challenge since disruption of established community spirit awakened determined opposition from the non-Christian authorities, from the level of village leaders to those at the centers of political power.[91]

In one important respect, however, women converts moved toward a more companionate or quasi-equal role for married Christians. As the mission work spread out into rural areas, converted catechists played a critical role in spreading the Christian faith, since they were fluent in the languages and customs of the population. By one estimate, from 1706 to about 1720, "about 500 Indians worked in different capacities in the stations of the Danish-Halle and the English-Halle mission." Only one of eighty catechists was a woman, but prayer leaders included women in the two urban parishes and four village congregations in Tranquebar. What is most striking is that the women prayer leaders who were sometimes authorized to repeat sermons given by either European pastors or the few converted Indian pastors were no longer spouses. They were "widows of former mission employees" who resurrected the duties of the widows and deaconesses of the ancient Christian church, designated as the guardians of the spiritual welfare of other women.[92]

Ende des Jahrs 1767 fortgesetzt von Michael Meier, Prediger zu Garz bei Ruppin (Halle, 1772), p. 224.

91. On the European consequences, Pamela Biel, "Let the Fiancees Beware: Luther, the Lawyers and Betrothal in Sixteenth-Century Saxony," in *Protestant History and Identity in Sixteenth-Century Europe II: The Later Reformation,* ed. Bruce Gordon, 2 vols. (Aldershot, U.K., and Brookfield, Vt., 1996), pp. 121-41, at 141.

92. Heike Liebau, "The Indian Pastors in the Danish-Halle and the English-Halle Mission," in *Halle and the Beginning of Protestant Christianity in India II,* pp. 719-34, at 720, 722.

Contrary to later, nineteenth-century British assumptions about the restriction of education in the Madras Presidency solely to males of the "higher castes," schooling in Tamil villages roughly matched the levels of their English counterparts, and the educated did not come from the "twice-born" of *varna* classifications of Brahman, Kshetriya, and Vaisya, but from the *shudras* — the majority classification of Tamil society among whom the Halle missionaries had labored. They constituted the biggest percentage of villagers attending schools. Educated girls remained a comparative rarity, though some may have been educated at home, and the continued acquisition of literacy and cultivated elegance Ziegenbalg had reluctantly admired among the *devadāsīs,* or temple dancing girls, persisted a century after his death.[93] Against this positive record, however, the consistory court in Tranquebar seemed to single out women for correction and punishment, especially for sexual transgressions. The missionaries worried about popular beliefs, especially if they stemmed from social or economic pressures that threatened to separate married couples, even temporarily, as the letters surrounding wet nurses demonstrated.

The ideal missionary, in Francke's mind at least, would remain immune from popular beliefs and would also remain celibate. The realization among the men sent to India that they were unlikely ever to return home to marry and take up pastoral work emboldened Ziegenbalg and his colleagues to contest Francke on this point. But Polycarp Jordan and Nikolaus Dal had already learned that intermarriage with converted Indian women was impermissible. Perhaps even more significantly, the parents of the intended Tamil bride had seen no advantage for their daughter in marriage to a European and also opposed the union, a clear signal from the perspective of Tamil-speakers that marriage that violated or endangered the social-economic values of *jāti* could not be risked despite a common commitment to Protestant Christianity.

The refusal to allow for European-Indian marriages produced a missionary strategy by which converted women had to be educated in the mission school in order to gain entry to women's quarters to which neither European missionaries nor their wives could gain access.[94] But the hesitation to

---

93. Dharampal, *The Beautiful Tree: Indigenous Indian Education in the Eighteenth Century* (New Delhi: Biblia Implex Private Limited, 1983), pp. 11-53, at 14-15, 20, 36-37. Dharampal's conclusion remains largely unchallenged by scholars to this day: "the decay noticed in the early 19th century and more so in subsequent decades originated with European supremacy in India" (p. 53).

94. Heike Liebau, *Die indischen Mitarbeiter der Tranquebarmission (1706-1845): Kate-*

trust the judgment and abilities of indigenous women meant that the first converted Tamil women to work as catechists only began their labors some seventy years after the mission's founding. The dilemma the missionaries had created by relying on converted women for access intensified since, by violating the social norms regulating gender relations, a woman daring to teach underwent a rupture with her family. To counteract this problem, the married catechists could teach unmarried younger women from a village in the home of the woman catechist. The standing of women as married or unmarried had little to do with a theological understanding of the importance of spousal friendship in marriage, and everything to do with the strategy of ensuring the mission's success.[95]

Because of these practical — but plausibly also theological — issues that surrounded spousal relationships, converted Indian pietist married couples did not work together as teams. Here again, the caution with which Ziegenbalg and his coworkers treated *jāti* played the decisive role. For, "while daughters of the higher castes lived protected from the outside world at the onset of menstruation, and were only allowed in public with an escort but even after marriage could manage the business affairs of the household, such norms were not as rigid for women from the . . . [lower *varna*] families." Nonetheless, the missionaries did not bring forward the example of the married couples from their own lower-order converts when they tried to attract the attention and financial support of Europeans. Rather, they singled out widows. Widows who were not employed by the mission but who had simply lost their converted husbands — by 1734-35 between 104 and 123 persons — received monthly alms.[96]

Despite European assistance collected for converted Indian widows, the missionaries made little effort to help sustain spouses during marriage. Ziegenbalg acknowledged from the very beginning of the mission that the example of chaste marriages would hasten the conversion of families to pietist Christianity. By midcentury, however, the dangers of unmarried poor women falling into "idleness and disordered ways" spurred pietist authorities in Cuddelur to create spinning centers in the hopes that an occupation and income would help them avoid sexual misconduct and scandal.[97] The

---

cheten, Schulmeister, Übersetzer (Tübingen and Halle: Max Niemeyer Verlag, 2008), pp. 358-82, 359-61, 365.

95. Liebau, *Die indischen Mitarbeiter,* pp. 365, 366.

96. Liebau, *Die indischen Mitarbeiter,* pp. 372-73.

97. The generosity of a donor making the wool-spinning experiment possible was reported in *Hallesche Berichte* IV (1752), p. 363.

pietist concern about insufficiently supervised village spinning evenings in Württemberg found its way into the Indian context to aid a deliberate program to construct occasions for Christian female sociability — but under tight supervision. It was precisely the influence of the non-Christian family, the missionaries reported, that continued to change the minds of those contemplating baptism and accepting the duties of Christian spouses. The pietist pastors did not know how to employ converted women as allies in the missionary enterprise, in part because of the marginal status of the Indian women who were the objects of missionary efforts.

Instead of reporting on success in recruiting better spouses, the missionaries had to inform their European superiors of unfortunate instances when converted Christian women caught in adultery underwent public shaming in trials where converted Indians sometimes served as judges. These reports of marital discipline are striking not because of the concern shown for order and social control — that was commonplace also in European villages. Rather, the reports made no mention of influence or guidance given by the Christian women themselves, either the pastors' wives or the catechists' wives or the lay pietist women, the very people who gave the southeast Indian pietist community its character. While married women exercised a degree of control over male behavior in the German southwest, they enjoyed no comparable institutional framework to give them such a voice in the Indian pietist settlements. Their silence revealed the extent to which the converted Tamil women shared with their European counterparts a declining status. But Tamils suffered from an even lower degree of companionate sharing in spiritual and material advancement than did married women in pietist-dominated European localities. The deep ambivalence Ziegenbalg's official theology imposed on his struggle to understand Tamil women had surfaced very early in a 1708 report on the customs of the Tamils. In praising the honor in which children held father and mother as the "first gods" they encountered, Ziegenbalg nonetheless also reiterated the official Tamil theology that wives should be obedient to their husbands and preserve chastity at all costs. In passing on wisdom about "worldly uprightness" (weltliche Gerechtigkeit), however, he signaled the mistrust of wives who should never be left alone in their houses, and to whom no husband should confide any secret or private matter.[98]

98. *Bartholomaeus Ziegenbalg's Kleinere Schriften,* ed. W. Caland (Amsterdam: Koninklijke Akademie van Wetenschappen, 1930), p. 55 *(Kondei Wenden, oder Malabarische Moralia); (Ulaga Nidi oder weltliche Gerechtigkeit),* p. 80.

Without warning, however, by the 1730s the inadequacy of official pietist theology to address the challenges raised by the customs of the Tamils, the misbehavior of transplanted Europeans, and the rather desperate reach for discipline and order in the form of the imported Danish marriage court no longer held the attention of the theologians in Halle. Whatever connections between the erotic and the divine that emanated from India and so troubled European Christians in the previous decades paled now by comparison with a challenge that erupted from the preaching and writing by an alumnus of Francke's Foundations. The Moravian "sex-positive" argument that the sexual act in marriage was sacramental pushed the dangers posed by the *devadāsīs* of the Indian temples out of the light and refocused attention away from India and back to Europe, and very quickly thereafter, to North America.

CHAPTER 5

The Moravians, the Church, and Marriage

As Christian Thomasius lay near death in September of 1728, his servants declined a request from a supplicant begging for an audience with the great man. Frustrated in his attempt, Nikolaus Count von Zinzendorf nonetheless wrote to Thomasius on the day before he died in Halle that "my love and respect for you was always great and I possess an entirely unpartisan veneration for one of the first bulwarks of the truth in the German empire."[1] Soon to suffer exile from Saxony in that same empire, Zinzendorf would also now contribute a massive new impulse to the debates over the nature and meaning of marriage as new currents in theological anthropology began to swirl through European Protestantism. In his exaltation of human erotic love, Zinzendorf may well have been aware that Thomasius himself appeared to have understood erotic love and friendship as partaking of the same moral virtue.

Perhaps more ominously, at least in the opinion of Zinzendorf's opponents, the count may also have believed that Thomasius held that even unmarried persons could engage in erotic love, although since homosexual liaisons were forbidden by law, perhaps the same prohibition applied — at the discretion of the prince — as with polygamy or polyandry. But as Thomasius himself had earlier argued, by "law" he meant the law of the prince, since he had spent much of his life denying that there was a "natural" or "biblical" law in which to ground such teachings.

The question of how men and women related to one another, whether

---

1. Werner Schmidt, *Ein vergessener Rebell: Leben und Wirken des Christian Thomasius* (Munich: Eugen Diederichs Verlag, 1995), p. 197.

146

genuine friendship between them was possible, and what implications such a question held for the marital relationship intensified in the 1730s. The leader of the recently renewed Moravian Brethren would play a large part in those debates. His own struggle with marriage, sexuality, and the teachings of the Reformation that he had imbibed in his student days at Halle now led to increasingly frequent confrontations with other alumni and admirers of the renowned center.[2]

Few students of Christianity today claim deep familiarity with the Unitas Fratrum, but they may recognize the Moravians, as they are more commonly known, for their success in Protestant missions. Moravian advances in establishing congregations from Greenland to South Africa during the eighteenth century alarmed their European critics. Never numbering more than perhaps 10,000 European souls in the eighteenth century, this group that claimed continuity with the Bohemian reformer Jan Hus, who died at the stake in Constance in 1416, agitated the already contentious Protestant debate over marriage into acute crisis in the 1740s. No more than the Lutherans with whom they claimed affinity, however, did the Moravians intend for such a debate to occur. At first, the ambitious plans of Zinzendorf for pan-Protestant cooperation ruffled the feathers of the recognized European confessions, and by the late 1730s some of his speculations about Trinitarian doctrine appear to have alarmed still others.

These dogmatic and ecclesiological critiques, however, included almost from the outset attacks on Moravian teachings about sexuality and marriage. Coming hard on the heels of the disquieting evidence from India that a teaching on monogamous spousal relationships would not easily transform the profoundly traditional social and familial beliefs of the subcontinent, the controversy with the Moravians moved the official theology of Lutheran pietists decisively away from the founding generation's willingness to talk about the marriage relationship in quasi-sacramental terms of cooperative friendship. Language that had hinted at "union" with God and the transformative capabilities of a privileged order of creation now became altogether too dangerous.[3]

---

2. For the analysis of Thomasius on erotic love and friendship, see Werner Schneiders, *Naturrecht und Liebesethik: Zur Geschichte der praktischen Philosophie im Hinblick auf Christian Thomasius* (Hildesheim and New York: Georg Olms Verlag, 1971), pp. 169-254, at 178-79 and n. 98 on the interpretation of Thomasius's essay "Einleitung zur Sittenlehre." Despite the claims of Zinzendorf and others, Schneiders denies that Thomasius was ever a genuine pietist — see pp. 229-31.

3. For an excellent introduction to the origins of the Brethren, see Craig D. Atwood, *The*

What maddened Lutheran pietist opponents most about the Moravians' teaching on the marriage relationship was that Moravians were so bold as to call the act of human coitus sacramental. They taught that in that act a form of "union with God" became possible for spouses, and that not only the particular marriage, but also the entire believing community, thus realized the relationship of Christ to his church. They pointed consistently to the teaching of Ephesians 5 as the basis for their belief. This conclusion, however, exceeded any hopes for better spouses that Luther or Spener had envisioned. We can only appreciate the virulent reaction Moravian teaching provoked among their opponents by noting that Lutheran pietist attitudes toward sexuality were so fraught with misgivings that non-Moravian Protestants found the Brethren challenge embarrassing. The Moravian teaching on the marriage relationship assumed massive importance not only because it obviously drew upon elements of Lutheran pietism but also because it just as clearly broke the boundaries of that tradition. Frustration with what pietists since the 1690s had expressed about the state church's inadequate expression of a genuine community of believers now found a particular expression in the Moravian vision of the intimate connection between spousal relations and their view of the church's relationship to Christ.

What, precisely, did Nikolaus Graf von Zinzendorf believe and teach about the marriage relationship and the church? His thinking on this topic matured over the decades, of course. But from an early age, he appears to have been convinced that the marriage relationship should be characterized by a cooperative friendship between partners whose objective in getting married was to strengthen each other's service and devotion to the broader Christian community. In setting down his famous "Seventeen Points of Matrimony" in 1740 (a text that remained unpublished but in circulation within the Moravian community), Zinzendorf clarified beliefs he had begun to develop years earlier.[4]

Marriage, divinely instituted, reflected God's intention for all humans,

---

Theology of the Czech Brethren from Hus to Comenius (University Park: Pennsylvania State University Press, 2009); on Protestant debates over the nature of the church intensified by Moravian attempts to be defined as "church" and not as a sect of dissenters, see Roeber, "The Waters of Rebirth: The Eighteenth Century and Transoceanic Protestant Christianity," *Church History* 79, no. 1 (March 2010): 40-76.

4. The following relies on Peter Vogt, "Zinzendorf's 'Seventeen Points of Matrimony': A Fundamental Document on the Moravian Understanding of Marriage and Sexuality," *Journal of Moravian History* 10 (2011): 39-67 (hereafter Zinzendorf, "Seventeen Points"). I have substituted my own translation since Vogt left some of the original German points untranslated.

although God certainly made room for celibate exceptions to this godly order. The husband-wife relationship reflected in a visible, tangible manner Christ's relationship to the church, even though the "mystery" of that relationship noted by Ephesians 5 remains beyond human comprehension. Zinzendorf re-iterated what Luther and Spener also believed, namely, that husband and wife remain sinners, but the grace of God in marriage clearly outweighs the lapses of men and women. God's intention is clear: marriage is a "holy union" *(eine selige Gemeinschaft)*. This "unchanging relationship" *(beständiger Umgang)* accomplishes in communion what no individual can. It might indeed some-times happen that to fulfill a particular duty or office *(Amt)* a husband might not be able to fulfill all the obligations of this holy estate *(Stand)*. But except in such rare occasions, husband and wife were to share in everything, heeding the scriptural teaching that the husband was to protect his wife and overlook any weaknesses. The wife, however, in her role as the church, should find her husband the vessel into which she could pour every thought, concern, or con-viction. She was obligated to support him, but the relationship was not en-tirely an equal one because he carried the greater obligation to improve and bear with her *(heben und tragen)* in all circumstances.[5]

Had Zinzendorf contented himself with these first ten points, many Lu-theran pietists might well have applauded his reiteration of Luther's and Spener's beliefs. At some point during his years after leaving Halle, however, Zinzendorf began to express the convictions that now found their way into the stunning conclusions he set down in the remaining seven points of his treatise.

The creation of a new — and apparently successful — sense of commu-nity centered on the marriage relationship that was managed by the entire *Gemeine* may have stung Lutheran critics who had failed to reform Lutheran village marriage customs and moreover had been shocked by the radical pietists' alternatives of repudiating sexual relations altogether, or in the case of the infamous Buttlar scandal, of promoting union with God through pro-miscuous sex with the group's female leader. Zinzendorf himself had been well aware of the earlier scandal at the time he married his cousin Erdmuth Dorothea von Reuss. From his teenage years onward, both he and Erdmuth had apparently concluded that their marriage should reflect not romantic personal attraction, but the good of a larger community in which not only his own but also her formidable intellectual and theological acumen would find room for expression. Marriages among the Moravians modeled on this

---

5. Zinzendorf, "Seventeen Points," points 9, 10, pp. 47, 48.

belief "were arranged by the leaders according to the economic and religious ends of both the individuals and the Gemeine. This was in accordance with Zinzendorf's concept of the *Streiter Ehe,* such as he had contracted with Erdmuth, in which the emotional aspect of marriage is circumscribed for the communal/religious purpose of the Brüdergemeine. Moreover, many of the vocations were restricted to married persons, such as many mission stations. But even the marriages of common artisans and tradesmen were also arranged since their activities were part of the overall mission."[6]

Yet even this subordination of the particular marriage relationship to the good of a larger community might have escaped Lutheran pietist censure. Some might have worried over the eleventh point of Zinzendorf's teaching, when he identified the true beginning of marriage with a sequence: the forgiveness of sins, the reception of the Holy Spirit "in the blood of Jesus," and an anointing. This sequence binds the marriage partners into a true, spiritual common life of genuine holiness with each other that might look like the previous mere "fleshly citizens" *(leibliche Bürgerschafft)* but was clearly something quite different. The schocking implication of this point, however, only became clear when the following point explained that the "anointing" meant the reception by the woman of the husband's semen, described as "a Balm and an anointing oil of the holy marriage covenant." To be absolutely certain that no ambiguity surrounded the teaching, Zinzendorf explicitly termed this act sacramental, restoring a "sacred harmony" between husband and wife on the same level as Jesus' giving to the church "his mystical body." Wasted semen through accident or carelessness is a "scandalous" misfortune and a "loss," but in marital intercourse *(in der handlung der Ehe)* the "greatest and most respectable of all the mysteries of body and soul."[7]

By comparison with this stunning revelation, the remaining points Zinzendorf laid down could only be described as anticlimactic. Undue pleasure or lust in the act is to be avoided; children are indeed a blessing, but in-

---

6. Craig D. Atwood, *Community of the Cross: Moravian Piety in Colonial Bethlehem* (University Park: Pennsylvania State University Press, 2004), pp. 184-85; on Erdmuth Dorothea, see Erika Geiger, *Erdmuth Dorothea Countess von Zinzendorf, Noble Servant,* trans. Julie Tomberlin Weber (Winston-Salem, N.C.: John F. Blair, 2006), and for further details on the background to Zinzendorf's first marriage, see Truus Bouman-Komen, *Bruderliebe und Feindeshaß: Eine Untersuchung von frühen Zinzendorftexten (1713-1727) in ihrem kirchengeschichtlichen Kontext* (Hildesheim, Zürich, and New York: Georg Olms Verlag, 2009), pp. 213-27. Bouman-Komen argued that "there is no agreement concerning the question to what extent bridal mysticism and asceticism belong to Lutheran Orthodoxy" (p. 212).

7. Zinzendorf, "Seventeen Points," points 11 and 12, pp. 47-48.

tercourse remains holy even if progeny are not the result. Zinzendorf did not shrink from reinvoking explicitly the teaching that parents participate in creating a being that while "unlike" God and "subaltern" to God is nonetheless made "in the image of the Creator."[8]

Some Lutheran pietists may have labored to bring Luther's and Spener's insights on the marriage relationship into their renewal movement, but they had only limited success. The reliance upon Luther's theology of the cross; the marriage of the soul to God; the insistence on the sacrificing love of the husband — these elements in a renewed theology of marriage that the aggrieved Lutheran women had deployed with such force before the consistory in Holstein all originated in Luther's high vision of marriage.[9] But the additional Moravian teaching points now added more impetus for those who had chosen to emphasize the marriage relationship as a form of social discipline — those who had fought off Indian polygamists as well as those aghast at what they (correctly) suspected lay at the heart of the challenge emanating from the Unitas Fratrum.

Lutheran theology had affirmed that God was present when the Word was joined with water in baptism, for example, or with bread and wine in the Lord's Supper. Why then, given a prelapsarian command to "be fruitful and multiply, and fill the earth and subdue it" (Gen. 1:28) and Jesus' statement that "in the beginning" a union of one man and one woman was "so" (Matt. 19:8), should not marriage and sexual union be just as "sacramental"? This, in essence, was the unnerving question the Moravians now raised, and Zinzendorf answered with a shocking boldness — but only within the confines of his community. In doing so, the Brethren awakened ancient fears that centuries earlier had caused the early Christians to put as much distance as possible between their defense of sexuality and the ritualized temple prostitution of the late ancient Mediterranean world. Coming hard on the heels of the polygamy debates, the question could not have been more ill-timed or more unwelcome among Lutheran pietists.

The delay by pietist Lutheran critics in perceiving the threat Zinzendorf posed to marriage stemmed in part from the cases the Halle faculty was asked to adjudicate. By examining those cases, then turning to the vexed attitudes toward sexuality that began to circulate in the 1730s, we can better appreciate

8. Zinzendorf, "Seventeen Points," points 13-17, pp. 49-52, quotation at 51.

9. Atwood, *Community of the Cross*, pp. 91-100; Erich Beyreuther, "Ehe-Religion und Eschatology," in Beyreuther, *Studien zur Theologie Zinzendorfs: Gesammelte Aufsätze* (Neukirchen-Vluyn, Kreis Moers: Neukirchener Verlag der Buchhandlung des Erziehungsverein, 1962), pp. 35-71.

both the delay and the intensity of the reaction to the Moravians by the middle of that decade. In part, the lack of a positive theology of marriage as companionate friendship may have flowed not only from indecision in the aftermath of the Thomasius challenge. The hesitation also reflected the questions put to Halle's theological faculty. Although the records remain incomplete, 42 of the 120 surviving petitions sent to the faculty from the 1690s through 1799 dealt with marital questions. The overwhelming majority asked about degrees of consanguinity and permission for marriage or divorce.

At first, the faculty provided the model for what their students on the consistory in Holstein would articulate: a husband who failed to "carry out his responsibilities" *(üble Aufführung)* was guilty of deserting his wife, and the absence of evidence of changed behavior justified separation from bed and board — plus, he was to bear the costs of the proceedings.[10] A husband married since 1673 accused his wife of being unloving, of threatening him and the children, and of trying to poison him. His wife demanded separation for his misbehavior. Local pastors ordered trial separations five years into the marriage and again a decade later, but the faculty debated whether the estate of marriage was made worse by infidelity or malicious desertion. In the end, they deemed the man responsible for attempting reconciliation since his wife had indicated a willingness to try again. They admonished another couple for not trying hard enough to reconcile and reminded the couple that even if they allowed separation from bed and board the marriage bond remained inviolate. The husband was obliged to provide his wife with support or to return her marriage portion as laid down by Carpzov's treatise on ecclesiastical law.

Most of the cases, however, offered no opportunity for more than decisions about the marriage of near relatives, in many cases after the death of a spouse. The faculty was clearly shocked by a man who had gotten his aunt pregnant, but who had married with the knowledge of the pastor anyway. Was it better to tolerate this kind of incest, or would it be a greater scandal to dissolve an entire household?[11]

---

10. Martin-Luther Universität Halle-Wittenberg Archiv (Theology Faculty), Rep 27/1280 Nr. 16, December 1698.

11. Martin-Luther Universität Halle-Wittenberg Archiv (Theology Faculty), Rep 27 IV c:5 Nr. 1281; Nr. 36; Nr. 20 (15 November 1701). See Nr. 39 for the case of a widower asking to marry the niece of his deceased wife and the opinion of the faculty that no consensus existed on the question since some theologians cited Old Testament precedents. Most agreed that whatever the degree of consanguinity in this case, the greater danger lay in the consciences of the parties who might discover that the basis of their marriage was so dubious that "lack of unity, depression, carelessness, poverty and similar misery would result."

At first, Halle's theologians may have worried that the issue of polygamy alone, and not friendship and male-female roles in marriage, would stir controversy beyond the bounds of Brandenburg-Prussia. Correspondents initially confirmed their anxiety. Francke had been dismayed to learn in December of 1710 from a pastor in Württemberg that the emerging dispute with Thomasius and the subject of polygamy had already resonated there. Andreas Adam Hochstetter reported that at the recent meeting of the Württemberg synod, his father, a leading theologian from Bebenhausen, was shocked to hear of a "Doctor of Theology who studied at Rostock" willing to defend polygamy. "Oh God, into what matters is our church fallen!"[12]

But by 1724, just as the controversies in Britain over clandestine marriage began to prompt renewed demand for legal reform, the theology faculty at Halle had to conclude that it was not just polygamy that stimulated dangerous speculations and teachings. The deeper questions of male and female roles in marriage and of the exclusive friendship associated with monogamy had to be addressed as well. The faculty now became embroiled in the aftershocks of Thomasius's questions and the renewed controversy over the true nature of marriage and the duties of each spouse in the estate.

In Jena, a student's dissertation aroused the ire of authorities who asked Halle's theology faculty to determine whether students should be allowed to write on topics that disturbed public peace and brought the church and the Bible into disrepute. The dissertation (*De connubiis infantum* — "Concerning the marriage of the underaged") seemed innocuous at first glance. But the young author had interpreted *porneia* in Matthew 19:9 in such a way as to question the grounds for divorce, and more dangerously, to suggest that perhaps marriage was not indissoluble and that women as well as men were free contracting agents. Polygamy and divorce threatened the order of the household and of society, his critics pointed out. But the faculty found especially unnerving the student's argument that men had no premier rights in marriage that could be supported by arguments from the law of nature. Rather, such notions were but mere conventions and could only be defended from the standpoint of political governance and convenience. The associated question that troubled the faculty had to do with damage control: Were not

---

12. Stab/F 10, 217, 104 (Film 7 AFSt), 29 December 1710, letter to Francke from Andreas Adam Hochstetter, 0689-90. On Hochstetter and his father Johann Andreas, the "Spener of Württemberg," see *RGG* III, pp. 1813-14.

153

such writings intrinsically scandalous since a few "journalists" stood ready to defend the author's argument?[13]

Such cases showed that controversy over men's and women's roles in marriage could no longer be restricted to abstruse exchanges among the theology and law faculties. The Jena incident demonstrated that certain "journalists" were determined to make known to a broader public the potentially unsettling arguments about the purely pragmatic basis of marital roles. Although Halle's theologians could not avoid fielding questions about the contested borders of consanguinity, the spreading interest in debates about Protestant marriage suggested the need by the 1730s for renewed attention to the proper teaching on the estate.

The failure to produce just such teaching stemmed in part from the declining fortunes of Halle's theology faculty. Moreover, what the faculty did teach appears to have left many young men with a decidedly ambivalent attitude toward their own sexuality and toward even the possibility of holiness in marital union. As unimpressive figures such as the pious but unproductive Liborius Zimmermann joined that faculty in the early 1730s, it seemed to reflect the lack of "an agenda of research and a rigorous method" that could come to grips "with the new science and other contemporary intellectual currents." When a younger generation of talented theologians such as Siegmund Jacob Baumgarten did join the faculty during this decade, their attempts to reconfigure the pietist conviction "that the true end of Christianity and thus of all theology was the 'union' of man with God" provoked inquisitions. In Baumgarten's case, a 1736 investigation proceeded with the plain intent of having him dismissed. The internal tensions among the faculty by the time of the elder Francke's death had pitted Breithaupt and Baumgarten against Lange in the struggle to shape the future of the Foundations, a tension the hapless younger Francke had to mediate and keep under control.[14]

13. Martin-Luther Universität Halle-Wittenberg Archiv, Rep. 27/1283: Nr. 110, 18 February 1726 (Jena disputation was 29 December 1724 — unpaginated, but by my counting, at 1 verso, 50 verso, 51 recto and verso, 60 and 61, recto and verso). The intent of the complainants in warning of "journalists" remains unclear since this was not a term in common use, nor would prevailing censorship laws have made it easy for a writer for a learned journal or officially sanctioned newspaper to publish something so controversial. See Johann Christoph Adelung, *Grammatisch-kritisches Wörterbuch der hochdeutschen Mundart: mit bestäandiger Vergleichung der übrigen Mundarten, besonders aber . . .* , revised and corrected by Franz Xaver Schönberger, 4 vols. (Vienna: Bauer, 1811), p. 1441. See also Jacob Grimm, *Das Deutsche Wörterbuch von Jacob und Wilhelm Grimm auf CD-ROM und im Internet,* vol. 10, col. 2238-40 (http://dwb.uni-trier .de/; accessed 20 July 2011).

14. David Sorkin, "Reclaiming Theology for the Enlightenment: The Case of Siegmund

We cannot easily reconstruct what young men in Halle learned about sexuality, marriage, friendship, and celibacy under the tutelage either of the older or the newer faculty as these subjects became increasingly fraught with controversy. No complete course of lectures survives, nor can we even say with certainty what books were available in the university's or the Foundations' library to shape the debate between Halle and the followers of Zinzendorf. An occasional reference to the work of the Jena theologian Johann Franz Buddeus (his *Institutiones theologiae moralis* of 1711) that finally saw German translation in 1719 hints that long after Buddeus's exodus from Halle to Jena in 1705, the faculty might have used his exposition of ethics to instruct future pastors. Reconciling notions of sexuality, friendship, and holiness — even within the estate of marriage — apparently did not come easily to some of those who received their training at Halle as the faculty who had surrounded August Hermann Francke faded from the scene.[15]

The lecture notes in moral theology taken by the later India missionary Christian Friedrich Schwartz during 1748 as he was teaching in the girls school suggest that most of the instruction focused on the "duties" owed to God, to others, and to oneself. No particular regard was paid to sexual mores or marriage duties.[16] Among the students who struggled, as Schwartz did, with questions of sexual and marital obligations, Samuel Theodor Albinus, who finished his studies in 1738, seems to have suffered especially. Born in 1718 in Tremmen, just as the controversy over marriage and polygamy had vanished temporarily from public dispute in Brandenburg-Prussia, Albinus

---

Jacob Baumgarten (1706-1757)," *Central European History* 36, no. 4 (2006): 503-30, at 508, 509. See for biographical sketches of the faculty, Christian Stephan, *Die stumme Fakulät: Biographische Beiträge zur Geschichte der theologischen Fakultät der Universität Halle* (Doßel: Verlag Janos Stekovics, 2005), pp. 28-30, 41-49. On Baumgarten and the expulsion of Spangenberg (mostly at the insistence of Joachim Lange, the self-appointed guardian of the legacy of August Hermann Francke and the recently deceased Joachim Justus Breithaupt), see W. R. Ward, *The Protestant Evangelical Awakening* (Cambridge: Cambridge University Press, 1992), pp. 139-41.

15. Buddeus, *Gesammelte Schriften,* 10 vols. (1999-2006); vol. 6, ed. Walter Sparn, 2nd ed. (Leipzig, 1727; reprint, Hildesheim and New York: Georg Olms, 2007). For the work's existence in London among Ziegenhagen's library acquisitions, see AFSt Teilnachlass Ziegenhagen und Pasche, Karton 2:1 "Books of the late Rev. Mr. Ziegenhagen and Pasche."

16. UTC Bangalore Library Archives, SPG Records, Films, Reel 1: C/IND India General, Box 1 (3), Schwartz's notes "on a divinity lecture at Halle" (unpaginated, but dated 1748). I believe Schwartz's notes, however, probably reflect the Latin lectures delivered first in 1738 and published in German in 1750 by Siegmund Jacob Baumgarten. On his work and its implications for post-1750 teachings on marriage, see below, chapter 7.

must have imbibed no good impressions of marriage during his student days at the pietist center.

After finishing his studies, Albinus served between 1741 and 1743 in the *Paedagogium* of the Foundations, but he emigrated in 1743 to London, where he joined Friedrich Michael Ziegenhagen as preacher at the Court of Saint James. Seven years later, at the age of thirty-two, he experienced a crisis of conscience and an emotional breakdown and committed himself to write a confession of his position on marriage for Ziegenhagen's examination and support. The "explanation of his heart," as he put it, had revealed his "inward disgust and hatred against all lusts of the flesh." The revulsion resulted in a "stark horror against the marriage estate," because he could not believe otherwise than that this estate was "fodder for fleshly lusts." Only gradually had he managed to accept that God hallowed the estate, since Jesus blessed it at the wedding in Cana, and that marriage was "the means by which his Kingdom is maintained on earth." He then exposed the practical dangers he faced as an unmarried pastor, especially in dealing with "awakened" women. He suffered from the beginning of his time in London from a "very weak and very sensitive nature" that caused him to faint so often that those who sought him out did so more "out of necessity than good will." His concern to avoid scandal or give anyone grounds for complaint now led him to reconsider his early disgust with marriage and sexuality.[17]

The written deposition would be a singular curiosity were it not for the fact that its author seems to have imbibed at Halle the preference of the elder and younger Francke for celibacy for those intent on a pastoral career as a missionary. This became painfully clear when Albinus — apparently successful in reversing his ideas about marriage — again sought out Ziegenhagen, but this time for support to marry. He met an outraged refusal. In a long and pained explanation in 1754, Albinus recounted Ziegenhagen's fury that the young man had written some observations that reflected poorly on his older colleague. Ziegenhagen "would never give his consent to my marriage because he believes that the married estate would be detrimental for me and the work of God." Ziegenhagen now insisted that Albinus leave their dwelling and find a place of his own in the area of Saint James that, Albinus explained to the Halle fathers, was ruinously expensive and thus no solution.[18]

---

17. See Albinus to Sebastian Andreas Fabricius, AFSt/M1 E9, 17 February 1747; and AFSt/M 1D1b:51, 21 November 1750, for the quotations.

18. AFSt/M 1/De: 55 and 59, 16 May 1754, 23 July 1754, 55: r, recto No. 3; on Albinus's fruitless search for a house of his own, 55: 1 recto and verso.

156

Albinus finally quit London and ended his life in the Holy Roman Empire in a quiet pastorate and, as far as we know, a happy marriage. His slightly older contemporary Obuch had been active in both the Latin school and the girls school and had already departed for Vienna in 1734. Unlike Albinus, he promptly married (twice), apparently without the same sense of distress but, as his comments from India also indicated, without giving marriage any comment or status in his reports, content to label it a part of the "worldly" aspects of his life.

By the time Albinus had begun his studies in Halle, he had, in the person of Obuch, encountered the sole attempt made by Francke to provide not only young men but also pious women with the opportunity for education in a pietist context. Francke gradually abandoned the possibility of educating such women as potential future spouses of pietist clergy and laity. With that abandonment, positive reinforcement of attitudes that would have reassured pious young men about sexual relations with equally pious young women also suffered accordingly. Supported originally by the monetary contributions of the same eminent theologian and pietist Johann Samuel Stryk, whose 1704 essay had figured in the debates over marriage and polygamy, the Gynäceum had been formally separated from the Foundations in 1709 and left to fend for itself. Organized on lines of strict, quasi-monastic discipline and rules of dress and behavior, the experiment never received the wholehearted support of the elder Francke. It seemed to decline more or less on the same schedule as his relationship to his spouse and his increasing preference for celibate missionary pastors.

Although the Halle pietists continued to give some attention to the condition of single women, by 1740 the Gynäceum had closed after training no more than 100 girls. The original daughters of Silesian and Saxon nobility gave way steadily to Halle and Glaucha children of the middling sorts, who in the end concluded, like their social betters, that Protestants need not support the education of women outside the context of marriage and family in their own homes. In any case, the project of educating young women in institutions directly supported by the throne never caught the attention of the Brandenburg elector. Halle's theologians had abandoned it financially even before the Foundations received the renewal of their privileges in 1713.[19]

The question broached by Thomasius about the role of men and women and the place of friendship in the estate of marriage intensified again during

---

19. This summarizes Ulrike Witt, *Bekehrung, Bildung und Biographie: Frauen im Umkreis des Halleschen Pietismus* (Tübingen: Max Niemeyer Verlag, 1996), pp. 136-45.

Albinus's and Obuch's time in Halle. The noble and middling estates of the Reich produced some of the major women benefactors of the pietist movement. Correspondence within these circles cultivated friendship among pietist-inclined women. But friendship across the gender line was not a significant topic of interest. Rather, the difference between the reborn and the unconverted allowed pietists to lay aside social and hierarchical conventions.

Friendship within marriage likewise did not interest these correspondents.[20] Often enough, building on patterns inherited from medieval customs and networks, the letter writers equated in principle the concepts of friendship and relation by marriage. But whereas older notions of friendship had emphasized "fidelity" in the sense of a vassal's bond to a lord, by the 1730s authors explored more often the concept of trust, a notion relevant to a middling class that valued equality of intellectual standing, and open exchange of opinion. For some, however, the Moravians' willingness to pursue such notions extended far beyond what Lutheran pietists could accept, since they had inherited the conviction that even in marriage sexuality was almost always fraught with the sin of lust.[21]

Only belatedly, in 1743, did Halle decide to republish the 1741 treatise by Johann Jakob Moser that addressed sexual relations in marriage and a theology of the body.[22] Moser reached back to Spener, noting that the famous pietist father had been the only person willing to discuss marital relations and sex without shame in his *Theologische Bedencken* (1700-1702). Too many

20. Jutta Taege Bizer, "Freundschaft zwischen adeligen und bürgerlichen Frauen im frühen Pietismus — Die Briefe der Anna Elisabeth Kißner an die Gräfin Benigna von Solms-Laubach," in *Alter Adam und neue Kreatur: Pietismus und Anthropologie. Beiträge zum II. Internationalen Kongress für Pietismusforschung 2005*, ed. Udo Sträter and Hartmut Lehmann et al. (Halle and Tübingen: Max Niemeyer Verlag, 2009), pp. 445-58, at 455.

21. Elisabeth Quast, "Schwägerinnen: Adlige Frauen in der Frühphase der Halleschen Medikamentenexpedition," in *Medical Theory and Therapeutic Practice in the Eighteenth Century: A Transatlantic Perspective*, ed. Jürgen Helm and Renate Wilson (Stuttgart: Franz Steiner Verlag, 2008), pp. 281-307, at 299. On the older patterns, see Karl-Heinz Spieß, *Familie und Verwandtschaft im deutschen Hochadel des späten Mittelalters: 13. Bis Anfang des 16. Jahrhunderts* (Stuttgart: Franz Steiner, 1993); Wolfram Mauser, "'Ich lasse den Freund dir als Bürger': Das Prinzip Vertrauen und die Freundschaftsdichtung des 18. Jahrhunderts," in Ute Pott, *Das Jahrhundert der Freundschaft: Johann Wilhelm Ludwig Gleim und seine Zeitgenossen* (Göttingen: Wallstein Verlag, 2004), pp. 11-20, at 12-13. Mauser identifies this shift as beginning with Thomasius's 1692 essay on *Sittenlehre*.

22. Johann Jakob Moser, *Theologische Gedancken von der ehelichen Beywohnung unbekehrter, erweckter und wiedergebohrener Personen: Nebst des seeligen D. Speners Bedencken hievon und einem dreyfachen Anhang* . . . (Züllichau: In der Waysenhaus-Buchhandlung bey Joh. Jac. Dendeler, 1743), AFSt 34 M. Page references have been placed in the text.

of the truly converted, Moser argued, were embarrassed and would not raise important issues except to near relatives. But Scripture itself reveals that it is acceptable to learn about sex in a godly manner, and the converted should neither abuse sex in marriage nor turn to celibacy. Both partners must respect the rights of the other, though Moser distinguished sex among the unconverted (pp. 17-27), the "awakened" (pp. 28-39), the "re-born" (pp. 39-103), and the converted with an unconverted spouse. Even in that context, Moser defended "married love and friendship" (p. 104) and denied that children were the sole purpose of marriage. Abstinence from sex during pregnancy was unnecessary, as was abstaining for three nights after marriage, as in the example of Tobias; such practices smacked of "spiritual arrogance" or "legalistic fear" (pp. 44-53, 58-60, 94).

Less than a decade later, proof emerged that a broader audience existed for those writing on marriage. The threat posed by the Moravians finally began to attract serious attention. This is exemplified in a pamphlet published by Christian Friedrich Demelius in 1735. Demelius, one of a rising generation of theologians fascinated by close empirical observation of natural phenomena, had already in 1732 authored a pamphlet in which he asked whether reports of vampirism in Hungary could not, in the end, be explained by recourse to rational principles of nature. But his "thorough" as well as "historical" and "theological" report of 1735 on "nature" focused on its subversion by the unnatural teachings of the Moravian Brethren.

Demelius emphasized appropriate and inappropriate behavior by women but even more by men. It was alarming, he believed, that Moravian women were instructed to "please" the men sexually. It was more alarming that the men "affected" a suspiciously feminine manner of sighing and crying. In derisively fencing out the Brethren from the company of those who understood nature, Demelius sneered at Zinzendorf as a "master of ceremonies" who was not German in his understanding of the proper role of men and women in society, but some unnatural creature "wholly other."[23] If some quarters of European opinion softened the tradition of "elective friendship" — that is, of marriage into a family or by choice of a friend — Demelius's scorn suggests that some boundaries of socially accepted behav-

---

23. Cf. Demelius, *Vollständige so wohl Historisch als Theologische Nachricht von der Herrenhuthischen Brüderschafft . . .* (Frankfurt am Main, 1735), pp. 95-96. On Demelius and his earlier essay, *Philosophischer Versuch, ob nicht die merckwürdige Begebenheit derer Blutsauger in Niederungarn, anno 1732 geschehen, aus denen principiis naturae erleutert wurden* (Vienna, 1732), see Paul Peucker, "'Inspired by Flames of Love': Homosexuality, Mysticism, and Moravian Brothers around 1750," *Journal of the History of Sexuality* 15, no. 1 (2006): 30-64, 53 n. 71.

ior could not be crossed with impunity, or at least, not without the transgressor becoming the target of satire or outright denunciation.[24]

As Zinzendorf's ally August Gottlieb Spangenberg made his fruitless journey from Jena to Halle and Demelius published his essays in the early 1730s, views of men and women and of marriage continued to shift rapidly among the literate middling sorts of the Continent. The Eisenach physician Johannes Perlargius Storch contributed to the heightened interest, for this author of the eight-volume work on the diseases of women managed to combine "traditional body perceptions of his female patients" with knowledge "about the medical theories of the time." Storch did not do examinations since physical touching was allowed only to those in carefully guarded "legitimate" relationships of intimacy, but he exemplified the new interest in the close description and "enciphering" of human activity. He shrugged off the earlier attempt "to read and decipher creation, the book of god."[25] By the 1730s, the entire enterprise that had preoccupied theologians and jurists since Thomasius first contested with Pufendorf over the question of human sociability had changed. The earlier attempt "to establish a sound and coherent image of man as the firm ground of natural law had collapsed." Despite the absence of a coherent theological anthropology, some intrepid authors demonstrated renewed determination to explore the physical and lived reality of male and female relations within marriage. That determination now manifested itself from within the group that had been the object of Demelius's 1735 attack.[26]

Nikolaus von Zinzendorf's theology of the heart appealed to a growing European appreciation for sentiment, affection, and physical intimacy. His willingness to consider sexuality in the light of how men and women actually behaved now began to emerge in his teaching about marriage. In his

24. On the plasticity of gender roles among some of the middling and well-to-do English speakers, see Richard Godbeer, *The Overflowing of Friendship: Love between Men and the Creation of the American Republic* (Baltimore: Johns Hopkins University Press, 2009), pp. 8-12.

25. Barbara Duden, *The Woman beneath the Skins: A Doctor's Patients in Eighteenth-Century Germany,* trans. Thomas Dunlap (Cambridge, Mass., and London: Harvard University Press, 1991), pp. 8-9, quotation at 50, 84-85, 170-71, 177. On Halle pietists' difficulties reconciling empirical and cognitive notions of the body, see Jürgen Helm, "'Erde, Fettigkeit, subtiler Schleim und Wasser': Der Pietismus und die Leiblichkeit der Menschen," in *"Der Herr wird seine Herrlichkeit an uns offenbahren": Liebe, Ehe und Sexualität im Pietismus,* ed. Wolfgang Breul and Christian Soboth (Halle: Harrassowitz, 2012), pp. 183-237.

26. Michael Kempe, "The Anthropology of Natural Law: Debates about Pufendorf in the Age of Enlightenment," in *The Anthropology of the Enlightenment,* ed. Larry Wolff and Marco Cipolloni (Stanford: Stanford University Press, 2007), pp. 252-61, quotation at 259.

own estimation, he drew his conclusions from the implications of the Lutheran tradition in which he had been raised. His high view of the marriage relationship, so he claimed, drew upon Luther and Spener. His indebtedness to eclectic readings of less orthodox theologians of the preceding century emerged in his understanding that "union with God" was a "progressive and dynamic process of further development . . . [since] the heart is the foundational capacity of all religious life." Zinzendorf's "heart religion" did not automatically identify the Brethren as a "novel" or "fourth" religion within the legal-constitutional framework of the Reich. Since the Treaty of Westphalia had not formally recognized the ancient Unitas as a legitimate church, the "renewed" Moravians under Zinzendorf emphasized that they were but a renewal cell within the recognized Lutheran confessional tradition. Nor were their theology of the "heart" and their emphasis upon the marriage of the soul to God anything new. As far as this initial argument went, it appeared plausible to some of Zinzendorf's defenders within the ranks of Lutheran theologians. Gradually, however, and shockingly so, the count's insistence that the physical act of marital intercourse constituted the sacramental outward sign of mystical marriage, that is, communion with God, changed the identity of the Moravians and solidified Lutheran pietist theologians' hostility to anything even remotely smacking of the quasi-sacramental when describing the marital relationship.[27]

Zinzendorf's awareness of the importance of marriage in "heart religion" may have stemmed from his exposure to the debates over polygamy that began when he was a student in Halle. Arriving as a precocious youngster in 1710, he listened with rapt attention as the reports of Ziegenbalg, Plütschau, and Gründler were read to the faculty and students in the Foundations in 1714 after Ziegenbalg arrived to inform Francke of the Indian mission's progress. Although Zinzendorf left Halle for law study in Wittenberg in 1716, he remained a close observer of the pietist center's activities. During the count's own life, Moravians did not enter into debates over marriage with Halle's missionaries in India. Only in 1760 did the "Brothers' Garden" in

27. Michele Cassese, "Herkunft der Herzensreligion von Nikolaus Ludwig von Zinzendorf," in *Interdisziplinäre Pietismusforschungen: Beiträge zum Ersten Internationalen Kongress für Pietismusforschung 2001*, ed. Udo Sträter et al., 2 vols. (Halle and Tübingen: Max Niemeyer Verlag, 2005), 1:187-99, quotation at 198; the argument for a Moravian radical theology of gender and proto-feminism is Aaron Fogelman, *Jesus Is Female: Moravians and the Challenge of Radical Religion in Early America* (Philadelphia: University of Pennsylvania Press, 2007). I am unconvinced that novel ideas about women's roles account for the hostility since the focus of so much Moravian sexual and marital teaching remained on the male body.

Tranquebar serve as the platform for a disastrous attempt at a mission in the Nicobar Islands. Since the Moravians in India made few converts (three before 1775), they did not find occasion to engage in the Tamil context in disputes over marital relationships. The missions to both African slaves and Native Americans in the Western Hemisphere, however, would raise disturbing questions about polygamy, premarital intercourse, and divorce.[28]

Zinzendorf's activities in Europe and North America reopened debates on male and female sexuality that had been closed off in Christian circles since the fifth century. The apostle Paul's call for lifelong virginity (in anticipation of an imminent Second Coming) had given the edge to celibates. Some medieval writers had suggested that even the estate of marriage was open to the possibility of "voluntary transitions from normal conjugal relations to chastity" and "spiritual marriage." By the eleventh century, bourgeois or noble women (hardly ever those of lower economic and social status) had initiated such transitions. In the minds of some critics, at least, the Moravians now threatened to reopen issues long thought to have been settled among Protestants.[29]

Zinzendorf's comments in the "Seventeen Points" suggest that, like the Christian Alexandrian theologians of the fourth and fifth centuries, he found a remote image of "God the Father" too inaccessible. His emphasis upon Christ as "the human face of God" sprang from both his own family history and his reading of the church fathers. His notion that God the Son was the creator of the world depended on some of the Greek Fathers who had also seen in the Genesis account God's "speaking" the creation into existence as the "Word" Christ. But as Zinzendorf read the patristic sources, Luther, and Spener, he also recalled the controversies that had swirled around the more radical mystical tradition inherited from Jakob Böhme and the English Philadelphians — a tradition that had been manifest in the work of Gottfried Arnold by the early 1700s. The notion of a pre-Fall androgynous

28. Thomas Ruhland, "The Moravian Brethren and the Danish-Halle Mission in Tranquebar — the 'Garden of the Brothers' at the Centre of a European Conflict," in *Halle and the Beginning of Protestant Christianity in India II: Christian Mission in the Indian Context,* ed. Andreas Gross, Y. Vincent Kumaradoss, and Heike Liebau (Halle: Verlag der Franckeschen Stiftungen zu Halle, 2006), pp. 743-66.

29. Peter Brown, *The Body and Society: Men, Women, and Sexual Renunciation in Early Christianity* (New York: Columbia University Press, 1988), remains the standard summary for early Christian views; see also Dyan Elliott, *Spiritual Marriage: Sexual Abstinence in Medieval Wedlock* (Princeton: Princeton University Press, 1993), pp. 25-60, 86-93, and 266-67, 300, quotation at 83.

humanity was (again) not new; at least hints of the notion can possibly be found in the works of Origen. But the majority of Christians had rejected such views.[30]

By the mid-1730s, one anonymous pamphleteer assessed the all-too-optimistic teachings of the Brethren on the human condition, an optimism he concluded revealed itself in their willingness to challenge conventional ideas of male and female. From Gotha in Thuringia, this critic described the peculiarities of the night vigil, foot washing, and the separate groupings of married and unmarried males and females. Although admitting with some admiration that these disciplines were intended to replicate the virtues of the first Christians, the observer wondered whether such measures were altogether fitting and useful in contemporary Europe. The essay then focused more intently on the teachings of the Moravians "by which they make themselves objects of suspicion."[31]

Frustrated by the lack of a clear summary of Moravian teaching, the author suggested that Moravian hymnals revealed their fascination not so much with the "great nothing and visible darkness in the souls of humanity" as with the "breaking out of the glowing spark, the painful birth-giving," the "breaking in with force to God," and similar unclear notions. Dubious attempts to improve on Luther's Bible translation did little to enlighten ordinary believers, the critic charged, and the Moravian conviction that they possessed a special sense to interpret Scripture revealed a dangerous reliance upon the subjective and corrupted heart they were loathe to admit. Some among them apparently rejected the notion of God as commonly confessed among Lutherans, and rather than speak of Christ as the mediator, Moravians accentuated "the Christ in us as [for what he has done] for us." Attacking Moravians' naïve notion that so much of the original image and likeness remained in humankind that baptism, the Lord's Supper, and the struggle for repentance were no longer of great importance, the critic ques-

---

30. On Origen's fragmentary speculations, see Peter C. Bouteneff, *Beginnings: Ancient Christian Readings of the Biblical Creation Narratives* (Grand Rapids: Baker Academic, 2008), pp. 106-12, at 109. On Zinzendorf and the Alexandrians, see Craig D. Atwood, "'He Has Carried You My Members': The Full Humanity of Christ and the Blessing of the Physical Body in Zinzendorfian Piety," in *Alter Adam*, pp. 197-207, at 198-200, and Wolfgang Breul, "Gottfried Arnold und das eheliche und unvereheliche Leben," in *Alter Adam*, pp. 357-69.

31. *Ausführliche Historische und Theologische Nachricht von der Herrenhuthischen Brüderschafft* . . . (Frankfurt, 1743), in *Antizinzendorfiana aus der Anfangszeit 1729-1735*, edited and introduction by Erich Beyreuther, 2nd ser., vol. 14 (Hildesheim and New York: Georg Olms Verlag, 1976), pp. 7-102, at 102.

tioned whether primitive notions of holding all goods in common did not lead to disorder rather than virtue among ordinary people.[32]

But, the anonymous critic concluded, the "most astonishing of all [teaching] we encounter in their marriages." The use of the lot to link a man declaring his desire to marry to any one of the available women was supposed, the critic noted, to redirect what might be purely sexual lust to a more spiritual end. In fact, he concluded, "it is easy to see that these [practices] are stark innovations in the household," and seen together with the wrongheaded estimation of how men and women really are in this world, such novelties demonstrated the Moravians' erroneous understanding of both God and humanity.[33]

The more traditionally Lutheran, early Zinzendorf who had not yet revealed just how far he was willing to push the boundaries of union with God in marital relations made a major impact upon a brilliant Württemberg theologian, Friedrich Christoph Oetinger (1702-82). The young man fell under Zinzendorf's spell, and then spent most of the 1730s attempting to extricate himself from the count's influence. Eventually, Oetinger devoted his life to probing questions about the body as the location of the soul. He also drew attention for his contributions to the debates over sexuality and marriage. Oetinger was unique among Lutheran theologians because he did not, as his patristic and medieval mystical predecessors were inclined to do, locate the soul in the "heart." Rather, for him, the soul acted vaguely as some kind of "electricity in the body."[34] His speculations in the realm of a possibly novel theological anthropology, however, did not allow him to remain in sympathetic alliance with Zinzendorf's all-too-optimistic views, nor Zinzendorf's emerging teaching on sex and marital relations.

Oetinger took his time deciding how to deal with marriage and the threats Moravian theology posed to the estate. In the aftermath of the fierce

32. *Ausführliche Historische und Theologische Nachricht,* pp. 103, 104-20, at 120.

33. *Ausführliche Historische und Theologische Nachricht,* pp. 136-67, at 167. See also the Wittenberg faculty's condemnation of the hymn contents and the "invention" of the lottery in marriage by which anyone living in Herrnhut can "lose his natural freedom he was born with," the marriage lottery practice being not only against nature but also a "dangerous disorder," in *Der Historische und Theologische Nachricht . . .* (included in the same volume), pp. 82-128, at 107.

34. Martin Weyer-Menkhoff, "Herzsorge, Gott und Körper bei Friedrich Christoph Oetinger," in *Interdisziplinäre Pietismusforschungen,* 2:611-18, at 615. On Oetinger, see Martin Brecht, "Der württembergische Pietismus," in *Geschichte des Pietismus: Der Pietismus im achtzehnten Jahrhundert,* ed. Brecht et al. (Göttingen: Vandenhoeck & Ruprecht, 1995), pp. 225-95, at 269-78.

criticism he unleashed on the Moravians, he paused to develop the idea of a "biblical dictionary," which he completed in 1759 and revised in 1776. His earliest definition of marriage defended the estate against the accusation that it had "animal" qualities because of coitus, which was as far as he was willing to go in defending Zinzendorf's far more aggressive defense of sexual relations. Oetinger noted with Luther that God "extended his cloak" over the estate and made it holy. He likewise sneered at those who despised marriage in favor of celibacy, a point of view those who knew of his youthful determination to remain unmarried would have found ironic. Oetinger pointed to the words of Jesus that in the resurrection, men and women would no longer marry. Nonetheless, we live in the here and now, he wrote, and both virgins and the married should equally "rejoice in the Lord, but not after the spirit of the world." For Oetinger, the transformative nature of marriage appeared in Paul's teaching that the holiness of the Christian partner would make the unbelieving spouse holy.[35]

It is not so clear that Oetinger had always thought this way. If the Brethren were shocked by his decision to attack them, they had good grounds for surprise, for he had long counted himself among their friends. His published attack came a decade after he had been an apparently appreciative guest in Herrnhut in the Upper Lausitz in 1730 and had assured Zinzendorf by letters from Halle that he would not turn against the count because of the younger Francke's animosity. Upon his return to Tübingen, he became one of Zinzendorf's ardent defenders. By 1736, however, he became a doubter again, repeating a pattern in the relationship between the two men that lasted until a decisive break in 1741. His decision to publish his critical essay in the 1740s suggests that the original bridegroom mysticism Zinzendorf found in Johann Arndt, the author favored by the early pietists, had turned in an all-too-worldly fashion to include the notion that human sexual ecstasy between men and women had quasi-sacramental significance. Even worse, as the 1740s turned into the "Sifting Period," genital sex among a group of Moravian males at Herrnhaag intensified scrutiny of Zinzendorf's teaching on sex and marriage, prompting Oetinger to clarify where he stood.[36]

Like anyone else familiar with Luther's translation of the Bible, Zinzen-

---

35. Oetinger, *Biblisches und Emblematisches Wörterbuch,* ed. Gerhard Schäfer et al., 2 vols. (Berlin and New York: Walter de Gruyter, 1999), 1:84.

36. Martin Brecht, "Zinzendorf in der Sicht seiner kirchlichen und theologischen Kritiker," in *Zur Rezeption mystischer Traditionen im Protestantismus des 16. Bis 19. Jahrhunderts: Beiträge eines Symposiums zum Tersteegen-Jubiläum 1997,* ed. Dietrich Meyer and Udo Sträter (Cologne: Rheinland-Verlag, 2002), pp. 207-28, at 211-14.

dorf and Oetinger had to grapple with Luther's decision to translate Paul's observation in 1 Corinthians 6:13 that although the body and food were made for each other, God would "put both to death" *(hinrichten)*. Although the Latin Vulgate used the word "to destroy" *(destruet)*, the original Greek *(katayesei)* had conveyed neither the sense of destruction nor especially the sense of "execution." All commentators could agree with the apostle's conclusion that the body was made for the Lord, not for fornication *(Hurerei)*. But Zinzendorf developed an elaborate schema that understood this "destruction" to eliminate male sexual genitalia in order to allow men to return to the feminine soul qualities already enjoyed by their female counterparts.

In an equally scandalous manner, Zinzendorf insisted that in the coming kingdom, the role of Christ as the original creator of the world and his appearance as a fully male human required that only he retain his male genitalia. None of these teachings were yet obvious in the 1730s and only began to emerge clearly after Zinzendorf's break with Oetinger and his equally frustrating failure a year later to convince North American German speakers to accept his theological teaching. Oetinger had already clearly stepped away from such speculations as he approached his own wedding day in 1738.

The influence of the count on Oetinger's marriage was twofold: it allied Oetinger with a woman who ended his peripatetic wanderings to Halle and Herrnhut, and Oetinger composed a hymn for the occasion that he stipulated was to be sung to the same tune Zinzendorf had chosen for his "Jesus, Still Lead On." The Oetinger composition of 22 April 1738, however, drew more on Drese's original than on Zinzendorf's 1721 adaptation, paraphrasing "Bridegroom, Jesus, Lamb of God" to "sweet Bridegroom, beautiful Lamb of God" *(Holder Bräutigam, Schönes Gotteslamm)*. But Oetinger tied such mystical language directly to the bridal couple by writing: "can souls who show themselves your own as bride and bridegroom escape from Egypt's distress?" Oetinger affirmed that they could, and continued in his version to reflect that grace accompanied the man who sought out as a bride a sister who also knew God; that the marriage estate, though it might be accompanied with considerable sorrow, was blessed by God's love; and that "you will our flesh and bones to become eternal and to recognize us in love." This was as close an approximation of Spener's and Luther's transformative hopes for marriage as any European Lutheran writer of the eighteenth century was to achieve.[37]

---

37. Oetinger, *Geistliche Lieder,* edited and with an introduction by J. Roessle, *Zeugnisse der Schwabenväter,* Band IV (Metzingen and Württemberg: Verlag Ernst Franz, 1967), pp. 114-15.

Oetinger confined his comments about this occasion in his autobiography to the terse observation that "I married therefore in my 36th year and produced children." Elsewhere he claimed to be impressed that his wife was so modest she would hardly even shake his hand and that he himself was not in the least mesmerized by her charms. Christiane Dorothea Linsenmann, whatever his description of her, appeared to share at least some of his admiration for the renewal of spiritual life Oetinger had located among the Moravians — but not the count's attempt to explain how both males and females would be the brides of Christ.[38]

Zinzendorf in his youth had admired German mystical writings that emphasized the possibility of "union with God" that so interested Oetinger. But by 1734 the count claimed that he had turned against such teachings and devoted himself increasingly to a strict version of Lutheran emphasis upon justification by faith alone. It may have been this apparent reaffirmation of a more "orthodox" Lutheran position that made Oetinger reluctant to join in 1735 the pamphleteers who moved openly against Zinzendorf.[39]

Oetinger's own marital life undoubtedly played a role in his decision as well. Infatuated with the young Anna Nitschmann during his visits to Herrnhut, Oetinger had returned to his homeland and, finding an unusual degree of peace in his marriage with a woman whom apparently he regarded as a genuine friend, began work on the essays that he would finally publish in 1748. His need to make clear his true assessment of Zinzendorf intensified because of attacks initiated by the Straßburg polemicist Johann Leonhard Fröreißen. The latter, devoted to Halle's version of pietism, suspected Oetinger of still harboring Moravian sympathies. Oetinger lamented his condition as a latter-day Job, abandoned by friends. He now claimed that he had been worried about Moravians and the marriage issue since 1730 but only recently decided to set forth his reflections in the format of the book of

---

38. Friedrich Christoph Oetinger, *Genealogie der reellen Gedancken eines Gottes-Gelehrten: Seine Selbstbiographie,* ed. Dieter Ising (Leipzig: Evangelische Verlagsanstalt, 2010), p. 128; see also Martin Weyer-Menkhoff, *Christus, Das Heil der Natur: Entstehung und Systematik der Theologie Friedrich Christoph Oetingers* (Göttingen: Vandenhoeck & Ruprecht, 1990), pp. 110-11, and Julius Rauscher, "Die Auseinandersetzung zwischen Chr. Fr. Oetinger und Zinzendorf," *Blätter für württembergische Kirchengeschichte* 39 and 40 (1935, 1936): 131-48 and 107-135, 40, 110-11.

39. On this shift in Zinzendorf's views of mysticism, see Dietrich Meyer, "Cognitio Dei Experimentalis oder 'Erfahrungstheologie' bei Gottfried Arnold, Gerhard Tersteegen und Nikolaus Ludwig von Zinzendorf," in *Zur Rezeption mystischer Traditionen im Protestantismus des 16. bis 19. Jahrhunderts,* pp. 223-40, at 231-35.

Job as "A Conversation between a Mystic, a Philosopher, and a Law-Fanatic. . . ."[40] The essay made it clear where Oetinger believed the count had fallen into error on the proper function of the law of God, on the doctrine of the Trinity itself, and on the right understanding of marriage.[41]

Although the Moravians might claim affinity with the great Lutheran Johann Arndt, he noted, they derived their understanding of God and the church excessively from the humanity of Christ. Weak on the notion of original sin, the Moravians had unduly elevated marriage and given women an "ascendant" role over their husbands because the "original human" was female and the male sex only an afterthought of the Creator. Logically, therefore, all souls were female with Christ as the bridegroom, just as Zinzendorf taught. The Moravians forgot, Oetinger warned, that we remain "children of this world" in the body; they attempted to make sexual congress itself into a work of justification, forgetting the three conditions of humanity that the apostle Paul spoke of — those under the law, those under grace, and those beyond the law. Forgetting to tie the sufferings of Christ to the wrath of God, the Moravians dared to suppose that union with God could be obtained here and now without spiritual struggle and repentance; their desire to affirm the godliness of the physical in this world overlooked the necessity of Christ's suffering by which humans would be saved and in which they participated under the cross.

Oetinger confessed that he had originally been willing to overlook the novelty in Zinzendorf's marriage notions because he thought they were merely "fleeting thoughts" *(fliegende Gedancken)*. Instead, a mere two years after Zinzendorf had last preached in Oetinger's parish, the Württemberger began to discover that the count's emphasis upon Christ as the bridegroom to all his members implied that "Polygamy can be a better picture of Christ and his Bride than monogamy according to his doctrinal concept." Zinzen-

---

40. Oetinger's essay is bound with *Das rechte Gericht* . . . (Esslingen: Gottlieb Mäntlern, 1748); I have used this edition from the United Library Seabury Theological Seminary Special Collections. The *Gespräch eines Mystici, eines Weltweisen, und eines Gesetz-Eyferers* . . . begins at p. 268 in this edition. On Fröreißen, see Erich Beyreuther, ed., *Antizinzendorfiana II: Aus den Freien Reichsstädten Hamburg, Lübeck, Frankfurt am Main und der ehemlas Freien Reichsstadt Straßburg*, with an introduction by Erich Beyreuther (Hildesheim and New York: Georg Olms Verlag, 1982), 2nd ser., vol. 15, "Introduction," pp. 62-103; for Fröreißen and Halle and his 1742 and 1743 pamphlets, pp. 29-108.

41. Martin Brecht, "Zinzendorf in der Sicht seiner Kritiker," in *Neue Aspekte der Zinzendorf-Forschung*, ed. Martin Brecht and Paul Peucker (Göttingen: Vandenhoeck & Ruprecht, 2006), pp. 207-28, especially 211-14.

dorf had, Oetinger concluded, even changed his notion of the Trinity to "accommodate . . . his sensuous marriage-secret" teaching, moving from a Trinity that was merely three appearances of a godhead to one where the Father was now a mere helper in the creation, the Holy Spirit a mother of the congregation, and the Son the commanding officer in charge of the war against sin *(Kriegs-General Amt)*. Oetinger's decision to cast his observations in the form of a conversation among the three figures intentionally called to mind Job's fair-weather friends who had betrayed declarations of loyalty and provided false and misleading counsel when he most needed sound advice, a not-so-veiled revelation of how Oetinger had come to view Zinzendorf.[42]

By the time Oetinger's attack became available in print, however, Zinzendorf had good grounds to conclude that it was he who deserved iconic identification with the hapless Job who was attacked by supposed friends. He had last visited Oetinger to give a sermon at the latter's request in the parish of Hirsau in July of 1739. Although Oetinger dedicated an essay to the count shortly thereafter, his ruminations on the gospel amounted to a declaration of independence from Zinzendorf and a refusal to pursue further the emphasis on Jesus as the soul's bridegroom. Oetinger could not have known too much about the developing marriage theology of the count since the Holy Spirit appeared as the mother of the community first in 1739; the "Seventeen Points," although composed in 1740, were not made public; and not until 1743 did Moravian hymnals include materials that concentrated on the circumcised Christ and urge meditation upon this wound, the one that prefigured his ultimate suffering on the cross.

The evolving emphasis upon the veneration of Christ's male member and the holiness of sexual coitus that became obvious to Zinzendorf's critics by the late 1740s, especially in his talks given at Zeist, however, may also have been spurred by the count's disappointments with both the Schwenkfelders and the Ephrata community. He visited these North American groups in 1742 with high hopes of securing their endorsement of his vision for a renewed Christian church.[43]

---

42. Oetinger, *Gespräch,* pp. 298, 307-8.

43. For the sequence of Zinzendorf's evolving teaching on the holiness of human sexual activity in marriage, see Peter Vogt, "'Er ist Mann': Die Männlichkeit Jesu in der Theologie Zinzendorfs," in *"Der Herr wird seine Herrlichkeit an uns offenbahren": Liebe, Ehe und Sexualität im Pietismus,* pp. 183-237; Craig D. Atwood, "Christ and the Bridal Bed: Eighteenth-Century Moravian Sex-Positive Spirituality as a Possible Influence on Blake," in *Re-envisioning Blake,* ed. Mark Crosby, Troy Patenaude, and Angus Whitehead (New York: Palgrave Macmillan, 2012), pp. 160-79; Paul Peucker, "Wives of the Lamb: Moravian Brothers and Gen-

Conrad Beissel, the troubled genius whose thought dominated the experimental community at Ephrata, Pennsylvania, agreed with Zinzendorf's speculations about humankind, at least on certain points. Both men drew upon Johann Georg Gichtel (and perhaps ultimately Origen) to say that an androgynous male-female creature preexisted the Fall into male and female. But Beissel's agreement with Zinzendorf ended here. There had been no sex in paradise, Beissel taught; circumcision was a sign of God's revulsion at the animal qualities of human coitus, and since marriage was a post-Fall concession by God, it could be dissolved for the higher purpose of pursuing a celibate life. Beissel had no use for Zinzendorf's emerging piety venerating the circumcised member of Christ, and although he shared the latter's fascination with the side wound of Christ, for the Ephratans this representation of the maternal and vaginal was the point of contact with the banished Sophia, the original feminine soul the celibates were attempting to connect with and to venerate properly. This theosophical emphasis depended upon a reading of Jakob Böhme's teachings. It set Beissel at odds with Zinzendorf, who had rejected the Böhmist conclusions. Instead, the circumcision of Christ had restored male and female sex organs to their original capacity to reflect the image and likeness of God. Logically then, sexual coitus itself could be understood as a form of liturgical worship. This was no mere "fleshly" procreative act but one that realized the union of Christ and his church.[44]

Zinzendorf's stormy confrontation with Beissel contained none of the poignancy of the former's rupture with Oetinger, a culminating break between old friends. The aristocratic Lusatian count and Beissel, the baker's son from Eberbach in the Palatinate, spoke different versions of the German language and lived their lives in social circles that rarely intersected. Zinzendorf met with an equally decisive but for him more bitter rejection at the hands of the Schwenkfelder community, which had arrived in Pennsylvania in 1734 after being sheltered by the count on his estate at Herrnhut.

---

der around 1750," in *Masculinity, Senses, Spirit,* ed. Katharine Faull (Lewisburg, Pa.: Bucknell University Press, 2011), pp. 39-54.

44. This paragraph summarizes Peter Vogt, "'Ehereligion': The Moravian Theory and Practice of Marriage as Point of Contention in the Conflict between Ephrata and Bethlehem," and Jeffrey Bach, "Ephrata and Moravian Relations: The View from Ephrata," both in *Communal Societies* 21 (2001): 37-48 and 49-60, respectively; see also Bach, *Voices of the Turtledoves: The Sacred World of Ephrata* (University Park: Pennsylvania State University Press; Göttingen: Vandenhoeck & Ruprecht, 2003), pp. 13, 33-59, 97-114. On the medieval theological speculations on Christ as mother, see Caroline Walker Bynum, *Jesus as Mother: Studies in the Spirituality of the High Middle Ages* (Berkeley: University of California Press, 1982).

His rejection by people Zinzendorf justifiably thought of as owing him *Treue* — the older notion of "friendship" as "loyalty" to their former patron — stung worse than Beissel's hostility. Zinzendorf apparently had never been fully convinced that the Schwenkfelders were theologically sound. Tracing their own heritage to Caspar Schwenkfeld, the sixteenth-century theologian whom Luther dismissed as a radical enthusiast, this small group of Protestants preferred a profoundly internalized understanding of the church and of the individual soul's and the community's relationship to Christ. They regarded external signs such as baptism and the Lord's Supper as purely spiritualized in ways that Luther had found insufficiently attentive to an incarnate God's presence in the world. Why Zinzendorf believed that the Atlantic passage would have altered the Schwenkfelders' beliefs remains a mystery. He returned to Europe in March 1742 with nothing to show for his efforts to bring Ephratans and Schwenkfelders into his vision for a pan-Protestant church.[45]

The gathering storm over the suspected Moravian marriage teachings now affected the German-speakers who had crossed the Atlantic during the 1730s. Although the Schwenkfelders were used to accusations of heterodoxy hurled by Lutheran and Reformed theologians, they were stunned to discover within a few years of Zinzendorf's failed American journey that Europeans thought of them as his close allies. Oetinger's attack that finally appeared in 1748 took aim at the Moravians, but it also (erroneously) accused the Schwenkfelders of sharing radical notions of an androgynous Christ and of holding the heretical and dangerous views of sexual love that had corrupted Zinzendorf's teachings. Oetinger's publication and the potential damage his writings could wreak upon the reputation of the small Schwenkfelder group demanded a response. From Pennsylvania, the Schwenkfelder physician Abraham Wagner now answered Oetinger's assault in a handwritten memorandum that made its way back across the Atlantic for circulation among the friends of the tiny group of Protestant dissenters.[46]

---

45. Horst Weigelt, "Zinzendorf und die Schwenckfelder," in *Neue Aspekte der Zinzendorf-Forschung*, pp. 64-96; on the earlier history of the Schwenkfelder, see Weigelt, *Spiritualistische Tradition im Protestantismus* (Berlin and New York: De Gruyter, 1973), pp. 239-76; Brecht, "Das Aufkommen der neuen Frömmigkeitsbewegung in Deutschland," in *Geschichte des Pietismus*, pp. 113-203, at 118-23.

46. The text of Wagner's response and the matrimonial poem he composed in defense as cited here have been reproduced in Andrew S. Berky, *Practitioner in Physick: A Biography of Abraham Wagner, 1717-1763* (Pennsburg, Pa.: Schwenkfelder Library, 1954), pp. 72-74, 126-30. The original answer to Oetinger is in the Schwenkfelder Library Archives, Pennsburg, Pa.,

Wagner had much earlier compiled a poem praising marriage. He decided to publish it after deferring its appearance for a decade because of the urgent need to respond to Oetinger. His memorandum first refuted Oetinger's fears about the Schwenkfelders by referring Lutherans back to their own Apology of the Augsburg Confession and the mystical prototype of marriage found in Ephesians 5. That the Schwenkfelders (and by implication Oetinger among the Lutherans) felt threatened by their association with the "sex-positive" Moravian defense of coitus became clear in Wagner's refutation. Wagner's marriage poem pointed only to the descent of Christ to rescue his bride, the church (Heb. 2:14). Only a "water baptism in the Word" makes for purity in preparation for heaven; marriage, he insisted (echoing Luther himself), is a "likeness" *(Gleichnis)* of the relationship of Christ to his church, but finally it remains, as in Ephesians 5, a great mystery ("Das Geheimnis ist gross/Christi und Seiner Braut").

Wagner then turned to the roles for man and woman in marriage. At first he appeared to reject any notion of friendship in his theology of spousal relations. The pious wife is obedient to her husband and is his subject — she owes him fidelity *(Treue)*. Nonetheless, Wagner could not bring himself to jettison the elevation of marriage that Luther had brought to Protestantism, for just as Christ gave himself for the church, so must the man love and honor his "marriage companion" *(Ehgnoss)*.

What did ordinary people make of the intense international theological disputes about marriage that now raged among pietist and Moravian leaders? No diary entries, no letters from German-speaking Schwenkfelder or Ephrata believers survive that allow us to conclude with certainty whether they accepted the official view, the more legal/contractual position that corresponded to the sociopolitical dimensions of real married life, or the unofficial, more mystical-companionate view of marriage as a created order and icon of the church. Nor can we track with certainty the fate of Wagner's missive and whether it effectively exonerated the Schwenkfelders in European circles by saving them from guilt by association with the marriage theology of Zinzendorf and his followers.

Abraham Wagner Collection, VS 4 1; the handwriting is not Wagner's but that of an unknown contemporary from the mid to late eighteenth century who notes "Folgendes hat A[braham] W[agner] geschrieben und den Briefen nach Deutschland Beylegen lassen." I am grateful to Hunt Schenkel for his assistance in checking the original paper quality for dating purposes. On the larger practices of scribal publication, see David D. Hall, "Scribal Publication in Seventeenth-Century New England: An Introduction and a Checklist," *Proceedings of the American Antiquarian Society* 115, part 1 (2006): 29-80.

As the Moravian-pietist confrontation now shifted to North America, the combatants took sides on the issue of marital friendship but largely ignored the vexed issue of polygamy. In their Caribbean missionary efforts, the Moravians opposed polygamy, although they had made a reluctant compromise by 1749 to allow "converts with more than one wife before baptism . . . to retain them." Similarly, in their efforts among the Lenape of the Middle Atlantic, the Moravians went to some lengths to combat the absence of lifelong commitment to a single spouse, and by the 1770s explained that they expected converted Lenape to "maintain order among themselves since they [were] now somewhat settled in." In admonishing the married Lenape, David Zeisberger made it a point to review again their rules, "and this satisfied all the Brothers and Sisters, because many Brothers and Sisters, and especially new ones who came to us several years ago, were under the illusion that their children could not marry among us." The observation covered the reality that "the native practices of premarital sex, serial monogamy, and polygamy appalled the Moravian missionaries." To some degree, converts internalized the Moravian teaching on monogamous Christian marriage, but placed more importance upon the matrilineal control of degrees of kinship in determining who might be allowed to marry whom, even among the converted.[47]

Activities among both Native Americans and Africans did not come to the attention of pietist critics nearly as often as did practices among Europeans. Among those activities, the resurgence of iconography among the Moravians signaled to viewers a potentially alarming theology. Alone among the eighteenth-century European Protestants, the Moravians devoted considerable attention to religious paintings. Perhaps precisely because of the controversy about marriage, the estate found almost no direct resonance in the work of Johann Valentine Haidt or the anonymous artists who provided these pictures in Herrnhut, London, and North America. Sexuality, however, did. A double portrait in Herrnhut of the Protten family with their daughter and one of Johann and Susann Nitschzmann in Bethlehem along with an engraving of multiple married couples at Herrnhaag before their departure for Pennsylvania exhaust the marriage theme. The focus of the Moravian

---

47. Quotations above come from Jon F. Sensbach, *Rebecca's Revival: Creating Black Christianity in the Atlantic World* (Cambridge: Harvard University Press, 2005), pp. 90-91; *The Moravian Mission Diaries of David Zeisberger, 1772-1781*, ed. Hermann Wellenreuther and Carola Wessel, trans. Julie Tomberlin Weber (University Park: Pennsylvania State University Press, 2005), pp. 125-26, at 125, 145-46; and Jane T. Merritt, *At the Crossroads: Indians and Empires on a Mid-Atlantic Frontier, 1700-1763* (Chapel Hill: University of North Carolina Press, 2003), pp. 135-43, at 140.

theology upon the male body, the maleness of Christ, however, was abundantly clear in Haidt's work.

Converted from his Lutheran heritage in London in 1738, Haidt moved to Herrnhut and in 1740 began work that by the latter part of the decade presented Zinzendorf as the *Teacher of the Nations* (1747) and the *First Fruits* of the converted (1747) in which the muscular, idealized male form of the converted African and North American Native Americans stands out in intense light, in sharp contrast to the (consistently) modestly clothed and postured women. Not surprisingly, his *Christ Scourged, Thomas Doubting,* and *Lamentation over the Body of Christ* also make unmistakably clear the focus on the male body and Christ as the bridegroom of believers. In the 1750 work *Band of Maidens* Christ's nearly naked body is surrounded by demurely clothed women, the Virgin Mother portrayed by Zinzendorf's second wife Anna Maria Nitschmann, and the count himself in the role of the virginal John the Beloved Disciple.[48]

By 1746, with the marriage of his own daughter Benigna to Johannes Langguth, Zinzendorf's marriage teaching matched Haidt's portrayals. Zinzendorf had by 1740 developed his "Seventeen Points on Matrimony," although the details of instructing newly married Moravians in acceptable sexual practices remained a closely guarded secret within the community. So, too, did the existence of the so-called Blue Cabinet that referred to an actual room (or in some cases, a portable chamber or bench) upon which intercourse took place. The Moravians clearly understood that not the marriage rite or the institution but rather "intercourse was considered sacramental." But even without express knowledge of these internal practices, Halle polemicists like Joachim Lange and Siegmund Jacob Baumgarten (though not particularly of one mind on many aspects of the pietist movement) put aside their differences and with the aid of their allies in Wernigerode sought to undermine any claim the Moravians put forward to be considered subscribers to the Lutheran Confessions and orthodox teachers on the topic of marriage.

---

48. I am indebted to Paul Peucker for confirming my own survey of the surviving images. No systematic study of Moravian iconography has been done. On Haidt, see John F. Morman, "The Painting Preacher: John Valentine Haidt," *Pennsylvania History* 20, no. 2 (April 1953): 180-86, and the Bethlehem Digital History Project: http://bdhp.moravian.edu/art/paintings/paintings.html (accessed 11 February 2011). For the analysis of the *Jungfernbund* portrait, see Gisela Mettele, "Das Gedächtnis der Bilder: Malerei und Memoria in der Herrnhuter Brüdergemeine," in *Gendering Tradition: Erinnerungskultur und Geschlecht im Pietismus,* ed. Ulrike Gleixner and Erika Hebeisen (Korb: Didymos-Verlag, 2007), pp. 149-69, at 159-60.

Upon his return from North America, Zinzendorf discovered that Baumgarten (among others) had identified the count as the author of what was in fact a collective effort that appeared as *Siegfried's Modest Illumination*. Baumgarten's attack on the Brethren, however, focused on their right to be thought of as part of the confessional tradition; they were instead a separatist sect whose leader had hidden his real intent of creating a new church order in Europe. For the moment, the marriage question among Moravians was overshadowed by this intense polemical exchange that lasted until the year before the marriage of Zinzendorf's daughter.[49]

Appearing to focus on the political implications of Moravian confessional soundness, Joachim Lange's last major work, *Fatherly Warning* (1744), did disavow sensationalist scandalmongering about Moravians. Nonetheless, he could not avoid confronting the issue that by now had become a recognized peculiarity of the Moravians' beliefs about the relationship of God to humans, namely, marital relations, sexuality, and the openly sacramental claims that proclaimed union with God now, in this physical world.[50]

Lange's attack on the Moravians and marriage revealed the underlying hesitancy that had prevented Halle theologians from defining the estate ever since the controversy with Thomasius had first brought the question to light. Unwilling to elevate the definition of the estate of marriage to the level of an article of faith, Lange insisted that the Moravian "material on marriage belongs, it is true, not to dogma, but rather to the light and right of nature; nonetheless it is especially important in and of itself, especially when man considers it according to how it enlightens and regulates [sexual matters] as holy Scripture has handed down to us; and how perverted it is within the Herrnhuter form of a church."[51] Reaching back to evidence from Moravian writings in 1733, Lange made it clear that he did not intend for anyone to understand him to be a defender of licentiousness given the "fallen nature" of

---

49. The above summarizes discussion of the authorship of *Siegfrieds Bescheidener Beleuchtung* and the resulting polemics; see Erich Beyreuther, ed., *Antizinzendorfiana III: Aus der Hallenser und Jenenser Theologischen Fakultät im Zusammenhag mit "Siegfrieds Bescheidener Beleuchtung" 1742-1749*, introduction by Erich Beyreuther (Hildesheim and New York: Georg Olms Verlag, 1982), ser. 2, vol. 16, pp. 1-30. For the quotation and the treatment of the "Blue Cabinet," see Paul Peucker, "In the Blue Cabinet: Moravians, Marriage, and Sex," *Journal of Moravian History* 10 (2011): 7-37, at 12.

50. *Väterliche Warnung an die der Theologie ergebene Studirende Jugend vor der Herrenhutischen Kirchenform . . .* , in *Antizinzendorfiana III*, pp. 251-358. See also Beyreuther's introductory comments, pp. 44-49.

51. *Väterliche Warnung*, p. 263.

humankind. Nonetheless, too high a demand on conscience, he concluded, would only result in worse sexual excesses. Marriage among the Moravians was so highly praised as the condition in which the participants experienced the indwelling of God and enjoyed the realm of grace that this teaching threatened the entire fabric of the gospel.

The notion that no one could contract marriage before being completely convinced of forgiveness by God, Lange wrote, was as unrealistic as the Moravian refusal to take the words of Paul seriously — that it was better to marry than to burn with lust (1 Cor. 7:9). Instead, he concluded (on the basis of Moravian writings) that the Brethren rejected the whole concept of restraining lust or seeing in marriage a "remedy" for such passions since the truly converted should not think of sexuality in such negative terms. Since the Moravians taught that no special grace was needed to be sexually continent, they must also not take seriously the observation of Christ (Matt. 19:11, 12) that only those who felt that they were able to remain celibate for life should attempt it. The Moravians seemed to deny that casting lustful glances (Matt. 5:27-28) was a problem for the truly converted. In short, their whole marital teaching rested on a defective, hopelessly naïve, and optimistic theological anthropology, one founded on a twisted reading of Scripture.[52]

The increasingly vitriolic and at times prurient obsession with the supposed sexual debauchery of the Moravians accelerated as the Frankfurt polemicist Johann Philip Fresenius took up the fight against the Brethren. Unlike Lange and Baumgarten, Fresenius scoured sources to find particularly savage attacks on the Moravians. Yet for all the heated polemical rhetoric, it seems unlikely that European villagers "who had been busy having premarital sex followed by a public marriage ceremony . . . had a problem with semipublic consummation of marriage." Rather, it was the claim that coitus was sacramental that transgressed the boundary of the hesitant church Lutheran pietist hopes for the semisacramental quality of the estate. The positive assessments of Luther and Spener had failed to produce a succeeding generation capable of sustaining a vigorous, pro-marriage position within Lutheran church pietist circles.[53]

The real victim of these polemical exchanges, however, turned out to be neither Zinzendorf nor any of his opponents. Rather, as the rhetorical attacks increased in bitterness and intensity, what vanished over the horizon of meanings was the vision of marriage as a genuine partnership of friends,

52. *Väterliche Warnung,* pp. 265-74, at 265; 269-70, at 273.
53. Fogelman, *Jesus Is Female,* p. 150.

male and female, who in this godly estate journeyed together toward God, as Luther and Spener had hoped true Christians would recognize it. Their vision suffered as the lines defending gender roles and social order hardened to exclude any ambiguity about the proper portrayal of male and female in European Protestantism. In Wernigerode, a collection of poems by Henrich Ernst, future count and ally of Halle's version of pietism, appeared in 1748, standing at the end of a mystical tradition that Lutherans would increasingly find unacceptable. Baumgarten provided an introduction to the collection, apparently without any second thoughts regarding the mystical imagery of Christ that appeared in one of the poems entitled "Refuge in the Motherly Heart of Jesus." Another, entitled "Renown of Jesus' Motherly Fidelity," included lines that praised "the milk of your motherly breasts [that] infuses Spirit, Soul, Marrow and Bone. . . . You allow me to nurse with joy."[54]

Wernigerode's future count was not the only Lutheran pietist to indulge a peculiar reading of an obscure set of passages from Isaiah, who had promised that Israel would enjoy "the milk of nations [and] suck the breasts of kings" (60:16). Most Christian commentators had overlooked this difficult passage in favor of images of the church offering "consoling" breasts where believers might "drink deeply with delight" (Isa. 66:11). Oetinger apparently shared a fascination with the Isaiah imagery because his oddly titled *A Wholesome System from the Gospel (Etwas ganzes vom Evangelio)*, written in 1739, had expounded upon Isaiah 40 to 66 at some length. Still, for Oetinger, these obscure passages taught something about the plan of salvation, and he did not mention the odd gender imagery. Although dedicating the work to Zinzendorf, Oetinger had used his investigation of Isaiah to strike out indirectly at Zinzendorf's reducing the Bible and the Trinity to bridegroom imagery — it was a "whole system" of salvation that had to be pursued and the Isaiah passages were a reminder of just how obscure much of the Old Testament was, its clarity not to be revealed simply by concentrating upon Jesus as bridegroom.[55]

---

54. *Geistliche Gedichte: Erste Samlung Mit einer Vorrede Sigm. Jacob Baumgartens* (Halle: Gebauer, 1748), no. 69, 150; no. 54, 153. Baumgarten may have had Zinzendorf and the Moravians in mind in writing in his introduction of a lament of supposedly Christian poets who suggested that the natural recognition of God was possible by heathens "without the revealed truths of Christianity and the Order of Salvation that pertains to it," nearly as reprehensible as those who twist the meaning of Scripture in a shameful attack not only on sound reason but in a misuse of Christian teaching (7, 8). I have used the two-volume collection of the three editions, 1748, 1749, 1752, in the Herzog-August Bibliothek Wolffenbüttel (Lo 7403.1.)

55. On the use of Isaiah, see John F. A. Sawyer, *The Fifth Gospel: Isaiah in the History of Christianity* (Cambridge: Cambridge University Press, 1996), pp. 63, 73, 234; see also Joseph

Why did the Moravian veneration of the circumcised penis of Christ, the identification of the Holy Spirit as "mother," and the apparently naïve invocation of an image of a believer suckling male breasts became so intensely controversial between the late 1730s and 1750? Late medieval imagery of both the Virgin and Christ had included images of Christ with engorged breasts and as an infant, or more rarely, as an adult, with male genitalia. But such images did not necessarily mean that those who viewed them would automatically "associate either penis or breast primarily with sexual activity." If those who decisively counted themselves outside the realm of Moravian error continued this older tradition, why did the Moravian teaching on marriage and the reflections upon the male sexual identity of Christ, which affirmed the incarnational teaching of historic Christianity, elicit such virulent responses between 1735 and 1750?[56]

No single answer can adequately account for the pattern of the polemics. Still, Lange's reproach to Zinzendorf — written even before the full impact of the "Sifting Period" became more widely known in the late 1740s — remains suggestive. Lange, the last of living theologians who had been an active and aggressive participant in the disputes with Thomasius, advanced no convincing theology of marriage on Halle's own behalf in his *Fatherly Warning*. And in this, he was not an outlier or relic of a bygone age, but thoroughly representative of Halle's unhappily unsettled thinking on the problem of marriage. On balance, the observation of a twentieth-century commentator tends to ring true: "Halle pietism show[ed] itself on the theme of marriage to be prudish and remarkably taciturn."[57]

The correspondence, the sermons, the hymnody, the pamphlets produced during these tumultuous decades by the Halle-Wernigerode opponents of Zinzendorf appear so striking precisely because of their failure to produce a positive alternative reading of the issues of marriage, friendship, and sexual relations between husbands and wives, and any accompanying joint pursuit of holiness. As the assaults on the Moravians increased after

---

Blenkinsopp, *Isaiah 56–66*, Anchor Bible Commentaries 19B (New York: Doubleday, 2003); Oetinger, *Etwas Ganzes vom Evangelio nach Jesajas 40–66, oder evangelische Ordnung des Heils* (Tübingen: Johann Heinrich Phil. Schramm, 1739); see also on Oetinger's intentions in publishing the essay, Weyer-Menkhoff, *Christus, Das Heil der Natur*, pp. 63-69, 75-93.

56. See "The Body of Christ in the Later Middle Ages" and "The Female Body and Religious Practice in the Later Middle Ages," both in Carolyn Walker Bynum, *Fragmentation and Redemption: Essays on Gender and the Human Body in Medieval Religion* (New York: Zone Books, 1992), pp. 79-117, 181-238, Figure 6.9 at 213, quotation at 87.

57. Beyreuther, *Antizinzendorfiana III*, introduction, p. 47.

1735, Halle's London representative, Friedrich Michael Ziegenhagen, did have access to a source employed by his fellow Protestant Philip Doddridge that at least hinted at a more hopeful, if perhaps somewhat sentimental, view of the spousal relationship.

Philip Doddridge (1702-51) had been raised in a nonconforming household, and his maternal grandfather Johannes Baumann had fled the Continent in search of religious refuge in England. A close friend of Isaac Watts (a correspondent and occasional dining companion of Ziegenhagen), Doddridge began his ministry in 1723 as the drive to reform the laws on clandestine marriage in Britain began to accelerate. Among his many publications, his six-volume work *The Family Expositor* that first appeared in 1739 found its way into the London library of Ziegenhagen and his associate Friedrich Wilhelm Pasche. Doddridge offered readers an interpretation of the New Testament that integrated the four Gospels into a historical review of Jesus' life. Commenting upon Jesus' first miracle at Cana, Doddridge waxed eloquent about marriage in a manner that might have profited Halle's divines. The presence of Jesus at the marriage feast, he wrote, was "a testimony borne to the honour and purity of that happy state on which so much of the comfort of the present generation and the existence of the future, regularly depends."

The pietists, however, would not have appreciated Doddridge's admonition against censuring others "for innocent liberties at proper seasons of festivity and joy" such as weddings. Doddridge's analysis of the teachings of Jesus on divorce presented an even more stunning proclamation of marriage as a true partnership. Reflecting on the Genesis foundation of Jesus' teaching, he concluded that we should adore such a God for having made "for his new formed creature *Adam* so suitable and amiable a companion, to enliven every other object of delight, and to crown the pleasures of *paradise* itself." Nor was this state of affairs entirely lost in the Fall. For to this present day, Christians enjoy in marriage a "mutual tenderness for each other which the purest bosoms may feel and avow, and which is the foundation of such an union of souls as no other friendship will admit." The indissoluble friendship of marriage, he concluded, was blessed, but so was the single life. Jesus now revoked "some indulgences which the law of *Moses* gave," and Christians "have a sublime master, and are to *do* and forbear *more than others.*"[58]

58. Doddridge, *The Family Expositor,* 6 vols. (London, 1739-56), available online as archive .org/stream/familyexpositor1831dodd; this is the 1831 reprint version of the London original, here: I: Section 23 for the wedding at Cana, p. 54; and on marriage and divorce, Section 134, pp. 235-36, at 235.

Doddridge's volumes may have found a place on Ziegenhagen's library shelf, but the fragmentary evidence that survives suggests that the Halle pietist only heeded Doddridge's admonitions to children and servants on the necessity of obedience to authority. Nothing on the topic of friendship in marriage attracted his attention or merited his approbation.[59] If the middling sorts of readers in Britain and Europe became increasingly exposed to the literature on sensibility and the importance of human affections, that shift in emphasis, which might have opened a new perspective on the standing of women and the possibility of marital friendship between women and men, as a joint journey toward holiness, eluded the Halle pietists. That fact may account in part for the attraction many devout Protestants initially felt for the Moravians. The Hallensians had been unable to muster a consensus on the volatile topic of marriage after the Thomasius furor, and they remained in a purely defensive posture in the face of the Moravian challenge. By 1766, a decade before Ziegenhagen's death, the Reverend James Fordyce's immensely popular *Sermons to Young Women* summarized what had become the prevailing understanding of "sensibility" among English-speakers. Although later critics would dismiss the "sentimental" Fordyce's description of women as naturally pious, the Anglophone literature of the century emphasized women's capacity to bring a unique companionship to marriage. The use of the word "friend" and the implications for the marital relationship its use implied did not, at least at the official level of theology, penetrate pietist circles on the Continent, in India, or in North America.[60]

59. AFSt: Teilnachlass Ziegenhagen und Pasche; 184Z 1720-67, Karton 5, Verschiedene Briefe "Gottlich-Vermahnung an die Kinder" (undated); Karton 2:1, "Books of the late Rev. Mr. Ziegenhagen and Pasche." The London pastors also had a copy of Oetinger's *Erklärung des Buches Hiob* that includes the defense against Fröreißen noted above. For the connection to Watts, see his letter to Ziegenhagen dated 23 October 1736 notifying Ziegenhagen of a present of John Jennings's *Discourses concerning Evangelical and Experimental Preaching,* which had been translated into German, and issuing an invitation to dine with him. Johann Adam Steinmetz translated Doddridge's work into German, but I have found no references to or reliance upon the translation with regard to marriage and family in any surviving sermons, letters, or books in use among German-speaking pietists in North America, India, or Europe. For an attempt to reconstruct Ziegenhagen's theology and perspectives, see Christina Jetter, "Halle, England und das Reich Gottes weltweit. Friedrich Michael Ziegenhagen (1694-1776): Pietist und Londoner Hofprediger" (Ph.D. diss., University of Tübingen, 2011), pp. 59-60, on Ziegenhagen and marriage and the possible influence during his student years at Halle exercised by the faculty member Johann Daniel Herrnschmidt (1675-1723). I am grateful to Dr. Jetter for discussing Ziegenhagen and permission to cite the dissertation.

60. G. J. Barker-Benfield, *Abigail and John Adams: The Americanization of Sensibility* (Chicago and London: University of Chicago Press, 2010), pp. 101-13.

180

Neither from Halle, nor from Wernigerode in the 1735 revision of its hymnal, did anyone undertake to advance Lutheran pietist reflections on the spousal relationship. The marriage of Johann Liborius Zimmermann to the sister of Gottlieb Friedrich Lange that took place in Wernigerode in May of 1728 had revealed in the presence of the count and his family the desired profile of a solemn (and to most ordinary believers, uninspiring) pietist wedding. The small party gathered at 5:00 P.M. in the home of the court preacher. The court deacon Lau presided over the ceremony, and the bride's father gave the blessing. The party then retired to "a simple festive meal," but all was done as quietly as possible. After Zimmerman's death, his widow remarried in March of 1738 the court deacon Jacob Hildebrandt, with as little ceremony as had attended her first wedding.[61] Their time consumed with battling both pastoral and popular resistance to the bans on wedding festivities, Wernigerode's consistory members produced nothing of a positive nature that might have answered the Moravian challenge on the status of marriage, either for the congregations in the small territory or for their allies in Halle.

If the objective of promoting a Christian orphanage modeled on Halle's example was to showcase Wernigerode's pious support of marriage, children, and family (and to show why the Moravian option was the wrong one), the behavior of the "Orphan Father," the Magdeburg stocking-weaver Johann Hahn, recruited to manage the new institution, undercut Christian Ernst's hopes. The original orphanage had been overseen by a preceptor (usually a theology student in his last year of preparation for ministry). But a new administrative regime had created the new positions of a married "father" and "mother" to the orphans, stipulating that they were to lead by example and to show kindness toward the children and toward one another. From the date he assumed his duties until his death in 1768, however, Hahn was notorious for the brutality of his regime, beating the orphans regularly, and making his position so noxious that upon his death the count refused to name a successor.

Perhaps in defiance of such brutal treatment, the children brought under the care of the Hahns reacted with behavior that led one observer to conclude that they were thieves and liars who engaged in unchaste behavior

---

61. Eduard Jacobs, "Johann Liborius Zimmermann und die Blütezeit des Pietismus in Wernigerode," *Zeitschrift des Harzvereins* 31 (1898): 121-226; reprinted Wernigerode (B. Angerstein, 1898), pp. 41, 45-46. Jacobs extracted his evidence from the family archive before it was scattered in the 1930s.

shocking for children of their age. The children of the laboring poor who spent most of their time on the streets of the town also engaged in mischief and were also no testimony to the sanctity of married family life. The continued resentment of the population against pietist attacks on traditional marriage customs and festivities manifested itself further as voluntary contributions solicited for support of the pietist orphanage stagnated by 1740 and remained at that level for the next decade.[62]

The deepening interests of a literate, middling audience of European Protestants in the themes of friendship, sensibility, and marriage made an engagement with these topics unavoidable for Lutheran pietists by the 1740s. Neither in Halle, nor in Wernigerode, nor even in the diaspora community in London, however, did the clergy seem up to the task. Of all the contexts where a literate, moderately prosperous, demographically booming, and religiously tolerant climate might have encouraged a real engagement with such issues, the German-speaking settlements of North America provided the ideal setting. Zinzendorf's journey to Pennsylvania in 1742 had revealed that the debates over marriage that had begun in Europe and spread to India now intensified because of his own claims to have realized the full implication of Luther's and Spener's high view of the estate. In the pietist experimental community at Ebenezer, Georgia, and in Lutheran communities in Pennsylvania, however, the weakness of ecclesiastical legal instruments, a secular law that placed special value upon the importance of property and contract, and the transplanted deep inclination of Halle-trained clergy toward demanding disciplined spousal relations guaranteed the further eclipse of an unofficial theology that nonetheless still kept alive some aspects of the companionate vision of the spousal relationship.

---

62. Silvia Maier, "Studien zur Geschichte des Waisenhauses in Wernigerode im 18. Jahrhundert" (M.A. thesis, University of Leipzig, 1993), pp. 26-28, 33-34, 69-70, 55-56; Roeber, "Constitutions, Charity, and Liberalism by Default: Germany and the Anglo-American Tradition," in *Republicanism and Liberalism in America and the German States, 1750-1850*, ed. Jürgen Heideking and James A. Henretta (New York and Washington, D.C.: Cambridge University Press, 2002), pp. 79-81.

CHAPTER 6

Marriage in North America:
Social Discipline and Cultural Diversity

On 24 December German-speaking Lutherans and Catholics in central and eastern territories of the Holy Roman Empire unofficially observe the Feast of Adam and Eve. The original "Paradise Tree" — little more than a crude wooden pyramid structure hung with ornaments to represent the tree of life in Eden — over time came to include a crèche with the Child and some representation of the Virgin. Adam and Eve never achieved official, universal status in the Christian church as saints, despite a late iconographic representation of their rescue by Christ in his "Harrowing of Hell." No one can document how the popular devotion to the first pair managed to penetrate central and eastern Europe either from the Byzantine or the Roman centers of Christianity.[1]

At some point during the eighteenth century, unknown artisans in the mining town of Johanngeorgenstadt in Saxony fashioned a metal candleholder in the form of an arch, detailing at its center the Genesis story of the expulsion. Johannes Paulus Teller (1682-1732) created a version of this folk

---

1. The icon of the resurrection or "Anastasis" in the East or West cannot be dated earlier than the eighth century; Western representations of the "Harrowing of Hell" that occur in stained glass figures in both northern Italy and the western German-speaking lands roughly parallel the Byzantine dates. See Leslie Ross, *Medieval Art: A Topical Dictionary* (Westport, Conn.: Greenwood, 1996), pp. 10-11; the classic older study is J. A. MacCulloch, *The Harrowing of Hell: A Comparative Study of an Early Christian Doctrine* (Edinburgh: T. & T. Clark, 1930); for a summary of more recent literature and disputes, see Alyssa Lyra Pitstick, *Light in Darkness: Hans Urs von Balthasar and the Catholic Doctrine of Christ's Descent into Hell* (Grand Rapids: Eerdmans, 2007).

Figure 4. Adam and Eve, Paradise, and Expulsion (Saxon Folk Art 1794). "Schwibboggen, Erzgebirge" [Das Evangelium in den Wohnungen der Völker / Sammlung Gertrud Weinhold, Museum Europäischer Kulturen / Staatliche Museen zu Berlin]. Reproduced with permission.

art in honor of the miners in this profitable village in the Ore Mountains on the border with Bohemia. Teller may or may not have constructed the very first of these arches on which a Christ candle and twelve others burn in honor of the days of Christmas. Other examples survive from 1778 and 1796. The folk belief contrasted Christ and Mary, the "new Adam" and the "new Eve," with the original spouses. The original, and intended, order of the spousal relationship in creation and now its restoration by Christ through his mother's giving him birth continued to preach a more hopeful view of the human condition.[2] (See Figure 4.)

Far more common than the arched candelabra, the "Tree of Paradise" had evolved also in Saxony as the most primitive form of what later became the "Pyramid," and much later the "Christmas Tree." The more elaborate representation of the tree of life found its way beyond this seasonal celebration of Christmas. In certain locales, Lutheran church chancels boasted a

---

2. Christian Teller, "Der Schwibbogen der Fundgrube 'Neu Leipziger Glück,'" *Erzgebirchische Heimatblätter* 6 (1986): 151-54.

pulpit located directly above the altar, flanked by the tree of the knowledge of good and evil with Eve and the serpent on the viewer's left and Adam on the right.[3]

Never receiving enthusiastic endorsement from the Saxon electoral church, such folk art representations reflected the centrality of the original spouses in everyday beliefs and practices. By the mid–eighteenth century, these expressions of piety that connected the original spouses to the central theme of redemption and restoration of Paradise found little favor with pietist reformers.

For its part, the Saxon clergy's growing concern about pietist incursions into "orthodox" Lutheranism of the official or unofficial version had already surfaced in a bitter struggle over proposed revisions of the Lutheran hymnal at Nordhausen in 1735. The controversy focused on a supposed weakening of the teaching on justification by faith and a creeping emphasis on "good works." But the exclusion of many of Luther's old hymns, though lamented, paled in comparison to the accusation that the revisers had smuggled in medieval mysticism and overemphasized the transformation or "sanctification" of believers. The orthodox suspected Moravian influence and the baneful influence of Halle's hymnal.

Worse yet, the pastor of the Frauenberg church, Friedrich Christian Lesser, a follower of August Hermann Francke, and since 1724 the administrator of the local orphanage, dedicated himself to nature study. This unwelcome focus on the worldly, with the objective of teaching the unbelieving or the weak in faith from the book of nature through the use of new hymns, alarmed the critics. Lesser and his colleagues Johann Christoph Tebel and the jurist Chilian Volkmar Riemann all felt compelled to respond. In classic pietist fashion, they described the three categories of humanity in the Christian world. Only a minority of the "truly awakened" graced Protestant parishes; most people belonged among the so-called worldly Christians, content to observe "external" formalities of religious ritual such as these folk art fancies. Finally, morally conscientious but misguided Christians confused by such controversy could, with proper instruction, be brought to see the error of folk customs and mere "external" observances in favor of heartfelt religion.[4]

---

3. Johannes Just, *Sächsische Volkskunst aus der Sammlung des Museums für Volkskunst Dresden* (Leipzig: VEB E. A. Seemann Verlag, 1982), pp. 223-36, illustration 157.

4. Freidrich De Boor, "Der Nordhäuser Gesangbuchstreit 1735-1738," *Pietismus und Neuzeit* I (1974), pp. 100-113.

August Hermann Francke's vision of a global renewal based on genuine conversion of the heart had run into serious opposition in Saxony since his student days in Leipzig. Reform of marriage customs never got very far in the electoral Saxon church for the simple reason that the threat of pietism overshadowed worries about village practice. Still, had a consensus emerged about spousal relationships and their connection to the images of Adam and Eve in pietist Lutheran circles, an extraordinarily influential newspaper, begun in 1731, could have disseminated the correct theological interpretation. The paper became a model for pietist communication to support networks that spread throughout central Europe and North America. Immanuel Traugott Jerichovius's *Collection of Selected Materials for the Building of God's Kingdom* produced enough resonance to warrant a continuation after his death under Johann Adam Steinmetz's editorship that produced first a competitor, Steinmetz's subsequent "improved" collection, and a final series that appeared with a Magdeburg publisher. Awareness of the Moravian Brethren's activities in Lusatia and Halle's confrontation with Zinzendorf escalated through the dissemination of such media and increasingly brought transplanted German-speakers, including Saxons, in North America into the debates over marriage.[5] That part of the world had remained outside central European pietist interest until 1711, when Francke's New England correspondent Cotton Mather began to share his own endorsement of "a practice of devotion and good works that answered to the religious and social needs" of a renewed Protestantism. Mather corresponded with the Halle missionaries in Tranquebar as well.[6]

Some of the migrants to North America whose devotion to "heartfelt religion" was not really in doubt wanted to maintain certain marriage customs that caused Halle-trained pietist pastors considerable worry. The high hopes represented by Spener's vision of the spousal relationship as a full-blown friendship struggled for survival in North America, dwarfed from the very outset by the official theology whose pastoral articulators took up the

5. *Die Sammlung Auserlesener Materien zum Bau des Reiches Gottes* . . . (Frankfurt, Leipzig, and Magdeburg: Samuel Benjamin Walter, 1731-39; Christian Leberecht Faber, 1737-43). On the collection's impact in Georgia, see below. For the founding of the series, see Rainer Lächle, *Die Sammlung Auserlesener Materien zum Bau des Reiches Gottes zwischen 1730 und 1760* (Tübingen: Max Niemeyer Verlag, 2006), pp. 4-5; for the various editions, 295-310.

6. Oliver Scheiding, "The World as Parish: Cotton Mather, August Hermann Francke, and Transatlantic Religious Networks," in *Cotton Mather and Biblia Americana — America's First Bible Commentary: Essays in Reappraisal,* ed. Reiner Smolinski and Jan Stievermann (Tübingen: Mohr Siebeck, 2010), pp. 131-66, at 148.

more pressing need (as they saw it) for discipline among spouses that had been pioneered in Wernigerode and was now imported with mixed results to pietist settlements in the North American British Protestant settlements.

A sufficiently large number of Lutherans had settled in New York, Pennsylvania, and Georgia during the 1730s to provide a market opportunity during the next decade for those who offered religious news and devotional aids in the form of imported German-language texts. The early classics of the pietist movement, Johann Arndt's *True Christianity* and a collection of his morning and evening prayers, found buyers. Spener's works enjoyed a more curious popularity. Surviving inventories, book sales, and records of purchase suggest that none of his printed sermons on marriage ever appeared in the New World advertisements, imprint lists, or import registers. Availability was not the issue; the 1691 Frankfurt edition of the sermons merited a 1719 reissue and was surely known to pastors in training at the Francke Foundations (Figure 2). By the late 1760s, importers and printers of German texts judged some of Spener's other essays to be of sufficient interest to merit advertisements. These included his essay "Nature and Grace," a polemical work against indulgences and the Roman Year of Jubilee; reflections on the work of the Holy Spirit in the process of making humans blessed; sermons on the comfort offered by the gospel, another on the duties of a true evangelical life (both in a yearly cycle). Sermons on the *Small Catechism* and essays in defense of pietist renewal attempts buttressed church pietism against both "fanatics" and orthodox critics.[7]

The market for marriage materials by the 1760s had apparently grown sufficiently to encourage the importation of Cyriacus Spangenberg's (1528-1604) *The Marriage Mirror* that Heinrich Müller offered for sale. Whether the book found a buyer and what influence it might have had, however, remain unanswerable questions. A German translation from a Latin edition of

---

7. Karl John Richard Arndt and Reiner C. Eck, eds., *The First Century of German Language Printing in the United States of America*, 2 vols. (Göttingen: Niederschäische Staats-und Universitätsbibliotek Göttingen, 1989), 1:34 (1745), 82 (1751); for the various offers by Spener, see *Catalogus von mehr als 700 meist Deutschen Büchern* . . . (Philadelphia: Heinrich Müller, 1769) (HSP), nos. 4, 58, 130, 143, 147, 174, 178, 195, 198, 481, 491, 599, 600, 606, 651; AFSt 4 F 6/2 (*Rechnungen, 1746/47–1768*); Roeber, "German and Dutch Books and Printing," in *A History of the Book in America I: The Colonial Book in the Atlantic World,* ed. Hugh Amory and David D. Hall (Cambridge: Cambridge University Press, 2000), pp. 298-313, 579-83. Spangenberg, *Ehe-Spiegel, das ist, Alles was von den heylige Ehestand nutzliches nötiges und tröstliches mag gesagt warden in LXX Brautpredigten zusammen verfasset* (Strassburg: Theodosius Rihel, 1578). On Spangenberg, see Jens Wolff, *Cyriakus Spangenberg, RGG* VII, pp. 1536-37.

Augustine's *Two Books on Adultery* may have mildly alarmed pietist pastors because it used John 8:1-11 to encourage spouses to forgive even lapses in marital fidelity. Perhaps more unsettling was the anonymous *Wholesome Means of Recovery and Help for Adulterers, Visitors of Whores and Whores*, a text that all too clearly underscored the failure of fidelity and friendship in marriage and the need for good order in spousal relationships.[8]

Despite the clamor that surrounded real and imagined Moravian teachings about the sanctity of conjugal sex in Europe, neither in the market for German-language imports, nor in Georgia's nor Pennsylvania's Lutheran congregations did the official or unofficial theology of most German-speakers focus on the Moravian innovation. In Georgia, the Moravian "threat" disappeared quickly. Instead, for a brief time an official theology emerged that emphasized wives' submission and their "helping" role in marriage. Unofficially, among both the Halle-trained clergy and the laity, an unofficial theology that granted a more companionate role to both partners may have flourished briefly before the prevailing economic and legal issues in Georgia swamped both in favor of securing property rights for sons, with less attention given to the critical role wives had actually played in helping a pietist experiment survive. In Pennsylvania's more diverse population, both the ambivalence of Halle-trained pastors and a robust importation of unofficial folk beliefs about marriage followed a similar pattern. There too, however, the hopes for a spousal relationship characterized by mutual fidelity and friendship fell victim to similar practical concerns, an equally weak ecclesiastical shepherding of marriage, and the secular law's preference for contractual understandings of the estate.

Despite the relative paucity of printed materials that directly addressed spousal relationships, the issue emerged both at the level of unofficial piety and in official theology represented by the writings of Halle-trained pietist pastors in both colonies. These men struggled to impose discipline upon the same kinds of unwanted village mores that their counterparts in Wernigerode fought to suppress. Because of the relative isolation of transplanted Salzburgers in Georgia, the Wernigerode model in the hands of a clergy that

---

8. *Catalogus,* no. 53, *Aur. Augustini zwey Bücher vom Ehebrecherlischen Heyrathen. Aus dem Lateinischen überseßt . . . ;* no. 56, *Heilsame Genes-und Hülfmittel für Ehebrecher, Hurer und Huren;* no. 685, *Spangenbergs Ehespiegel.* For a summary of all known titles among the Salzburgers at Ebenezer, see the appendix 7.3, "Buchbestand in Salzburg und Ebenezer," in Charlotte E. Haver, *Von Salzburg nach Amerika: Mobilität und Kultur einer Gruppe religiöser Emigranten im 18. Jahrhundert* (Paderborn, Munich, Vienna, and Zürich: Ferdinand Schöningh, 2011), pp. 420-32.

exercised both civil and ecclesiastical power appeared, briefly, to work. By the 1740s, however, the opportunity to shape marriage along official pietist lines began to fade as the legal and ecclesiastical climate in North America encouraged a far more pragmatic concern for property and the succession of male heirs, and little room for wives who could function as actual partners in the worldly affairs where marriage increasingly seemed to belong. In Pennsylvania, by sharp contrast, no group of pietist believers lived with a pietist pastor isolated from polyglot, rapidly expanding communities. Here, the unofficial theology that centered on remembrance of the first humans and the songs, hymns, and rituals accompanied Lutheran and Moravian emigrants and at first seemed to promise a triumph of the more hopeful relationship between spouses in a context rich in new opportunities. Arrivals from the southwestern territories introduced even more of their village customs in Pennsylvania. In them, one catches a glimpse of marriage understood by believers who did not necessarily agree with the theology of the pietist clergy who promulgated Halle's anxieties that focused on the need for submissive wifely helpers and sober, responsible husbands. A hint of how Halle's transplanted pastors thought officially about marriage surfaced in the memorial sermon pamphlet they knew of after it appeared to honor the death of Gotthilf August Francke's first wife, Johanne Henriette (Rachhals). Lauded for her many virtues, she had personified the model of the "faithful wife and helper in marriage" *(treue Frau Ehe-Gehülfin)*. The more generous image of a woman as a partner, friend, and companion to pastors and laymen would gradually be adopted unofficially by the transplanted Halle clergy, but it remained only an unofficial theology, endangered from the earliest plantings of both pietist and nonpietist believers to Georgia in the 1730s. Almost universally, the official theology of the pietists described a pastor's wife solely as a "helpmeet." In the face of disease, grief at child mortality, and the indispensable contribution of women to the Salzburger experiment, however, the unofficial theology of friendship eventually, temporarily, modified somewhat the official version.[9]

9. AFSt [Bib] S/A: 1119 [15], Johann Justus Gebauer, *Bey dem unvermutheten seligen Hintritt der Hoch-Edelgebornen Frauen Frauen Johanna Henrietta Franckin, geborenen Rachhalsin . . .* (Halle: J. J. Gebauer, 1743). The description of both laywomen and pastors' wives as "helpmeets" can be followed in *The Letters of Johann Martin Boltzius, Lutheran Pastor in Ebenezer, Georgia: German Pietism in Colonial America, 1733-1765,* ed. and trans. Russell C. Kleckley, in collaboration with Jürgen Gröschl, with a foreword by Ann R. Purcell and Thomas Müller-Bahlke, 2 vols. (Lewiston, Queenstown, and Lampeter: Edwin Mellen Press, 2009); e.g., 1:144, 259, 303; 2:469, 506, 540. On Boltzius's relationship to his own wife and marriage, see below.

I

The colony of Georgia welcomed nominal Lutheran dissenters whom the archbishop of Salzburg expelled in the winter of 1731-32. Both they and their fellow exiles who settled in East Prussia struggled with indebtedness, a condition that often dictated spousal choices and instilled a fear of what impoverishment might do to surviving spouses and children.[10] In this context, pastoral concerns aimed at curbing economic and social disorder outdistanced concerns about spousal partnership and friendship. Pastor Johann Martin Boltzius's remarks on marriage reflected the challenges he faced in shaping a community from a mixture of Salzburgers, Palatines, Kraichgauers, and eventually Swabians. A Saxon arrived from Chemnitz and expressed amazement at a pastoral visit because "they consider it something great and unusual for a minister to visit healthy people unsummoned."[11] Boltzius's comments on marriage in this mixed community reflected both his deep anxiety and his desire to isolate his charges from the baneful influence of their nonpietist neighbors.

Born in Forst on the Neisse River in the lower Lausitz, Boltzius held no high opinion of mainstream Lutheranism in his childhood territory or in Saxony. Saved, as he thought, from the danger of education at Wittenberg and Leipzig, he instead absorbed Halle's version of pietist renewal and, throughout his pastorate, maintained connections to colleagues who ended up serving in Tranquebar and Europe.[12] Ordained in Wernigerode in November 1733 along with his first colleague, Christian Israel Gronau, Boltzius arrived in Georgia to shepherd the experiment. Using the newly revised Wernigerode hymnal, he kept in touch with the town of his ordination. At noon on 30 June 1751 a fire broke out that in the next few hours leveled 300 buildings, erasing much of the urban landscape Boltzius and Gronau had known. The fledgling community in Georgia was able to keep abreast of news from Wernigerode, Tranquebar, and Halle, albeit with some delay, and learned of the shocking destruction (via Pennsylvania newspapers) on 1 February 1752.[13]

10. Mack Walker, *The Salzburg Transaction: Expulsion and Redemption in Eighteenth-Century Germany* (Ithaca, N.Y., and London: Cornell University Press, 1992), pp. 146, 160-61.

11. George Fenwick Jones and Renate Wilson, eds. and trans., *Detailed Reports on the Salzburger Emigrants Who Settled in America . . . Edited by Samuel Urlsperger*, 18 vols. (Athens: University of Georgia Press; Rockport, Maine: Picton Press, 1968-95), 15:149.

12. *Letters of Johann Martin Boltzius*, 2:536, 556, 559, 569.

13. Jones and Wilson, *Detailed Reports*, 15:159.

Boltzius kept abreast of the southeastern India experiment, and he lifted straight from Ziegenbalg a defense of the "equality between Christian and heathen children regarding the spiritual misery in nature," taking "the *East Indian Reports* to church with me . . . [reading] some important passages as remarkable examples, from which we can learn what [is] the Christian's duty toward the slaves that come into our power."[14] On the topic of spousal relations as they were being debated in Wernigerode or in Tranquebar, however, Boltzius remained silent. That silence did not extend to marriage among non-German-speakers in British North America, on which he often commented bitingly, or disguise his own failure to deal with the question of spousal relationships among enslaved and freed Africans.

Georgia trustees and pietists agreed on the aim of promoting independent, familial, nonslave-holding, and productive believers. That shared vision raised issues about marriage. According to the dictates of the trustees, marital property was to be settled in male tail alone. Criticized as unrealistic and as a disincentive to some widows who saw no reason to invest in such a colony, the scheme was abandoned by Georgians by 1739. But other questions persisted.[15] As senior pastor, Boltzius sat until 1755 alongside two village elders to preside over all legal and moral matters. He informed his European correspondents that he intended to reform Salzburg baptismal celebration customs that threatened the good order of the settlement and encouraged a frivolous atmosphere of celebration. He also disliked jocundity at weddings, and he reflected on the need for pious wives. "Until mid-century, the Georgia diaries are full, often to excess, of the minister's Pietist concern for women in terms of their state of salvation, physical and spiritual health, and church discipline and as Christian agents of successful marriage and community life in the Lutheran tradition."[16]

Over the course of his ministry, Boltzius entered observations, laments,

---

14. Jones and Wilson, *Detailed Reports,* 7:125; 17:237. In July 1747 Boltzius received news of the death in Tranquebar of Gottfried Wilhelm Obuch, "who still is well known to me," and the departure of Jakob Klein and Johann Christian Breithaupt, the cousin of the Wernigerode pastor, for Tranquebar. See *Letters of Johann Martin Boltzius,* 1:475.

15. "Male tail" refers to lands given solely to male heirs; for details, see A. G. Roeber, *Palatines, Liberty, and Property: German Lutherans in Colonial British America* (Baltimore and London: Johns Hopkins University Press, 1993), pp. 158-61.

16. For details, see Roeber, *Palatines,* pp. 158-64; quotation in Renate Wilson, *Pious Traders in Medicine: A German Pharmaceutical Network in Eighteenth-Century North America* (University Park: Pennsylvania State University Press, 2000), pp. 167-68; for Boltzius's disapprobation of the baptismal ceremonies, see Jones and Wilson, *Detailed Reports,* 3:190.

and praises for marriages that reflected the vagaries of the pietist experiment. Between 1733 and 1760 he mentioned the issue 90 to 100 times; observations peaked between 1739 and 1742 but dwindled to 3 to 7 a year by the mid to late 1750s. In part, the pattern reflected his declining eyesight,[17] but Boltzius and Gronau also had to abandon an approach to marriage that depended heavily upon their capacity to insulate the pietist community from temptations.[18] The concern for order emerged both from their European training and from the sometimes shocking irregularities in marital life they encountered in their new surroundings.

Initially, in a flurry of some 22 observations for 1734-35, Boltzius predicted the victory of sober pietist marriage reform, but over time the comments changed in tone. He displayed a classic Lutheran concern for marriage as part of civil society ("law") but also for its divine origin, blessing, and purpose (not quite "gospel"). Only gradually did an "unofficial" endorsement of marriage as friendship emerge from his experiences. Boltzius saw marriage as a matter of public concern, and Samuel Urlsperger promoted this view as he edited the pastor's rehearsal of English laws, banns, and civil jurisdiction. But Boltzius also reflected at some length on the "internal" aspects of marriage — its purpose, its theological basis (reflected in the texts and hymns), and the proper roles of husbands and wives.

Boltzius refused to become involved in marrying the English settlers whose spiritual care lay outside the bounds of his own pastoral calling. Scrupulously careful to inform James Oglethorpe of any requests that might suggest that he was overstepping his bounds, Boltzius also conveyed to the readers of his edited diaries his scorn for the purely "external" formalities of marriage. Often enough, all English-speakers wanted were ministers "who [would] please them and do what they wish."[19] His pietist disdain for the external formalisms of marriage rites included biting comments about the newly arrived John Wesley's anxious insistence upon episcopal ordination of pastors, an indication of "papist" sophistry Boltzius condemned as much as he did a Reformed catechism and the threat of transplanted Moravians. Indeed, it was Wesley's infatuation with the wrong kind of pietists — the Moravians — that led Boltzius to question how long their bonds of "friendship" could endure. Despite theological differences with the more Reformed-influenced George Whitefield, it was the latter's more law-driven

17. Jones and Wilson, *Detailed Reports,* 17:55.
18. The tabulations are taken from the eighteen volumes of the *Detailed Reports.*
19. Jones and Wilson, *Detailed Reports,* 8:505 (1741).

theology that Boltzius approved of heartily.[20] By 1756 Boltzius wrote to Gotthilf August Francke summarizing more than thirty years of grappling with the correct public order surrounding marriage. Boltzius's first concern had been to maintain pietist marital cohesion by discouraging his charges from marrying anyone outside the Salzburg settlement. "People of all races, languages, and religions marry each other . . . and there are, unfortunately, very evil marriages. German women marry English, Scottish, Irish, and French men and vice versa, from which there generally arises a very unchristian child rearing." How much more would exposure to outright pagan notions of marriage portend failure for the Christian upbringing of children?[21]

The public face of marriage could hardly have been more disfigured than in the behavior of the colony's governor, John Reynolds, who lived "with his wife, with a German girl, whom he clothe[d] as his daughter," who ate with the family and, according to rumor, was pregnant. "He has not married her, and no one knows whether he intends to do so."[22] The spectacle reinforced Boltzius's conviction that New World spousal relations amounted to disorder and a lack of household governance, an insight underscored by historians' own conclusions that "80 percent of the population in the thirteen colonies was comprised of *legal* dependents." A generation after Boltzius's death, not a single one of the new mainland independent states ventured "to void irregular marriages, including those in which minors had not obtained parental consent."[23]

20. *Letters of Johann Martin Boltzius,* 1:194-95; 2:539; Jones and Wilson, *Detailed Reports,* 1:411, 204; 4:118. Boltzius felt compelled to correct Wesley's naïve acceptance of the Moravian Gottlieb Spangenberg's claim that he had been called to Halle as Breithaupt's successor. Boltzius seems not to have known or commented on Wesley's own anguish over his failed wooing of Sophia (Hopkey) Williamson, whose husband finally drove Wesley from North America. For the episode and Wesley's own sad marriage, see Bedford W. Coe, *John Wesley and Marriage* (Bethlehem, Pa.: Lehigh University Press, 1996); Stephen Tomkins, *John Wesley: A Biography* (Grand Rapids: Eerdmans, 2003), pp. 51-56, 135-48. On the ambivalence of Methodists in general about marriage versus celibacy, see Anna M. Lawrence, *One Family under God: Love, Belonging, and Authority in Early Transatlantic Methodism* (Philadelphia: University of Pennsylvania Press, 2011), pp. 96-157.

21. Stab, Francke Nachlaß, Boltzius to Francke, 12 August 1756: F: 32/892-99; this letter has been translated and published: "A Letter by Pastor Johann Martin Boltzius about Bethesda and Marital Irregularities in Savannah," with an introduction by George Fenwick Jones, *Georgia Historical Quarterly* 84, no. 2 (Summer 2000): 283-94; I cite Jones's translation unless otherwise noted; quotation here at 293. The letter is also reproduced in *Letters of Johann Martin Boltzius,* 2:641-47.

22. Jones, "A Letter," p. 293.

23. Carol Shammas, *A History of Household Government in America* (Charlottesville and London: University of Virginia Press, 2002), pp. 31, 99.

193

Boltzius proved himself a shrewd observer of the weakness of the relationship of many husbands and wives. Before arriving in Georgia, several Salzburgers had been married "properly and in Christian fashion, after having been previously admonished. This took place for 5 couples on the day of St. Matthew, Sept. 21st, and for another couple, with permission from the Protestant council, on the following day."[24] Such orderly spousal relations collapsed in the colony. In a rare relaxation of his usual strictness about avoiding outsiders, Boltzius presided over the marriages of several persons because, as they explained, their "local pastor has been away from home for several months" and they had received written permission for him to marry them.[25]

More dangerous threats lurked in the form of Georgia's secular, supposed guardians of marriage. When challenged about the legitimacy of his marrying a servant to one of his flock, Boltzius contacted the unpopular but powerful magistrate in Savannah, Thomas Causton, who in Oglethorpe's absence presided at court but also controlled the stores provided to the colony. Causton relinquished jurisdiction over this marriage at Ebenezer. In a letter that probably misled Boltzius into thinking he had absolute jurisdiction over all aspects of spousal issues in the Ebenezer settlement, Causton wrote that "I have no objection to that matter, nor to anything else of that nature with respect to your Congregation, that Shall be agreeable to your Judgment. His intended Wife Shall be accepted after matrimony as one of your people."[26]

By 1738 Boltzius had grown pessimistic about the capacity of English ecclesiastical law to support his efforts to bring order to the spousal relationship. A Savannah German-speaker had married a servant after having lived "in open sin during the voyage," only to have his prior marriage in Germany catch up with him. Boltzius declared the second marriage void but had to contact Oglethorpe and the trustees even though "the civil authorities do not deal with such matters as belong to the bishop and his court."[27] The reach of the bishop of London to Georgia, however, Boltzius opined, was highly overrated. When George Whitefield was scheduled to take his place in Savannah, his predecessor lodged a complaint with the hierarch, leading Boltzius to observe that "This good man imagines the Bishop to have greater power in this colony than the Lord Trustees have granted him, for they do not wish to relinquish the right to accept such chaplains or court preachers

24. Jones and Wilson, *Detailed Reports,* 1:13.
25. Jones and Wilson, *Detailed Reports,* 2:99.
26. Jones and Wilson, *Detailed Reports,* 2:164.
27. Jones and Wilson, *Detailed Reports,* 6:81, 82, 108.

as please them and send them here — a privilege also enjoyed by other Lords in England. None of the provinces in America, with the exception of Carolina, acknowledges the power of the Bishop in ecclesiastical matters, as is shown by the fact that he has a *commissarius* nowhere else but in Charleston, who acts in his name and corresponds with him."[28]

In 1760, with a full generation of conflicts and the royalization of the colony behind him, Boltzius still hoped for resolution of marital scandals by English church law. A German mason reported that his "pregnant wife had been seduced by a Spaniard and had come with him to Bethany. He is making use of the local authorities to take her from this scandalous life and to bring the adulterer to justice. In this and the neighboring colony (indeed in all America) such sins are neither noticed nor punished, rather the plaintiff is referred to the Episcopal court in London, which means almost nothing."[29]

But Boltzius was realistic. He knew that in law the Church of England retained jurisdiction over divorce, decisions on impediments, and degrees of consanguinity or affinity. It could annul marriages tainted by forced consent or underage status. Divorce for adultery did not bring with it freedom to marry again, and in royal colonies "absolute divorce was unknown . . . where the Church of England was established by law. America lacked the church courts as well as the bishops who would have supervised them, though county courts occasionally granted separations for causes such as desertion, cruelty, and bigamy." Boltzius knew that ecclesiastical law remained a dead letter.[30]

Boltzius nowhere indicated that he had studied the debates over clandestine marriage in Britain, but in 1749, four years short of the Hardwicke Act, he reported another Savannah marriage of four couples, "Some English,

28. Jones and Wilson, *Detailed Reports*, 6:170-71.

29. Jones and Wilson, *Detailed Reports*, 17:30.

30. Thomas E. Buckley, S.J., *The Great Catastrophe of My Life: Divorce in the Old Dominion* (Chapel Hill and London: University of North Carolina Press, 2002), pp. 16-17, at 17; Shammas, *Household Government*, p. 50. On Virginia and an argument for the ineffectiveness of Anglican clerical attempts at imposing order, see Jacob M. Blosser, "Irreverent Empire: Anglican Inattention in an Atlantic World," *Church History* 77, no. 3 (September 2008): 596-628. Boltzius does not name Alexander Garden, the South Carolina commissary who served from 1726 to 1749, attempted to impose ecclesiastical discipline on his clergy, and clashed with George Whitefield, who openly disdained Garden's authority as the bishop of London's representative. For details, see Harry S. Stout, *The Divine Dramatist: George Whitefield and the Rise of Modern Evangelicalism* (Grand Rapids: Eerdmans, 1991), pp. 67, 95-96, 110-12. Whitefield managed to alienate both New York Commissary William Vesey and Philadelphia's Archibald Cummings, as well. See Frank Lambert, *"Pedlar in Divinity": George Whitefield and the Transatlantic Revivals* (Princeton: Princeton University Press, 1994), pp. 174-76.

some German," in which for the English, according to license, he had used the rite prescribed by the *Book of Common Prayer*. He noted that this use of Anglican ritual had little to do with spousal piety. "They all want to be distinguished people so they perform it like the people in England who let themselves be married in private without public notice after having received a license and the regular minister makes no scruple of this. I do not let myself get involved with such licenses and the marriages of the English and the French if there is a preacher in the country in Savannah."[31]

The other — far more sensitive — question about the spousal relationship found Boltzius uncertain and hesitant. Some years after chattel slavery had acquired legal standing following Georgia's royalization, Boltzius found himself accosted on the way to Zion church by

> an old Negro who showed me two documents which proved that he was a freed Negro and could thus go about freely. He was baptized in Virginia, but beyond the Lord's Prayer and the Apostles Creed he has very little knowledge of the Christian religion. For five years he has been living with a Palatine woman near Augusta, but they are not married. He wants to move into our district and asked me to marry them when they have settled, but I was not able to promise this to him. I must first inquire what the law of the land is in this matter. His poor English, having always been a slave, and the unchristian lives of many so-called Christians are the main hindrances to the conversion of these poor heathens.[32]

Interracial marriage remained possible only in regions where no one version of Protestant Christianity enjoyed a monopoly that allowed closer supervision. Demographic evidence suggests that "African American and Indian conjugal relationships" were common, but "discriminatory marriage laws did have an important effect . . . when a man and woman of European descent cohabited for a long period of time, the supposition — unless challenged publicly by an interested party — was that they were married and their children were legitimate. No such presumption would or could be made for a mixed race couple." In fact, despite the evidence that "marriage laws were loose even in areas that one might think would have been of central concern — miscegenation and incest[,] the only colony to void interracial marriages was Georgia."[33]

31. Jones and Wilson, *Detailed Reports*, 13:75-76.
32. Jones and Wilson, *Detailed Reports*, 17:19.
33. Shammas, *Household Government*, pp. 44, 102.

Boltzius shared with his contemporaries a sense of ethnic hierarchy that placed the Native American population just beneath the Jews and left the enslaved Africans a distant third. Although not profoundly disturbed by the remote possibility that the immigrant Saxon Christian Gottlieb Prieber would realize his utopian ambitions among the Cherokee, Boltzius cryptically alluded in 1747 to Prieber's endorsement of polygamy, the right of divorce, and egalitarian male-female relationships.[34] Boltzius wanted no spousal ties to bind Native Americans or transplanted Africans as members of the body of the pietist church.

Boltzius's views about spouses reflected in part the grim demographic realities of the colony and the evolving character of his own marriage. The four initial transports had deposited 249 souls to the Ebenezer settlement, but by the end of 1742 the population stagnated due to "the ravages of childhood diseases and high infant mortality." Migration in the 1750s brought another "150 adults, many of them young males," so that by 1754 the 650 souls of Ebenezer "and its sister congregations Bethany and Goshen" comprised "between 12 and 14 per cent of the total European population of Georgia."[35] The demographic challenge undercut Boltzius's dream of copying the Halle philanthropic model that by 1737 included the fledgling orphanage, which was intended to house not only orphans but also widows and the poor. Beginning with seven children, the orphanage by 1750 cared for only sixteen, almost exclusively children or the indigent. In any event, as he himself reported by 1744, "there have been no more widows in the orphanage after one moved to her blood relations in Savannah and the other to her son-in-law, and they are very well cared for."[36] Nonetheless, in sharp contrast to the grim picture of authoritarian control over orphans exercised by the married overseers in Wernigerode, Boltzius could boast that Ruprecht and Margaretha Kalcher "maintain fine, Christian order and know how to deal with the

---

34. For more details, see Roeber, "'What the Law Requires Is Written on Their Hearts': Noachic and Natural Law among German-Speakers in Early Modern North America," *William and Mary Quarterly,* 3rd ser., 58, no. 4 (October 2001): 883-912, at 883, and on Prieber, Claus Bernet's biographical sketch in the *BBK,* 1132-38.

35. Renate Wilson, "Land, Population, and Labor: Lutheran Immigrants in Colonial Georgia," in *In Search of Peace and Prosperity: New German Settlements in Eighteenth-Century Europe and America,* ed. Hartmut Lehmann, Hermann Wellenreuther, and Renate Wilson (University Park: Pennsylvania State University Press, 2000), pp. 217-45, at 224.

36. Wilson, "Public Works and Piety in Ebenezer: The Missing Salzburger Diaries of 1744-1745," *Georgia Historical Quarterly* 77, no. 2 (Summer 1993): 336-66, at 347 n. 29. *Letters of Johann Martin Boltzius,* 1:401 (4 June 1744, to Gotthilf August Francke).

children in a genuine fatherly and motherly manner." To another correspondent, he expressed his wish for "such upright in heart, capable, and selfless people for all good institutions."[37]

As Boltzius began dealing with spousal problems within the constraints imposed by high mortality, he himself married. Whether he had intended to do so, or, in accord with August Hermann Francke's wishes for all overseas missionaries to follow the Pauline example, to remain celibate remains unclear. In his letters to his mother and to Gotthilf August Francke in September of 1735, he alluded both to a promise made to his mother to return to Germany and to Francke's "last words . . . upon my departure, namely, that I might come again to Germany after a few years and look about there for a helpmeet according to divine will." But in justifying his marriage to Gronau's sister-in-law Gertraut Kroeher, Boltzius cast the decision in pragmatic terms of health, and his "external material care." To his mother, he explained the marriage by "my physical circumstances" and "love for my congregation." To his own married sisters he urged an upright life in "the state of marriage in faith and according to God's will," and to his mother, God's "consolation and support in your state of widowhood."[38]

His early letters routinely described Gertraut as "my helpmeet." Unusually skilled and a quick learner, she helped dispense Halle's pharmaceuticals to customers and objects of charity, and also contributed to the success of the silk culture in one of Ebenezer's economic experiments. The birth and loss of children and his close friend and colleague Gronau in 1745, however, altered Boltzius's written references. He and his wife were devastated by the death of thirteen-year-old Samuel Leberecht. The diphtheria epidemic then took their younger daughter Christiana Elisabeth six days later. Gertraut's grief was so deep that Boltzius confessed that "her mind is oppressed and comfortless to such an extent that I myself am thereby discouraged." Increasingly he referred to her as "my dear spouse," the children's "mama." He wrote to Francke, congratulating him on his second marriage and expressing a hope that he and his new wife would "live for many years in a delightful and blessed state of marriage and long enjoy mutual aid and comfort in this difficult pilgrimage."[39]

37. *Letters of Johann Martin Boltzius,* 1:239, 215.

38. *Letters of Johann Martin Boltzius,* 1:145, 148, 149 (1 September 1735).

39. *Letters of Johann Martin Boltzius,* 2:567-600, quotations at 585, 587; 655 "we parents"; 718 "my dear wife"; 732 "my dear spouse"; and in opposing the return of his younger son to succeed him in Georgia, "I wish also with my spouse," 777.

Upon the death of Gronau, Boltzius wrote to Samuel Urlsperger in Augsburg announcing that his sister-in-law would continue living in the Gronau house until a replacement pastor could be sent. In referring to her as *Gevatterin,* Boltzius deployed a term common in Saxony and lower Lusatia (borrowed from medieval baptismal sponsorship) that in colloquial use conveyed the status of a good neighbor or family member.[40] Despite the use of the pietist hymnals that are replete with images of Christ as the bridegroom, Boltzius only rarely slipped into this language, though in urging careful preparation for marriage he did once refer to "Christ and His Spirit, the bride suitor and best man" *(Braut-Weiber und Braut-Führer).*[41]

In choosing texts upon which to preach at marriages, Boltzius ranged widely, at times opting for classic passages such as Ephesians 5, or the Gospel of Matthew and Christ's blessing of the estate. Couples seeking betrothals sometimes asked him for the "blessing of the Lord through [his] office." When he used Ephesians at the wedding ceremony, Boltzius emphasized the duty of the wife to be submissive rather than pointing to the self-sacrifice demanded of the husband. But he compared marriage to the Old Testament covenant in Exodus 20:2-3, and found 2 Peter 2:9 useful to admonish the newly married that "The Lord knows how to rescue the godly from trial." Most of his texts were admonitory, and Romans 14:17-18, reminding the bridal party that the "kingdom of God is not meat and drink," left little room for doubt about his attitude about wedding celebrations. Zechariah and Elizabeth ought to stand as models of Christian marriage.

Only very rarely did his observations reveal genuine pleasure in weddings, though in May of 1736 he declared himself delighted when three couples invited two other betrothed couples "who [were] very poor" to sit down for a meal marked by "good conversation and . . . much sincere love and intimacy." By midcentury, he turned to the wedding feast at Cana to underscore

---

40. See the etymology and use in the Grimm *Wörterbuch:* http://dwb.uni-trier.de/Projekte/WBB2009/DWB/wbgui_py?lemid=GA0001 (accessed 20 October 2011). I prefer instead of Kleckley's translation, "close friend," since the term is quite distinct from *Freund* or the concept of *Freundschaft;* "close relative" might be more accurate. See also *Letters of Johann Martin Boltzius,* 2:484, and a description of the difficult Ebenezer physician Christian Ernst Thilo's "unusual friendships in Savannah" *(Gevatterschafft).* I would translate this as "unusual comrades, or compatriots."

41. *Letters of Johann Martin Boltzius,* 1:347 (13 March 1742 to Gotthilf August Francke). Boltzius uses this bridegroom imagery rarely; he describes Francke's first mother-in-law Henriette Rosine Goetze as "very worthy as a bride of the Lamb." See 2:535.

"the importance of Christian marriage," and noticed the level of devotion shown by a wife reading to her dying husband Hosea 2:19, "I will even betroth thee unto me forever."[42]

Boltzius defended conventional views of the roles and expectations of marriage partners. He pleaded for "Christian, unmarried women" for transport to the colony,[43] and both sexual misconduct and the refusal of subservience to husbands provoked him to demand public penance. Sexually scandalous women stood with their prospective husbands before the congregation. But never, as far as the records reveal, was public penance demanded of potential husbands. Rather, Boltzius criticized men in his journals for being disorderly, lazy, drunken, and unproductive householders, precisely the grounds upon which women brought complaints before consistory courts in Europe.[44]

In accord with the expectations of the trustees, Boltzius recruited equivalents of village elders acquainted with legal custom to serve with him as *Schöffen,* and in drawing upon their sense of right and wrong, described the court as one of "conscience." Forced to preside over the court when the de jure justice Johann Ludwig Meyer failed in his duties, Boltzius translated into German William Wilson's *The Office and Authority of a Justice of the Peace* for his own instruction.[45] He complained to Friedrich Michael Ziegenhagen in London that in discharging his duties as justice, he found "no reception with my spiritual office."[46] Boltzius regarded the court and all such civic matters as "external things that [have] been required on behalf of the community by the authorities in the land and in London." Five months later, however, he complained to Francke in Halle that he needed a free hand in disciplining the Ebenezer community rather than having to put up with "what they here call English freedom . . . [that] agrees rather much with the so-called academic freedom (which better might be called more of a misuse of freedom and a punishable license)." To his mind, the trustees had failed to give "us full power of authority to settle our things without the authorities in Savannah and to remove vexation."[47]

---

42. For the various citations to biblical texts, see Jones and Wilson, *Detailed Reports,* 6:152, 300-301 (1739); 7:146-47, 249 (1740); 8:296, 427, 504, 538 (1741); 15:149-50 (1751/52); 16:208 (1753/54); for the engagement blessings, 9:210 (1742); 10:118 (1743).

43. *Letters of Johann Martin Boltzius,* 1:179.

44. See Jones and Wilson, *Detailed Reports,* 7:81-82, 230; 8:46, 53, 302, 338; 15:227; 17:5-7.

45. Roeber, *Palatines,* pp. 163-64.

46. *Letters of Johann Martin Boltzius,* 1:336.

47. *Letters of Johann Martin Boltzius,* 1:336, 406.

Only by 1755 did Boltzius find at least a modicum of satisfaction in the royal governor's appointment of four justices who sat (as he continued to describe them) as a court of conscience with a competence over noncapital offenses and small claims. Even better in his opinion, "there is no appeal to another court."[48] The typical mixed jurisdiction of both common law and equity in local courts established by royal authority could not, however, maintain cohesion over a community that had become larger, more diverse, and geographically scattered. He disliked presiding over disputes of an "external" rather than spiritual nature, but the boundaries became increasingly indistinct.

Warning his congregation against sexual impropriety and imposing occasional public confession and penance, Boltzius evidently believed that the proper forums for premarital and marriage conflicts were the pulpit and his study. If so, he apparently wanted to keep the issue of the marital relationship within the purview of the church except when crisis involved property disputes or public scandal. No records remain to document the congregation's views of his teaching. Only forty-one wills from the eighty-nine that German-speakers in Georgia actually wrote survive for the last two-thirds of the eighteenth century. Of those, fourteen suggest that perhaps Boltzius's fixation upon the pious wife may have influenced his congregants. "Fourteen of the surviving forty-one wills provide wives with more than the usual thirds; several make explicit reference to pre-marital contracts, and to what the wife had brought into the marriage . . . fifteen of the forty-one named the wife as executrix or coexecutrix."[49]

Shortly before Boltzius died, he noted that he had performed at least 178 marriages; he solemnized some 56 in his own community, or about 5 a year between 1734 and 1756. By the time of his death, however, the pietist vision that had idealized obedient wives and sober, productive husbands had vanished. His parishioners apparently did cultivate a more companionate if unofficial theology on husbands' affections and responsibilities for surviving wives than could be found in his official admonitions. But the long-term trajectory of concerns about property and succession issues did not produce a triumph of marital friendship. As for Boltzius himself, even he had softened his official theology with age and sorrow. At his death, however, Ebenezer re-

---

48. *Letters of Johann Martin Boltzius,* 2:615.

49. Roeber, *Palatines,* p. 170; for more details, see 166-74. On the critical role of women in the survival of the colony prior to royalization, see Lee Ann Caldwell, "New Deal on a New Frontier: European Women Colonists and Trustee Policy, 1733-1752," *Journal of the Georgia Association of Historians* 16 (1995): 106-26.

sembled the more thickly settled German-speaking communities far to the north, where diverse opinions on spousal character and behavior elicited even more ambiguous proclamations about the meaning of marriage and its place in the New World.[50]

II

Boltzius's counterpart in Pennsylvania, Henry Melchior Mühlenberg, shared his Georgia colleague's frustration about wedding revelries and village customs. In 1747 he performed a ceremony after which he condemned in his journal the "frivolity" of dancing and "sporting" as part of the "deplorable . . . conditions here." He commented acidly on the indulgent view of young people expressed by "my neighbor, the old Reformed pastor, Mr. Böhm, [who] tells his people that one cannot keep young people tied up in a sack; they must have their fun, and dancing has its place, too. My other neighbor, Pastor Andreae, not only approves of this sensuality, but is even the instigator of it."[51]

Mühlenberg kept up an astonishing number of observations about marriages of all sorts and kinds until his death in 1787. He married twenty-three couples in a single year (1749), and his more than sixty entries on marriage for the first twenty-one years of his pastorate in North America increased to at least sixty-eight during the political crisis from 1764 to 1776. Even as his health declined and he was removed in 1779 from his Philadelphia parish, he still received requests to perform marriages. He entered some 156 records, comments, and observations, noting the last marriage two months before his death in October of 1787.[52]

This native of Einbeck and proud graduate of the university in Göttingen had intended to remain celibate and serve in the new Bengal mission field, but in 1745 he married Conrad Weiser's daughter Anna Maria.[53] A

50. For the statistics, see entries in George F. Jones and Sheryl Exley, eds. and trans., *Ebenezer Record Book, 1754-1781: Births, Baptisms, Marriages, and Burials of Jerusalem Evangelical Lutheran Church of Effingham, Georgia, More Commonly Known as Ebenezer Church* (Baltimore: Genealogical Publishing Co., 1991), pp. 84-92, and entries in the eighteen volumes of *Detailed Reports*; Boltzius's figure of fifty-six marriages from 1734 to January 1745 is at 18:163 (1744-45).

51. *The Journals of Henry Melchior Muhlenberg*, ed. Theodore G. Tappert and John W. Doberstein, 3 vols. (Philadelphia: Muhlenberg, 1952-58), 1:136-37, quotation at 137.

52. The statistics are taken from the Tappert and Doberstein edition of *Journals of Henry Melchior Muhlenberg*.

53. *Journals of Henry Melchior Muhlenberg*, 1:102.

cryptic comment in his autobiographical statement noted that the price of an organist's position in his homeland had been "with the condition of entering into marriage," a step he concluded "might have proved ruinous to his soul."[54] His recollections of a wedding attended when he was but a "half-grown boy" focused on the embarrassing conduct of a financially secure but stingy pastor. Passing around the customary plate for freewill offerings to speed the newlyweds on their way, the cleric put nothing in himself, justifying his abstention by quoting Acts 3:6, "silver and gold have I none . . . ," to the outrage of the parish that knew his income. Mühlenberg was determined not to fail by giving bad example, but his first comments about his wife hardly reflected a positive view of marital friendship or partnership. At least for the record he emphasized, like all the Halle-trained clergy, the purely pragmatic motive of seeking someone to take care of his "earthly" needs. He made no attempt to cast his relationship with Anna Maria Weiser as friendship or in mystical terms that reflected the relationship of Christ to his church as Ephesians 5:21-33 taught. Instead, Mühlenberg cited the need for a "female servant," "pious, simple-hearted, meek, and industrious" who would be "*convenable* both for myself and my work."[55] Like Boltzius, Mühlenberg initially described his spouse only as a "helpmeet." Anna Maria, afflicted with fainting fits and lacking advanced education, knew, however, how to argue about the spousal relationship.[56]

54. *Journals of Henry Melchior Muhlenberg,* 1:1, 102; Wilhelm Germann, *Heinrich Melchior Mühlenberg: Patriarch der lutherischen Kirche Nordamerikas: Selbstbiographie, 1711-1743. Aus dem Missionsarchiv der Franckeschen Stiftungen zu Halle. Mit Zusätzlichen Erläuterungen* (Allentown, Pa.: Brobst, Diehl, 1881), p. 2.

55. *Journals of Henry Melchior Muhlenberg,* 1:102; compare Kurt Aland et al., eds., *Die Korrespondenz Heinrich Melchior Mühlenbergs aus der Anfangszeit des deutschen Luthertums in Nordamerika* (Berlin and New York: Walter de Gruyter, 1986-2002), 1:193, 195 n. 10 (hereafter Mühlenberg, *Korrespondenz*); and *Journals,* 2:495, for his boyhood memory of a wedding in Einbeck. Some comments on marriage survive in the diary of Johann Friedrich Handschuh (AFSt 4H 10) and his correspondence with Francke (AFSt 4C 33). Unless specifically noted, I cite the excerpts from his diary as they appear in heavily edited *Nachrichten von den vereinigten deutsch-evangelisch-lutherischen Gemeinde in Nord-America, absonderlich in Pennsylvanien,* with an introduction by Johann Ludewig Schulze, 2 vols. (Halle: In Verlegung des Waisenhauses, 1787), cited below as *HN (Hallesche Nachrichten).* Both Handschuh's and Brunnholtz's woes in searching for wives as expressed in their diaries and letters do not reveal a view of proper spouses other than as helpmeets.

56. Her illness may have been epilepsy; that she ordered very large amounts of the Halle medications can be demonstrated, but the family relied also upon the treatments of their neighbor Abraham Wagner, who was very conservative in his use of mercury preparations. See Wilson, *Pious Traders,* pp. 141, 170-73, 187.

Upon being called to sort out internal disputes in the Lutheran congregations in Ebenezer and in Charleston, South Carolina, the aging pastor in August 1774 wrote his will, put his affairs in order, said good-bye to friends, and made ready to depart on a journey from which he did not expect to return alive. Determined not to expose his wife to undue danger, he insisted that she stay home. To his consternation — but not wholly to his surprise — Anna Maria refused. What did it profit, he confided to his journal, to argue "with the weaker vessels, especially with hypochondriacs and hysterics, either with valid or invalid arguments? Mere sensual perception drowns the so-called *intellectus purus*." The manuscript copy of his entry concluded: "She would not be persuaded by any arguments to remain at home: she appealed to the marriage formula."[57]

The "marriage formula" laid out his responsibilities to treat her with respect as a partner, and obedience did not, in her opinion, require that she concede her rights in the relationship — a perspective Philipp Jakob Spener had tried to convey in his sermons on marriage. The pattern of marriages at which Mühlenberg presided, the occasional observations about the meaning of the spousal relationship among his congregants, and his own marriage convey the strong impression that his wife taught him something about the estate. For her part, "Mary" Weiser Mühlenberg only rarely reflected on her relationship with her husband in the few letters to her family that survive. Mostly she lamented the state of her health, but this burden meant that she and her "dear husband" "need each other now more than ever. He would not get along well without me, and I — hopeless without him."[58]

Mühlenberg's journal and correspondence entries reveal that marriage in Pennsylvania — despite its legal standing as a public act performed by a licensed clergyman — remained more a private than a public occasion. Between 1742 and 1752 he never noted the existence of a license at all in his comments on marriages he performed. Most of the marriages at which he officiated took place in the afternoons or evenings, usually in his house or the houses of parishioners or friends. Elaborate wedding processions or ceremonies were the rare exceptions to simple, quasi-private occasions. He also made a point of informing his European superiors that "when poor people marry, I have accepted nothing from them."

57. *Journals of Henry Melchior Muhlenberg*, 2:563.

58. Muhlenberg Family Letters, American Philosophical Society Microfilm [Peter Goetz Collection; formerly the property of Fredrick Nicolls], 26 March 1779, p. 1; she addresses her "dear husband" in the letter of 31 May 1775, p. 1. I am grateful to Lisa Minardi for discussing Maria's letters and this solitary spousal observation.

In part, as he himself noted at a marriage in New Jersey, he was simply adapting himself to the prevailing custom among Pennsylvania Lutherans. His early observations excoriated the poor housekeeping and drunkenness of husbands, lamented the prevalent dangers of intermarriage across confessional lines, and decried the loss of young people "by fashionable and rich marriages." Not averse to exercising discipline, Mühlenberg had forced a public apology from a woman taken to court for spreading the calumny that he kept two whores; he reconciled a woman excommunicated for having a child out of wedlock, and he deplored the scandal of a Lancaster bigamist. He used 1 Peter 3:1 to remind wives to be subject to their husbands, and on only one occasion hinted at sympathy for "spiritual marriage" (as Boltzius had done) by using Hosea 2:19-20 in commenting upon the "spiritual marriage" of Christ "and his believing bride," the church. After the sermon, he invited the assembled to sing the hymn "O Jesu mein Bräutigam."[59]

He doubted, however, the propriety of hymns that others found salutary. He told his North American colleagues that "I . . . have not included those which, inspired by the Song of Solomon, are composed too close to the verge of sensuality, and also those that dally with diminutives — for example, 'little Jesus,' 'little brother,' 'little angels,' etc. These appear to me to be too childish and not in accord with Scripture, even though they were intended to be childlike and familiar."[60] The *Halle Reports* from North America reflected a shared view of the spousal relationship among the Halle clergy serving in the Middle Atlantic colonies. When Friedrich Handschuh joined Mühlenberg in Pennsylvania, he never mentioned meeting the latter's wife, and the published reports consistently used the word "helper" solely to mean the schoolteachers or newly arrived pastors, not the wives of pastors. Mixed marriage dangers surfaced in Handschuh's diaries, and when he noted the time of day for marriages, evenings outnumbered mornings two to one. He never indicated sermon texts, but he singled out women for public penance for sexual misconduct and deplored scandalous Lancaster weddings. He did describe one newlywed woman as one of the "awakened" who,

59. *Journals of Henry Melchior Muhlenberg;* on the times and customs of weddings, 1:322, 331, 613, 639, 766; on poor housekeeping, 1:133, 144, 147, 148, 149, 232; on the dangers of intermarriage, 1:149, 151, 288, 367, 508-9; on the public apology and the disciplining of the woman and the Lancaster bigamist, 1:96-97, 102, 134, 90; for the sermon texts, 1:134, 186. On taking no stipend from poor couples, see Mühlenberg, *Korrespondenz,* 1:155 (1745).

60. *Journals of Henry Melchior Muhlenberg,* 3:524 (21 January 1783); compare with his silence in Mühlenberg, *Korrespondenz,* 5:495-512.

he hoped, would manage to keep the "spark" of grace from being "entirely extinguished" in her married life.[61]

In 1749 Mühlenberg hinted that marriage might mean more than what was implied in the *Halle Reports* — a matter of pragmatic convenience and legitimate for the begetting of children. When Anna Stephenson wed the schoolmaster Frederick Vigera, Mühlenberg lauded this woman who had been a Quaker, a convert of George Whitefield, and then a Lutheran. He described her as "another Phoebe," a partner and helpmeet and shining example. He concluded the service with the hope that "these two persons in this newly begun marriage may lose nothing, but daily grow in grace and attain the end of faith, the salvation of their souls." This was as close as he ever came to describing the estate of marriage as an occasion of grace.[62] Still, the marriage relationship ended in this life. Mühlenberg deplored the Moravian practice of parading after "the dead with violins and bagpipes[;] that would be a great affectation and contrary to the nature of the case." Rather, Mühlenberg praised a "converted" widow because her behavior put to shame the "fleshly" bereaved who "clasp their hands over their head, pull out their hair, wail dreadfully, and even try to leap into the grave, and then, a month after the funeral, go running around again, become lascivious, and carry on courtships." Despite his apparent preference that widows and widowers not marry again (reflecting the ancient Pauline teaching), Mühlenberg nevertheless concluded, "When widows sorrow, but not like the heathen, let no one judge them."[63]

More typically, even when given the chance to comment favorably on a wedding celebration, Mühlenberg skipped over the more positive endorsement of marriage in Matthew 19. He preached instead on Matthew 24:38-40, that before the flood men and women were eating, drinking, and "marrying and giving in marriage," only to be swept away by God's wrath. The pastor's tendency to regard the spousal relationship in contractual terms surfaced when he was forced to confront a German-speaking husband's wife from a mixed Baptist/Presbyterian family background. Eventually convinced of the need for adult believers baptism, the woman provoked a family crisis since her husband argued that if she were free to break her baptismal covenant

61. This paragraph summarizes the *HN* entries for 1:45, 115 on "helpers"; 1:520-22 for women suffering public denunciations; 1:401-2 on the scandalous "Godless" Lancaster wedding; for hopes that his sermons appeared to have some impact upon others judged by external appearances (including Quakers doffing their hats), see 1:399, 525, and for the quotation, 1:421.

62. *Journals of Henry Melchior Muhlenberg*, 1:219-20, at 220.

63. *Journals of Henry Melchior Muhlenberg*, 1:214-15.

made in the Presbyterian church, he in turn was free to break the marriage covenant. Mühlenberg attempted to reason with the wife, noting that a repeated baptism would be an offense not just to Presbyterians but to the "whole Christian church." He did not choose to commit to writing his conclusions as to the husband's theology, at best a misinterpretation of the famous "Pauline privilege" by which the Christian spouse of a pagan determined to end the marriage was held to be blameless and "not bound" (1 Cor. 7:10-15). In interconfessional disagreements, most Protestants would still have insisted that the man was enjoined not to "put away his wife." But a unilateral change of confession might, plausibly, have been argued to constitute a form of desertion — grounds for dissolution in Lutheran canon law implemented by many a consistory. In a long encomium about a faithful, elderly Lutheran man who had arrived as a youngster in North America, the pastor praised his beliefs and his books, noted his many children and grandchildren — but said not a word about the rather key role played by the man's wife. Over the course of his first quarter-century of pastoral service in North America, Mühlenberg learned to deal with his own wife's serious illnesses; he countered attempts made to create scandal around the marriage of his fellow pastor Friedrich Handschuh to his much younger maidservant; he tried his best to pass on years of accumulated wisdom to a bachelor colleague intent on marrying the late Handschuh's daughter Henriette. Long experience inclined him to counsel the man, but "old bachelors," Mühlenberg concluded, "cannot comprehend that marriage can take a course other than the customary one."[64]

Because marriages did not always conform to settled custom, Mühlenberg began in 1752 to record the public details and the legal standing of the marriages he performed. Like Boltzius, he initially hesitated to marry anyone not under his pastoral charge. Pressed by Protestants of Reformed, Presbyterian, and Anglican convictions, however, he began systematically to note the correct publication of banns, the "permission from the Governor according to the laws of this province," the consent of parents or guardians, and the licenses themselves, including their cost. The potential for liability when he married persons outside his communion partly explains his diligence. He had to admit an error later in his ministry when he attested that he

---

64. *Journals of Henry Melchior Muhlenberg,* 2:139, 465 for the sermon texts; 2:161-62 on the woman and adult baptism; on the elderly Lutheran, 2:474; on Handschuh, 1:240-41; on bachelors, 2:521. On Handschuh, see also Mark Häberlein, *The Practice of Pluralism: Congregational Life and Religious Diversity in Lancaster, Pennsylvania, 1730-1820* (University Park: Pennsylvania State University Press, 2009), pp. 72-79.

had married a couple in 1763 but the official entry at St. Michael's and Zion recorded that the marriage took place in 1766. As a result, "this has caused litigation." Unlike his hapless contemporary in Wernigerode, Mühlenberg insisted upon a testimony from "Mr. John Earl, a sergeant of the Lord Cavendish Regiment," attesting that John Closs, "a German soldier born in Alsace," could marry without *"impediment."*[65]

Of the forty-eight entries on marriages made between 1764 and 1776, more than half focused on the public, legal dimension of the estate; only rarely did Mühlenberg reflect on the theological meaning. His rare comments revealed an increasing adjustment to a predominantly Reformed-Augustinian focus on procreation as the "first" good of marriage. In explaining Matthew 22 in 1764, Mühlenberg summarized the purpose of marriage: "marrying and giving in marriage are necessary for the propagation and preservation of a mortal race. But when mortality ceases, propagation is no longer necessary: *currant caussa* [*sic*], *cessat effectus*" [when the reasons have run their course, the purpose ceases]. Nothing in his later official or public comments repeated his 1749 description of marriage as an occasion of grace.

When an elder of the Lancaster congregation, Bernhard Hubele, fell into scandal, Mühlenberg must have wished that he, too, had remained a widower. He doggedly focused on the man's licit standing under the secular laws of the colony. Hubele's first wife had become insane and died. Wishing to remarry, he had courted his twenty-six-year-old housekeeper but failed to secure his grown children's consent to a second marriage. Under Pennsylvania law, he was within his rights. Still, because of his origins in the German southwest (and since his first wife was the sister of the Halle-trained pastor Handschuh), he must have known the canonical requirements in the German territories that children of the first marriage consent to the second and that the new couple guard those children's property rights. His young future wife became pregnant and Hubele confessed the fornication. Despite Mühlenberg's developing sensitivity to the need for banns and the consent of relatives, he excused Hubele and argued that he had been quietly married "on the basis of a legal license." Mühlenberg's terse entry — "the *lex forensis* has no hold on him" — suggests that he anticipated criticism from Halle

---

65. *Journals of Henry Melchior Muhlenberg,* 1:322 for quotation on the laws of the province, and according to "custom," 1:331; 1:417, 427, 471, 481, 486, 509, 524, noting servants with master's consent; 1:526, 536, 537, 564, 584, 618, 639 on Closs; on the danger of orphans and non-Lutheran guardians, 1:509, and HSP Philadelphia Orphans' Court Records Books 1-6 XWO Pa PH-2: VI: 1761-63, 23 April 1762. See *Journals,* 3:548 (1783) for the 1763/66 marriage confusion.

since the Lancaster congregation disapproved of his decision. Outraged women and men alike had demanded a public ecclesiastical trial, but Hubele rescued Mühlenberg from the conflict between present secular law and inherited canonical norms. He resigned his position.

Mühlenberg had refused to hear accusations of fornication against Hubele and fell back on the legality of the license. Since he was lawfully married in the eyes of the proprietary colony, Hubele could not be tried in a *forum ecclesiasticum*. Mühlenberg did avoid the gender-specific insults he had made in an earlier case, when he dismissed the criticisms of "those who may be classified as women, i.e., several elders." In fact, as he knew well from experience in the colonies, married women often signaled by their judgments and open protests that the issue of proper spouses and behavior remained very much within their purview and control, never mind what secular authorities — or Halle pastors — might say about it.[66]

No evidence remains that prospective couples had access to premarital advice, pamphlets, sermons, or other pastoral aids beyond a cursory monitory address or reference to the Lutheran catechism's Table of Duties. European pietist couples may also have lacked practical advice. Although Moser's pamphlet on sexual conduct in marriage could be obtained from the Halle printing house, it did not make its way across the Atlantic. In part, the turmoil and diversity of North American society help explain why the Halle pietists preferred to impose order and avoid scandal. Mühlenberg explained much in his journal entry of August 1764: "At home I was besieged by people with matrimonial quarrels and troubles."[67]

Domestic violence caught the pastors' attention as a signal of the social and household disorder they decried.[68] Mühlenberg mentioned one German-speaking husband in New York who had disciplined his wife by hitting her with a bound copy of the Augsburg Confession. Conrad Weiser in Reading had to deal with the case of George Reichman, who had arrived home to find "one Jacob Kinterman" in "Clandestinal dealings"; Reichman crept under the bedstead and then emerged to find "the Said Kinterman in

---

66. *Journals of Henry Melchior Muhlenberg,* 2:139 on procreation; 2:452 on "academic differences"; 2:424-26 on Hubele; 1:239 on "women elders." See also on the Hubele affair Häberlein, *Practice of Pluralism,* pp. 93-94. On the history of the legal maxim, see Hermann Krause, "Cessante causa lex," *Zeitschrift für Rechtsgeschichte Kan. Abt.* 46 (1960): 81-86.

67. *Journals of Henry Melchior Muhlenberg,* 2:114.

68. Rainer Beck, "Traces of Emotion? Marital Discord in Early Modern Bavaria," in *Family History Revisited: Comparative Perspectives,* ed. Richard Wall et al. (Newark, Del., and London: University of Delaware Press and Associated University Presses, 2001), pp. 135-60.

action with his wife." He pulled Kinterman out of bed by his hair.[69] Weiser also took a deposition in 1753 from Rebecca Wortman against her husband Gabriel for beating her. In Philadelphia Elizabeth Keihle filed a petition against her husband George for turning her out of his house, but when he answered the summons to appear, he brought against her a charge of adultery.[70] The legal dilemmas resulting from spousal misconduct — over disorder, debt, and property — tended to increase in direct proportion to the distance in time of arrival from Europe, and trust in the oversight of pastors and German-speakers acquainted with Pennsylvania law. The pietist pastors, for their part, had at their disposal only fragile legal mechanisms in the secular realm to help them promote better conduct among spouses, and none at all from their own canonical tradition. Moreover, they continued to be vexed by their own uncertainty about how to reconcile their official theology with the behavior and beliefs of their parishioners.[71]

But clerical perspectives that placed a high premium upon the authority of husbands and good order over obedient wives jostled for place along-

69. For the New York incident, see Mühlenberg, *Korrespondenz,* 3:231-53, at 239; HSP Weiser Papers, Correspondence Vol. 1: "Examination of George Reichmann," 26 March 175[5?].

70. Hence the difficulty of assessing where German Lutheran pietists do or do not fit into the picture offered in Sharon Block, *Rape and Sexual Power in Early America* (Chapel Hill: University of North Carolina Press, 2006), that depends upon 912 incidents for the whole of the continental British North American colonies from 1700 through 1820; her appendix A (p. 249) documents 42 sexual coercion incidents to 1760 for Pennsylvania (compared to a mere 10 in New York and 29 in New Jersey, and the singular observation of Mühlenberg [*Journals of Henry Melchior Muhlenberg,* 1:265] of a German-speaker attempting to rape a servant woman). On the problem of Pennsylvania's criminal records, see Donald Fyson, review of *Troubled Experiment: Crime and Justice in Pennsylvania, 1683-1800,* by Jack D. Marietta and G. S. Rowe, *American Historical Review* 113, no. 4 (October 2008): 1150-51. Rowe and Marietta rely on the records for Chester County, but its high concentration of free-church dissenters sheds no light on the majority "church" Lutherans and Reformed; see *Troubled Experiment* (Philadelphia: University of Pennsylvania Press, 2006), pp. 68-73; and pp. 80-88 on morals prosecution and the decline of enforcement of the laws against fornication. None of the cited examples drawn from the case records include German-speakers; pp. 118-20 on the prosecution of infanticide in counties heavily settled by both church and free-church German-speakers. For various incidents of drunkenness and its role in marital strife, see Christine Hucho, *Weiblich und fremd: Deutschsprachige Einwandererinnen im Pennsylvania des 18. Jahrhunderts* (Frankfurt am Main, Berlin: Peter Lang, 2005), pp. 473-86. For the Philadelphia incident, see HSP Philadelphia Court Records, Mayor's Court Docket (AM 30353 1769 *King v. Eliz. Keemle* and 1770 *King v. Elizab. Kehmly*). This is perhaps the St. Michael's shopkeeper Georg Adam Kehmle and spouse.

71. The incidents of marital violence resulting in criminal prosecution in Philadelphia cannot be documented since the criminal dockets are missing prior to 1759.

210

side unofficial companionate visions of marriage and pragmatic concerns for the protection of property that over time overshadowed worries or moral qualms about indebtedness. Pennsylvania law protected to some degree the welfare of a surviving widow, and married women from German-speaking Europe brought with them a sense of their customary rights, which encouraged them to prefer a public, witnessed, solemnized marriage ceremony in case they should in future become endangered, physically or economically.[72] Pastors like Handschuh might consent to perform weddings in private homes, even in one case between a Mennonite and a Lutheran, but married women watched over both weddings and other parish affairs that guarded and shaped the future roles of young men and women. In Germantown, as candidates for confirmation were marched, two by two, into the church to the altar for examination, the elders led the young men, their married wives, the young women.[73]

The protection of a stable marital relationship in North America could not be accomplished without facing the dangers posed by indebtedness. To leave a widow hopelessly encumbered with debt reflected badly on the moral standing of a head of household, at least in the minds of Massachusetts judges and justices. Whether the German-speaking arrivals into a common law jurisdiction understood the issue in quite that light, however, Mühlenberg could not say, nor can we, more than two centuries later. The sharp increase in German-speakers arriving in Pennsylvania after 1727 had produced a full generation of men and women by the 1740s who could utilize in a rudimentary fashion the legal instruments of the courts to handle issues of indebtedness and the preservation of spousal rights. A pietist conviction — shared by both church and separatist pietists — that urged the moral view of debt as sinful, however, did not fall on fertile ground in Pennsylvania, as preaching on this moral lapse had done in Massachusetts, or even, briefly, in Georgia. In the New England colony where Cotton Mather had cultivated early connections to Halle and the Francke Foundations, moral obligation to both the household and honoring one's word as bond came to be reflected in a severe enforcement of debt collection. The stern moral view about creditor-debtor relationships in that jurisdiction strictly separated chancery causes and remedies from those available at law, and it was the latter, more severe application of the law that won out. In Pennsylvania, the early obser-

---

72. On the influence of married women over such issues, see Hucho, *Weiblich und fremd*, pp. 479-82; Roeber, *Palatines*, pp. 59-61, 151-54, 169-70, 224-26, 229-30, 314-16.

73. *HN*, 2:474, 557.

211

vations on the nature of law penned by Daniel Francis Pastorius had given pride of place to doing "justice" (by which he meant that magistrates should protect widows, orphans, and the poor). But the teaching apparently had only limited impact upon German-speaking litigants who appeared in the proprietary colony's courts. Pastorius had insisted, as had Massachusetts preachers, that debts were to be avoided, and when contracted paid in full; best of all, "he is rich who has no debt."[74] Absent a written set of reflections by German-speakers who were the pietist pastors' auditors, we are hard pressed to determine exactly their unofficial view of spousal rights and the dangers posed to them by debt. A few cautious generalizations may be risked on the sinfulness of debt and the primary obligation of the husband to honor marriage as a responsible head of the household, gleaned from the behavior of these Continental arrivals in the courts of Pennsylvania. Indices of wills and bequests, how juries were used, and the records of the Orphans' Courts remain, however, fragmentary and ambiguous.

In neighboring New York, by 1750 jury trials were used to recover for injuries, and not for mere enforcement of commercial obligations.[75] In Lancaster County, Pennsylvania, a decade earlier, as Emmanuel Zimmerman took his place as a justice, in one session of the Common Pleas Court in 1741, out of sixty-three causes, only eleven involved German-speaking plaintiffs or defendants. Lancaster's population grew steadily between 1740 and 1800, but the Lutherans, the primary targets of pietist pastors' preaching, declined from a 1741 percent of 9.2 to 7.9 over those decades. Increased overall population and pressures on land provided grounds for these people to turn to the courts in settling marital property issues or in assisting children approaching adult status and eligible marriage age. But litigation in proportion to German-speakers in the general population did not increase. Jury trials that might have matched New York for this period — with suits for slander, assault and

74. On debt as a moral issue, see David Konig, "The Virgin and the Virgin's Sister: Virginia, Massachusetts, and the Contested Legacy of Colonial Law," in *The History of Law in Massachusetts: The Supreme Judicial Court, 1692-1992,* ed. Russell K. Osgood (Boston: Supreme Judicial Court Historical Society, 1992), pp. 81-115; on the connection to Pennsylvania, George L. Haskins, "Influences of New England Law on the Middle Colonies," *Law and History Review* 1 (1982): 238-50. For the Pastorius quotation, see Alfred L. Brophy, "'Ingenium est Fateri per quos profeceris': Francis Daniel Pastorius' *Young Country Clerk's Collection* and Anglo-American Legal Literature, 1682-1716," *Roundtable: A Journal of Interdisciplinary Legal Studies* 3 (1996): 638-734, at 665.

75. Deborah Rosen, "The Supreme Court of Judicature of Colonial New York: Civil Practice in Transition, 1691-1760," *Law and History Review* 5 (1987): 213-47.

battery, and recovery of debt — did not occur. Indeed, the opposite pattern emerged. The continuance docket for 1759 reveals that most causes had begun as long as eight or more years prior and abated due to the death of the plaintiff; were discontinued for failure to appear; or were continued for arbitration or further action. For causes that actually went forward, attempts to recover debt by writ of case *(assumpsit)* guaranteed the possibility that once contractual agreement had been proven, (consideration) damages for inconvenience suffered by the plaintiff could be secured. Most of the cases in the 1750s also revealed that defendants entered the plea of *non assumpsit* — that is, the general denial of having promised or undertaken an obligation. But the full rigor of the action *indebtitatus assumpsit* was never imposed here as it was in Massachusetts. By May of 1771, from a total of 149 appearances and judgments for recovery of debt, a lower proportion of German-speaking plaintiffs and defendants was involved than had been the case in 1751.[76]

In Philadelphia's Court of Common Pleas, the number of litigants increased sharply after 1757, and that pattern matched Lancaster's. Simple pleas of *non assumpsit* and failure to appear characterized the dockets. The patterns suggest how increasing caseloads reflected the arrival of disputants from a different private law system. But the use of courts to secure debts and to deal with family property issues brought no stigma of being a debtor or of being litigious, nor as sharp a rise in numbers of cases as a percentage of the German-speaking population as one might expect.

Just over the border from Lancaster in Maryland, Frederick County had become the destination of poor German-speaking tenants. Export of lumber and grain from the second-largest city in the colony that boasted one-seventh of Maryland's population, however, did not create conscientious at-

---

76. This and the following paragraph utilize sources I cite elsewhere in examining patterns of property stewardship. See Roeber, "'Troublesome Riches': Protestant and Catholic Stewardship of a Capitalist World, 1698-1815," *Amerikastudien/American Studies* 42, no. 3 (1997): 357-75, at 371; Philadelphia City Archives, Court of Quarter Sessions Dockets, 1753-70; Court of Common Pleas Appearances and Executions Dockets, 1769-1776; Philadelphia Mayor's Court Dockets, 1756-1772, Society Collections, HSP and Philadelphia Common Pleas Issues Dockets, 1752-1755; Philadelphia County Court Dockets, 1758-1776. Lancaster County Courthouse Archives: Execution and Continuance Dockets for 1731, 1741/42, 1765; Book C: Executions, Lancaster Historical Society Archives, Appearance Dockets. Since the 275 boxes of unsorted materials related to Common Pleas appearances begin only in the 1780s, the Philadelphia record for German-speakers and indebtedness remains beyond recovery. For the relative size and growth of the Lancaster Lutheran population, see Rodger C. Henderson, *Community Development and the Revolutionary Transition in Eighteenth-Century Lancaster County, Pennsylvania* (New York and London: Garland Publishing, 1989), table 3, p. 43.

tention to fulfillment of debt obligations. Only occasionally did judges impose additional penalties for nonfulfillment of agreements through *indebtitatus assumpsit,* issue bench warrants compelling debtor appearance, and undertake *voir dire* examinations of witnesses. Civil causes involving debt resolution were dwarfed by the administrative details of binding out orphans and apprentices. When jury trials did occur, they never exceeded more than two per sitting of the court, never over ten for an entire year. The general picture of pleas entered followed that in Pennsylvania: some defendants confessed judgment; most causes began with a general plea of *non assumpsit;* only rarely can one find a plea of *son assault demesnes* involving trespass on the case where the plaintiff's own original assault occasioned the action. Throughout the 1760s pleas for debt relief increased; jury trials did not. Sheriffs routinely returned writs of execution *nulla bona;* plaintiffs indicated willingness to accept payment in whatever currency could be found, or in one case, released the debt upon payment of costs.

Between 1763 and 1773 fewer jury trials dealt with matters of conscience over nonpayment of debt than dealt with trespass (killing animals); verdicts on assault, slander, and defamation, and — a novelty by 1765 — six instances of trover and conversion, penalized those who had misused animals, or slaves. German-speakers were not bashful about pressing for collection of debt, but they appear to have been far more exercised about abuses against their animals or their reputations. The number of debt cases did not increase in proportion to the growing number of Germans. The forty-eight German-speaking creditors and thirty-three debtors who regularly appeared before the court constituted a very small percentage of a population that comprised a near-majority of the county by 1775.[77]

These patterns suggest a rather ambiguous view of obligations due a surviving spouse by men who resorted to a public forum to resolve difficulties or clarify their obligations both within families and in the broader community. Despite patterns of litigiousness that can be traced back to village conflicts in Europe, German-speaking litigants in debt causes did not pursue creditors with the rigor private law remedies in the Middle Atlantic offered them. Where indebtedness was concerned, the litigants apparently associated no particular moral stigma to that condition. Similarly, jury trial did

---

77. Frederick County Maryland Court Minutes and Judgments, 1750-62; 1763-68; 1769-1775, Maryland Hall of Records Microfilms; see also Elizabeth Augusta Kessel, "Germans on the Maryland Frontier: A Social History of Frederick County, Maryland, 1780-1800" (Ph.D. diss., Rice University, 1981), pp. 260-65.

not expand in proportion to population as a mechanism for enforcing the conscientious recovery of debt. If rigor in pursuing one's rights on behalf of spouse and family had been a high priority, the court records would read differently. In places of known pietist activity where Halle's pastors were active (Lancaster, for example), attention to coreligionists did manifest itself in the building of churches and schools, but only slowly.[78]

Indirect confirmation that German-speakers were not entirely of one mind on the question of obligations due spouses emerged in advertisements in the colony's German-language newspapers about wives who had abandoned the household. Warnings were given by English-speaking husbands informing creditors that the husband would not be held responsible for an absconded spouse. But German-speaking wives occasionally challenged such notions, accusing their men of failing to be providers, of excess drinking, and of violating the agreed-upon mutual obligations within marriage. The *Pennsylvanische Berichte* notices (forty-two in 1745 and seventy-seven in 1755) reflected a cautious resort to defending marriage as a partnership in which specific duties, when left unfulfilled, gave the basis for a claim to a violated right by the aggrieved spouse.[79]

Puzzling inconsistencies surrounded the manner in which Continental husbands in the Middle Atlantic dealt with widows. Maryland outstripped New York, New Jersey, and Pennsylvania in providing liberal dower rights to widows in personalty. Conveyancing rights of women also came under close superior court scrutiny there, while New York and Pennsylvania shrugged off objections over lack of form by pointing to an official signature to a deed as adequate proof. Pennsylvania had said nothing about dower in 1711. On paper, the Quaker colony appeared to favor creditors more than did Maryland, but creditors relied on Quaker affirmations of indebtedness.

In Maryland by 1750, and even before that in New York and Pennsylva-

---

78. Häberlein, *Practice of Pluralism*, p. 222.

79. Two historians have analyzed the advertisements; see Hucho, *Weiblich und fremd*, pp. 509-12, and Kirsten Sword, *Wives, Not Slaves: Marriage, Authority, and the Invention of the Modern Order* (Chicago: University of Chicago Press, forthcoming), chapters 3 and 5. The ex-convert Moravian printer Heinrich Miller (who rejoined the Brethren in 1773) exploited the imagery of a woman bearing a cross in his 1770s notices for these cases but provided no commentary, assuming that the imagery of the cross and spousal abandonment spoke for themselves, or that for women beyond the protection offered by the Moravian community, marriage was more likely to be endured as a cross. For details, see Sword, chapter 6; on Miller, see Roeber, "Henry Miller's *Staatsbote:* A Revolutionary Journalist's Use of the Swiss Past," *Yearbook of German-American Studies* 25 (1990): 57-76.

nia, few male heads of household designated wives as executrices of wills. Concern for the disaster that might befall surviving heirs if a wife unaccustomed to dealing with English-language laws and obligations had to serve as executrix accounts for such patterns among the Continental arrivals. But inattention to drawing up such prophylactics against disaster also played a role. The lack of concern for proper form in contracting marriage led Pennsylvania in 1730 to admit that efforts to stop clandestine marriage had failed. By insisting upon parental consent to those under the age of twenty-one seeking to marry, the Assembly at least implicitly admitted that it worried about households in which the families could be relied upon to pay their debts and secure the next generation's welfare. The trend among wealthier English-speakers of pursuing debtors through writs of case and bonds had been encouraged before the Halle pietist pastors arrived to express their shock at the disorder of irregular marriages they discovered among their flocks. But their charges did not apparently find access to the courts sufficiently compelling to take up the opportunity to do so.[80]

Although eighteenth-century German-speaking migrants to Pennsylvania initially came mostly as family groups, the arrival of unmarried males in the second half of the century also contributed to conditions that rendered hopes for spouses — never mind better ones — only a remote possibility for English-speaking and, soon, German-speaking male servants. William Moraley joined the ranks of arrivals where "men outnumbered women by eleven to one . . . [and] prosperity and marriage were intimately linked but difficult to obtain for propertyless former male servants."[81]

---

80. Marylynn Salmon, *Women and the Law of Property in Early America* (Chapel Hill and London: University of North Carolina Press, 1986), pp. 20-22, 29-37, 149-51, 163-67, 234 n. 98; Carol Shammas, Marylynn Salmon, and Michael Dahlin, *Inheritance in America from Colonial Times to the Present* (New Brunswick, N.J., and London: Rutgers University Press, 1987), pp. 59-61; table 2.12, pp. 212-13; Mary M. Schweitzer, *Custom and Contract: Household, Government, and the Economy in Colonial Pennsylvania* (New York: Columbia University Press, 1987), pp. 21-34; Shammas, *Household Government,* p. 100; on the chancellor's role in the orphans' court and charity cases, see Roeber, "The Long Road to *Vidal:* Charity Law and State Formation in Early North America," in *The Many Legalities of Early America,* ed. Bruce Mann and Christopher Tomlins (Chapel Hill: University of North Carolina Press, 2001), pp. 427-30.

81. *The Infortunate: The Voyage and Adventures of William Moraley, an Indentured Servant,* ed. Susan E. Klepp and Billy G. Smith, with an introduction and notes (University Park: Pennsylvania State University Press, 1994), p. 33; for the changes in the numbers and composition of German-speaking arrivals, see Marianne S. Wokeck, *Trade in Strangers: The Beginnings of Mass Migration to North America* (University Park: Pennsylvania State University Press, 1999), pp. 37-58, at 49.

The later laments of the last Swedish Lutheran pastor at Gloria Dei in Philadelphia, Nils Collin, about misbehavior that surrounded spouses and families echoed what his German-speaking counterpart recorded during his ministry. Collin's refusal to marry people without evidence of the consent "of their parents, guardian or master" caused him to turn away applicants in droves. Moreover, "few middle- and lower-class parents even attended the wedding ceremony of their children." Urban Philadelphia undoubtedly provided more opportunity for escaping close oversight and over time became "a conglomeration of individuals each going his or her own way." But securing an understanding of the spousal relationship as one that required the witnessing and consent of a larger believing community had never been a teaching easily imposed upon the settlers.[82]

Patterns of marriage also reflected a mix of the pragmatic and the inherited folk wisdom about the timing of weddings. The yearly crop and weather cycle overlapped with the need to marry when a minister was present. Traditional peasant beliefs about the right time to contract a marriage — and when the time was unpropitious — eventually fell victim to both practical concerns and the willingness of pietist pastors to set aside those beliefs. The Reformation was supposed to have ended the medieval practice of marrying between Christmas and Shrovetide, and Protestant authorities had tried to suppress such peasant practices as forcing peasant girls who had refused marriage to haul a plow on Shrove Tuesday. By the late seventeenth and eighteenth century, upper-class Protestants and Catholics were mimicking these old customs, including practices that seemed to make fun of marriage itself. Various pithy statements survived customary rituals: "marriage is like grating horseradish: you cry the whole time but enjoy eating it all the same."[83]

Practical needs and agricultural demands in Pennsylvania encouraged intermarriage of Lutheran pietists with the Reformed, seldom with Moravians, and even more rarely with Schwenkfelders, Amish, or Mennonites. These rhythms and intermarriages reflected patterns in the German southwest in the eighteenth century. Despite the constitutionally guaranteed standing of the three major confessions in the Holy Roman Empire after 1648, an

82. *Life in Early Philadelphia: Documents from the Revolutionary and Early National Periods*, ed. Billy G. Smith (University Park: Pennsylvania State University Press, 1995), pp. 177-218, at 179, 181, 183.

83. Norbert Schindler, *Rebellion, Community, and Custom in Early Modern Germany* (Cambridge: Cambridge University Press, 2002), pp. 146-92, at 146-52; 184-87, quotation at 186 n. 134.

aggressive re-Catholicization (for example, in the Palatinate) intensified Protestant antipathy to Catholic teaching that marriage was a sacrament. The right of the father to determine the religious confession of his children came to be interpreted so aggressively that a deathbed conversion of a father to Catholicism could compel a widow to raise her erstwhile Protestant children in the Catholic faith or authorize their removal from her care by force. A 1705 declaration that permitted a surviving woman to raise in her own confession the children of a mixed marriage languished without enforcement. Lutheran-Reformed intermarriages may have accounted for around 20 percent of marriages in some parts of the Palatinate, but Catholic-Protestant mixed marriages were rare. The privileging of the father's wishes over legal liberty of conscience aroused antipathy.[84] Especially in those areas where mixed confessions were common due to shifts in political and confessional allegiances by rulers, Lutheran and Reformed intermarriage was not unusual. In certain locales intermarriage with Roman Catholics increased briefly, but it declined as the century wore on.[85]

Just so, emigrants resettling in North America tended to marry those from their own region and religious confession. Second marriages sometimes violated these boundaries, and pietist Lutheran pastors encouraged marriage with others of the "reborn." Dates for marriages usually coincided with the presence of an itinerant pastor or occurred during milder seasons of the year. Harsh winters conspired against the old Christmas-to-Shrovetide marriage customs. Despite the increasingly regular practice of reading banns and in-

84. Dagmar Freist, "One Body, Two Confessions: Mixed Marriages in Germany," in *Gender in Early Modern German History*, ed. Ulinka Rublack (Cambridge: Cambridge University Press, 2002), pp. 275-304, at 280; Freist, "Religious Difference and the Experience of Widowhood in Seventeenth- and Eighteenth-Century Germany," in *Widowhood in Medieval and Early Modern Europe*, ed. Sandra Cavallo and Lyndan Warner (New York, 1999), pp. 164-77, at 173. For further examples, see Freist, "Der Fall von Albini — Rechtsstreitigkeiten um die väterliche Gewalt in konfessionell gemischten Ehen," in *Frauen vor den höchsten Gerichten des Alten Reiches*, ed. Siegrid Westphal (Cologne and Vienna: Böhlau, 2005), pp. 245-70.

85. See Rosalind Beiler, *Immigrant and Entrepreneur: The Transatlantic World of Caspar Wister, 1650-1750* (University Park: Pennsylvania State University Press, 2008), tables 3 and 4, pp. 62-65, on mixed marriages in this region where the law dictated that the father's religion determined that of children, and evidence that both Reformed and Roman Catholic pastors violated the norm by baptizing children into other confessions. Beiler estimates that mixed marriages accounted for somewhere between 20 and 25 percent of the total population. For tendencies to intermarry with those of one's own region and confession, but with changes over time largely within the language group, see Häberlein, *Vom Oberrhein zum Susquehanna*, and his *Practice of Pluralism*, pp. 138-54.

volving parents in betrothal and marriage, pietist pastors in North America only occasionally bound together "awakened" couples.[86]

The Church of England's partial retention of medieval regulations meant that at least in theory the colonists did not usually marry during Lent, the "Rogationtide," specific fast days tied to the agricultural cycle, or Advent. By the seventeenth century, however, the Rogation prohibitions had vanished; the Advent sanctions perhaps survived into "the early eighteenth century, but the Lenten proscriptions were still leaving their mark on the seasonality of weddings in the second half of the eighteenth century" even in England.[87]

Halle-trained pastors such as Boltzius were willing to transgress such norms. Boltzius explained in 1740 that Lutheran pietist pastors did not "hesitate to marry those who wish to be married during the passion period or even, as occurred today, during Holy Week. I believe that even the very fact that such an important act is performed on a holy occasion can impress them all their lives, especially if they are told that the crucified Jesus with His reconciliation can and must be their only concern in their married state, if their married life is to be refreshed and blessed and if all the trials in it are to be salutary and bearable." In Pennsylvania, the record of marriages in German-speaking congregations still reveals a seasonality that suggests the mix of the pragmatic with the inherited customs of European seasonal times. Intermarriage in urban Philadelphia, while increasing over the course of the century, did not become the pattern for the more typical rural and village settlements. As the German minority of Philadelphia (about 12 percent in 1710, 35 percent by 1765) increased, the willingness to marry outside confessional bounds also rose. Before the second wave of migration of 1740-53 peaked, mixed marriages had remained rare, with perhaps 90 percent of marriages remaining "in-house," a pattern that waned after the migrations and the Seven Years' War.[88] The seasonality of marriages in the villages and

---

86. This paragraph summarizes my compilation of marriages from the three volumes of the *Journals of Henry Melchior Muhlenberg;* J. H. C. Helmuth's diaries (Lutheran Archives Center, Philadelphia, PH 48/A 1769-1810). The hostility toward Moravians and the refusal of the Lutheran and Reformed pastors to countenance intermarriage with them (especially given the number of initial converts to the Brethren from the confessional churches) have been amply documented for towns such as Reading and Lancaster; for details, see Häberlein, *Practice of Pluralism,* pp. 100-105, 142-54. For an early example of Mühlenberg singling out the dangers of mixed marriage with Moravians, see his *Journals,* 1:149-51 (June 1747).

87. R. B. Outhwaite, *Clandestine Marriage in England, 1500-1850* (London: Hambledon Press, 1995), p. 57.

88. This summarizes the research of Marie Basile McDaniel, "Divergent Paths: Processes

rural areas suggests that economic considerations and the availability of a pastor especially influenced decisions about partners and about timing, with April outpacing all other months of the year, for example, in Trappe.[89]

The pastoral struggle to adjust to such cycles deepened their concern for order, the understanding of wives as "helpers," and a preference for lifelong celibacy among missionaries. In 1779, Mühlenberg counseled a young pastor, Johann Ludwig Voigt, to take the promising Anna Maria Söllner as his bride. A widow with landed property, Söllner embodied, from Mühlenberg's perspective, the ideal solution to Voigt's dilemma. In journals sent to the Halle fathers, Mühlenberg revealed that Voigt had visited him to complain of an insubordinate maidservant who had left his service: "The man is unlucky with his maids. They rob and plunder him and then run away. He will have to get married yet."[90]

Mühlenberg reprimanded Voigt for his disinclination to marry, a scruple he appears to have shared with his contemporary Samuel Theodor Albinus. In this case, the older pastor subordinated his pragmatic views on spouses to the more Luther-like and Spener-like urging to view marriage as a mystery. He reminded Voigt that marriage was a union "between Christ and humanity." Even if two people were of different temperaments, a person informed "through reason and revelation" and the "higher powers of the soul" would see marriage differently than someone informed only by the "lower powers" of the body and sensuality, such as Ahab's lust for Jezebel or the homoerotic lust of the Sodomites. Mühlenberg allowed for the possibility of celibacy for missionaries, but he accented the church pietists' preference for the spousal union of one man and one woman, and preferably with the knowledge and consent of parents and community.

Ephesians 5 provided the Protestant norm — "when Christian husbands love their wives as Christ loves his congregation," they represent in miniature the relationship between Christ and the church. But how can someone in the pastoral office teach the obligations of the household if he does not exemplify them? Even eunuchs from birth would be wise if they

---

of Identity Formation among German-Speakers in Eighteenth-Century Philadelphia," in *"A Peculiar Mixture": German-Speaking People in the Middle Colonies from 1709 to the Revolution,* ed. Jan Stievermann and Oliver Scheiding (University Park: Pennsylvania State University Press, forthcoming, 2013) (cited with permission). For Boltzius's comments, see Jones and Wilson, *Detailed Reports,* 7:82.

89. Don Yoder, introduction to *Pennsylvania German Church Records of Births, Baptisms, Marriages, Burials, Etc.,* 3 vols. (Baltimore: Genealogical Publishing Co., 1983), 1:429-61.

90. *Journals of Henry Melchior Muhlenberg,* 3:257.

took someone of a like mind or a widow who was no longer interested in having children so that at least they would enjoy the second purpose of marriage — "namely help and care."

Missionaries in the New World who remained celibate, Mühlenberg continued, would have to develop the talents of a true pioneer — doing their own household chores. Lodging permanently with a sympathetic family of the congregation was unwise — Mühlenberg had tried that. Marriage would be advantageous for an aging bachelor who should have confidence in his ability to support a wife and be ready to lay down his life for the church. Marrying a young woman ran the risk of the pastor's dying and leaving a widow and orphans in a land without orphanages.[91]

This late-eighteenth-century reflection — written as private, unofficial theology, not as a public, official declaration — still retained a degree of the early pietist hope that pointed to the mystery, the iconic relationship of husband and wife. At the same time and in the same exhortation, the aging Lutheran pastor also concluded that the primary purpose of marriage was procreation — a move away from Spener. Mühlenberg reanchored marriage in the New World within the predominant Augustinian-Reformed understanding. The advantage of marrying a propertied partner reflected both the socioeconomic realities and an emphasis upon marital property alliances that had also begun to transform marriage patterns in many territories of the Holy Roman Empire by the 1750s.

Why did the more "mystery-centered" theology not become official? By the time Mühlenberg advised his colleague, he had been removed from office, and disputes with congregations in Germantown, Philadelphia, and Lancaster may well have suggested to him how dangerous it could be to push analogies of the spousal relationship of Christ to his church to present human realities in the face of such quarrelsome and fractious members of the "body of Christ." Did the Halle fathers also play a role in shaping Mühlenberg's evolving notions of the spousal relationship? No one knows. The arrival of a letter from the younger Francke in October of 1751 — less than a decade after the beginning of the Pennsylvania pastor's ministry — must have had some influence on "the preachers in Pennsylvania." Francke had written that he had learned from his father that "through a single marriage everything suddenly" could be ruined, but he made it clear that he would not think the less of anyone for marrying, and he expressed pleasure that many already were blessed "with helpmeets" *(Gehülfinnen).* Glad to hear

---

91. Mühlenberg, *Korrespondenz,* 5:244-48, citations at 244, 245, 246, 247.

that older pastors were not dissuading younger ones from marriage, he observed that the need for caution was "self-evident" *(eine ausgemachte Sache)* for pastors, even more than other Christians. Pastors required God-fearing spouses of an appropriate disposition so that a wife would not "in future inner and exterior conditions make for more vexation and hindrance rather than support." On the possibility of marital friendship or partnership, however, Francke remained silent.[92]

In 1748, Mühlenberg turned his attention to writing a common order of service for the German-speaking Lutherans, and shortly thereafter began work on a rite for marriage, which he copied both from the Savoy Chapel Liturgy that had been in use among London Lutherans and from rituals common in the north-central territories of the empire.[93] He retained Luther's prayer that the married couple remember their creation in God's image and likeness and recall that marriage reflects the "secret of the union between your beloved Son Jesus Christ and his bride the Church," an estate reflecting "your creation, order, and blessing." The Swedes in the Delaware River Valley had also retained this kind of language for their rite when they founded New Sweden in the 1630s. They retained that tradition even after they revised their rituals in 1686 and Swedish pietist preachers like Andreas Rudman arrived in the early 1700s. Rudman's hymns — pietist in sentiment and tone — stimulated debates over the necessity of ordained clergy and the appropriateness of certain hymns deemed doctrinally suspect, but he did not include any specific hymns for weddings. Typically, he did include one that referred to the soul's bridal relationship to Christ, the theme Freylinghausen had chosen to highlight in his hymnal. The Swedish ritual for marriage avoided any covenant or contractual language.

92. Mühlenberg, *Korrespondenz*, 1:432-36, at 435, 434.

93. The next paragraphs appeared in slightly different form in Roeber, "Creating Order with Two Orders of Creation? Halle Pietism and Orthodox Lutherans in the Early American Republic," in *Halle Pietism, Colonial North America, and the Young United States,* ed. Hans-Jürgen Grabbe (Tübingen, 2006), pp. 1-20, at 14-16. I am indebted to Mr. John Petersen, archivist at the Lutheran Archives Center, Philadelphia, for his aid in locating both editions in the Krauth Memorial Library. The formal title is *Kirchen-Ordnung der Christlichen und der ungeänderten Augspurgischen Confession zugethanen Gemeinde in London, Welch, Durch Göttliche Verleyhung, Im 1694 Jahre, Am 19. Sonntage nach dem Fest der Heiligen Dreyfaltigkeit, Solenniter eingeweyhet und eingesegnet worden In St. Mary's Savoy.* See pp. 84-90 for the 1718 edition; pp. 92-99 for the 1743 edition. I am indebted to Kim-Eric Williams for his aid in examining and translating the Swedish rituals of betrothal and marriage and for discussing Rudman's hymns, a translated edition of which Williams is preparing for publication. Private communication to author, 9-10 May 2006.

Mühlenberg wrote that his final order of divine service reflected the influence of north-German rites, the *Kirchenagenda* known in Lüneburg, Calenberg, Brandenburg, and Saxony, in addition to the London service.[94] He adopted almost verbatim for the marriage service the version in use in 1718 at the Savoy Chapel. It contained four passages of Scripture that taught the proper doctrine of marriage. Genesis showed that marriage originated in Paradise. Ephesians drew the analogy between Christ creating a perfect bride through holy baptism for himself, namely, the church; by analogy, this showed the proper relationship of man and woman in the marriage estate. Genesis revealed that the Fall required the man and woman to bear the cross in life — travail in childbirth for the woman and subordination to her husband; hard labor in life for the man, and at the end, death. And Genesis also revealed that God created male and female in his image and likeness, and that marriage, even despite the Fall, remains a blessed estate. The concluding prayer of the 1718 rite (unchanged in the 1743 edition) returned to Ephesians 5, pointing to "the secret of the union between your beloved Son Jesus Christ and his bride, the Church" being signified in marriage. The prayer concluded by asking for the maintenance of this "your creation, order, and blessing."

The only alterations Mühlenberg made for the German-speakers in North America suggest that they were not as willing as pietists in England to adapt themselves to Anglican custom. The Savoy rite included a provision for the exchange of rings; the North American version instructed the married couple to join hands. The printed version of this rite included in the 1786 Lutheran Agenda retained most but not all of Mühlenberg's original language. Minor wording changes *(untersuchen/examinieren* or the more updated *zur Ehe schreiten* instead of the Savoy version's *die Ehe greifen wollen)* altered none of the original intent. More significantly, the original rite had included a stipulation that only those who had been baptized could be married, or if they had not been, that they, in the presence of witnesses, be baptized as soon as possible — a provision omitted from the 1786 ritual. But the 1748 rite insisted that marriage be solemnized in the church building, *und nicht ohne Not in den Häusern* (and not in homes except in emergencies), even though quasi-"private" ceremonies had quickly become the norm in Pennsylvania.

94. "Vierter Abschnitt: Vom Ausrufen und Trauen," in *Kirchen-Agende der Evangelisch-Lutherischen Vereinigten Gemeinen in Nord-America* (Philadelphia: Melchior Steiner, 1786), pp. 39-48, quotation at 47-48. For the original rite I have consulted the Van Buskirk manuscript, Lutheran Archives Center at Philadelphia, Ministerium of Pennsylvania, Ordnung 1763 (N2/1748B). I thank John Peterson for his aid in procuring copies of both of these sources.

By 1786, pastors were told that the rite could occur either in a church or in a house — both were now equally acceptable, a confirmation of unofficial practice but a further step away from a quasi-sacramental or churchly setting. A further index of growing Anglican/Protestant influence surfaced in the vows in which man and wife promised to remain faithful until death and to behave toward one another as befitted a Christian husband or wife "in love and suffering, in evil and good times" *(in Lieb und Leid, in bösen und guten Tagen).* The North American marriage prayer ended the ceremony in the words of the Savoy rite.[95]

The German Lutherans' Schwenkfelder neighbors, by contrast, understood marriage as almost strictly contractual. Any mystical understanding played a minor role in their teaching. When the English-language version of Christopher Schultz's Schwenkfelder catechism appeared in 1863, Daniel Rupp, the translator, retained the confusion of Luther's three orders of creation with the "estates" that Schultz had introduced in his German-language version in 1763. Where Luther had placed marriage second among the prelapsarian orders of creation (after the church), Schultz ignored creation and ordered the estates as the church, the "temporal magistracy," and third, marriage. His definition of marriage was succinct: "an indissoluble contract between a man and a woman." This contractual notion had its origin in the Garden, but the design or purpose of marriage was "the propagation and preservation of the human race." The catechism did note a "further design," namely, "a type of the mystical union between Christ and his church; yea, between Christ himself and every believing soul." Under this "further design," the mutual obligations were love, protection, honor, and obedience.[96]

Schultz's version of the orders resembled a version of marriage teaching

---

95. *Kirchenbuch für Evangelisch-Lutherische Gemeinden,* ed. Allgemeine Versammlung der Evangelisch-Lutherischen Kirche in Nord Amerika (Philadelphia: United Lutheran Publication House, 1877), pp. 223-27, citation at 226. See Mark Oldenburg, "The 1748 Liturgy and the 1786 Hymnal," in *Henry Melchior Muhlenberg — the Roots of 250 Years of Organized Lutheranism in North America: Essays in Memory of Helmut T. Lehmann,* ed. John W. Kleiner (Lewiston, N.Y.: Edwin Mellen Press, 1998), pp. 61-76. The Agenda of 1748 was not printed but circulated only in manuscript copy, of which only a few survive. Peter Mühlenberg used the Agenda in conjunction with copies in both English and German of the marriage service from the Anglican *Book of Common Prayer.*

96. Christopher Schultz Sr., *Short Questions concerning the Christian Doctrine of Faith . . . ,* trans. I. Daniel Rupp (Skippackville, Pa.: J. M. Schuenemann, 1863), pp. 93-106, and for the marriage quotations, 103, 104, 105-6. The original German is Christoph Schultz, *Catechismus, Oder Anfänglicher Unterricht Christlicher Glaubens-Lehre . . .* (Philadelphia: Henrich Miller, 1763).

that emanated from the Halle-trained (and lifelong celibate) Peter Brunn-holtz. His 1752 edition of the *Small Catechism* dominated Lutheran instruction for the rest of the eighteenth century in North America. Brunnholtz's estates consisted of the teaching, ruling, and family orders, a reflection of Halle's insistence, after the confrontation with the jurists, that the teaching function of the church and its ministry be understood as superior to that of lawyers and statesmen. Marriage, however, occupies the third-place standing that Melanchthon had assigned to it. By the mid–eighteenth century, this shift from the orders to estates reflected the gradual movement away from the initial hopes for the marital relationship pietist Lutherans had learned from Spener, hopes that had never been very robust in North America, at least officially.[97]

Efforts to simplify marriage rites in order to enhance the official theology's desire for ordered spousal lives and to overcome unedifying village customs may not have been universally popular judging from the iconography of Adam and Eve. The market for this particular iconography testified to the preservation of a more companionate, if unofficial, sense of the spousal relationship. As those who studied them have concluded, "among the most popular of the illustrated broadside prints of the Pennsylvania Dutch people were the Adam and Eve ballad broadsides." The extension of the medieval liturgical drama, the broadside ballad ensured that ordinary German-speakers would associate their own marriage with the story of Genesis, but the role of the spouses in that story received its own interpretation in these unofficial sources of belief.[98] Pastoral indifference if not hostility toward the

---

97. On Brunnholtz's catechism, see Roeber, "Creating Order," p. 11.

98. See Mary-Bess Halford, *Lutwin's Eva und Adam: Study-Text-Translation* (Göppingen: Kümmerle, 1984); Halford, *Illustration and Text in Lutwin's Eva und Adam* (Göppingen: Kümmerle, 1980); Philip C. Almond, *Adam and Eve in Seventeenth-Century Thought* (Cambridge: Cambridge University Press, 1999), pp. 210-14, on the marginalization of traditional views of the Genesis story by the 1670s in England; Michael E. Stone, *A History of the Literature of Adam and Eve* (Atlanta: Scholars, 1992); Brian O. Murdoch, *The Fall of Man in the Early Middle High German Biblical Epic: The "Wiener Genesis," the "Vorauer Genesis," and the "Angaenge"* (Göppingen: Kümmerle, 1972). On the Saxon traditions that rejected blaming Eve for the Fall, see Scott H. Hendrix, "Christianizing Domestic Relations: Women and Marriage in Johann Freder's *Dialogus dem Ehestand zu Ehren*," *Sixteenth Century Journal* 23, no. 2 (1992): 251-66. See also Christa Pieske, "The European Origins of Four Pennsylvania German Broadsheet Themes: Adam and Eve; the New Jerusalem — the Broad and Narrow Way; the Unjust Judgment; the Stages of Life," *Der Reggeboge/The Rainbow: Journal of the Pennsylvania German Society* 23, no. 1 (1989): 6-32, at 22-25. Don Yoder, *The Pennsylvania German Broadside: A History and Guide* (University Park: Pennsylvania State University Press, 2005), quotation at p. 294, and pp. 254-61, at 255, on certificates.

creation of elaborate, decorative marriage commemorations may have played at least a minor role in the curious absence of such documents, and those lacunae may be an index of the pietist pastors' mixed success in trying to reconcile official teachings with unofficial theologies and practices.

The creation of family registers emerged first as a peculiar North American custom, one that reflected the absence in many places of complete church and court records. Lutheran and Reformed Christians sometimes wrote broadside versions of records by hand, later printed them, and occasionally illustrated them by hand or through block printing, especially in order to preserve the baptismal records, the *Taufscheine*. These proofs were needed for a request to a pastor to regularize a marriage. Halle-trained ministers insisted on them partly to avoid alienating British authorities by deviating from legal regulation of their pastoral duties. But celebratory folk art marriage certificates were rare. Mühlenberg wrote that he provided an attestation or simple certificate when requested, but these uninteresting legal records apparently did not inspire folk artists to transform the marriage occasion into a celebratory, illustrated commemoration.

Family lists for German-speakers also emerged by midcentury, but no "family tree" competed with contemporary New England practice (with the parents as roots and children as branches). Nor were trees used to illustrate such records. The "Adam and Eve" broadsides and the very few marriage certificates that survive used vivid colors — reds, yellows, and greens — with the heart as the most common motif, often rendered with clasped hands between two hearts. The most common phrase for marriage was simple: "these two persons entered marriage" or, sometimes, "married one another" ("haben sich in dem Ehestand begeben"; "sind mit einander verheyratet"; "haben sich zu den Heil. Ehestand begeben").

The combination of this elegiac but pragmatic view of marriage also appeared in Bible-entry registers, which suggests that perhaps 30 percent of "families of Pennsylvania-German heritage appear to have been unwed at the conception of their first child — or they had premature babies." Nonetheless, at least in Philadelphia the number of bastard children whose names appeared in the court records reveals that "Germans . . . were noticeably underrepresented, comprising only 9 percent of the fathers and 11 percent of the mothers. . . . Germans engaged in sexual intimacy as part of courtship but moved more easily from premarital sexual intimacy to marriage, and discouraged bastardy."[99]

99. Clare A. Lyons, *Sex among the Rabble: An Intimate History of Gender and Power in the*

The search of his records of 1763 marriages at St. Michael's most probably prompted Mühlenberg to reenter dates because of subsequent evidence of premarital pregnancy, a task he undertook without comment in his surviving letters or journals. Although medieval practices had recognized betrothal and only subsequent blessing of the marriage, pietist pastors condemned such customs, especially because they created problems over property claims.[100] Married men and women also tended to approach the Lord's Supper in nearly equal numbers from the 1730s to the 1770s. The slightly higher number of women meant simply that widows lived longer and were more numerous than widowers. A mix of unofficial, somewhat idealized views of marriage beyond mere civil contract functioned alongside earthy views of the spousal relationship among German-speaking families who listened to Halle's version of pietism.[101]

The largest collection of broadsides identified so far (some 1,800 items) includes approximately 69 examples of the "Adam and Eve" illustrations and poems; only 7 appear explicitly to address the spousal relationship by incorporating this mixture. They hint at an estate blessed by God meant for the mutual aid and support of the spouses.[102] A group of 154 broadsides from the eighteenth and early nineteenth centuries that boasts four "Adam and

---

Age of Revolution, Philadelphia, 1730-1830 (Chapel Hill: University of North Carolina Press, 2006), pp. 69-71, at 70. The same pattern prevailed in Germantown.

100. I suggest a different interpretation about pastoral attitudes regarding such incidents based on the crossed-out entries in the St. Michael's and Zion marriage records from that suggested by Stephanie Graumann Wolf, *Urban Village: Population, Community, and Family Structure in Germantown, Pennsylvania, 1683-1800* (Princeton: Princeton University Press, 1976), pp. 259-60.

101. Corinne Earnest and Russell Earnest, *To the Latest Posterity: Pennsylvania-German Family Registers in the Fraktur Traditions* (University Park: Pennsylvania State University Press, 2003). This samples about 1,000 printed registers, freehand examples, preprinted forms both in Bibles and as individual sheets, freehand registers, and handwritten registers; for specifics see pp. 2-4, 19-21, 31-33, quotation at 88 based on a sample of 118 names in the first three volumes of *German-American Family Records in the Fraktur Tradition.* For the patterns of communicants, see Hucho, *Weiblich und fremd* (for Germantown, Providence, New Hannover, Reading), pp. 375-76; for St. Michael's and Zion, Philadelphia, see Roeber, *Palatines,* pp. 245, 250-51, 400 n. 12.

102. This summarizes extracts from the Databank of German-language Broadsides Project begun with a German Research Council grant to Prof. Dr. Hermann Wellenreuther, who collaborated with the late Dr. Carola Wessel, and Reimer Eck at the University of Göttingen. I am grateful to them and to their assistant Anne von Kamp for assistance in searching the databank of some 1,800 broadsides published between 1730 and 1830. The complete, online version will appear under the auspices of a joint research project of the German colleagues, Pennsylvania State University Press, the Penn State Libraries, the Max Kade German-American Research Institute in 2014.

Eve" commemorations includes not a single marriage certificate. Instead, baptismal, confirmation, or death certificates constitute the largest number of examples having to do with life cycles. The Adam and Eve representations in all surviving collections invariably show the woman taking the fruit from the serpent with one hand while giving Adam another piece with the opposing hand. In some cases Adam is posed on the left of the viewer; in other instances the first couple's positions are reversed. The poetic verses reflect upon the creation, Fall, and redemption — and at first glance appear to be silent about the spousal relationship.[103]

A closer look at the version of the broadside that was reprinted and sold most often, however, suggests that an unofficial theology of spouses survived sufficiently to create a market for this depiction of the first married couple.[104] The most popular version that enjoyed a market sale of between 12,000 and 45,000 copies in the century after 1730 includes a long explanation of the biblical text. In it, God addresses Adam, but not with the curse of death. Instead, the words of Genesis spoken to Eve on "enmity" between the serpent and the woman's child are directed at the husband. Moreover, the explanation describes Adam and his "whole generation" or "race" as enslaved to sin. It is not Eve who bears responsibility for the Fall, nor Adam alone, since God speaks the curse of mortality to all of humanity, including "the wife," who is here not represented as "his" wife as the Luther translation of Genesis 2:23 and 3:6-21 renders the original. Although Adam is the primary interlocutor with God, partnership emerges in the text and reflects the survival of an unofficial theology that harkens back to Luther's reading of women in Genesis and not strictly to the official gender roles prescribed by the public theology of later Halle pietism.[105] (See Figure 5.)

Luther reached his first conclusions about spouses as a young exegete, and in that iteration defended hierarchy and scorned Eve; later, in his mature

103. The Penn State University collection includes 154 items with four "Adam and Eve" samples that date from around 1800 to 1820. See http://collection1.libraries.psu.edu/cdm4/results.php? A more extensive analysis of the European background of the broadsides is provided in Wellenreuther, *Citizens in a Strange Land: A Study of German-American Broadsides and Their Meaning for Germans in North America, 1730-1830* (University Park: Pennsylvania State University Press, forthcoming, 2013), chapters 1 and 2.

104. Wellenreuther, *Citizens in a Strange Land,* chapter 2, part VI. My interpretation of the contents, however, differs somewhat from his.

105. See Wellenreuther's discussion of broadsides 16-20; the German text for the longer version ("Als Gott die Welt erschaffen" [Ephrata: Samuel Baumann, 1810, No. 1776] is: "Adam Du bist gefallen, Du und Dein ganz Geschlecht/Mußt nun in Kummer wallen/und bleibt der Sünde Knecht."

Figure 5. Adam and Eve, Pennsylvania Broadside ["Als Gott die Welt erschaffen," Ephrata, Pa. Baumann, 1810?-1820?]. Reproduced with the permission of Rare Books and Manuscripts, Special Collections Library, The Pennsylvania State University Libraries.

works, he insisted that "the dominion they shared pertained only to the creation over which they ruled together, and not to their relationship to one another."[106] The Adam and Eve figures, from the popular representations in

106. Mickey Mattox, *"Defender of the Most Holy Matriarchs": Martin Luther's Interpretation of the Women in Genesis in the "Enarrationes in Genesis," 1535-45* (Leiden and Boston: Brill, 2003), pp. 29-108, quotation at 74.

the Saxon Ore Mountains to the Pennsylvania broadsides, suggest that later Lutheran laity somehow held both to an unofficial theology of common and shared friendship and to more official versions. Lewis Miller, the most famous artist of Pennsylvania German life, produced his work in the late eighteenth century and failed to render a single marriage scene. The omission may be a peculiarity attributable to his own unmarried status, or alternatively, to the fact that the unofficial theology of the spousal relationship had gradually declined by the time he began his attempt to document the culture of his hometown. The latter interpretation appears to be the more plausible.

Born of immigrant parents who arrived from Schwäbisch-Hall and Heidelberg in 1771, Miller grew up in the York Lutheran parish, attending the parochial school, and by around 1818 began the "Chronicle of York." His detailed renderings complete with poems, observations, wordplays, and scenes of everyday life encompass cradle-to-grave incidents — with one glaring exception. Not a single sketch details how Yorkers married. Instead, he recorded the marital disorder lamented by the pietist pastors. Aside from one sketch in which a man hurries to save a woman's modesty as her dress is caught upon a saddle, the remaining incidents are uniformly grim, or satirical.[107] (See Figures 6-9 for these incidents.)

Miller noted the discovery of a foundling child; the widow Herman in jail awaiting hanging (though pardoned by the governor in 1811); a sketch of "Mr. Knaub & wife . . . on their way to a wedding" in 1801; the victims of "an English man" who "had a bad practice [of] pouring out of the upper window his filthiness" that landed on a woman's silk dress. Miller's eye and ear for rough marital humor included the depiction of "old Schreck" sawing a two-inch toenail from his wife's foot while he gave her "a Sly Squeeze." She in turn yelled "save my toe" and "kicked him over[,] it tickled her almost to death." Their repartee ended with "you old Canalia, can't you keep still?" "She: you old hangman — go under the gallows[;] you want a lock on your muzzle! He: What! I'm sprung from the nobility!" More sobering was Miller's recollection of a visit to Dr. John Morris's office to be cured of ringworm as a boy:

107. Lewis Miller, *Sketches and Chronicles,* introduction by Donald A. Shelby (York, Pa.: Historical Society of York County, 1966), pp. xv-xvi on Miller's life; the incidents noted below are found at pp. 5, 20, 38, 46, 62, 77, 94, 97, 114. I am grateful to the director and librarian Lila Fourham-Shaull and the staff at the York County Heritage Trust for their help in examining the unpublished balance of Miller's work. No sketch of an actual marriage was made, or if made, survives.

Figures 6-9. Lewis Miller's Depictions of Married Life (ca. 1814-20). Lewis Miller Collection "Chronicle of York," reproduced with permission of the York County Heritage Trust.

Figure 7

Figure 8

Figure 9

Alas! Alas! That painful consciousness in my own heart was to me worst Suffering and Seeing now Mistress Morris [who] Sits — within her chamber[;] after being passed in review as it were, by the malicious eyes of Mrs. Morris and the icy Stare of Mr Morris and a few who knew me would recognize me in that Sad way[.] Mrs Morris with her hands clasped in her lap, and gazing outwards, with eyes of vacancy, the very picture of despair. If we Knew, if we Knew the woe and heartache waiting for us down the road, if our lips could taste the wormwood, if our backs could feel the load, would we waste the day in wishing for a time that ne'er can be, would we wait in Such impatience for our Ships to come from Sea[?]

His remaining depictions of spouses were equally unedifying. An 1806 sketch of Henry Sheffer and his wife Annamaria displayed her caught in a door, him behind her yelling in German, "now I have you, you red-beet grater!" Miller added his own conclusion: "the[y] had been quarreling[;] it was their tempers and dispositions, no peace." His pessimistic folk wisdom followed: "in these cases in that line, marry, yes, in that crooked line, O that present word to damnation." Jacob Kauffelt presented an equally unsavory image of a brutal husband, addressing his wife: "good woman I told you to boil me some eggs. She saying I bought them to make sugar cake. Take care of me. He threw a dish full of broken eggs on her head[.] She was not able to speak. A covering for a woman's head."

The lifelong bachelor depicted a final scene on the consequences of adultery, as he sketched the gallows in Lancaster. There, on 24 October 1822 one Loechlor was "hung for shooting Hack's wife after night, in her bed. Hack made to[o] free with Loechlor's wife, and to revenge himself he shot Hack's wife out of mistake. He was in the kitchen and shot through the door with his pistol. Hack and his wife were both in bed. The[y] hearing him outside rattle and made a noise. Loechlor killing his wife the same night."

These depressing recollections that are offered in a satirical, bittersweet set of sketches suggest the fragility of companionship in the marriages the pietist pastors solemnized in the community where Miller was born and raised. But Miller's detailed descriptions of buildings, trades, professions, properties, and foodstuffs also reflected the growing contractual emphasis on marriage as a key element in the important goal of pursuing prosperity and protecting property rights. The English common law tradition came increasingly to dominate and transform village notions of property and the role of married women. German-speakers had adjusted by the 1770s to the predominant legal definitions of married women dictated by British-American law and custom. Spener's vision was forgotten.[108]

As a context for understanding this declination over time in the unofficial theology of marital relations, we need look only to a fictitious conversation written by the most influential pietist-inspired printer and publisher in Pennsylvania. Christopher Saur offered marriage advice in a pamphlet *The Mirror of the Married*. Appearing from his Germantown press in 1758, the pamphlet's title both invited self-examination and evoked memories of the title *Martyr's Mirror*, a pamphlet produced at Ephrata in 1748.[109] Saur warned his readers primarily about suffering in marriage. He discouraged mixed marriages and explored the reasons why "many people change from one religion to another." Saur's wife, Maria Christina, had abandoned the family for a brief sojourn in the experimental ascetic community at Ephrata that officially shunned the fleshly aspects of marriage in favor of the spiritual pursuit of Sophia. She must have found the opportunity gratifying since she rose to serve as the subprioress "Sister Marcella." Since his wife remained with him only six years before joining Beissel's community, her behavior helps explain the bitter tone of this 1758 screed.

The essay excoriated women for insubordination and for being too ready to intervene when fathers should properly exercise discipline over children. The essay's attack on weak husbands and fathers is both self-reproaching and aimed at Beissel, whose understanding of "the female as a person who lacked male attributes" led him back to the radical marriage mysticism that had emerged in late-seventeenth-century Europe. Beissel's version of "Sophialogical" mysticism encouraged both dissolution of marriage in favor of celibacy and the quest for males to "seek the missing female qualities through spiritual rebirth in Christ/Sophia, resulting in a celibate restoration of primeval divine androgyny." Saur's essay title reemphasized at least one aspect of Luther's own teaching, that marriage is a way of the cross — but in Saur's opinion, especially so for naïve, uninstructed males.[110]

---

108. Roeber, *Palatines*, pp. 135-282.

109. For the 1748 volumes, see *The First Century of German Language Printing in the United States of America*, ed. Karl John Richard Arndt and Reimer C. Eck, 2 vols. (Göttingen: Hubert & Co., 1989), 1:54-57.

110. The pamphlet is *Ein Spiegel der Eheleute Nebst schönen Erringerungen vor Ledige Personen, Welche willens sind sich in den Stand der Ehe zu begeben. Wie auch Etwas von den Ursachen, warum viele Menschen aus einer Religion in die andere übergehen. Vorgestelt in einem Gespräch zwischen einem Jüngling und Meister* (Germantown, Pa.: Christoph Saur, 1758); on the earlier model of the conversation between the settler and the newly arrived, see Roeber, *Pala-*

Aghast at the revival of radical "marriage religions" in their New World surroundings, Lutheran pietists such as Mühlenberg defended officially the proper roles of obedience and submission, as did Saur, and distanced their theologies from mystical notions of marriage's transformative possibilities, whether of the Moravian or Ephratan variety. Officially, the canonical legal tradition continued to support a theology that elevated the authority of husbands, and the obedience of wives. This teaching, buttressed by secular law, continued to shape public pronouncements, sermons, and admonitions among both Lutheran and Reformed pietists. Unofficially, the experience of marriage and hints of joy at weddings reflected a gentler, if still muddled, appreciation for marriage that nonetheless waned for lack of defenders among the pietist clergy or canonical courts such as those that had bolstered the claims of the wives in Holstein.

In 1783 Mühlenberg's maidservant celebrated her wedding. He wrote, with a touch of humor, that he paid for a dinner that entertained an obviously celebratory crowd of "Twenty-three stomachs. Stomachs swelled, minds slept, tongues sang several stanzas of hymns. Paid 3s 9d to the cook." But old habits die hard. Mühlenberg could not forbear adding: "'In the world there is no pleasure that rests the soul,' etc."[111] In his descriptions of his own spouse, the Pennsylvania pastor, like his long-deceased Ebenezer counterpart, now referred not to his "helpmeet" but to "Mama" as he made an account of expenses "to Mary Bradford for knitting two pairs of stockings."[112]

In his later years, Mühlenberg mainly recorded licenses, told how they were paid for, wrote about bonds that stood surety for the costs, and noted that witnesses were present. He could be caustic, as when a Montgomery County pair appeared, she already pregnant. A witness "half-intoxicated" attempted to snatch away the license before it had been properly filled out and then "insisted noisily" that the license did not cost twenty-five, but only ten, shillings in Pennsylvania currency.[113] Moreover, as the press of business and the darkening horizon of warfare between Britain and France dominated reports, he began to omit any reference to the number of marriages at which he presided.[114]

---

tines, pp. 189-96; on the Saurs and the Ephrata Community, see Jeff Bach, *Voices of the Turtledoves: The Sacred World of Ephrata* (University Park, Pa., and Göttingen: Pennsylvania State University Press and Vandenhoeck & Ruprecht, 2002), pp. 109-14.

111. *Journals of Henry Melchior Muhlenberg*, 3:543.

112. *Journals of Henry Melchior Muhlenberg*, 3:574. For other examples where he refers to her as "my poor wife" or "poor Mama" in describing her seizures, see 3:634, 727.

113. *Journals of Henry Melchior Muhlenberg*, 3:277.

114. *HN*, 2:641 (1754); 2:693 (1756); 2:739-40 (1758).

In his own reading habits, however, Mühlenberg showed himself fascinated not with external matters of marital order and obedience, but rather with interior notions of gradual sanctification — a difficult theological position for a strict Lutheran to adopt as public doctrine without being accused of "works righteousness." In 1779, Mühlenberg noted that he had spent the better part of the day reading a moral theology text by Christian August Crusius. First published seven years earlier, Crusius's work had established his reputation as a Leipzig theologian and opponent of the philosopher Christian Wolff. Despite his identification with the orthodox Lutheran center in Saxony, Crusius took for granted the importance of being "reborn" as the basis for morality. He made no compromises on the "natural corruption" or depravity of the human condition. But when he wrote about marriage, he depicted it as an example of "sanctification or renewal" *(Heiligung oder Erneuerung)* when used as God intended it. It was an institution that could nurture "renewal."

The conclusion stuck in Mühlenberg's memory because four years later he returned to Crusius on the topic of "sanctification." He saw the passage as an occasion for "self-examination and prayer." He then wrote in his journal about an incident that reminded him of his care for his wife. In that care he had discovered far more about the spousal relationship, both as cross and opportunity for growing together in Christian love, than his initial comments about "convenient helpmeets" ever allowed him to admit openly. The softening of his own personal stand from official to unofficial, however, could not disguise the fact that in the North American legal and ecclesiastical context, Luther's and Spener's hopes for spouses had by his death largely succumbed to pragmatic concerns for property succession, the legal dimension of the relationship between spouses, and a reaffirmation of the husband's authority. Both Boltzius and the transplanted Einbecker in Pennsylvania never quite sorted out how to negotiate the boundaries between official and unofficial theologies of marriage in this profoundly different political and social context. In that, they were anything but singular among late-eighteenth-century church pietists.[115]

---

115. *Journals of Henry Melchior Muhlenberg,* 3:679; Crusius, *Kurzer Begriff der Moraltheologie . . . Erster Theil* (Leipzig: Ulrich Christian Saalbach, 1772), available online at http://www.archive/org/stream/KurzerBegriffDerMoraltheologie1/Crusius_1772_Moraltheologie-1#page/n/9/mo. Part VII, pp. 837-39. (Accessed 28 June 2011.) On Crusius, see Friedrich Wilhelm Bautz, "Crusius, Christian," in *BBK,* 1:1174.

238

CHAPTER 7

After Pietism, after the Church:
Romance, Companions, Contracts

During the bitterness of the Second World War, a German refugee and now schoolmaster Peter H. Wiener, educated in both Berlin and France, published a pamphlet entitled *Martin Luther: Hitler's Spiritual Ancestor.* Wiener concluded that Luther had destroyed all sense of morality among Germans. Nowhere in Wiener's polemic did his indignation with Luther rise to more towering heights than in his third chapter, "Luther and Marriage." The scandal of Luther's own marriage to the former nun Katharina von Bora and his endorsement of sexual license, Wiener wrote, demonstrated beyond a doubt that "the degradation of womanhood and the taking away of all the sacred character of marriage is one of the main reasons why Germany with Luther began its unchristian way down the hill."[1]

Germany's modern opponents traced its apostasy to Luther's marriage at least in part because the National Socialist regime had conducted a massive propaganda campaign during the 1930s to demonstrate the peculiarly "Germanic" and pre-Christian nature of marriage. German Lutherans might well have retorted that it took some cheek for Anglicans to suggest that Luther was to blame for the decline in an official theology exalting the sanctity of the spousal relationship. Henry VIII's marital adventures made the marriage to a divorcée by the recently abdicated Edward VIII appear trivial by comparison. But the misbehavior of the rich and the powerful should have reminded all

---

1. Peter H. Wiener, *Martin Luther: Hitler's Spiritual Ancestor,* Win the Peace Pamphlet no. 3 (London, New York, Melbourne, and Sydney: Hutchinson & Co., 1942). The book has been reprinted under the same title (Cranford, N.J.: American Atheist Press, 1999), quotation at p. 36.

the combatants that the hopes for better spouses had never managed to reform the spousal failures of those at the upper end of the European social hierarchy. In a bid to claim that spousal morality was the very hallmark of "ordinary" Germans, the National Socialists endorsed and sometimes subsidized various "folk" histories. Among them, Eugen Fehrle's *German Marriage Customs* argued that the "true" German marriage was pre-Christian in its customs and meaning. The alien and elitist Roman Church had introduced a "foreign language" (Latin) and replaced the practice of *Trauung* (plighting troth) with rites that put the power of creating a "copulation" in the hands of celibate priests who confirmed it "with the Hebrew final word: Amen." Only now were Germans recovering the "old Aryan" understanding of marriage as a simple consent of two "equal, healthy, young people just as Tacitus described it" and the Third Reich promoted it.[2]

This distorted appeal to an invented memory of what Luther had taught about the spousal relationship received a quasi-official approbation from at least some German Protestant theologians. Particularly at Erlangen, pronouncements emphasized with the Party the importance of "traditional" marriage roles. So close did that connection appear to critics that the teaching of marriage as the second order of creation fell under suspicion. This remained true after the collapse of the Third Reich. In the 1950s, conservative Lutheran pastors began to question the legitimacy of emergency ordinations of women to the pastorate that had occurred during the war. Their recourse to the orders-of-creation argument reinforced negative associations with the now-suspect teaching on gender and spousal roles in marriage and the church.[3]

The long-standing tension between official and unofficial understandings of the marital relationship, the failure of pietists to convince the rich and the powerful of the need to take spousal fidelity and love seriously, and the continued alienation of many "ordinary" German-speakers did not, however, only become evident in the twentieth century. That rupture had already occurred two hundred years earlier. Dismay with the confessional

---

2. Fehrle, *Deutsche Hochzeitsbräuche* (Jena: E. Drederichs, 1937), pp. 16, 18. Fehrle's main enemy seems to have been the Catholic Church; he makes no mention of Luther or how such "Old Germanic" customs might have been considered restored by Luther's quarrel with the Roman Church.

3. See Richard V. Pierard, "The Lutheran Two-Kingdoms Doctrine and Subservience to the State in Modern Germany," *Journal of the Evangelical Theological Society* 29, no. 2 (June 1986): 193-203. For the rather bitter exchanges between Emil Brunner and Karl Barth, see Peter Fraenkel, trans., *Natural Theology: Comprising 'Nature and Grace' by Professor Dr. Emil Brunner and the Reply 'No!' by Dr. Karl Barth* (Eugene, Oreg.: Wipf and Stock, 2002).

churches had produced in the hands of various Protestant renewal groups the shunning of human sexual activity, and in the hands of the Mother Eva group and then the Moravians, an exalted, explicitly sacramental role for conjugal sex, beyond or within the bounds of a monogamous, heterosexual relationship. The renewers within the confessional church, however, had not found a way to defend the quasi-sacramental understanding of the marriage relationship understood as friendship, and even less, to tie that teaching to a coherent understanding of what they meant by the church. The radical pietists could locate marriage in their smaller communities, but in ways most Protestants found unappealing or unconvincing. The tendency among many of the confessional Protestants to seize upon the spousal relationship as a condition in need of serious discipline, based on the inherited canonical and secular legal tradition, led unintentionally, but increasingly, to understanding marriage as a civil and worldly relationship. By the early nineteenth century, social and economic shifts also conspired in Europe to make access to marriage difficult for those on the lower rungs of society. And nearly everyone had forgotten that Protestants had once cherished hopes that marriage might mean something more than being considered a pragmatic alliance useful for cementing social and economic standing, or alternatively, a highly romanticized and sentimental locus for private aspirations of the middling sorts. Those grander Protestant hopes had foundered for lack of an adequate official theological defense because the canonical legal teaching, itself swamped by the trajectory of secular marriage regulation, had never caught up with the hopes Luther and Spener had struggled to articulate.

The foundering of hopes for better spouses did not occur because the Reformation had opted for some version of "secularization." The protagonists had no desire to see the legal standing of marriage or the understanding of the marriage relationship between spouses fall exclusively into the hands of princes. Still, neither in Europe, nor in southeast India, nor in North America did Protestants either officially or at the level of lived religion successfully locate where on the precarious intersection of the ineffable and the created the spousal relationship belonged. Nor, indeed, have today's Protestants, Roman Catholics, or Orthodox Christians been much more successful.[4] Protestants in Europe, southeast India, and the fledgling United States differed not only about marriage but also about what it meant to be a

---

4. For the literature on the "secularization" debates and my argument for a further "Protestantization," see Roeber, "The Waters of Rebirth: The Eighteenth Century and Transoceanic Protestant Christianity," *Church History* 79, no. 1 (March 2010): 40-76.

Protestant Christian or to be married within a Protestant context. Among Europeans and North Americans, marriage came to be defined sometimes in companionate language, sometimes in adversarial legal and contractual terms, sometimes in the romantic imagination of Luther's marriage to Katharina. In none of these options did marriage remain tightly bound to the hopes for mutual holiness implied in Ephesians 5, and as a bellwether of what the church itself meant. This had always been the Achilles heel of Luther's own hopes for the estate. As a result of that weakness, the spousal relationship, understood in various ways among his many spiritual descendants, now limped into the nineteenth century.

I

In late-eighteenth-century Europe, the pasquinade had made its way into German letters in the form of pamphlets, essays, and books that took aim at various absurdities of the human condition. Effectively quashed since the 1730s, a cautious form of satire resurfaced in 1781 in an anonymous series of "promenades" set in or near Leipzig. The description of the village wedding took merciless aim at the ponderous solemnity of pastors and the pretended reverence of the new spouses and villagers. Echoing the conclusion to J. S. Bach's "Peasant Cantata," which lauded the playing of the bagpipes (*Dudelsack*), this paean to the peasantry opened with praise for "Kaspar with the Dudelsack" and described young and old hopping about, the woods ringing with their congratulatory jubilation in honor of the bridal pair. The pastor arrived "with heavy step — his body, eyes and chin reveal his thoroughly studious mind, and his office is shown in his gait." "Those who so recently were dancing, hopping and springing about with song now moved neither foot nor mouth — and far more effective than the staff of the civil authority is the black robe of the clergy!" The marriage ceremony complete, however, the festivities resumed in full force, though, the observer suggested: "It appeared to me the pastor was no friend of fiddles, flutes, horns, dance and game because he disliked them, and seemed at least to suffer as the feast began."[5]

5. Gertraude Lichtenberger, ed., *Promenaden bey Leipzig* (1781; reprint, Leipzig: F. A. Brockhaus Verlag, 1990), pp. 37-54, at 37, 46. On the early origin and history of the pasquinade, see Kurt Stadtwald, *Roman Popes and German Patriots: Anti-Papalism in the Politics of the German Humanist Movement from Gregor Heimburg to Martin Luther* (Geneva: Libraire Droz, 1996), pp. 179-203. On banishing popular satire, see Helmut G. Asper, *Hanswurst: Studien zum Lustigmacher auf der Berufsschauspielerbühne in Deutschland im 17. und 18. Jahrhundert* (Ems-

The failure of the pietist renewal movement to impose its ascetic standards upon either prosperous newlyweds or poor newlyweds from the villages did not however leave German village culture unindicted by critics who still kept alive the high hopes of Luther and Spener. Friedrich Christoph Oetinger's marriage to Christiane Dorothea Linsenmann produced ten children before his death in 1782. His wife survived him by fourteen years, dying at age seventy-nine and outliving some of their children. Oetinger had particular reason to mourn the judgmental, censorious character of Württemberg village pietism. In 1757 rumors began to circulate through his parish that his daughter's piano teacher had impregnated both the daughter and Oetinger's wife. Unable to bear the whispering campaign, his wife fled to her father's house where she lost two unborn daughters during a premature delivery. Oetinger bitterly remarked that his wife had never harmed anyone and that her very mistakes were more impressive than the hypocritical "virtues" of many a village pietist.[6]

Twenty years later, Oetinger wrote his 1777 essay on marriage, dedicated to "researchers after the truth." In it, he returned to the original Luther-Spener grounding of marriage in the relationship of Christ to the church. But Oetinger insisted on a number of preconditions for a genuine Christian marriage — chastity during engagement, the signing of a contract in the presence of witnesses, the full ceremony in the presence of the "priest," and significantly, a marriage celebrated with real festivity *(Feyerlichkeit)*. Furthermore, after the ceremony "the marriage of the spirit" had to be accompanied by the union of flesh, and only thus would it become "a complete marriage." Reflecting back on the controversies with Zinzendorf and the disputes with Thomasius, Oetinger struck at polygamy and dismissed other cultures and ancient times. The only true marriage was marked by genuine friendship between one man and one woman, and any so-called Christian who disregarded the iconic relationship of Christ to his church — his sole wife — was not worthy of the name Christian.[7]

---

detten: Lecthe, 1980); Agatha Kobuch, *Zensur und Aufklärung in Kursachsen: Ideologische Strömungen und politische Meinungen zur Zeit der sächsisch-polnischen Union (1697-1763)* (Weimar: Hermann Böhlaus Nachfolger, 1988); Paul Spalding, "Noble Patrons and Religious Innovators in 18th-Century Germany: The Case of Johann Lorenz Schmidt," *Church History* 65 (1996): 376-88.

6. Oetinger, *Genealogie der reelen Gedancken eines Gottes-Gelehrten, Eine Selbstbiographie,* ed. Dieter Ising (Leipzig: Evangelische Verlagsanstalt, 2010), pp. 158-59 n. 849.

7. Oetinger, *Freymüthige Gedanken von der ehelichen Liebe nebst einem Anhang verwandter Materien für Wahrheitsforscher, welche prüfen können* (Ludwigs Maximilians-Universität München

The decline of pietism in central Europe by the late eighteenth century generated a retrospective criticism typified by Oetinger's attempt to recapitulate the high hopes he himself had struggled to realize in his own marriage. But demographic and social conditions also allowed a companionate and celebratory vision of the estate of the sort he championed only among the propertied, even as they guaranteed the exclusion of large numbers of the population. As a result, marriage remained an elusive dream throughout the lives of many European Christians. People at the lower edges of European society knew little of an estate specially blessed as one of the orders of creation. Local courts and authorities, adjudicating marital estates, increasingly preferred to transfer property "from females to males." With a remarkable determination to turn a blind eye to these grim realities, pietist women who began to write the history of the movement constructed a collective memory that said nothing about the importance of marriage as a means of renewal. Nor could they acknowledge the sometimes abusive relationships in pietist pastoral households that gave the lie to any notion of the "companionate" vision. Far more often, what scholars would later identify as the "narration of self-identity"[8] that had sprung from the pietist fascination with the conversion of the individual heart marooned the marital relationship itself from the pietist notions of the church, the renewed body of believers.

Hopelessly mismatched from the time of their betrothal, Beate Hahn and Karl Friedrich Paulus entered marriage in 1800. She found that her strict pietist morals and his urbane enjoyment of Trollinger wine made for a miserable household. Ambitious for the education of her sons (and ignoring her daughters almost entirely), Beate Hahn retreated into the form of piety that allowed her to construct an inner sanctuary from which she could criticize her often drunken and abusive spouse, freeing herself from her recognized obligation to honor him as husband and as pastor of the church. By the Advent and Christmas season of 1818, the marriage had become so brutal that "the results of his violence and drinking [were] becoming ever harder and more frightful," leading her to conclude that despite his New Year's wish that they live "in peace," no realistic prospects for improvement would ever be forthcoming.[9]

Open Access URN: nbn:de:bvb:19-epub-10773-6 OPAC Signature: 0014/W8 Theol. 5319 #2), pp. 31-32, 34.

8. The term is associated with the work of Anthony Giddens, *The Transformation of Intimacy: Sexuality, Love, and Eroticism in Modern Societies* (Stanford: Stanford University Press, 1992). Sheilagh Ogilvie, "How Does Social Capital Affect Women? Guilds and Communities in Early Modern Germany," *American Historical Review* 109 (April 2004): 325-59, quotation at 348.

9. Ulrike Gleixner, "Memory, Religion and Family in the Writings of Pietist Women," in

The harrowing conditions of the Hahn marriage and Beate's search for her own identity did not stand for all marriage relationships among those in the later stages of European pietism who chronicled such stories. Still, even in instances where a genuine sense of companionate friendship clearly existed, the crafted memories of various heroes and heroines of the movement passed on no such recollections to their descendants. A perfect opportunity presented itself in the marriage partnership of Anna Schlatter-Bernet and her husband Hector, but their example fell into obscurity along with Oetinger's writing.[10]

Beyond the ranks of the middling, as for example in Fellbach, one of the pietist "hot spots" in the Duchy of Württemberg, the chances for companionate marriage declined as the line between the truly poor and the precariously situated smallholders in the village grew ever thinner by the 1790s. Local officials increasingly turned down petitions for permission to marry on the basis of insufficient means to sustain a household.[11] In Neckarhausen, over the course of the century, people of differing social and economic conditions no longer contracted marital alliances. The grounds for divorce also changed, without reference to pietist hopes for better marriage partners. Rather, the old complaints of drunkenness, abusive behavior, and wasted resources still led to decrees of separation and, sometimes, divorce. But marital conflicts intensified when "marital alliances connected people of equal wealth, and . . . people with power constructed alliances among themselves." The changes produced no move toward deeper companionate marriages; they instead produced "more disputes over the dividing lines between gender spheres of authority."[12]

In Wernigerode, interest waned during the later eighteenth century in

---

Gender in Early Modern German History, ed. Ulinka Rublack (Cambridge: Cambridge University Press, 2002), pp. 247-74, quotation at 247. For Beate Hahn's strategies and objectives see Ulrike Gleixner, ed., *Beate Hahn Paulus: Die Talheimer Wochenbücher 1817-1829* (Göttingen: Vandenhoeck & Ruprecht, 2007), pp. xvi-xix; diary entries 29-30 November 1818, pp. 8-9; for her husband's poor management of the property and resultant poverty, pp. 22-23.

10. Ulrike Gleixner and Erika Hebeisen, eds., *Gendering Tradition: Erinnerungskultur und Geschlecht im Pietismus* (Korb: Didymos Verlag, 2007), especially Marianne Jehle-Wildberger, "Zwischen Heiligsprechung und Domestizierung: Anna Schlatter-Bernet (1773-1826)," pp. 47-66, at 50.

11. For details, see Hans-Volkmar Findeisen, *Pietismus in Fellbach, 1750-1820: Zwischen Sozialem Protest und Bürgerlicher Anpassung: Zur historisch-sozialen Entwicklungsdynamik eines millenaristischen Krisenkults* (Tübingen, 1985), pp. 95-114.

12. David Warren Sabean, *Property, Production, and Family in Neckarhausen, 1700-1870* (Cambridge: Cambridge University Press, 1990), pp. 245-46, quotation at 246; on the divorce cases and the grounds (drinking and wasting of property) endangering the welfare of wives and children, see 214-22.

promoting that territory's long-standing determination to impose ascetic standards upon prospective spouses. Faced with continued popular non-compliance, the ruling house and its consistory gave way. The commonly accepted custom of a "private marriage" in the parsonage without previous announcement of banns continued despite attempts at reform. Investigated in the 1750s, these cases continued to occur into the 1780s despite repeated warnings. The old question of whether a widow and widower also had to proclaim banns remained alive given the common custom of such people living together before marriage, a practice that had the potential to create gossip and scandal in a congregation.

Moreover, partners who remarried were still not careful about securing the rights to property of their children by the first marriage. An official ceremony (priesterliche Copulation) — though stipulated by law — became a matter of choice and not part of the believing community's concern. By December of 1780, pastors asked for a clarification from the consistory since social customs often required them to bless arrangements that were not God-pleasing. People presented themselves as unmarried, but after the pastor had presided at the ceremony, "shortly after a few months or even weeks had gone by, their drunken misbehavior becomes public and we, the pastors must in such cases be seen to have blessed a lie."[13]

Poverty continued to conspire against marital piety as well. August Gottfried Donath had waited three years after approaching the parents of his future bride for their blessing, but Christian Heber, a cloth maker, refused. He and his wife were so poor they could not provide anything for their daughter on the occasion of the wedding. The lack of sufficient funds to care for children of a prior marriage, to secure proper documents, and to have banns proclaimed according to law undercut the drive for more orderly marriage laws. The 1752 prohibition that forbade unmarried persons, children, and those who were not yet communicants to stand as sponsors at children's baptisms had to be repeated again in the 1780s. The repetition testified to the limited success of pietist reformers even in this Prussian territory.[14]

By the early 1800s, alarmed theologians began to identify the state's con-

13. AuBKS, E 3: II: 1/788, "Verordnung, keine Person sine praevia proclamation zu copuliern" (29 February 1750; 11 October 1782; 3/790, "Verordnungen, daß Verlobte die Vollziehung der Ehe nicht über 2. Bis 3. Monate aufschieben . . ."; 4/791, 27 January 1762; 1762; 4/791; "Strafe bei Verheulung der Schwaengerung bei bestellten Aufgebot" I, 18 December 1780.

14. AuBKS 5/792 "Dispensationene in Ehesachen Haustrauungen" I: 1757-1842; 11 October 1792; 16 October 1792; II: G 11 813: "Acta der Graeflichen Consistorii zu Wernigerode betr. Verordnungen wegen der Anzahl der Taufzeugen."

trol of marriage as an index of the church's failure to proclaim the sanctity of the spousal relationship. The view of marriage as an estate officially of "this world" had proven to be the source of mischief. Local princes and other civil authorities had demonstrated both the ability and intent to regulate spousal relationships and to turn them into contractual arrangements in which the disposition of property lay at the heart of the spousal relationship and around which controversy continued to swirl.

Critics unhappy with the trajectory of the eighteenth-century debate turned away from the official theological emphasis on "forensic" justification and simple "declarations" that human beings were saved, or that marriage was merely juridically "ordained" by God. Instead, they sought a way back to the views of marriage the early Luther supposedly had preached, unaware that some of the pietists they excoriated had aspired to achieve just that. What these latter-day critics managed to create, however, was a peculiarly romantic view of Luther, his family, and a "middle-class" urban view of marriage and family. This reincarnated version of spouses, however, emphasized individual choice, particularly by propertied white males. Among a younger generation of more elite German thinkers, traditional religious teaching seemed unconvincing since the view of nature and where men and women fit into it did not seem to require reconciliation with a biblical account of sex and marriage. The attempt to derive a full-blown theory about the nature of humans from a broader law of nature had already collapsed by the 1730s; by the late eighteenth century, the official theological worries of the pietists about such questions appeared quaint and irrelevant.

A combination of romanticized and companionate notions of the spousal relationship could comfortably fit into early-nineteenth-century *Bürgerlichkeit,* but it left unaddressed the indifference or the alienation of the upper and lower orders. The appearance of an ordered household as the icon around which Protestant defenders of conservative political and social relationships gathered, however, had little to do with the theological debates of the previous century. Very little of this central European shift in attitudes about marriage affected the later history of Christianity in southeast India, where a new elite order was imposed in the form of British colonialism, and Christianity remained overwhelmingly the marginal faith of the socially marginalized as well. Continued exchanges across the Atlantic with North American Protestants, however, guaranteed that in that context the understanding of the spousal relationship would reflect the legal and political perspective of white male property holders who demonstrated little interest in the theology of the marital relationship — official or unofficial.

II

The triumph of British imperial colonialism put an end to the patient compromises of pietists in the Tranquebar colony, where they had made at least some progress in educating Christian women and bestowing upon them a highly qualified but real self-understanding of spiritual equality with their spouses. Almost exactly a century after Ziegenbalg's untimely death in 1719, indigenous protest against British interference with marriage practices suggested that the stark simplicity of the marriage ceremony favored by Ziegenbalg's successors had not dislodged deeper cultural customs or attitudes among converted Tamils. As a new generation of evangelical Anglicans arrived in India, they began to assault the compromises the Danish-German Lutherans had made to prevailing Indian customs, with devastating results.

One bitter attack on these "reforms" came from Nellaiyan Vedanayakam Sastriar, the Tamil poet and singer who idolized Christian Friedrich Schwartz, with whom he had lived since the age of twelve. His *Dialogue on the Difference of Caste* defended the long-standing respect for the realities of Tamil society that distinguished Brahmins from *paraiyar,* and the middling group of *vellalar,* nominally *shudras* in Tamil society. Europeans had sat separately from *vellalars* in pietist congregations, who in turn insisted upon separation from *paraiyar* (and by gender and age). Among his denunciations, Vedanayakam now excoriated those who forbade such segregation, disapproved the use of flowers for weddings, and presumed to encourage marriage across the lines of *jāti* and *vamsha* (birth and lineage).

If Vedanayakam's protest can be read as an index of prevailing customs, it would appear that a more elaborate celebration of marriage had survived, at least among the more affluent converts.[15] What such protests also disguised, however, was the price paid by the pietist experiment in deciding that *jāti* was not a religious matter but mere social custom. Effectively, by ordaining exclusively *vellalar* candidates for the pastorate and excluding *paraiyar* and all those who later adopted the name *dalit,* the pietists replicated in miniature the European church pietist successes among the middling sorts of society. But in so doing, they postponed what has remained until today the explosive and unresolved issue — the continued discrimination against

---

15. *Dialogue on the Difference of Caste* (Jatiyacaracampavinai, 1829). See for a discussion of the crisis touched off by the arrival in Madras of Archdeacon Thomas Robinson and the "Rhenius Affair," Robert Eric Frykenberg, *Christianity in India: From Beginnings to the Present* (Oxford: Oxford University Press, 2008), pp. 249-60; on the importance of the *Dialogue*, 259-61.

dalit Christians in all Orthodox, Catholic, or Protestant forms of this world religion.[16]

Among the pietist community in the Tamil areas, almost nothing remained of Ziegenbalg's own "companionate" version of marriage or his hopes for his converts. A small group of Europeanized clergy, like their Danish and German-speaking counterparts, had begun acknowledging the important role their spouses played in Christian ministry, but only much later in the eighteenth century. When the indigenous widow/concubine Raja Clarinda (Kohila) rose to eminence in Tanjavur by the 1780s, official theology's concern for order in spousal relations dovetailed with political and social disorder and the gradual absorption of the Danish-German experiment into the world of East India Company, and eventually, the British Empire.[17]

Although the community had celebrated in July of 1756 fifty years of the mission's presence, over 400 members would die of dysentery within two years as famine followed in the wake of war between the Tanschauer and Tranquebar regimes. When Christian Pohle wrote to Halle expressing his longing for a good wife, he reported that his own health remained sound so far, but the climate was so hard that he despaired of finding a Christian spouse. Someone had recommended the daughter of a Swedish pastor, but the probability of a short life in difficult conditions where Protestants enjoyed no privileges discouraged him. Whatever his theology of marriage, Pohle wrote only of the practical, grim social and political realities he was convinced would keep him single.[18]

Church pietists in India found little opportunity for developing the

16. For a survey of the problem, the literature, and recent developments in one Tamil area, see Rev. D. Peter Paul Thomas, "The Role of Violence in Dalit Liberation: A Study of Dalit Movements in Cuddalore District" (Ph.D. diss., Tamilnadu Theological Seminary, Arusadi, Madurai, 2001). For the later disputes among Protestants in nineteenth-century India on the "caste" issue, among others, see Joseph G. Muthuraj, *We Began at Tranquebar*, 2 vols. (Delhi: ISPCK, 2010), vol. 1, *SPCK, the Danish-Halle Mission, and Anglican Episcopacy in India (1706-1843)*, pp. 150-218; vol. 2, *The Origin and Development of Anglican-CSI Episcopacy in India (1813-1947)*, pp. 136-91.

17. Eliza F. Kent, "Raja Clarinda — Widow, Concubine, Patroness: Women's Leadership in the Indian Church," in *Halle and the Beginning of Protestant Christianity in India II: Christian Mission in the Indian Context*, ed. Andreas Gross, Y. Vincent Kumaradoss, and Heike Liebau (Halle: Verlag der Franckeschen Stiftungen, 2006), pp. 659-83.

18. For the issues surrounding women and events leading to the 1756-57 warfare, see Niekamp, *Kurzgesfaßte Missions Geschichte, oder historischer Auszug der Evangelischen Missions-Berichte* . . . (Halle: In Verlegung des Waisenhauses, 1772), pp. 238, 321-22, 363, 416-31. Pohle to Johann Ludwig Schulze, AFSt M 1C 27: p. 31, 11 October 1786.

friendship dimension of the spousal relationship, an emphasis that had proved impotent in the face of the new anthropology rising in Europe that had no use for a divinely ordered creation and no particular interest in a sanctified estate among its human members. Upon their arrival at the end of the century, larger numbers of Anglican missionaries began a drive to stamp out concubinage and to tighten discipline over the spousal relationship.

Arguably the strongest Christian community in India by the end of the eighteenth century that produced the outraged pamphlet by Vedanayakam sidestepped the question of pious spouses in the person of its influential, permanently celibate pastor. Christian Friedrich Schwartz began his spectacularly successful pastoral duties in India in 1750.[19] Despite his obedience to his mentors' wishes — that he remain unmarried in order to devote himself unreservedly to his pastoral ministry — Schwartz suffered from scruples about his integrity, and it appears, about his capacity for celibacy.[20] In an agonized exercise of self-accusation, he wrote of the sins of his careless youth, but now yearned to have a child of his own. As a result, "when I dream at night that I was in Europe, I've dreamed in my sleep about women, that I might have opportunity with regard to this matter." He ended his ruminations by writing that he knew that his spiritual father had recognized his suffering, temptation, and trouble.

His struggles with celibacy apparently also pricked his memory to such a degree that he asked if he were not conscience-bound to make restitution for some petty theft committed while he was a student. Gotthilf August Francke responded (after consulting his colleagues) that indeed it was a principle of moral theology (learned from Augustine) that no sin could be remitted without a washing away by restitution. Nonetheless, since Schwartz had confessed to wrongdoing in writing, he should not exaggerate his guilt, since that would risk that "no one ever would be able to keep hold of a secure, peaceful humility" *(eine sichere Demuthsruhe).*

Apparently alarmed by Schwartz's sufferings, the Halle fathers arranged (without his knowledge or prior consent) to send Anna Sophia Pap to India to be his bride. Stunned by her unannounced appearance, he refused to

19. Robert Eric Frykenberg, "Raja-Guru and Sishiya-Sastriar: Christian Friedrich Schwartz and His Legacy in Tanjavur," in *Halle and the Beginning of Protestant Christianity in India I: The Danish-Halle and the English-Halle Mission,* ed. Andreas Gross, Y. Vincent Kumaradoss, Heike Liebau (Halle: Verlag der Franckeschen Stiftungen, 2006), pp. 471-91.

20. The following summarizes Schwartz's letter of 4 January 1754 to Francke, a second dated 25 May 1754 and the responses from Halle contained in AFSt/M B 43:9, *Brief der Herrn Missionarien zu Tranckenbar Madur und Cudelur . . . ,* p. 12, recto and verso; p. 31, 25 May 1754.

marry her. The crisis over his struggles with marriage had proven, however, to mirror a deeper uncertainty about the mystery for which it was a metaphor — the church. That uncertainty was signaled in 1751, a year after Schwartz's arrival in India, when an extraordinary "memorandum" was composed in Halle in response to the Tranquebar missionaries' pleas for guidance. The working draft of the memorandum reveals the difficulty the pietist center now faced as it came to a final, uncompromising declaration that marriage was to be defined and considered "a civil matter" *(res civilis)*.[21]

Gotthilf August Francke had given the request to his colleagues for discussion and formulation. Beginning with the problem of publishing banns before weddings, the instruction rehearsed the obvious danger that without such proclamations pastors might end up performing marriages for prostitutes — the old obsession with female Tamil morals. Parents who wanted to arrange weddings for their children needed to understand that "among Christians the consent of both parties must be demanded," and that the contract could not depend upon parents without the consent of the bridal pair, and especially not if a girl were still under the age of discretion. It was clear, the memorandum went on, that "for the sake of good order, instruction regarding marriage must be prepared in the Tamil language and made clear to the Christians and the catechists for their information and for the further teaching of Christians." At least as far as the surviving records show, the marriage instruction booklet in Tamil never came into being.

On the one hand, Danish law regarding marriage needed to be taught, although innocent customs of the native country were to be permitted. On second thought, as a marginal note inserted, pastors were not to change mere "externals" except in case of extreme need. Halle reminded everyone that the Tamil Lutherans were not to marry Catholics or pagans. Too often, in such mixed marriages, the Christian party departed for the other's village or family.

Returning to an earlier set of questions posed in a letter from 17 October 1750, Francke now attempted a further clarification. Except in cases of adultery, what conditions should guide the missionaries on the subject of divorce? Francke could only suggest that the missionaries pull together all the literature on divorce available in the library of the Foundations. Clearly

21. The following summarizes the document AFSt/M 1 C 19:25, 20 December 1751 (addressed to Jakob Klein [1721-90], missionary in the Tamil Tranquebar congregation). The composer is not identified but indicates he is summarizing the wishes of Gotthilf August Francke and other members of the faculty. The identification of marriage as a purely civil institution is at p. 2 verso.

wanting to avoid a potentially controversial topic that had political ramifications, Francke reinforced the correct supposition that the missionaries did not believe they could decide divorce cases on their own authority, "least of all on the territory of the [Danish East India] Company."

The lack of help from Halle left the missionaries in India on their own to negotiate marriage as a "civil matter" with the various territorial authorities. The diary entries of both Kiernander and Breithaupt during the 1750s reveal both their practical dilemmas and the unresolved tensions about spousal relationships. On the one hand, the sober, modest celebration of marriage continued when "a couple from our Tamil congregation married, who thereafter held a meal in the house of our catechists which to our joy went off in a very Christian manner." Joy, however, rarely surfaced in observations that increasingly referred to rumors of war, scarcity of rice, and the deaths of adults and children. A meeting with a married woman who asked if her husband shouldn't also drink of the milk of the gospel led Kiernander to respond that her husband's reaction to her when he returned would reveal whether he had an interest in conversion. Even if he did not, she should become a Christian anyway since God was offering the gospel to her first. A man whose wife came from an especially large and influential family noted his family's lack of interest as sufficient grounds to resist conversion, which would risk his economic and social standing; the missionaries replied that his example might convert them all, but the appeal failed. The missionaries noted in September of 1755 that they had baptized seven people and married two couples; they chose the burial of a child to remind bystanders that if they died unbaptized, "so must they most certainly go to hell." By October in Cuddelur a convert died away from home and the English were requested to allow burial in their graveyard. So many were dying in the hospitals by that time, they learned, that it had become necessary to bury six to twelve persons in one grave, a practice that reflected dire necessity but also underscored the indifference toward the burial of spouses in proximity to one another, another sign that marriage was a civil, worldly matter.[22]

Unofficially, however, some bereaved spouses identified their departed life companions as real friends. When Johann Friedrich Zscherpel buried his

22. The above summarizes AFSt/M 2 LG:3 *Cudelurisch Diarium de 1748 der beyden Missionarien Kiernander und Breithaupts auf Cudlur gemeinschafflich gefürtes Diarium vom 1. Jan 1748 bis d. 8. Jan. a.c.:* entries for 2 March, p. 11; 14 and 15 May, pp. 28-29; June 4, p. 34; 11 September, p. 16; 29 October, p. 26. The abolition of the Danish ecclesiastical marriage courts (the *Tamperret*) may have played some role in shaping Halle's responses and final definition of marriage as purely civil.

wife Christina, who died in her thirty-fifth year, her grave in St. Mathias churchyard in Madras lauded her "distinguished and most amiable Talents which endeared the Wife, Mother & Friend. He, with the trembling Hand of true affection inscribed this Stone to her virtues." In Tranquebar, the "sorrowing husband *(lugubris maritus)* of Susanna Jacoba Koenig nee Breithaupt mourned her 1777 death in childbirth and referred to her as 'the amiable and faithful spouse' *(amabilis et conjugalis fidelis).*"[23] Perhaps similar sentiments marked Tamil convert households, but the infrequency of such sentiments suggests that the Tamil converts retained the conventions of *jāti* and *vamsha.* The attempt to regulate Christian marriage that followed in the nineteenth century lacked any real engagement with the "remnants of the sacramental" and the hopes for simplified but transformative spousal relationships the early pietists had entertained. Those hopes, however, had also largely been abandoned by the latter eighteenth century by the missionaries themselves. Confronted with sexual misconduct by transplanted Europeans, but more concerned about sexual disorder they more often than not identified with the behavior of Tamil women, the missionaries had settled for what they hoped was at least a somewhat ordered view of Christian marriage that did not challenge too overtly the customary roles for males and females in Tamil society and culture. Moreover, the rise of British influence in southeastern India gave them little opportunity to operate without the protection of this emerging European power. Although the Tranquebar mission was fragile and small in numbers from beginning to end, its version of church pietism quietly adjusted to the prevailing political, economic, and social realities of the surrounding territorial rulers, and their eventual British overlords.

When the Erlangen theologian Werner Elert attempted in the 1930s to explain what had gone wrong with the Lutheran tradition by the nineteenth century, he rehearsed the history of marriage, excoriated the influence of Enlightenment rationalism, but noted specifically the baneful influence of the

---

23. Julian James Cotton, C.S., *List of Inscriptions on the Tombs or Monuments in Madras Possessing Historical or Archaeological Interest,* comp. Rao Bahadur and B. S. Baliga, rev. ed., 2 vols. (Madras: Government Press, 1945, 1946). Cotton's introduction to the first edition admitted that his was only a "select list of monumental inscriptions relating to Europeans buried in the Madras presidency . . . all epitaphs of adults earlier than 1800" (p. iii). For the inscription for Susanna Koenig, see 2:215. The Zscherpel inscription I copied in person in February 2011; a tablet in the wall of the Poryar Lutheran Church cemetery commemorates the Tamil pastors Ambrose (1777), Ryappan (1797), and Saveriryan (Xavier) (1817), but no inscriptions in Tamil referring to spouses exists.

253

Halle theologian Siegmund Jacob Baumgarten. The latter's lectures on moral theology delivered in 1738, Elert noted, reduced marriage to an institution that served the purpose of making life comfortable, begetting children, and perpetuating the species. But in the end, marriage was little more than a contractual agreement for entirely pragmatic, and private, ends.[24] Elert may have given Baumgarten more credit for influencing post-1750 views of marriage than the latter deserved, but he discerned correctly what was missing in the Halle professor's theology of marriage. Baumgarten's lectures discussed Christian duties in general and posited an overall moral nature of humans. But in the second part of his lectures on Christian duties, under his fifth heading, he discussed the "duties of social life." For Baumgarten, society was the mirror of the relationship of Christ to the church in the realm of nature. This reading of Ephesians 5, however, had not led Baumgarten to expound on the traditional view of the spousal relationship. Rather, in discussing marriage, he used "contract" language throughout and emphasized that the first purpose of marriage was the begetting of children, and the second was that partners had to be capable of this act; lastly, he discussed the degrees of kinship. Marriage, he concluded, required virtues of trust, dedication to work, patience, and the like, but all to the end of the raising of children. Marriage was a "mutual contract" *(gegenseitiger Vertrag)*. What it did not contain, in Baumgarten's exposition, was any mutual friendship, or connection to a struggle for mutual holiness and support.[25]

The decisive move in the Indian context of defining marriage as a *res civilis,* then, stemmed from the shift in official theological perspective emanating from Halle itself, and equally from the difficult political and social circumstances in which pietist Christians found themselves in southeast India after midcentury. As the subcontinent became more deeply enmeshed in European imperial struggles, debates also intensified in both Hindu and Islamic circles about social mores, especially the proper role of women and marriage. The traditional ban on the remarriage of upper-caste Hindu widows surfaced with sufficient intensity that in Bengal an assembly of scholars

24. Werner Elert, *Morphologie des Luthertums, Zweiter Band: Soziallehren und Sozialwirkungen des Luthertums,* 2nd ed. (Munich: C. H. Beck'sche Verlagsbuchhandlung 1953; orig. 1932), pp. 111-13.

25. Siegmund Jacob Baumgarten, *Unterricht vom rechmäßigen Verhalten eines Christen, oder Theologische Moral, zum academischen Vortrag ausgefertigt* . . . (Halle: Johann Andreas Bauer, 1750), para. 171, pp. 380-99, Ephesians reference at p. 380, contractual references at pp. 381, 395. Comparing Schwartz's student notes to the published edition confirms my judgment that Baumgarten provided Schwartz with his views on moral theology, and perhaps on marriage.

debated without resolution whether child widows (in unconsummated marriages) could be allowed to remarry. Even a fictional Bengali narrative poem touched on the imaginary debate (set between the Mughal emperor Jehangir and a Bengali nobleman). In the context of such potentially fraught questions and given their own precarious numbers and increased dependency upon British Company protection, pietist Christians may well have felt that leaving marriage defined as a purely civil matter in the hands of whatever political power controlled a region promised the safest recourse for their long-term welfare.[26]

III

J. H. C. Helmuth — trained at Halle, and ordained in Wernigerode before accepting a call to a parish in Lancaster, Pennsylvania, in 1769 — moved to the largest and most prestigious Lutheran pulpit of St. Michael's and Zion as second pastor in 1779. He eventually succeeded Heinrich Melchior Mühlenberg and his co-ordinand in Wernigerode, Johann Christoph Kunze, as senior pastor. By the time his observations reached the *Halle Reports* in the 1770s, the series had moved away from descriptions of pastoral activity to more general observations on the need for bigger churches, larger funds, and more pastors, and the deplorable political conditions. But some of Helmuth's diary entries did find their way into reports, and he could be forthright about his concerns regarding spouses.[27]

Like his older counterpart Obuch in Tranquebar, Helmuth wrote about his arrival in North America but passed over his own marriage except to observe, "I will add nothing more thereto, except that I believe from my heart that it was the will of God." In no subsequent report did he acknowledge the

26. Rasiklal Gupta, *Maharaj Rajballabh* (Calcutta: Roy and Co., 1902), pp. 192-99; Aloke Kumar Chakrabarty, *Maharaja Krishnachandra O Tatkalin Bangasamaj* (Calcutta: Progressive Book Forum, 1989), pp. 49-76; on the Bengali poem, see Bharachandra Roy, "Annadamangalkabya," in *Bharatchandra Granthabali,* ed. B. N. Bandyopadhyaya and S. K. Das (Calcutta: Bangiya Sahitya Parishad, 1962), pp. 305-8. I am indebted to my colleague Kumkum Chatterjee for alerting me to these debates.

27. The following paragraphs summarize the extracts from Helmuth's letters and diaries in *Nachrichten von den vereinigten deutsch-evangelisch-lutherischen Gemeinde in Nord-America, absonderlich in Pennsylvanien,* introduction by Johann Ludewig Schulze, 2 vols. (Halle: In Verlegung des Waisenhauses, 1787), cited below as *HN (Hallesche Nachrichten),* 2:1335 on his arrival and refusal to comment on his marriage; for the evening marriages, 2:1449, 1451-52, 1464, 1474.

aid or the socially prominent status of Barbara Keppele, daughter of the most influential Lutheran merchant in Philadelphia. Resuming his correspondence and forwarding his diary again in June 1783, Helmuth noted in the private entry evening weddings and spoke of his desire to counsel longer with prospective married couples that was thwarted by a lack of time. Worried over a recently married young man given to fits of melancholy, the pastor at least took heart that the wife, daughter of a Moravian father now relieved at her conversion, was a leader among the young women. Three years earlier, before her conversion, "she was one of the wildest girls in the city."

Hoping to curb off-color jokes and ribald comments among the unmarried who thronged to one such occasion, Helmuth lectured them on their need to pray for the newly wedded. More challenging, he thought, was the young sophisticate whose belligerent spirit he recognized from his time in Lancaster. The young blade had traveled through Turkey, Egypt, and Italy, was glib in his conversation, full of superstitions, and a perfect example of the wisdom that "he who goes on journeys and takes little religion with him will certainly bring none back with him." The sophisticated talk was little more than a cover for unbelief, Helmuth told the young groom, worse than superstition since the unbelief had its roots "in a malicious disposition." "Rather quickly without further complications we were finished with each other."[28]

Renowned more for his interests in education than for theological scholarship, Helmuth nonetheless published one treatise, *Reflections on the Evangelical Teachings of the Holy Scripture and Baptism* (1793). The work revealed how much an unofficial theology of nature, grace, and the marital relationship had survived in his own thinking. Intent on defending the sacraments of baptism and the Lord's Supper and the preaching office against the twin threats of Quakerism and Deism, Helmuth acknowledged that some aspects of the "image and likeness" of God might have survived the Fall. The family, he wrote, was the context within which a right faith would be nurtured, a faith "that changes the heart and transforms man into a new creature." His invocation of Adam and Eve as the first married couple led to the observation that "in the beginning, the family of God among human beings was small." Christ's coming established "a complete change in the housekeeping . . . the heathens were also supposed to be accepted into the school of God . . . and

---

28. *HN*, 2:1451 on the depressed bridegroom and formerly "wild" bride; 2:1468 on the attempt to quell ribaldry; 2:1464 for the confrontation with the world traveler.

256

again not only married men and women, because otherwise what would become of the young men and virgins, or those who never married?"

Helmuth emphasized that husbands and fathers were the heads of families but insisted that "all good things that came to him were also extended to the female gender." He presented an image of Adam and Eve that had less to say about Augustinian themes that emphasized the fall from "original righteousness" and more about motifs found in Byzantine Christian teaching. The first humans were immature children. And "due to their youth at that time, they have not been identified with attributes that indicate a certain number of years, but instead with a name which also belongs to the smallest of children." Membership in the "family of God," Helmuth taught, "this holiness of the children," born to Christian parents, was neither a "merely external or bourgeois cleanliness" nor a "moral, superior holiness of the heart" — but a transforming holiness of the entire person.[29]

Helmuth's treatise, never a best seller, remained on the margins of Lutheran theology in America. It marked the end of any serious reflection upon marriage as an icon of Christ and the church and the locus for a growth in holiness of partners made in the image and likeness of God. Lutheran theologians forgot his work in later discussions about the renewal of families or communities. Before his death in 1825, the marriage ritual, the hymnody, and the catechesis of Lutherans in North America drifted further away from reflection on the orders of creation. Pietist pastors began a long-standing tradition of putting in appearances at weddings and then departing before the dancing, singing, drinking, and eating.

It was not Halle pastors, however, but the more culturally dominant Reformed understanding of marriage as a covenant that helped to shape the secular law's trajectory on the law of marriage, and looked back to Luther for its own understanding of the marital relationship. Rooted in the "two kingdoms" theology of the early Luther, the Reformed were content to conclude that the spousal relationship was "to be regulated not by the church but by the civil authorities."[30] The elision of distinctions between "covenant" and "contract" language in the Reformed tradition may have misrepresented the difference between partnership in human affairs and the teaching that divine authorship was needed for a genuine covenant. As the Reformed tradi-

---

29. Helmuth, *Betrachtungen der evangelischen Lehre . . .* (Germantown, Pa.: Michael Billmeyer, 1793), pp. 4-5, 22, 224-25, 231, 262, 274.

30. James Turner Johnson, "Marriage as Covenant in Early Protestant Thought: Its Development and Implications," in *Covenant Marriage in Comparative Perspective,* ed. John Witte Jr. and Eliza Ellison (Grand Rapids: Eerdmans, 2005), pp. 124-52, at 127-29, quotation at 129.

tion's demographic dominance in North America came to influence late-eighteenth-century Lutherans as well, some of the latter, especially the pietists, nonetheless found the concept of "covenant" a reassuring halfway house between the overtly "sacramental" and a purely secular "contractual" definition of marriage. But scholars have also pointed out that in practice "the meanings of covenant in religious as well as legal parlance were not exhausted in the concepts of gift and command, equally unilateral. Word and idea also carried a freight of mutuality, of reciprocity, and crucially, of consent — all these being essential attributes of what seventeenth-century Englishmen and -women called 'contract.'" Reformed theologians had not intended, any more than did their Lutheran pietist cousins, to relinquish the definition of spousal relations wholly to the state. But the covenant/contract official language coupled with the secular law's focus on defining property rights, inheritance predominantly in male heirs, and gradually, the recognition of women as legal persons who might even pursue an adversarial legal relationship with a spouse moved marriage further away from the hopes Luther or Spener had for marital partners. The exclusion of German-speaking women from roles as executrices of wills on the part of husbands had already pointed toward a contractual vision of marriage that by the early nineteenth century reflected both official and unofficial, or lived, theology.[31]

Whether North American Protestants thought of marriage as "covenant" or "contract," by the end of the eighteenth century they had put aside any residual quasi-sacramental notions. Lutherans and Anglicans in North America had never faced a serious challenge posed by non-Christian marriage to their beliefs about the estate. The brief willingness among the Moravian Brethren to elevate both the baptisms and marriages of their Native American and African members to equal status with the rites in Europe also collapsed by the 1780s.[32] Protestant pastors in North America fretted over intermarriage between people of differing confessions and the persis-

31. Michael McGiffert, review of *Early New England: A Covenanted Society*, by David A. Weir, *William and Mary Quarterly*, 3rd ser., 63, no. 3 (July 2006): 600-604, at 603. And McGiffert, "Grace and Works: The Rise and Division of Covenant Divinity in Elizabethan Puritanism," *Harvard Theological Review* 75, no. 4 (1982): 463-502.

32. On Moravian missionaries and marriage issues among African Americans and the Lenape, see Jon F. Sensbach, *A Separate Canaan: The Making of an Afro-Moravian World in North Carolina, 1763-1840* (Chapel Hill and London: University of North Carolina Press, 1998), pp. 130-35, 197-98; Jane T. Merritt, *At the Crossroads: Indians and Empires on a Mid-Atlantic Frontier, 1700-1763* (Chapel Hill and London: University of North Carolina Press, 2003), pp. 135-48.

tence of peasant marriage customs. They could not always secure parental consent to marriage decisions, which further undermined the European legal and theological inheritance that had insisted on that public, familial participation. Both Anglicans and Lutherans postponed facing the internal tension within their theological heritage as they rallied around an emerging nation-state shaped by English and Continental Reformed legal and theological precedents, especially the English legal tradition governing marriage.

The instability, however, had been present at the outset of the Lutheran Reformation. Even in the hands of one of the most profound Lutheran theologians dedicated to defending Chalcedonian doctrine and an insistence upon the actual presence of God in physical things such as water and bread and wine, marriage remained problematic. In his brilliant defense of the presence of Christ on earth, in heaven, and in the Lord's Supper, Martin Chemnitz could refer to Ephesians 5:32 in listing various kinds of "presences" (Christ on earth, in heavenly glory, in the Lord's Supper, in the whole church, and in all creatures) — but not specifically in marriage.[33]

To one degree or another, a culture of personal consent, whether Catholic or Protestant, came to dominate the thinking of persons contemplating marriage, and that primacy of choice could be remarkably disconnected to any sense of "church." Partly because of modern feminist theology, nearly all contemporary Protestant — and some strains of Roman — theology tend to downplay the idea of orders of creation in marriage as constituting an attack on the dignity of women and a thinly disguised cover for misogyny.[34] The American Protestant construction of theological memory about marriage played a large role in that story, influenced by similar developments in Europe.

In 1833, eight years after Helmuth's death, and after a hiatus of some fifteen years, Halle's publishing ventures recovered influence in the United States. In Halle, Karl Eduard Förstermann (1804-47) published from the bookstore of the orphanage his two-volume *Urkundenbuch zu der Geschichte des Reichstages zu Augsburg im Jahre 1530*. Förstermann's work helped to further the renaissance of interest in strict subscription to the Unaltered Augsburg Confession. By the 1860s, that renaissance, led by Charles Porterfield Krauth (1823-83), resulted in the founding of the General Council and a new seminary in Philadelphia, Pennsylvania, and a decisive rejection of the

---

33. Chemnitz, *The Two Natures in Christ,* trans. J. A. O. Preus (St. Louis: Concordia, 1971), p. 448. The original text is *De Duabus Naturis in Christo,* published at Leipzig in 1578.

34. For a conservative Episcopalian attempt to respond to such suspicions, see, for example, Charles F. Caldwell, *Head and Glory: Sacred Order or Secular Chaos* (Swedesboro, N.J.: Preservation Press, 1996).

"American Lutheranism" advocated by the General Synod and its leading theologian, the Gettysburg Seminary president, Samuel Simon Schmucker.[35]

The story of early-nineteenth-century Lutheranism has rested on a narrative about a struggle for denominational order. The strict confessionalists and the "Americanizers" both concentrated on order within the churches, including the authority of the pastoral office and the correct interpretation of the Lutheran symbols. They had to attend to the relationship of Lutheran belief to political order, the "two kingdoms" teaching, and the border between "law" and "gospel." But except for a brief skirmish over whether to support Sabbatarian laws, blasphemy statutes, and similar state "police" powers over ethical-religious issues, politics did not preoccupy American Lutherans. Luther's and Spener's hopes for the spousal relationship played no part in the discussions of order.[36]

The orders of creation tradition, as it gradually became known to English-speaking students of theology in the twentieth century, came to be viewed from the predominantly Reformed perspective of European critics. The Erlangen theologians such as Paul Althaus became the objects of withering criticism from Karl Barth for endorsing a tradition that seemed to prescribe political passivity, even in the face of National Socialist attempts to establish a "German" Christianity. That entire exchange, however, focused primarily on political structures. Barth's dismissal shed no light on the original complexity of the three orders, especially not on marriage. But as the pietist renewers of Spener's generation had been acutely aware, Luther's theology had not only highlighted the worldly side of marriage, but had still fought to understand the spousal relationship as a mystery and a reflection in the created world of Christ's relationship to the church.[37]

---

35. Much of what follows in these paragraphs appeared earlier in a somewhat different version as Roeber, "'Creating Order with Two Orders of Creation'? Halle Pietism and Orthodox Lutherans in the Early American Republic," in *Halle Pietism, Colonial North America, and the Young United States,* ed. Hans-Jürgen Grabbe (Stuttgart: Franz Steiner Verlag, 2008), pp. 289-308, and appears here with the permission of the publisher. Förstermann's work comprises 12 vols. (Halle: Verlag der Buchhandlung des Waisenhauses, 1833-35; reprint, Hildesheim: G. Olms Verlag; Osnabrück: Biblio-Verlag, 1966).

36. See, for example, David A. Gustafson, *Lutherans in Crisis: The Question of Identity in the American Republic* (Minneapolis: Fortress, 1993), pp. 46-137.

37. On Pennsylvania German Lutherans and their adjustments to early republic political issues, see Steven M. Nolt, *Foreigners in Their Own Land: Pennsylvania Germans and the Early Republic* (University Park: Pennsylvania State University Press, 2002), pp. 89-108. For a summary of Barthian and Lutheran exchanges on this topic, see Gustaf Wingren, *The Christian's Calling: Luther on Vocation,* trans. Carl C. Rasmussen (Edinburgh: T. & T. Clark, 1952), and

Just as Luther's *Marriage Booklet* disappeared from later editions of German-language ritual books in Europe, so too in American Lutheranism, by the middle of the nineteenth century, "confessionalists" and "Americanizers" — both of whom believed themselves the true but improved inheritors of Halle's evangelizing and experiential religious insights — failed to recognize the larger problem they faced by forgetting or neglecting to reflect sufficiently on Luther's original teaching on how the spousal relationship meant more than authority and submission, and called partners to an ever-deepening relationship marked by the common quest for holiness. Lutherans eventually had to confront the increasingly unconvincing arguments their theologians struggled to maintain in the face of new knowledge about the observed behaviors of humans and the bewildering variety of sexual partnering in the animal world. Certainties that had once emerged from the province of natural philosophy gave ground to new "sciences" that appeared to provide reasonable grounds to challenge inherited teachings on the sanctity of the monogamous, male-dominated marital relationship. But the failure of Lutheran pietists during the previous century to articulate in official theology how marriage was more than a civil matter stood their heirs in poor stead for such challenges. Indirectly, Halle's pietist legacy informed both neo-confessionalists and those who sought a more radical adjustment to American Protestantism. That legacy left both sides poorly armed for articulating a more hopeful vision of the spousal relationship.[38]

Gustaf Wingren, *Creation and Law,* trans. Ross Mackenzie (Edinburgh: Oliver and Boyd, 1961). More specifically on the argument between Barth and Werner Elert, see Sigurjon Arni Eyjolfsson, *Rechtfertigung und Schöpfung in der Theologie Werner Elerts* (Hannover: Lutherisches Verlagshaus, 1994), pp. 23-29. On the conservative Lutheran free churches in Germany, see Manfred Rönsch and Werner Klan, *Quellen zur Entstehung und Entwicklung selbständiger evangelisch-lutherischer Kirchen in Deutschland* (Frankfurt am Main and New York: Peter Lang, 1987).

38. See Mickey L. Mattox, "Order in the House? The Reception of Luther's Orders Teaching in Early Lutheran Genesis Commentaries," *Reformation and Renaissance Review* (forthcoming); A. G. Roeber, "Pietists and the Orders of Creation," in *Interdisziplinäre Pietismusforschungen: Beiträge zum Ersten Internationalen Kongress für Pietismusforschung 2001,* ed. Udo Sträter et al., 2 vols. (Halle and Tübingen: Verlag der Franckeschen Stiftungen im Max Niemeyer Verlag, 2005), pp. 747-58; A. G. Roeber, "'What the Law Requires Is Written on Their Hearts': Noachic and Natural Law among German-Speakers in Early Modern North America," *William and Mary Quarterly* 58 (2001): 883-912; A. G. Roeber, "The Orders of Creation in Late Sixteenth- and Seventeenth-Century Lutheran Dogmatics" (paper presented at the Sixteenth Century Studies Conference, Denver, Colorado, 24-28 October 2001). The most comprehensive reassessment of Luther on marriage is Karl-Heinz Selge, *Ehe als Lebensbund: Die Unauflöslichkeit der Ehe als Herausforderung für den Dialog zwischen katholischer und evangelisch-lutherischer Theologie*

By the time "Americanizers" led by Samuel S. Schmucker sought to build upon Mühlenberg's supposed Halle legacy in North America, teachings on the spousal relationship were increasingly confined to pragmatic admonitions in marriage sermons or tracts about the duties of children to be obedient to parents. Schmucker thought he exemplified such filial piety. Educated in part by his father, who in turn was trained for the ministry under the last Lutheran pastors from the Francke Foundations before the Napoleonic Wars, Schmucker saw the future of American Lutheranism as a "union" church within the broader streams of North American Protestantism. So did Halle's theologians of the early nineteenth century, who were perfectly at ease with the Prussian Union. Schmucker and his allies valued the conversion experience and a subjective and emotive hymnody, and they exhibited indifference to liturgical ritual or sacramental piety. But willingness to adopt the "new measures" of the anxious bench, and in some cases engagement in controversial political issues such as abolitionism, exceeded the guarded and cautious policies Halle had once enjoined on its North American pastors to avoid confrontation with British authorities.

The gradual decline of the older pietist theology at Halle occurred at the hands of "neologist" theologians Siegmund Jacob Baumgarten (1706-57) and Johann Salomo Semler (1725-91), alarming some of their former students active in North America after the American Revolution. Anguished letters reached pastors like Helmuth, detailing the spread of infidelity and rationalist theology in the very halls that had once witnessed the rout of philosophers like Christian Wolff. The Americanizers in the United States appeared to confirm Halle's new direction, setting aside subscription to the Augsburg Confession as a prerequisite for ordination to the Lutheran ministry by the 1790s. That willingness to overlook a confessional subscription provided the springboard for Schmucker's attempt to reorder Lutheran identity in a form more compatible with evangelical and Reformed doctrine and practice in the New World.

On the surface, Halle's Americanized influence in Pennsylvania and neighboring New York appeared to receive renewed affirmation in 1837 when a group of New York Lutherans founded the Francke Evangelical Synod. Calling on the memory of "Luther, Arndt, Spener, and Francke,"

(Frankfurt am Main: Peter Lang, 1999), pp. 77-127. On the catechetical traditions and marriage, see Robert James Bast, *Honor Your Fathers: Catechisms and the Emergence of a Patriarchal Ideology in Germany, 1400-1600* (Leiden, New York, and Cologne: Brill, 1997), pp. 66-92. On catechisms in North America, see below.

they defended their endorsement of revivalist practices and their demand that converts testify to their "rebirth" by insisting that Old World pietism had demanded nothing less. They would not have countenanced contact with the Halle of the 1830s, because the theological and political climate in Prussia exhibited scant sympathy for republican tendencies in state, church, or society.[39]

Firmly rooted in the Prussian state tradition by the early nineteenth century, Halle's theological climate was now regulated by a faculty who hailed the Prussian Union of 1817. A positive view of "unionism" in Halle led the Americanizers to conclude that at least on this one point, both the university and the Foundations fit the program of American Lutheranism. Förstermann signaled his support for the Prussian Union by saying that he hoped his researches would promote the right understanding of the history of the Reformation and "our Church" "to the date of Melanchthon's or Calvin's death," signposts regarded as ominous by confessionalist Lutherans who hated the Union.[40]

But these apparent congruities of a unionist Halle and an Americanizing Lutheranism proved illusory and at least briefly seemed to promise a reengagement with the importance of marriage as something more than a purely civil matter. By the 1820s, theologians emerged at Halle who supported the Union but rejected rationalist theology. Among these, no one exercised more influence than Friedrich August Tholuck (1799-1877). His teaching and piety transformed the life of the young C. D. F. Wyneken, who years later would detail negative memories of his student days at Halle. Wyneken, a native of Hannover, seemed like a throwback to Heinrich Melchior Mühlenberg, having studied at both Halle and Göttingen before meeting Tholuck and undergoing what one can only describe as a conversion experience. Seeking contact with the Basel mission society and the "In-

---

39. See Gottfried Hornig, "Semlers Lehre von der Heilsordnung. Eine Studie zur Rezeption und Kritik des halleschen Pietismus," *Pietismus und Neuzeit* 10 (1984): 152-89. On Helmuth's exchanges with Europeans, see A. G. Roeber, "'Through a Glass, Darkly': Changing German Ideas of American Freedom, 1783-1806," in *Transatlantic Images and Perceptions: Germany and America Since 1776*, ed. David E. Barclay and Elisabeth Glaser-Schmidt (New York: Cambridge University Press, 1997), pp. 19-40. Quotation from *Lutheran Herald*, 15 March 1842, cited in Paul P. Kuenning, *The Rise and Fall of American Lutheran Pietism: The Rejection of an Activist Heritage* (Macon, Ga.: Mercer University Press, 1988), p. 83.

40. Karl Eduard Förstermann, *Urkundenbuch zu der Geschichte des Reichstages zu Augsburg im Jahre 1530*, 12 vols. (Halle: Verlag der Buchhandlung des Waisenhauses, 1833-35; reprint, Hildesheim: G. Olms Verlag; Osnabrück: Biblio-Verlag, 1966), 1:viii (note 1). For Förstermann's occupations see the title page of his volumes and the preface.

ner Mission" work pioneered at Hamburg, Wyneken became deeply involved in this domestic form of pietism before arriving in Baltimore in 1838 and moving to the Michigan and Indiana frontiers.

He emerged within a decade as one of the founders of what became the German Evangelical Synod of Missouri and Other States. His opinion of Pennsylvania Lutherans was not positive. These descendants of Halle pietism looked to him like Methodists, emphasizing conversion experiences and the use of such "new measures" as the anxious bench. The seminary at Gettysburg, "built largely with German money and maintained by synods as 'Lutheran,' is in their hands . . . instead of being a nursemaid of the Lutheran Church, if everything remains the same . . . will turn into a snake, which it has raised in its bosom, and into a powerful tool to help destroy the Church . . . [because of] the attempts at a union between Lutherans and Reformed."[41]

Tholuck's influence reached beyond Wyneken to English-speakers through the efforts of Charles Porterfield Krauth, who published the English version of Tholuck's *Commentary on the Gospel of St. John* in 1859. Krauth, the formidable enemy of the "Americanizers," received Tholuck's thanks for the translation and further affirmation from an American student at Halle who reported that the English version had gratified the Halle theologian.[42]

The German theologian who published Wyneken's *Notruf* also claimed no simple, direct lineage to Halle's pietist past. Yet Adolf von Harless was profoundly influenced by the themes of "rebirth" and "awakening" so dear to the pietist movement, and he proved to be as hostile as Krauth to the "Americanizing" tendencies in North American Lutheranism. Von Harless grew up in a household shaped by Nuremberg pietism, but no evidence survives that he was aware of Halle's eighteenth-century ventures in North America. Neither did his own piety reflect the influence of Spener on the issue of the spousal relationship in marriage. Only as a student at Halle beginning in 1826 did his encounter with Tholuck lead to a conversion experience based not on a deep study of the Lutheran Confessions but on his reading of Luther's *Bondage of the Will* and a book of excerpts from Luther's writings.

Alone among the "neo-confessional" theologians who contributed to the confessional revival in North America, von Harless recognized Lutherans'

41. F. C. D. Wyneken, *The Distress of the German Lutherans in North America*, trans. S. Edgar Schmidt, ed. R. F. Rehmer (Fort Wayne, Ind.: Concordia Theological Seminary Press, 1982). The original "Notruf" appeared in 1843 in Adolf von Harless's *Zeitschrift für Protestantismus und Kirche*; biographical details from introduction, pp. 1-16, quotation at 47.

42. Adolph Spaeth, *Charles Porterfield Krauth*, 2 vols. (New York: Christian Literature Co., 1898), 1:303-5.

failure to defend marriage as an integral part of the created order. His *Christian Ethics* appeared in 1842, and the work showed how indebted he remained to the pietist emphasis on rebirth, which also demanded a broader perspective on the signal importance of marriage and the profound implications the right teaching on the godly estate held for the church and society. Pietist renewal implied much more for von Harless than a personal quest for improved behavior. Deeply critical of his eighteenth-century predecessors, he concluded that they had abetted the Prussian state in understanding marriage not "as something which sprang from the Order of Nature carrying the very will of God, but a purely human-natural, godless relationship subordinated to human contract purposes and contractual rules." In truth, he insisted, marriage, even if not a sacrament and instead an estate defined under the law rather than the gospel, remained embedded in the natural law as part of the act of creation and an expression of the creator's will. In a later treatise on divorce, von Harless denied that ethical behavior between men and women in marriage could produce justifying grace. Marriage nevertheless remained "the vessel, which is prepared for the Spirit" even though "the heart of humans is inclined by nature to the abuse of God's Order."[43]

Two years after the appearance of the *Ethics,* Prussia issued a revision of its divorce laws, attempting to restore the function of the clergy in dissuading parties from seeking a divorce and thus promoting the sanctity of marriage. The liberalization of the Prussian Law Code of 1794 had been accompanied by a directive for correct procedure in the courts (the 1793 *Allgemeine Gerichtsordnung*). This procedural order had created a much larger responsibility for

43. Friedrich Wilhelm Kantzenbach, *Die Erlanger Theologie: Grundlinien ihrer Entwicklung im Rahmen der Geschichte der Theologischen Fakultät 1743-1877* (Munich: Evangelischer Presseverband für Bayern, 1960), pp. 115-20. Adolf Christoph von Harless, *Christliche Ethik* (Stuttgart: Samuel Gottlieb Liesching, 1842), pp. 22-24, 217-18; von Harless, *Die Ehescheidungsfrage: Eine erneuerte Untersuchung der Neutestamentlichen Schriftstellen* (Stuttgart: Samuel Gottlieb Liesching, 1861), pp. 123-24, 34-35. Von Harless is generally credited with having created a renewed interest in the orders, though in his work he employs the term *Schöpferordnung* (perhaps roughly: order of the Creator) rather than *Schöpfungsordungen.* For an overview, including C. F. W. Walther's enthusiastic response to the *Christliche Ethik,* see Edward H. Schroeder, "The Orders of Creation: Some Reflections on the History and Place of the Term in Systematic Theology," *Concordia Theological Monthly* 43 (1972): 165-78, 171. For an overview of the general pattern of Lutheran state churches' treatment of marriage, see John Witte Jr., *From Sacrament to Contract: Marriage, Religion, and Law in the Western Tradition* (Louisville: Westminster John Knox, 1997), pp. 42-73. Dirk Blasius, *Ehescheidung in Deutschland 1794-1945: Scheidung und Scheidungsrecht in historischer Perspektive* (Göttingen: Vandenhoeck & Ruprecht, 1987), pp. 52-80.

local judges, and reduced clerical oversight over potential divorces. Both Protestant and Roman Catholic protests in Silesia and later the Rhineland found a sympathetic ear in Friedrich Wilhelm IV, and his succession to the throne in 1840 helped pave the way for Friedrich Carl von Savigny's revisions of 1844. These developments could not disguise, however, the decline of clerical influence over marriage in the industrial areas of Prussia. American readers of the Erlangen theologians knew nothing of that failure.[44]

Von Harless was not alone in his criticism about teachings on the marriage relationship that emerged after a stay at Halle. His Erlangen colleague, Heinrich Schmid, after initial studies in Tübingen, also encountered Tholuck in Halle with similar results. A critical distance from the tradition that helped shape him and his university led Schmid to publish his history of pietism and a negative assessment of the Halle neologist Semler. But his definitive influence both in the United States and in Sweden stemmed from his systematic survey of Lutheran doctrine.[45] In some respects, Schmid appeared to buttress the "orders" argument von Harless had pioneered. Schmid's work, enjoying a translation and endorsement by Henry Eyster Jacobs, Krauth's ally among the confessionalists in Pennsylvania, reached back far more systematically into the sixteenth-century commentators for arguments than von Harless's did. Concerned to defend the Lutheran conviction that baptism regenerates and the Lord's Supper is where God is "truly" present, Schmid should have been the logical successor to his Erlangen colleague in teaching that marriage, the second of the created orders, was in some sense the context for the sanctification of believers. Yet, while calling it the "domestic estate" and the "seminary" of church and state in Melanchthonian fashion, Schmid in the end understood marriage as a legal institution. Distinguishing separation of bed and board from grounds for divorce — confined to adultery, cruelty, and desertion — he repristinated Melanchthon's approach, emphasizing a catastrophic Fall. In sharp contrast to the view of Helmuth — that Adam and Eve were immature children — Schmid defended the teaching of "original righteousness" and the desolate condition of humanity — including marriage — that followed the events recorded in Genesis. Any remnants of the original image and likeness of God, he wrote, echoing Chemnitz, Hollazius, and other systematicians before him, were now mere fragments. Both "civic righteousness" and ethics in

44. Blasius, *Ehescheidung,* pp. 209-10.

45. Olaf Willett, *Sozialgeschichte Erlanger Professoren 1743-1933* (Göttingen: Vandenhoeck & Ruprecht, 2001), pp. 205-14.

marriage remained wholly "external." Justification for Schmid was completely forensic — it "[did] not mean a real and internal change of man."[46]

Halle's earlier reputation for confessional pietism produced theologians who would eventually help to shape Erlangen's faculty. But Erlangen failed to populate the faculty at Halle. Erlangen lost a substantial number of its theological faculty to other German universities, especially in the first half of the nineteenth century. But Halle did not lure the newly "awakened" but confessionally committed away from Erlangen.[47] Whatever subtle differences separated the work of von Harless from Schmid or the other Erlangen theologians, all of them remained deeply indebted to the tradition of "rebirth" and "awakening" as they attempted to link these pietist themes to the principal teachings of sixteenth-century Lutheran confessional writings. That attempt, gathering momentum in the 1830s, suggests how Halle's view of the orders of creation in Mühlenberg's time continued to influence America. Both "Americanizers" and "neo-confessionalists" beyond the "direct" lineage of Pennsylvania clerics felt the impact of the old pietist center. But no quasi-sacramental teaching on marriage or how the marital relationship might be connected to the holiness of Christ and his relationship to the church emerged from these influences.

The most obvious struggle with Halle's role in shaping the pietist renewal movement surfaced in the assessment offered by Carl Ferdinand Wilhelm Walther, the Saxon pastor who gradually emerged as the primary theologian of the German Evangelical Synod of Missouri and Other States formed in 1847 in Chicago. In Walther's view, only such "old Lutherans" as his synodical group had escaped the baneful effects of pietism and rationalism. Halle's descendants in Pennsylvania, Walther concluded, had fallen victim to the maladies Wyneken had documented in his journey through Pennsylvania en route to the Indiana and Michigan frontiers. Walther's popular series of evening lectures, posthumously published and translated into English as *The Proper Distinction between Law and Gospel,* reviewed the history of pietism and the contribution of Spener, Francke, and the Halle theologians to its eventually disappointing performance. A rich irony undergirds

46. Heinrich Schmid, *The Doctrinal Theology of the Evangelical Lutheran Church, Verified from the Original Sources,* trans. and ed. Charles A. Hay and Henry E. Jacobs, 5th ed. (Philadelphia: Lutheran Publication Society, 1899); on domestic estate: pp. 582, 619-23; on sacraments and justification: 238, 265, 268, 424, 428. Originally published as *Die Dogmatik der evangelisch-lutherischen Kirche: Dargestellt und aus den Quellen belegt von Heinrich Schmid* (Erlangen: Heyder, 1843).

47. Willett, *Sozialgeschichte,* pp. 241-42.

the analysis, since Walther himself, like so many of the Saxon immigrants of 1838, bore the marks of pietist currents in the Leipzig circles of his youth. Similar experiences had also altered the careers of the Erlangen theologians von Harless and Schmid.[48]

Analyzing the mistakes of Halle pietism, Walther concluded that the "disciples, though not altogether faithful disciples, you know, of Spener, August Hermann Francke, and John Jacob Rambach," had overemphasized the importance of the exact moment of "conversion." For Walther, the word "pietist" had become nearly synonymous with "Methodist." He located the roots of the error in the "so-called pietists of former times" as well as the "preachers of the fanatical sects in our time." The priority of belief, followed by conversion — the true Lutheran doctrine, Walther insisted — had been compromised repeatedly by an undue emphasis on feeling and behavior. Yet, in the end, Walther's own past indebtedness to pietism persisted as he scorned the "spiritually dead" Lutherans who observed the externals of the faith but tried "to quiet their heart with the reflection that the Lutheran Church teaches that the lack of spiritual feeling is of no moment . . . [but] people in that condition have nothing but a dead faith of the intellect, a specious faith, or to express it still more drastically, a lip faith." Henry Melchior Mühlenberg would not have dissented.[49]

Like Wyneken, von Harless, and Schmid, Walther devoted his efforts to achieving order within the synodical structures and only rarely commented on marriage. When they did do so, Missourians and their counterparts in the Synod of Ohio reproduced the *Hauspostillen* of the sixteenth century. To supplement these guides to sound teaching, designed for fathers to read aloud to the family, pastors preached on the "Table of Duties" included in reprinted editions of Luther's *Small Catechism*. But neither pietist sources nor orthodox seventeenth-century theologians provided the "Missourians" with an understanding of marriage as anything other than the divinely ordained legal estate within which duties were to be fulfilled.[50]

48. Mary Todd, *Authority Vested: A Story of Identity and Change in the Lutheran Church–Missouri Synod* (Grand Rapids and Cambridge: Eerdmans, 2000), pp. 26-28.

49. C. F. W. Walther, *The Proper Distinction between Law and Gospel: Thirty-nine Evening Lectures,* ed. and trans. W. H. T. Dau (St. Louis: Concordia, 1929), pp. 193, 372, 195. Originally published in German as C. F. W. Walther, *Die rechte Unterscheidung von Gesetz und Evangelium: 39 Abendvorträge aus seinem Nachlaß* (St. Louis: Concordia, 1897).

50. For texts used see *Echt evangelische Auslegung der Sonn-und Festtags-Evangelien des Kirchenjahrs . . . ,* 7 vols. (St. Louis: Druckerei der Synode von Missouri, Ohio und anderen Staaten, 1872), 1:242-57; Matthias Loy, trans. and ed., *Dr. Martin Luther's House Postil; or, Sermons on*

When the Missourians reviewed the manner in which the orders appeared in earlier editions of Luther's *Small Catechism* in the early republic, they were dismayed. As a remedy, they imported the Dresden Holy Cross Church catechism, or tried to reprint the Darmstadt edition of Luther's work. Yet they mainly criticized alterations made by Americanizing pietists to the order of salvation. Among the imported and North American printed versions of the catechism, none had devoted much attention to the orders of creation. Justus Falckner's 1708 work had included a section on the orders (in an odd sequence) of family, state, and church. The influential edition of 1752 compiled by the Halle-trained pastor Peter Brunnholtz had set forth another curiously altered form of three "estates" *within* the church — the teaching, ruling, and family orders — a marked departure from the original conception of the *Schöpfungsordnungen* as well as of the three estates.[51]

Despite the neo-confessionalists' criticism of the earlier catechisms, Walther never clarified how the orders helped theologians handle difficult questions such as separation and divorce, or how they showed the way to reconcile alienated partners in a marriage. Even his letter of proposal to his future wife and reflections on that marriage shed only a little light on how he regarded spouses and the household. The chief purpose of marriage, he told Emilie Buenger, was to expand the number of Christians to create a "little house-church." In this, Walther held true to the first of Augustine's purposes of marriage, and to Luther's vision of the household as a domestic reflection of the entire church (Rom. 16:5), but he said nothing beyond this.[52] In the first collection of his essays, he presented no theology of marriage, but confined his observations to warnings about the difficulties that surrounded divorce and remarriage or the relationship of marriage to secular law.[53]

---

the Gospels for the Sundays and Principal Festivals of the Church Year, 2 vols. (Columbus, Ohio: Schulze und Gassmann, 1869-71), 1:206-12.

51. Arthur C. Repp Sr., *Luther's Catechism Comes to America: Theological Effects on the Issues of the Small Catechism Prepared in or for America Prior to 1850* (Metuchen, N.J.: Scarecrow; Philadelphia: American Theological Library Association, 1982), pp. 18-19, 47-57, 61-62, 75, 197-200.

52. *Letters of C. F. W. Walther: A Selection,* ed. and trans. Carl S. Meyer (Philadelphia: Fortress, 1969). See letters to Emilie Buenger, 10 August 1841, pp. 53-57; to Ottomar Fuerbringer, 19 April 1844, pp. 60-61; and to Hugo Hanser, 10 September 1856, pp. 87-90. The original German edition of his letters does not reveal anything more substantial. See Ludwig Fuerbringer, ed., *Briefe von C. F. W. Walther an seine Freunde, Synodalgenossen und Familienglieder,* 2 vols. (St. Louis: Concordia, 1915-16), 1:4-5 to his future wife, where he also suggests reading Luther's wedding sermons included in his *Hauspostillen* on the Epistles.

53. "Von Ehesachen," *Lehre und Wehre: Theologisches und kirchlich-zeitgeschichtliches Monatsblatt* 1 (1855): 289-93, 321-25.

If Missourians remained fixated on the covenantal view of marriage, a more romantic understanding also surfaced in nineteenth-century North America. It would be difficult to find any form of Lutheran pietism in the nineteenth century that could accurately be described as primarily "romantic." But at least a version did surface, and its official articulation came initially not from the pens of Lutheran historians or theologians. Henry Adams, in his 1876 lecture "Primitive Rights of Women," deserves credit for fashioning the image of Luther's domestic hearth.[54] The appearance in English of Luther's *Table Talk* in 1846 and an American edition of Jules Michelet's biography had helped to pave the way for what now became a romanticized, bourgeois image of Luther's marriage and domestic bliss. The unofficial endorsement of this romanticized iconography may also have begun in the pre–Civil War decades, but by the 1870s mass-produced certificates emanated from the Lutheran Publication House in Philadelphia with a rich iconography of angelic witnesses to the marriage of Luther and Katharina von Bora.[55] The 1840s became pivotal in this reinvention not merely because of the strife between "Americanizers" and "confessionalists" in American Lutheranism. Far more important to Christians of the Evangelical Alliance and most Protestant Americans, the emerging profile of Luther in the married estate created a non–Roman Catholic champion. That profile was now accessible to those beyond the bounds of Lutheran synods. Luther's marriage and family became objects of Protestant fantasy.[56]

Pseudoromantic and nonprofessional scientific treatises on "nature," within which this new Luther and his family could comfortably dwell, won a broad readership in the 1840s. No evidence suggests that Lutheran theologians in the United States felt any need to reconcile confessional views on the orders of creation with the new natural philosophy and science. In 1844, the anonymous work *Vestiges of the Natural History of Creation* created a sensation first in Britain, then in North America. Charles Porterfield Krauth owned the volume, but his marginal notations reveal no attempt to reconcile Lutheran teachings on creation to this volume on evolution, one Abraham Lincoln proclaimed to have read at one sitting.[57] Later, Krauth expounded a

54. Hartmut Lehmann, *Martin Luther in the American Imagination* (Munich: Wilhelm Fink Verlag, 1988), p. 144.

55. *The Pennsylvania German Broadside: A History and Guide*, ed. Don Yoder (University Park: Pennsylvania State University Press, 2005), p. 256, figure 9.24, p. 257.

56. Lehmann, *Martin Luther*, pp. 146-57.

57. Krauth's copy is in the Krauth Memorial Library, Lutheran Theological Seminary, Philadelphia. On the reception of the book and its significance, see James A. Secord, *Victorian*

correct anthropology and doctrine of original sin. But his review of various theories of preexistence, creationism, and traducianism never assessed the arguments in *Vestiges*. His romanticized essays on Luther's domestic life, moreover, including scenes around a fictitious 1542 Christmas tree, reveal how little attention Krauth devoted to marriage.[58] Nor was Krauth's indebtedness to Tholuck and a romanticized view of nature unique to Lutherans. Edward Robinson, professor of biblical literature at Union Theological Seminary in New York City, also fell under Tholuck's spell at Halle. Like Krauth, he remained committed to "an avowal of organic connection between the physical and spiritual, the material and the cultural."[59]

American legal doctrine on marriage, divorce, and the family bolstered yet another interpretation of Protestant marriage, one that recognized belatedly the rights of spouses but in a manner that could not be easily reconciled to the hopes for companionate holiness Luther and Spener had tried to articulate. State laws confirmed through the 1850s the authority of husbands and fathers. In fact, however, such legal commentators as St. George Tucker of Virginia prepared the ground for further change by emphasizing the civil/contractual understanding of marriage even as evangelicals were defining marriage as indissoluble because of "the destructive social effects of divorce on the community, family life, and women and children in particular." Protestant marriage could easily be construed in this new context as a legal contract, albeit still referred to in language of "covenant" rooted in a "two kingdoms" theology but "regulated not by the church but by the civil authorities." Even though courtroom divorce replaced legislative divorce, collusive divorce was almost unknown before the 1840s except in strict jurisdictions like New York, where only adultery legally justified absolute divorce, a legal act understood to be adversarial. These patterns, ironically, continued to offer reassurance to Lutherans in America. Slightly liberalized divorce laws that still left

---

Sensation: The Extraordinary Publication, Reception, and Secret Authorship of "Vestiges of the Natural History of Creation" (Chicago and London: University of Chicago Press, 2000), pp. 9-38.

58. Charles P. Krauth, *The Conservative Reformation and Its Theology: As Represented in the Augsburg Confession, and in the History and Literature of the Evangelical Lutheran Church* (Philadelphia: J. B. Lippincott Co., 1888), pp. 33-38 on the domestic Luther; 355-425 on the second article of the Augsburg Confession, "Original Sin."

59. Walter H. Conser Jr., *God and the Natural World: Religion and Science in Antebellum America* (Columbia: University of South Carolina Press, 1993), pp. 78-83, quotation at 79-80. Conser sees the broader dilemma of mainline Protestantism in terms of the declining social authority of ministers and the crisis of natural theology; pp. 8-36.

intact the understanding of marriage as contract and fathers as heads of households reaffirmed their own official, canonical tradition that had served the goal of imposing social discipline upon unruly spouses. Secular legal doctrine and social convention still underscored the importance of obedience by children and wives to husbands.[60]

The inattention of the American pietist pastors to these developments flowed from the illusion that the piety of practicing Lutherans needed no defense. The worship of ordinary Lutherans, however, suggests that pastors were overconfident. The appointed lectionary texts or pericopes for the church year provided some opportunity for pastors to expound on the estate of marriage. Luther's own impressive commentary on the wedding feast at Cana pointed to Christ's first miracle as the reaffirmation of marriage. This Gospel for the Second Sunday after Epiphany continued to be reprinted in the United States in the *Hauspostillen* German-speakers used for domestic devotions. Less frequently, they turned to commentary on the key Epistle text of Ephesians 5:21-33 — comparing the relationship of Christ to the church to the relationship of husbands and wives.

Von Harless's commentary on Ephesians remarked that "in the natural relationships ordained by God, none is so analogous as is marriage" to the relationship of grace and mercy God has to his church: for the apostle, "worldly, Christian marriage is a holy Mystery."[61] But neither von Harless nor any of the authors of surviving treatises on spousal relations focused on the sacrificial duty of husbands. The official theology of marriage mentioned only the need for submission and obedience by wives.

The hymnody that might have preserved Luther's more subtle hopes for spouses likewise did not unambiguously reflect his theology. Once the marriage service was over, Lutherans in North America had little opportunity or

60. Lawrence M. Friedman, *A History of American Law* (New York: Simon and Schuster, 1973), pp. 179-84; Hendrik Hartog, *Man and Wife in America: A History* (Cambridge, Mass., and London: Harvard University Press, 2000), relies on a data set from New York, California, Wisconsin, and Delaware to 1870, but even with these limitations provides insightful overview into the changing attitudes toward divorce and marriage while understandably relying on the New York cases that set the pace for overall liberalization of divorce law. See pp. 15-16, 79-86, 136-42, 176-92, 196-203, 242-75; see also Thomas E. Buckley, S.J., *The Great Catastrophe of My Life: Divorce in the Old Dominion* (Chapel Hill and London, 2002), pp. 46-79, at 50, quotation at 57; and James Turner Johnson, "Marriage as Covenant in Early Protestant Thought: Its Development and Implications," in *Covenant Marriage in Comparative Perspective*, pp. 124-52, at 127-29, quotation at 129.

61. Gottlieb Christoph Adolph Harless, *Commentar über den Brief Pauli an die Ephesier* (Erlangen: Carl Heyder, 1834), pp. 489, 513.

resources for calling to mind the theology of the orders of creation through hymnody or private piety. The longer Lutheran pietist families remained in North America, the more they fell under the influence of a general Protestant evangelical culture, one that elevated an understanding of grace as "the substitutionary atonement of Christ on the cross and the cosmological triumph of that atoning grace over death . . . because the doctrines of atonement, invitation, salvation, sanctification, witness, perseverance, death, and heaven articulated their direct, transforming experience of Christianity."[62] This view of the order of salvation overlooked the marital relationship as one in which the partners encountered grace as members of the larger church.

The eighteenth-century Lutheran hymns sung most often by worshipers, at least as described by Henry Melchior Mühlenberg and Johann Martin Boltzius, included those of Paul Gerhardt, which conveyed a warm, natural theology. Gerhardt's poetic gifts probably account for his hymns' continued popularity. Gerhardt had been committed to Luther's understanding of the orders of creation, but his influence dimmed in the ears and the memory of ordinary believers as they were instructed how to understand the spousal relationship.[63]

Gerhardt's hymnody survived both in Halle's editions of the *Geistreiches Gesangbuch* and in imported and translated hymnals, including the *Gesangbuch* of the nineteenth-century *Hannoversche Landeskirche* and the *Evangelical Lutheran Hymnal* issued by the Joint Synod of Ohio and Other States in 1880. Those still singing in German would turn to sections devoted to *Berufs- und Standeslieder* (hymns on callings and conditions) that included

---

62. Stephen Marini, "Hymnody as History: Early Evangelical Hymns and the Recovery of American Popular Religion," *Church History* 71 (2002): 273-306, at 302.

63. On the popularity of Gerhardt in colonial Lutheranism, see Roeber, "Lutheran Hymnody and Networks in the Eighteenth Century," in *Land without Nightingales: Music in the Making of German America,* ed. Philip V. Bohlman and Otto Holzapfel (Madison, Wis.: Max Kade Institute for German-American Studies, 2002), pp. 113-26. On Gerhardt and Lutheran natural theology, see Per Lonning, *Creation — an Ecumenical Challenge?* (Macon, Ga.: Mercer University Press, 1989), p. 213. For an overview of hymnals in North America, see Carl F. Schalk, *God's Song in a New Land: Lutheran Hymnals in America* (St. Louis: Concordia, 1995), and his appendix B, pp. 226-28, comparing the contents of the Halle 1741 edition of Freylinghausen's *Geistreiches Gesangbuch* and the 1786 Philadelphia edition of the *Erbauliche Liedersammlung.* The lists of hymns sung at Ebenezer are included as appendices to the *Detailed Reports* starting with vol. 6 (1739), pp. 321-22; although varying somewhat in emphasis given the fondness of Boltzius for the Wernigerode as well as the Halle hymnal, the Georgia record of hymnody parallels Pennsylvania's in the important respect that neither includes actual hymns specified to be sung at weddings.

hymns "für die drei Hauptstände" (the three estates) and especially Gerhardt's "Wie schön ist's doch, Herr Jesu Christ." That hymn pointed out that God ordained the order of matrimony and the household, and the Ohio Synod's English translation retained the sense of the German that "it was not we/Who first this order did decree; It was a higher Father."

By the 1840s, the high reputation of Mühlenberg's role in choosing hymns for the 1786 *Erbauliche Liedersammlung* had also dimmed and could not save this hymnal from decline. In 1849 Mühlenberg's second successor to the senior pastorate of St. Michael's and Zion, Karl Rudolph Demme, contributed the foreword to the new *Geistreiches Gesangbuch*. In defense of the new hymnal, Demme wrote that the old one had been too long and too expensive and that most congregations did not know many of its melodies. He estimated that only half of the hymns had ever been sung. But Demme insisted that the new hymnal uphold the Lutheran Confessions, to which the hymns by Luther, Gerhardt, Gellert, and Spitta gave voice. He repeated a claim that worshipers in Reformation Europe knew only 1,000 hymns, whereas by 1800 Lutherans had composed and sung fully 6,000 hymns in the German language alone.[64]

Demme's collection followed at least in part the structure of older hymnals and included a category for the "Order of Salvation" *(Heilsordnung)*, dear to pietist hearts. A section on "Creation" *(Schöpfung)* followed, but like Freylinghausen's hymnal and other eighteenth-century pietist compilations, Demme's hymnal offered no section for weddings. Marriage made a brief appearance in the American hymnody tradition as one of the hymns in the section "for special relationships and times," which often began with Gerhardt's hymn "Wie schön ist's doch" (no. 547) and Spitta's "O Seelig Haus" and "Ich und mein Haus." But the texts of the five hymns said nothing about the orders of creation, nor the marital relationship as a graced companionship, nor did they make clear its connection to the church. C. F. W. Walther and the Missourians attacked Demme's work because he had shortened and bowdlerized the texts, and they also found it offensive that Sam-

---

64. Karl Rudolph Demme et al., eds., *Deutsches Gesangbuch für die Evangelisch-Lutherische Kirche in den Vereinigten Staaten* (Philadelphia: L. A. Wollenweber, 1849), "Vorrede": pp. iii-vi. I have surveyed also the following, selected to reflect the various influences on German immigrant groups detailed in Schalk, *God's Song in a New Land; Evangelisch-lutherisches Gesangbuch der Hannoverschen Landeskirche* (Hannover: Schlüter, 1900); *Evangelical Lutheran Hymnal published by order of the Evangelical Lutheran Joint Synod of Ohio and Other States* (Columbus, Ohio: Lutheran Book Concern, 1870); *Kirchengesangbuch für Evangelisch-Lutherische Gemeinden . . .* (St. Louis: Druckerei der Synode, 1847).

uel S. Schmucker had served on the committee that had compiled the new hymnal.[65]

Walther should have been more charitable. On the one hand, the Missourians could rightly claim that they had preserved the original marriage rite language more faithfully than had the older congregations influenced by the language of Halle and the Savoy rite. The Missourians' rite replicated the 1539/40 edition of Duke Heinrich of Saxony's *Kirchenagenda* and remained unchanged throughout the nineteenth century. Luther's original language therefore shaped the Missourians' *Agenda.* When that set of rites appeared in English translation in the later nineteenth century, it survived intact through the publication of the 1941 *Lutheran Hymnal.* Yet while the rite remained unchanged, the Synod's 1847 collection of hymns, which endured unaltered for the balance of the nineteenth century, told a different story. Neither the German-language hymnal nor the English-language revision (1941) included Gerhardt's hymn, nor did the modern hymnals acknowledge the concept of the marriage relationship as one grounded in the orders of creation.

Among these conservative neo-confessionalists, the most popular collections of prayers did maintain a link to the older theology. The prayer prescribed for the couple on the day of marriage, for example, recalled the institution by God and included the following words: that "the Devil is the powerful enemy of this, Thine Order" *(daß der Teufel dieser deiner Ordnung mächtig feind ist).* Despite the Missouri Synod Lutherans' continued publication and use of these prayers, Lutherans in other synodical bodies showed no comparable inclination to teach about the orders of creation in manuals of domestic piety.[66]

Halle's theologians and pastors in North America hastened, but did not cause, the transformation of Protestant understanding of the marital relationship into that of a legal, civil contract. American Protestant culture, with its

65. For the criticism of the Demme hymnal, see Schalk, *God's Song,* pp. 135-38. On the Ohio Synod's more strictly confessional hymns in its German-language hymnal of 1879 and the Ohio Synod's English hymnal of 1880, see Schalk, pp. 138-41. In the 1941 Missouri Synod hymnal, marriage hymns occur under the general heading "The Christian Home" after seasonal liturgical hymns, "The Word," "The Sacraments," "The Redeemer," "Faith and Justification," "Sanctification (The Christian Life)," "The Church," "Cross and Comfort," "Times and Seasons," and "The Last Things," but before "Special Occasions" and "Carols and Spiritual Songs." See *The Lutheran Hymnal* (St. Louis: Concordia, 1941).

66. *Der Evangelisch-Lutheranische Gebets-Schatz: Vollständige Sammlung von Gebeten Dr. Martin Luthers . . .* (St. Louis: M. C. Barthel, 1864), no. 142, at p. 85. The more widely circulated version was probably *Der Kleine Gebets-Schatz . . .* (St. Louis: Concordia, 1869).

marketplace of denominations, invited Lutherans of the middling, property-owning ranks into a legal-secular view of marriage. Neither von Harless nor his American counterparts among the neo-confessionalists recovered Luther's insights into the more exalted possibilities of the marital relationship. Luther and Spener's vision of marital friendship and the relationship of this understanding of marriage to a doctrine of the church had slowly vanished in the long debates of the eighteenth century. North American Lutherans eventually made some progress achieving various kinds of synodical order as they adjusted to the political norms. But serious reflection upon the order of marriage and male-female relationships turned into sentimental invocations of domestic harmony or stern demands for patriarchal "government." The setting for a revolt against such notions by late-twentieth-century feminists could not have been better.

The erasure of memory about pietist discussions of the spousal relationship that began in the European retrospectives had spread also to the New World. The American heirs of pietism remembered none of the debates over monogamy, polygamy, the rights of a prince or state, and the relationship of marriage in the church. Consequently, the perceived threat of Mormonism arose in the 1830s, accompanied by an intensified anti-Catholicism. Those trends paralleled debates over the standing of marriage among Native Americans and produced arguments about the legal rights of "religion." But descendants of the Lutheran pietists remained on the sidelines. Their silence reflected an adjustment that justified temporarily clerical confidence that the Lutheran denominations had safely defined and defended the respective role of spouses in the United States. That satisfaction rested on an assumption that local and state authorities were competent to handle such questions because they agreed that the Founders had been "confident that the Protestant majority's correctly informed opinions would tolerate neither a 'national' religion nor non-Protestant religions."[67]

No less than their Canadian neighbors, the nineteenth-century German-speaking American descendants of the pietist settlers had adopted comfortable beliefs about marriage that "were open to United States–inspired changes in inheritance and marital property law that recognized the reality of widespread landholding and family capitalism, while adhering strongly to the ideal of the English patriarchal family in matters of divorce, illegitimacy, and

---

67. Roeber, "The Limited Horizons of Whig Religious Rights," in *The Nature of Rights at the American Founding and Beyond*, ed. Barry Alan Shain (Charlottesville and London: University of Virginia Press, 2007), pp. 198-229, at 211.

custody."[68] Because they had forgotten the eighteenth-century debate about the spousal relationship, their descendants would have been hard pressed to give theological justifications for anything other than a strictly legal, or perhaps romanticized, vision of marriage. Lutheran pietists now could also fit reasonably well into the search for "companionate marriage" that had begun by the late eighteenth century, "characterized by a pronounced emphasis on emotional, social, and sexual intimacy." Church pietists, given this pattern of adjustment to the prevailing legal and theological understanding of marriage, could have played a major role in fashioning the "narrative of self-identity" that emanated from European religious and marital ideals and commitments.[69] Not surprisingly, however, any indulgence in companionate self-expression that did emerge remained within boundaries that had deep roots theological and canonical authorities had planted "by developing rigid definitions of men's and women's positions in separate spheres and patriarchal households." Despite his mixed German-Swiss family background, for example, William Wirt deferred in his marriage to Elizabeth Gamble's Presbyterian family standards. Her decision to teach their children religion without recourse to a Presbyterian pastor she found "pompous" guaranteed that marriage, however the Wirts understood its companionate nature, would remain private, and have little connection to notions of the created order, or to the church.[70]

IV

After nearly a century of debate over spouses, Protestants who had originated the discussion in Europe found that it spread to India where, left as a purely "civil matter," the marital relationship would again cause controversy. British colonial officials lay and ecclesiastical would seek to impose yet again an official theology that paid scant attention to the dilemmas the Danish-

68. Philip Girard with Jim Phillips, "Rethinking 'the Nation' in National Legal History: A Canadian Perspective," *Law and History Review* 29, no. 2 (May 2011): 607-26, at 615.

69. For a survey of the literature from various ethnographic perspectives, see Jennifer S. Hirsch and Holly Wardlow, eds., *Modern Loves: The Anthropology of Romantic Courtship and Companionate Marriage* (Ann Arbor: University of Michigan Press, 2006), pp. 1-31, quotation at 8. Giddens, *The Transformation of Intimacy*, pp. 22, 94, 113-14.

70. Anya Jabour, *Marriage in the Early Republic: Elizabeth and William Wirt and the Companionate Ideal* (Baltimore and London: Johns Hopkins University Press, 1998), pp. 9-10, 14, 16, 123-24, 170.

German pietists had pondered during the previous century. The hopes for pious spouses had fallen on temporarily fertile soil among propertied coreligionists in North America reluctant to extend it to transplanted Africans and dispossessed First Peoples. For a time the unofficial theology of companionate friendship arrived with some German-speakers and enjoyed a temporary victory, at least among these white propertied believers in British North America and, later, the United States. That version, too, however, had begun to devolve into a romanticized vision that did not reflect the sometimes grim and adversarial realities of spousal relationships, especially among those trapped in harrowing economic and social circumstances.

Despite the Reformers' claim to have recovered the ancient Christian church from Roman innovation, they had failed, on the subject of the spousal relationship, to make their case. The failure resulted from more than Protestant uncertainty. The ancient church — whether Greek or Latin, Chalcedonian or non-Chalcedonian — had provided little substantive help in promoting a vision of the marital relationship as a partnership based upon friendship between men and women and a critical component of a journey toward holiness. Ancient pagan and Judaic wisdom doubted the existence of friendship between the sexes, and early Christianity only haltingly ventured into this territory, never quite successfully confronting especially deeply ambivalent feelings and teachings about female sexuality. Neither the Latin nor the Byzantine Christians had been prepared to reassess the practical consequences of defining marriage in such a profound manner, even if their official theology had occasionally been bolder in proclaiming such high hopes. In Orthodox Russia by the late nineteenth century, skyrocketing divorce rates that included both the privileged and the poor also revealed that an official theology of sacramentality did not dissuade litigants from casting their views of marriage in terms of defending the authority of husbands — or citing the failure of men to be genuine partners in marriage.[71] The disconnect between official and unofficial theologies of the marital relationship had both ancient roots and nearly global consequences. As one

71. Gregory L. Freeze, "Profane Narratives about a Holy Sacrament: Marriage and Divorce in Late Imperial Russia," in *Sacred Stories: Religion and Spirituality in Modern Russia*, ed. Mark D. Steinberg and Heather J. Coleman (Bloomington and Indianapolis: Indiana University Press, 2007), pp. 146-78, 168-69. For a comparative perspective on Orthodox, Roman Catholic, and Lutheran dilemmas over marriage, human sexuality, and the search for a theological anthropology, see Mickey L. Mattox, A. G. Roeber, and Paul R. Hinlicky, *Changing Churches: An Orthodox–Roman Catholic–Lutheran Theological Conversation* (Grand Rapids: Eerdmans, 2012), chapters 5 and 6 and Hinlicky's "Afterword," pp. 194-314.

scholar noted when someone learned he was working on an essay on the sacramentality of marriage in the Fathers, "my colleague responded by saying that would be a short essay."[72]

In North America, the sacramentality of Catholic marriage did not provide enslaved black Catholic spouses with protection against the law of the state, even when Catholic moral theology taught that the sexual abuse of enslaved blacks violated "the ethical demands of the natural law." Both John England and Patrick Kenrick by the 1830s distanced Catholicism from Protestant abolitionist thought but would not condemn the abuse of enslaved men and women whose *contubernium,* the "living in the same tent" of antiquity, even if officially blessed, could not prevent the destruction of de facto marriage and family.[73] European Protestants were no more farsighted, and the scorn with which the British regarded Indian peoples, and not merely as unsuitable marriage partners, launched years of resentment at the imposition of British-inspired marriage law reform.

Protestants had been forced to invent their hopes for the marital relationship drawing as best they could from both Scripture and scattered observations of ancient and medieval Christian sources. They were hampered in this task by a tradition of civil and canon law that reflected the preferences for patrilineal control of households and property. That canonical tradition, despite Luther's efforts at synthesizing it with his hopes for a theology of marriage superior to celibacy, never caught up with his aspiration for marriage's potential for partnership and holiness. Protestants' task became immeasurably more difficult as they had to match their continued belief in a unitary human "nature" with evidence that alien societies and cultures understood marriage in ways that challenged their delicate and unstable teaching that marriage was a godly estate that hovered between the sacramental and the profane.

Given the almost complete lack of ancient and medieval support for a more companionable vision, it is all the more astonishing that first Luther and then Spener advanced the hopes for spouses as far as they did. The persistent deployment of a sense of marital rights by Lutheran women suggests how important wives believed the relationship to be, and how willingly they

72. John C. Cavadini, "The Sacramentality of Marriage in the Fathers," *Pro Ecclesia: A Journal of Catholic and Evangelical Theology* 17, no. 4 (Fall 2008): 442-63, at 442.

73. On the American Catholic dilemma over slavery and marriage, see W. Jason Wallace, *Catholics, Slaveholders, and the Dilemma of American Evangelicalism, 1835-1860* (Notre Dame, Ind.: University of Notre Dame Press, 2010), pp. 119-26, quotation at 125; John T. Noonan Jr., *A Church That Can and Cannot Change: The Development of Catholic Moral Teaching* (Notre Dame, Ind.: University of Notre Dame Press, 2005), pp. 104-9.

embraced legal mechanisms to defend themselves and their marriages. One can legitimately argue that resting an official theology of marriage upon the work of the monastic Pseudo-Dionysius, who contributed a salutary mystical dimension to interpreters of the Genesis creation story but also conveyed preferences for hierarchy, earthly and divine, may have doomed Luther's hopes from the outset. Nor can one easily discern in the anonymous author of the "German Theology" or the works of Tauler a transparent source that helped theologians gain a perspective on the marital relationship that restored its holiness alongside that of lifelong celibacy.

Struggles in the North American context with failed marriages appeared to focus on wives especially as actual legal persons, but an unofficial, customary legacy of marriage as a covenant between unequal participants continued to confuse American Protestants about just what they did want to make of marriage.[74]

One way to account for the emerging nineteenth-century patterns has been to locate both companionate marriage and increased adversarial relationships in the history of the household form that emerged in northwestern Europe and North America just as the pietist debate over marriage intensified. In contrast to fathers in Europe, "American fathers did not have to endow their children at marriage . . . [and this] enhanced the power of the household head in the New World, but it also left him with fewer weapons to stave off premature household formation by his sons and daughters." For the propertied, whether in Europe or North America, somewhat different versions of a companionate marriage could emerge marked by considerable more personal freedom, choice, and control over fertility by women. Perhaps especially among the propertied in North America, "women's roles, parental responsibilities, economic possibilities, and political policies . . . emerged from those early personal decisions of women and men on the nature of the family, gendered equity, and the future of children."[75]

74. Norma Basch, *Framing American Divorce: From the Revolutionary Generation to the Victorians* (Berkeley, Los Angeles, and London: University of California Press, 1999), pp. 19-67: "compromise entailed more than adhering to a strict official code while tolerating a lax unofficial one: it invested wives with a measure of legal independence and then rhetorically obscured it or degraded it" (p. 61). More broadly, Roderick Phillips, *Putting Asunder: A History of Divorce in Western Society* (Cambridge and New York: Cambridge University Press, 1988); for marriage law and its dissolution in India from the 1872 Marriage Act, see William E. Pinto, *Law of Marriage and Matrimonial Reliefs for Christians in India: A Juridical Evaluation of Canon Law and Civil Law* (Bangalore: Theological Publications in India, 2000), pp. 30-211.

75. Carol Shammas, *A History of Household Government in America* (Charlottesville and

This interpretation about the emergence of personal choice as a primary market of the Protestant Reformation's impact almost always portrays the sixteenth-century event as the birthing room of "modern" notions of the self. That interpretation has been applied to the Danish mission to Tranquebar. In one observer's opinion, "from a historical perspective pietism, with its emphasis on personal piety, was instrumental in preparing the way for our modern individualism."[76] Yet in North America and Europe, where "the separate spheres of women and men in fertility and gynecology collapsed," little evidence demonstrates that such collapses stemmed from a successful theological redefinition — official or unofficial — of the marriage relationship.[77]

Reformed Protestantism had placed its hopes in the notion of "covenant" that had never been quite identical with mere "contract." Yet the trajectory of spousal relationships among Protestant church renewers in the Reformed tradition did move from covenant to contract, becoming evident in the changes in the law of marriage made manifest in the Hardwicke Act. Not without reason has one scholar concluded, "The harvest of Protestant 'covenantalism' is that the people must decide in their own hearts, minds, and communities of faith what is truly godly, loving, and just . . . [and that] the actual practice of the churches will likely include, as did the sacramental and covenantal traditions of the past, the element of legal contract; but it is also likely that the contractual element will come to dominance in legal theory for the foreseeable future."[78]

London: University of Virginia Press, 2002), p. 178; Susan E. Klepp, *Revolutionary Conceptions: Women, Fertility, and Family Limitation in America, 1760-1820* (Chapel Hill and Williamsburg, Va.: University of North Carolina Press, 2009), p. 286.

76. Jens Glebe-Moller, "The Realm of Grace Presupposes the Realm of Power: The Danish Debate about the Theological Legitimacy of Mission to the Heathen," in *It Began in Copenhagen: Junctions in 300 Years of Indian-Danish Relations in Christian Mission,* ed. George Oommen and Hans Raun Iversen (Kashmere Gate, Delhi: ISPCK, 2005), pp. 156-177, at 177. On the origins of "the self" for a classic text and reactions, see Charles Taylor, *Sources of the Self: The Making of the Modern Identity* (Cambridge: Harvard University Press, 1989), and the claim that a line can be drawn from Augustine through Anselm of Canterbury to Descartes on the "certainty of God within" (p. 140); for a more nuanced view of Augustine's role, see Philip Cary, *Augustine's Invention of the Inner Self: The Legacy of a Christian Platonist* (Oxford and New York: Oxford University Press, 2003); for the North American context, see Philip J. Greven Jr., "The Self Shaped and Mis-shaped: The Protestant Temperament Reconsidered," in *Through a Glass Darkly: Reflections on Personal Identity in Early America,* ed. Ronald Hoffman, Mechal Sobel, and Fredrika J. Teute (Chapel Hill: University of North Carolina Press, 1997), pp. 348-69.

77. Klepp, *Revolutionary Conceptions,* p. 214.

78. Max L. Stackhouse, "Covenantal Marriage: Protestant Views and Contemporary Life," in *Covenant Marriage in Comparative Perspective,* pp. 153-81, 180. See also John R. Witte Jr.,

Deciding "in their own hearts," however, left church pietist spouses without any explicit, joint connection to the larger church in the manner suggested by the difficult "mystery" Ephesians 5 holds up for emulation. The fragile condition of the marital relationship between better spouses linked by friendship and the pursuit of holiness had already dissolved at the level of official theology by the nineteenth century. That dissolution helps us to understand the ferocity of debates that have now broken out once again in defense of marriage as monogamous and heterosexual in the emerging Christian "global South." It may be true, as the influential anthropologist Bronislaw Malinowski once argued, that at some level, in all social systems and polities, "marriage carries some 'sacramental'; i.e. religious, significance." But what Protestants interested in church renewal in the early modern centuries dared to hope for in elevating the estate of marriage degenerated into the acrimonious debates we have excavated here, and then faded into oblivion. What they had hoped for had amounted to far more than a nebulous sacrality. Indeed, those hopes tried to articulate something not only about spouses, but about the church itself.[79]

In the global South, the Christian rejection of homosexual, polygamous, and polyandrous marriages illustrates how the unsettled understanding of what the spousal relationship, and therefore, the church "is" threatens to widen a gulf between European and North American Protestants and their coreligionists in Asia, Africa, and Latin America. In all these contexts, the understanding of marriage as a friendship between man and woman linked in the pursuit of holiness remains contested. A willingness by European and North American Protestants to define same-sex relationships as marriage represents for some the logical extension of the unofficial theology of marriage understood as friendship. For others, however, that move suggests a failure of nerve, a relapse into the ancient pagan disdain for friendship between men and women, but far more unsettling, an impermissible betrayal

---

From Sacrament to Contract: Marriage, Religion, and Law in the Western Tradition (Louisville: Westminster John Knox, 1997), who maintains that the Reformed covenant concept could not be sacramental since it "confirmed no divine promise" (p. 8) and the "freedom of contract" included in it amounted to the right choices of a spouse but not much more. Whether the covenant concept accelerated the tendency toward "a contractual view of marriage [that] has come to dominate American law, lore, and life" (p. 195), remains a topic of debate.

79. On Malinowski's conclusions, see Charles J. Reid Jr., "Marriage: Its Relationship to Religion, Law, and the State," in *Same-Sex Marriage and Religious Liberty: Emerging Conflicts,* ed. Douglas Laycock, Anthony R. Picarello Jr., and Robin Fretwell Wilson (Lanham, Md., and Boulder, Colo.: Rowman and Littlefield, 2008), pp. 157-88, at 177-79, quotation at 178.

of the iconic relationship between spouses whose gender identity is supposed still to say something about Christ's own relationship to the church Ephesians 5 testified to. The identification of both male and female spouses in marriage as "feminine" that Zinzendorf had argued for reaped hostility for his movement from without, and in the long run, abandonment from within the Brethren themselves.

Much of this Protestant uncertainty can be traced to the assignment of specific gender roles for women grounded in cultural assumptions. The uncertainty of Christian theologians about how seriously to promote marriage officially as friendship grounded in a mysterious relationship with God, and not primarily as a hierarchy defined by authority and submission, remained, from start to finish, the primary difficulty. Especially for women too often on the receiving end of male abuse, Paul's words in the book all Christians have long cherished, have rung with a bitter echo: "Suffering produces endurance, and endurance produces character, and character produces hope" (Rom. 5:3-4). Suffering in marriage, however, tended to be disproportionately the lot of subservient wives. The insistence in Ephesians 5:25, that husbands were to love their wives "as Christ loved the church, and gave himself up for her," seldom appeared in hymnody, sermons, pamphlets, or the legal dimensions of "official" theology in the pietist renewal movement. An unofficial theology that remembered this part of the admonition never vanished completely.

Despite the unfinished pietist agenda, most of the globe's two billion Christians appear even now to entertain the hope for better spouses. Pietists undertook to reinvigorate the church by changing behavior, beginning with conversion, the change of heart that distinguished true from merely so-called believers. On the vexed matter of spousal relations, however, the deeply ambiguous standing of marriage as quasi-sacramental fell on hard times as the canonical and legal synthesis Luther and Spener had struggled to maintain collapsed in the maelstrom of international debate. To understand why hopes for better spouses became so important in the Protestant view of church renewal, we have followed their uncertain and unresolved quest to articulate both an order and an estate. They dared to hope as they had been taught in Ephesians 5 that in some way marriage reflected, however inadequately, God's own relationship to them, the believers. This was a relationship under the cross, to be sure, but one in which they knew something about a God who no longer called them merely servants, but friends (John 15:15). In the end, despite the unfinished nature of their quest, they continued to hope for better spouses, and a renewed church. Their descendants, and many critics and skeptics, in all corners of a global Christianity, still do.

Index